Praise for *The Religious Revolution*

"Brilliant, witty, enjoyably idiosyncratic . . . [*The Religious Revolution*] is 'literary' as much as it is 'historical' . . . Part of what makes Green's narrative so beguiling is his strong sense of irony."
—John Wilson, *National Review*

"An incisive study of the Western world's shift from institutional religion to more personal beliefs in the second half of the nineteenth century . . . Throughout, Green draws illuminating connections between these transformational thinkers and briskly contextualizes the political, economic, and technological shocks of their epoch."
—*Publishers Weekly* (starred review)

"Dominic Green's focus on the second half of the nineteenth century as the moment when humanity started to look in a completely different way at everything metaphysical is inspired. His erudition is extraordinary as he takes the reader through the sometimes weird but occasionally wonderful worlds of alternative belief systems, mostly respectfully but with a pleasingly satirical edge for the more bizarre ones. I suspect this will remain the standard work on the subject for decades."
—Andrew Roberts, author of
Churchill: Walking with Destiny

"*The Religious Revolution* must be the most rollicking intellectual history of the Victorian age. It explains that Darwin, Madame Blavatsky, and Gandhi were carrying out a kind of common project, and it reveals why Nietzsche considered Emerson his 'Brother-Soul' in nihilism. Dominic Green is a consistently witty writer, and his book moves at the pace of a really good Victorian novel."
—Christopher Caldwell, author of *The Age of Entitlement*

"This beautifully written and deeply researched book by Dominic Green purports to be a work of history. But really, it is a work of contemporary spiritual anatomy. Green deals with a host of nineteenth-century mountaintops—Emerson, Ruskin, Nietzsche, Darwin, Whitman, and many others—but his focus is firmly on the human heart. This is a profound and moving investigation of mankind's deepest and most beguiling longings. *The Religious Revolution* is a book not for a season but for the ages."

—Roger Kimball, editor and publisher of *The New Criterion*

DOMINIC GREEN

THE RELIGIOUS
REVOLUTION

Dominic Green, PhD, is a critic, a historian, and the editor of *The Spectator*'s world edition. He writes widely on the arts and current affairs and contributes regularly to *The Wall Street Journal* and *The New Criterion*. He is the author of *Three Empires on the Nile*, *Benny Green: Words and Music*, and *The Double Life of Doctor Lopez*. A fellow of the Royal Historical Society and the Royal Society of Arts, he has taught writing, history, and politics at Brandeis University and Boston College. He lives in Cambridge, Massachusetts.

THE RELIGIOUS REVOLUTION

The Birth of
Modern Spirituality,
1848–1898

DOMINIC GREEN

Picador
Farrar, Straus and Giroux | New York

Picador
120 Broadway, New York 10271

Originally published in 2022 by Farrar, Straus and Giroux
First paperback edition, 2023

The Library of Congress has cataloged the Farrar, Straus and Giroux
hardcover edition as follows:
Names: Green, Dominic, author.
Title: The religious revolution : the making of modern spirituality, 1848–1898 /
    Dominic Green.
Description: First edition. | New York : Farrar, Straus and Giroux, [2022] |
    Includes bibliographical references and index.
Identifiers: LCCN 2021053951 | ISBN 9780374248833 (hardcover)
Subjects: LCSH: Religion—History—19th century. | Religions—History—
    19th century.
Classification: LCC BL98 .G65 2022 | DDC 204.09/034—dc23/eng/20220111
LC record available at https://lccn.loc.gov/2021053951

Paperback ISBN: 978-1-250-86314-0

Designed by Janet Evans-Scanlon

To Maja

We know that the world was made at one cast; what we find in ourselves, we recognize all around us. Whatever man sees, that he has a key to in his own mind . . . The religious impulse is the most revolutionary principle in human experience, uplifting and impelling the man beyond himself. Every nation of the globe is in our day, whether willingly or reluctantly, holding up its sacred books and traditions to our eyes, and we find in our mythology a key to theirs, and in our experiences a key to their experience.

—*Ralph Waldo Emerson, "Natural Religion" (1867)*

CONTENTS

Contents

THE RELIGIOUS
REVOLUTION

PROLOGUE: 1848

Great Expectations

Scything through sleeping woods, deaf to birds and blind to flowers, the Paris express thunders on through northern France. The earth shakes, the air sings, the beast breathes black smoke. Through the carriage window, the American passenger sees the old world in magic lantern images: a church spire and a flock of cottages, a stream and a green coppice, cattle and farmers like figures from a forgotten allegory. Overhead, a black spool of telegraph cable carries hidden code, a stutter of prices, politics, and gossip for the evening papers. The passenger feels his body vibrate.

A bishop blessed the first train to travel on this line. A band played *The Song of the Railways*, music by Hector Berlioz, lyrics by Jules Janin:

> *We, the witnesses to the marvels of industry,*
> *Must sing to peace, to the king,*
> *To the worker, the country,*
> *And to commerce and all its benefits.*

From Boulogne on the bare coast of Picardy, through Lille and Arras where cotton mill chimneys jostle the turrets of medieval belfries, down into the valleys of the green Somme and sleepy Oise, past the Gothic cathedral of Saint-Denis and the bones of dead kings, on

through the villas and factories, vegetable plots and grubby tenements, grand avenues and lightless slums, the train carves a straight
and graded line through the rippled surface of Earth and its topsoil of
human settlement until, in an ecstasy of brakes and whistles and
steam, it stops.

"From Boulogne to Paris fifty-six leagues, seven and one-half
mortal hours": the power and haste of modern life. A tall man with a
clerical air, a face of angles and planes, and dark hair turning to gray
steps onto the platform. It is May 1848, the "Spring of Nations," and
Ralph Waldo Emerson has come to Paris.

The sooty air is moistened by an unusually wet and cold spring.
These are Europe's Hungry Forties. The crops are rotting in the fields,
and food prices are rising. There are mobs in the cities, and famine is
in the country. There is mass starvation in Ireland, war in Italy, and
revolution in the German states. Emigrants crowd the ports; cholera
crosses to the New World in steerage. In Paris the streets are bare. Yet
another French revolution has begun. The plane trees have been
chopped down for barricades.

It was an age of grand ideas and great expectations, and it forged our
ecstasies and discontents. An age fascinated by speed and awed by
machines. An age of evolutionary biology and religious fundamentalism, of global powers and tribal politics. An age of glowing cities and
traditions lost, of the lone genius and the huddled masses, of restless
tedium and the torments of hope. An age that believed in the infinite
advance of knowledge, endured the infinite emptiness of a universe
without purpose, and succored a pantheon of new gods.

That age created global markets and global consciousness, but also
class war and scientific racism. It dreamed of peace and genocide,
chemical cures and chemical weapons. It overthrew the ancient authority of church and crown for the volatile gambles of democracy and the
market. It freed women, slaves, and serfs, but it harnessed children to
its factories and subject peoples to its empires. It was the New Age, the
era of democracy and emancipation, but the emancipated yearned to

elect new Caesars. Its vocabulary is ours: spirituality, evolution, ecology, crisis, culture war, diversity, Darwinist, fundamentalist, neurotic, organic, sadism, masochism, atomic power, karma, reincarnation. So are its pleasures: the department store (1838), the motor vehicle (1870), the telephone (1875), the moving image (1895). And also its consolations of knowledge and escapism: thermodynamic entropy (1851), the germ theory of disease (1870), synthetic opiates (1874), pornographic films (1895), the contents of the atom (1911). And so are its ideals, the transcendent principles that give meaning to life by appearing, like gods, to exist outside the world they create and explain.

Religion featured in few of these innovations but religiosity thrived amid them all. The age of scientific and technological discovery was also one of frantic religious creativity. Today, the world's largest democracies, the United States and India, are the world's most religious democracies. The market in spirituality is a multibillion-dollar industry, from package-tour pilgrimages to mail-order crystals. Two hundred years ago, perhaps a handful of Christians believed in reincarnation, and if they did, they were heretics. Today, at least a third of Americans believe not only that they have a soul that survives death, but also that it previously belonged to someone or something else. We want new cars and old souls: a life technological, founded on scientific rationality, but understood through our eternal wishes for meaning, endurance, and transcendence—the overcoming of mortality. This speculative realm of dreams and nightmares is the perennial province of religion, art, and sexuality. It is also the modern province of politics. As the net of technological civilization covered the globe, both provinces fell within the new empire of "spirituality," the distinctively modern experience of inner life as comprehensive and near simultaneous, novel in its infusion of biological ideas and technological metaphors, yet strangely familiar, even archaic.

We became like this in the late nineteenth century, when mass communications, mass politics, and global markets converged, transforming lives across the world. People, products, and ideas moved faster and farther than ever before. Travel and communication became standardized to Greenwich Mean Time. English became the global argot of trade. The erosion of inherited beliefs and customs, and the eruption of new ideas and experiences, forced a radical reordering of values. Nietzsche's "death of God" was only an obituary for the Christian deity, a clearing away of the old so that new ideas of divinity could flower. And reports of the Almighty's death turned out to be greatly exaggerated. Certainly, the established religions lost ground, especially where new ideas and institutions mimicked the old forms. But the weakening of organized religion liberated the religious impulse from the inherited restraints of hierarchy and dogma. Rather than atrophying like a superfluous evolutionary inheritance, religiosity surged in hypertrophic vigor.

The machine pulse of urban life and the rational proofs of science cracked the old barriers between the sacred and the profane. As the religious impulse flooded into all aspects of individual consciousness and collective endeavor, it sanctified all with transcendent significance, and disturbed the rule of Brahmins in Boston as in Bombay. Suddenly the heights of religious experience were no longer the privilege of hereditary male elites. Nor was religious joy the meager fruit of renunciation, abstinence, or retreat. Like Napoléon, who crowned himself emperor when the pope wavered, the modern individual personalizes his or her beatitude. And like Napoléon, who wanted to conquer India but never went there, the modern individual seeks to combine West and East, rational and sublime, personal and collective, science and spirit. As Emerson exhorted Margaret Fuller, "Write your own Bible!"

Emerson's "religious impulse" seems to be innate to our species. The oldest known human burial site is around one hundred thousand years old: a man daubed in red dust, curled in the fetal position, and cradling a wild boar's jawbone, an accessory for the afterlife. The evolutionary value of religiosity has become a modern commonplace. Transcendent ideas and experiences bond us to our kin and its goals. They explain the twin mysteries of life and death, and the "problem" of altruism. Religious ethics sustain society by restraining personal desires in the name of the common good, notably by controlling sexual and marital relations. As for the frustrations this might cause, religious ethics protect society by externalizing aggression and even rationalizing self-sacrifice as the ultimate altruism. Anthropologists have identified over one hundred thousand religions. All are the work of *Homo sapiens*, none the work of apes. Religiosity is a threshold of human consciousness. It is human to possess religiosity, but its possession does not protect against inhumanity.

Crudely, the difference between religiosity and religion is the difference between hunger and lunch. Hunger is a biological inheritance, its pangs inescapable proof of our nature. Lunch is a result of recent cultural evolution. The menu varies and is shaped by environment and appetite. Religion explains and organizes the experience of life, and when that experience changes, so does its explanation. The religious impulse endures but its forms are flexible, and its ideas and practices rise and fall like dynasties and empires. While biological evolution is glacially slow, culture evolves as far and fast as we can think—and sometimes faster than our minds and societies can bear.

Scientific ideas change our language and our minds, our perception of life. The application of scientific ideas through technology changes our experience of the physical world, compressing distance and increasing speed, creating new conjunctions and capabilities. Ours is the age in which science lifted the veil from the material world, from the dance of the planets to the epic of heredity. But this has not been enough. Different lives require new ideas, new personal and collective goals whose pursuit transcends the inchoate and mundane and gives meaning to life—or rather, transcendent meaning to life. For our age of scientific rationality, planned economy, and organized politics is also one of mass folly and biological mysticism. We venerate facts and we rely on technology, but we remain enchanted by the irrational, the mystical, and the metaphysical.

Our city life with machines created new social ideas and experiences, and these inspired new myths and ideals. These "spiritual" innovations are the common thread in the crazy quilt of modern life. Some responded to the weakening of traditional Christianity by fashioning a new faith. Éliphas Lévi's occultism, Auguste Comte's Religion of Humanity, Helena Blavatsky's Theosophy, and Nietzsche's Superman were all spiritual responses to science and the dilemmas of modern individuality. For others, notably socialists and nationalists, politics was the explicit heir to religion, with the state replacing the church, and race theory and the cult of blood replacing theology and miracles. Even the holy trinity of skeptical materialism, Marx, Darwin, and Freud, were resisted in their own fields. Marx struggled against the Christian socialists who preceded him and the Jewish and German socialists who followed him. Darwin contended with his own ambivalence about a purposeless universe, as well as Alfred Russel Wallace and the precursors of "intelligent design" theory. Freud could not prevent Jung from turning the biology of the mind toward racial mysticism.

The religious impulse demands explanations and purpose, images of perfection, and the logic of history and myth. Before we refashion Nature, nature fashions us. When innate religiosity interacted with science and the technological society it created, the results were the explosive "isms," the irrational appeals to salvation by nationalism, socialism, and racism that derailed the global civilization once in 1914 and again in 1939. This is what "New Age" originally meant: not an aisle of options in Whole Foods Market, but the total transformation of individual consciousness, a rebirth leading to a greater transformation, the remaking of the individual and society. Technology created the Agricultural Revolution and the Industrial Revolution. I call the modern transformation of inner life the Religious Revolution.

"All religious movements in history," Emerson observed, *"and perhaps* all political revolutions founded on Rights, are only new examples of the deep emotion that can agitate a community of unthinking men, when a truth familiar in words, that 'God is within us,' is made for a time a conviction." A movement to restore the individual's spirit

creates its social image. Protestantism made the personal political, because religion was now politics. The personal conviction that "God is within us" implied the political faith that "God is with us." The wars of religion led to the emergence of nation-states and national churches with vernacular Bibles. Their politics were thick with apocalyptic arousal. The communities led by Jan of Leiden, John Calvin, and Oliver Cromwell believed that their leap of faith would land in the last days of history. To hasten its joyous end and secure their permanent salvation, they sought to perfect society in the biblical image.

Religious impulses now expressed themselves in the new vocabularies of politics and science. While Henry VIII formed a national church, Copernicus placed the sun, not the earth, at the center of the universe. The ideal human became the hyphenated kind that Emerson's age called the "Renaissance man." Thomas More was a Machiavellian politician, a Platonic philosopher, and eventually a saint. Francis Bacon was an empiricist philosopher, the lord chancellor of a Protestant nation-state, and a practical scientist.

By the seventeenth century, Protestants were feeling "spiritual" and "soulful." Catholics, having fought the Protestant model, now adapted it and developed a competing brand, with a new technology, the confession box, as its incubator. As science emerged from the shattered unities of what was then called natural philosophy, so "spirituality" emerged from the cracked rock of organized religion.

The individual conscience found itself in an unmapped continent, an America of the inner world. It deciphered the mechanics and customs of this strange land with the telescope and microscope, observation and rational analysis. It appeared that the Renaissance rediscovery of pre-Christian philosophy and literature was not just a "rebirth" of scholarship and skeptical reason. When the new science viewed Nature without the aid of Christian dogma, it returned to Nature in its pagan sense. The universe was a vast, amoral theater of incomprehensible forces, the individual an actor in a drama without a script.

Until the nineteenth century, only the bold or reckless had dared to face the widening gap between Christian dogma and the new science. Pioneers like Jean-Jacques Rousseau, Thomas Jefferson, and William Blake had appeared in the salons of the Enlightenment and the antic parade of Romanticism. Similar sentiments had appeared sporadically among the leaders of the American Revolution, and prominently among the ideologues of the French Revolution, where the new spirituality confirmed its potential for tyranny and havoc.

The world, the poet Friedrich Schiller had complained, was "disenchanted," but the need for meaning, transcendence, and immortality persisted. The religious impulse, deprived of the next world, reoriented toward this one. It turned outward into society, to pursue redemption through "secular" politics and the Epicurean good life. And it turned inward, into consciousness.

The "once omnipotent traditions" might dissolve, Emerson wrote, but their "moral sentiment & metaphysical fact" survive as a permanent essence, expressed by each "new crop of geniuses." Heir to the early adopters of "spiritual" democracy and "soulful" religion, Emerson's significance for the Religious Revolution is akin to that of Benjamin Franklin for the American Revolution, or Rousseau for the French. He might not have caused it, but it would not have been the same without him.

In Emerson, the streams of a global tide met for the first time. In the 1830s, the young Emerson realized that seven generations of Puritan rigor had desiccated into the "famine" of Unitarianism, a faith that dominated New England's society while starving its spirit. If his defection from Christianity heralded the popular shift from "religion" to "spirituality," the direction of his spirit anticipated the modern movement. As an heir of Romanticism, Emerson revered nature and intuition as divine. He believed in Kant's promise that the mind was moral, and he expected that the materials of aesthetic and spiritual perfection lay in the mystic East, beyond the sources of Christianity. As an inhabitant of an age of empire, philology, and cheap print, Emerson could read sacred Hindu texts in English through the translations of the East India Company and the efforts of his aunt Mary, who supplied him with its publications. And as an English-speaking liberal, Emerson was also heir to the optimistic, tolerant strand of the individualist revolt. He linked freedom in religion to freedom in politics and commerce. He trusted that the freedoms of thought, religiosity, and commerce would, like the Three Musketeers, fight for one another: "The powers that make a capitalist are metaphysical."

So we can call July 15, 1838, the day that Emerson declared the Religious Revolution in the United States: the day that, speaking at Harvard Divinity School, he deliberately provoked the divines by contrasting "the Church with the Soul," and in a manner reflecting dimly on the Church and radiantly on the Soul. This, though, might have remained a purely Unitarian scandal, in the way that the Stamp Act might have remained a tax dispute or the Ninety-Five Theses a reform proposal. In the first decade of Emerson's century William Blake had cried, "Rouse up, O Young Men of the New Age," but few had listened. The difference is in the changes in environment—political, economic, and, above all, technological—that carried the Religious Revolution from the intellectual fringe to the mass market and catalyzed it into a global phenomenon.

Almost ten years to the day after the Harvard Divinity School address, Emerson stepped off the train in Paris. He had come from a lecture tour of Britain that, despite the acclaim that awaited him in every hall, had left him thoroughly discomfited. The cost of "metaphysical capitalism" was written in the flesh. Britain's cities were filthy. Its people were hard-eyed and brutal, and their ragged children begged in the rain. Coal dust and soot coated the entire island; in what remained of the countryside, they stained even the wool on the sheep.

The industrial city was the crucible of modern life. In Paris, Emerson recognized one of its products. Socialism, once a gospel of vegetarian cranks, now emerged as a "feature new to history," a doctrine of mass democracy. The rioting and rhetoric frightened him. The crowds seemed murderous and atavistic. The political rally was a primitive rite, a modern witch hunt: "Torchlight processions have a sleek and slay look, dripping burning oil drops, and the bearers now and then smiting the torch on the ground, and then lifting it into the air." The intuitions that Emerson prized as divine led the marchers toward appalling outcomes: hatred, violence, and a conformity in which one solitary walker was no different from another. The transition from the woods of New England to the cities of Europe confounded his inner Sybil. "For the matter of socialism, there are no oracles. The oracle is dumb."

Emerson knew his Hegel. The religious impulse never slept, never ceased "uplifting and impelling the man beyond himself." The forces that had unmade the old ways and faiths would also shape the new, universal, and absolute "Supreme beauty." One way or another, the revolutionary principle of the expanded soul would emerge from technical civilization. He must seek the biological pattern that lay behind the smoky, speed-blurred images of modern life. When Emerson returned to Concord, he took to a diet of scientific and economic literature. Poetry had brought him this far, but from here on, the "currents of the Universal Being" would speak the language of science.

This is the age of the Religious Revolution. It is also the age of science and race. This is the age of the Religious Revolution *because* it is the age of science and race.

PART I

The Development Hypothesis

1848–1871

But mankind are now conscious of their new position. The conviction is already not far from being universal, that the times are pregnant with change; and that the nineteenth century will be known to posterity as the era of one of the greatest revolutions of which history has preserved the remembrance, in the human mind, and in the whole constitution of human society. Even the religious world teems with new interpretations of the Prophecies, foreboding mighty changes near at hand. It is felt that men are henceforth to be held together by new ties, and separated by new barriers; for the ancient bonds will now no longer unite, nor the ancient boundaries confine.

—*John Stuart Mill, "The Spirit of the Age" (1831)*

1

THE NEW PROMETHEUS

Socialists and Spiritualists
in the Age of the Machine

> If there is any period one would desire to be born in,—is
> it not the Age of Revolution; when the old and the new
> stand side by side, and admit of being compared; when
> the energies of all men are searched by fear and by hope;
> when the historic glories of the old can be compensated
> by the rich possibilities of the new era? This time, like
> all times, is a very good one, if we but know what to do
> with it. —*Emerson, "The American Scholar" (1837)*

At Brussels, the wind whipped off the North Sea and through the
rooming house where Jenny Marx passed the first weeks of 1848.
She would have preferred to stay in Paris, but the iron laws of history,
represented here by the collusion of the Prussian and French police,
had cast her and Karl onto this bleak, blank-skied Eurasian shore.

Life with Karl Marx was never dull. He was a short man of excess
energy, intellect, and hair, with a bantam's barrel chest, a scholar's
wit, and a piercing, metallic voice that was a little too loud. Jenny had
no money and three children to feed, but there was still hope, the last
surprise in Pandora's box. Karl's father, a wealthy lawyer, had just
died, and an inheritance was in the offing. So too, Karl promised, was
the revolution in human consciousness.

"Until now, men have constantly had false conceptions of themselves, about what they are or what they ought to be." Men had invented ideas of God and illusions of a "normal man" whose body existed only as the vessel of his soul. They had bowed to these idols, and to the priests who curated them and the kings who protected them. Fortunately, the faculty that had led men to create and worship these spectral authorities now allowed men to see through them. Scientific knowledge of the physical world stripped Man of all illusions, religious, moral, and philosophical. The bedrock of Nature was the hard truth that Marx called "historical materialism."

Marx believed that the forms of human society came not from God but from technology. From the hand ax of the Neolithic hunter to the first civilizations, from the ancient empires to the medieval guilds, the surface patterns of class, power, and property reflected deeper currents: the creation, ownership, and use of technology. If, Marx argued, these forces of production evolved, then so must everything else. When Samuel Morse had tested his telegraph with the biblical inquiry, "What hath God wrought?" he had confused cause and effect. Man had always wrought everything in his world, God included. And now Man's latest historical movement, the bourgeois age of capital and democracy, steam engines and telegraphs, was crashing to its inevitable end.

"But what is most interesting," Lady Constance Rawleigh tells her guests, "is the way in which man has been developed. You know, all is development. The principle is perpetually going on. First there was nothing, then there was something; then—I forget the next—I think there were shells, then fishes; then we came—let me see—did we come next? Never mind that; we came at last. And the next change there will be something very superior to us—something with wings. Ah! that's it: we were fishes, and I believe we shall be crows."

Lady Constance has been reading *The Revelations of Chaos*. It is "all science": everything is explained by geology and astronomy. The stars are churned into light from "the cream of the milky way, a sort of celestial cheese," and the planets form and disintegrate in this cosmic dairy. "You see exactly how everything is made; how many worlds there have been; how long they lasted; what went before, what comes next." Man is adrift in the monstrous vista of evolutionary time, a transient life-form, a work of unknown authorship, a species fated to eclipse. "We are a link in the chain, as inferior animals were that preceded us: we shall in turn be inferior; all that will remain of us will be some relics in a new red sandstone. This is development. We had fins; we may have wings."

Lady Constance is a fiction from *Tancred*, Benjamin Disraeli's novel of 1847. The real *Revelations of Chaos* was *Vestiges of the Natural History of Creation* (1844) by Robert Chambers, a Scottish publisher and geologist. Chambers published it anonymously to protect his business and his reputation. More than a decade before Darwin published *On the Origin of Species*, "development" theory was familiar enough for Disraeli to spoof it in fiction. Yet the wider the commonplaces of development theory spread, the thinner they became. Every scientific doctrine speaks the language of its time, and in explaining grants cultural license: the image of Copernicus's heliocentric universe served the cult of the Sun King as well as the cause of individual Reason. But development, the idea that would be renamed "evolution" in the 1850s, was especially volatile. For if everything was evolving, then nothing could be permanent. There was no fixed hierarchy, no Great Chain of Being with God at one end and insects at the other, "the rich man in his castle, the poor man at his gate." There was only change, and the chain of development was its record. The world might have been "created at one cast," but its contents had not. Existence was not a fixed state of being but a fluid, uncertain process of "becoming."

For the scientific and commercial society, evolutionary thinking would fill the role that God had played in the Christian worldview: the creator and prime mover, the master idea and moral explanatory. Where the ancient bonds and boundaries failed, evolution would legislate anew. The ethics of evolution would often resemble the Christian eschatology they replaced. For social Darwinists like Herbert Spencer, change meant "progress," and specialization a purposeful movement toward perfection. This ideal would permeate the age so fully that even those who defied it would not deny it but endorse it by heresy. Disraeli's Tancred, appalled by Lady Constance's meaningless universe, searches for a "new crusade."

So far, the evolution of knowledge in the 1840s included rotary printing, the pneumatic tire, the planet Neptune, nitroglycerin, and the theory of the Ice Age. In 1848, while the infant Thomas Edison was conducting his first experiments in solid food, Lord Kelvin proposed the ideas of absolute zero in temperature and the entropy of molecular energy. The next five years would see the safety pin, the conical bullet, the refrigerator, the gyroscope, condensed milk, and the airship. In 1851 alone, Linus Yale would patent the cylinder lock, Isaac Singer would launch the single-stitch sewing machine, Henry Bessemer would invent a cheap process for deriving structural steel from pig iron, and Elisha Otis would design the other necessity of the skyscraper, the safety elevator.

Meanwhile Europe was ruled by a decrepit caste of emperors and aristocrats. Each morning, the Duke of Wellington tottered up to the ramparts of Walmer Castle to scan the English Channel for a ghost fleet of French invaders. Each morning, his friend Prince Klemens von Metternich bent to his desk in Vienna to fight democracy, nationalism, and socialism, the trio of evils unleashed by the French Revolution. Each morning, as the hungry peoples of Europe awoke to toil or starve, a shadow army of informers, eavesdroppers, censors, and jailers took up its posts. If scientific man was, as Mary Shelley had called Victor Frankenstein, the "New Prometheus," then the eagles that pecked out his liver each morning were imperial ones.

Europe's technical and social development was outstripping its political means. The scientific, commercial middle classes were growing in number and economic power, and they wanted their voices to be heard. Metternich and Wellington expected to witness the dissolution of the European system. Wellington had seen it coming in

1832, when middle-class troublemakers had taken their seats in a re-formed House of Commons. "I never saw so many bad hats in my life," he had sniffed. In 1830, the bourgeois bad hats of France had forced a similar reform, and substituted one dynasty for another in the process. Out of office, Alexis de Tocqueville had acquainted himself with the democratic future by touring the United States. Watching Europe's revolutions of 1848, he realized that revolutions occurred not only when people were hungry or hopeless but when they had hope too. The weakening of ancient bonds and boundaries, the sensation of affluence, and the promise of infinite possibility all encouraged a "revolution of rising expectations."

Marx hoped for a revolution of rising frustration: the revolt of the proletariat, the despairing and hopeless underclass. But in 1848, Europe barely had industrial cities, let alone working classes. The majority of Europeans were still tied to the land. Most northern Europeans were farmers, most southern Europeans peasants, and most Russians serfs. The French were political experimenters but the majority of their industrial output still came from family workshops. Only Britain, the "nation of shopkeepers," had the necessary density of factories and misery. One of them was a Manchester cotton mill supervised by Marx's friend Friedrich Engels.

No European nation had a workers' party. Europe's revolutionaries were fragmented and furtive, a rabble of wayward students and self-taught artisans. Their ideals were soaked in Christian metaphysics and abstractions of Justice and Reason, their methods in nostalgia for the French Revolution. Marx and Engels had spent much of 1847 scheming for control of the League of the Just, a London-based group of about eighty French and German artisans prone to secret conspiracies, sudden coups, and violently sentimental outbreaks of brotherly love. To Marx, the members of the league were utopians, dreamers, and fools. The revolution must commandeer the party, the machinery of politics.

By the end of 1847, the League of the Just had renamed itself the Communist League. The almost Christian slogan "All People Are

Brethren!" had become a selective call to class salvation, "Workers of All Countries, Unite!" Engels sketched a new constitution, a "Communist Catechism," its points of doctrine structured like a Christian confession of faith. He asked Marx to draft its final version. Marx began, but suffered one of his frequent attacks of procrastination. The New Year passed. The London committee grew restive.

"Think over the confession of faith a bit," Engels suggested. "I think it would be better to drop the catechism form and call the thing a communist manifesto."

Two days after Engels suggested that Marx "drop the catechism," John Humphrey Noyes fled south on the rutted roads from Putney, Vermont, pursued by warrants for adultery.

"God has set me to cast up a highway across this chaos," Noyes believed, "and I am gathering out the stones and grading the track as fast as possible."

In 1834, studying at Yale Theological Seminary, Noyes had reached Rousseau's conclusion that Man was not born wicked: he became wicked in society. Sin was not in the heart but in civilization. Most of what passed for Christian civilization was "the work of Antichrist." The Kingdom of God was not in the afterlife; it was here and now on Earth. The Second Coming had occurred at the destruction of Jerusalem in 70 CE. The Kingdom of Heaven had existed on Earth since then, and the Apocalypse of Revelation was imminent.

Expelled for preaching his revelation, Noyes spent eleven years in the wilderness, wandering through the leaderless network of Perfectionists, rogue Methodists who believed in the perfectibility of human conduct and society. Some of Noyes's hosts had dispensed with property like the early Christians did, others with monogamous marriage as an obstacle to the expression of love. In 1845, Noyes led forty young followers back to Putney. They settled near his parents and began to "redeem man and reorganize society." In 1848, Noyes wrote the other communist manifesto, *Bible Communism*, as a handbook for his elective community.

Before socialism became scientific, it was religious. The Putney Association of Perfectionists practiced "true holiness" and "true spirituality." The Bible was their "creed and constitution." They had no weekly Sabbath, for if all life were holy, then there were "seven holy days in a week, and twenty-four holy hours in a day." They corrected unloving behavior by "mutual criticism," group truth-telling sessions. They shed their possessions and took to the fields as equal workers, each sharing the earth's bounty with all. Then they shed their inhibitions.

"Reconciliation with God opens the way for the reconciliation of the sexes," Noyes explained. The "sin-system" of sexual guilt underpinned the "marriage-system" of monogamy and the family unit. These incubated guilt and jealousy, and that "condensation of interests" fed the greed and acquisitiveness of the "work-system." Modern life was really a spiritual "death-system," in which sexual repression fostered economic exploitation. There was an alternative, however. A "vital society," its energies harmonized with the biological truth of Creation. A society of economic and sexual equality, where men and women were true partners, where work was "sport, as it would have been in the original Eden state," where sexual desire could be enjoyed without sin. Noyes called this "free love," or "complex marriage."

The flaws of human nature meant that the sexual economy was a command economy, more complex than free. Left to its own devices, the community would founder amid erotic anarchy. The women would be constantly pregnant or nursing, and unable to work. When the men weren't fighting over their children's paternity, they would struggle to feed their growing population. As in economic life, the division of sexual labor must be reformed, and desire must be redirected toward a more perfect consummation in which all hold equal shares in joy. The community must separate sexual pleasure from its infant products, "amative" acts from "propagatory" consequences. Noyes trained his male Perfectionists in male continence, the deferral of ejaculation, and coached them to be more generous lovers. Slow learners received practical training from Perfectionist women past the age of menopause. "First we abolish sin; then shame; then the curse on woman of exhausting child-bearing; then the curse on man of exhausting labor; and so we arrive regularly at the tree of life."

It was all too much for Noyes's neighbors. Cast out of his Eden at Putney, Noyes fled to a Perfectionist commune in Brooklyn, New York. In late January 1848, some admirers offered a haven where Noyes could pursue his prophet motive. The elect reconvened at four farmhouses, a barn, and a sawmill upstate at Oneida, near Syracuse. The world remained poised between the redemption of true holiness and the Apocalypse of the Beast. Only those who understood the signs of the time would survive.

"Between this present time and the establishment of God's kingdom over the earth lies a chaos of confusions, tribulation and war, such as must attend the destruction of the fashion of this world, and the introduction of the will of God as it is done in heaven."

The Greek for "revelation" is apokalypsis, *a "lifting of the veil," the* laying bare of sacred mysteries. The people, Marx believed, must be forced to confront the historical revelation happening before their eyes. *The Communist Manifesto,* published in German on February 21, 1848, was his technological apocalypse.

The revolution had already begun. There had never been a man more godlike than the middle-class Faust. Europe's bourgeois manufacturer overthrew kings and sacked churches. He jumbled the classes and races. He declared republics and rewrote the law. He moved mountains and remade Earth in his image: "subjection of Nature's forces to man, machinery, application of chemistry to industry and agriculture, steam-navigation, railways, electric telegraphs, clearing of whole continents for civilization, canalization of rivers, whole populations conjured out of the ground."

The bourgeois "sorcerer" had grown rich from the "constant revolutionizing of production" and "the uninterrupted disturbance of all social conditions." Now, like Faust, he was losing control of the "powers of the nether world." When the bourgeois took the peasants from the fields and conscripted them into his industrial army, capitalism created its destroyers. A "perfect hierarchy of officers and sergeants" kept the workers enslaved to the machines. Noise and monotony stupefied the workers into "commodities" to be formed, used, and discarded. As competition pushed wages down, the workers competed for the scraps, shedding nationality, family ties, morality, religion, and all the other "bourgeois prejudices." But they could not evade the logic of capital. They were now waste products, a "passively rotting mass" to be mulched into the "social scum," the "swindlers, confidence tricksters, brothel-keepers, rag-and-bone merchants, beggars, and other flotsam of society." They were reborn as proletarians.

In ancient Rome, the *proletarius* was a citizen of the lowest class, his children fodder for the projects of the state. When the modern proletarians sensed their degradation, they would tear off their chains like Spartacus. The revolution would begin with individual nations and states, because the bourgeois had created the nation-state as the tool of capital and property. Though the world's economies were at different stages of development, the spread of modern industry across the world would drag more and more peoples into the bourgeois phase of economic development. The destiny of capitalism was to lay the tracks of a global revolution. When the bonds of property and law dissolved, Man would finally be free and the state would wither with its creator. There was no danger of the vanguard becoming permanent dictators: economic liberation would straighten the kinks of capitalist personality, and innate goodness would flourish. Those who did not flourish satisfactorily would receive compulsory "social education" until they did.

There would be no more uncertainty and no more agitation because there would be no more development. When Man maximized his industrial potential, he would complete the evolution of consciousness. History would enter a coda and Heaven, pleasant and monotonous, would arrive on Earth. The revolutionary leap forward landed in the verities of the preindustrial past: a little hunting in the morning, a little fishing in the afternoon, a little philosophy in the evening.

The natural man would be like a Neolithic flâneur, or a leisured Prussian gentleman—Friedrich Engels, perhaps.

Shortly after calling for the abolition of hereditary wealth, Marx received his share of his late father's estate. He gave some of the money to his socialist friends in Brussels. They spent it on knives and revolvers. On March 3, 1848, Marx was ordered to leave Belgium at once. Jenny was packing when the police burst in. Though Karl protested that he was leaving anyway, they arrested him. When Jenny followed him to the police station, they incarcerated her for "vagabondage," and added a night in a cell to the novelties of life with Karl.

Released without charge next afternoon, the Marxes had two hours to gather their children and leave. Jenny sold some of their few possessions and left her silver and linen with a friendly bookseller. The police escorted the Marx family onto a train and out of Belgium. They reached Paris early the next morning. In February, the Parisians had overthrown a monarchy for the third time in living memory, but Marx, confined in Brussels, had only watched. He informed the Communist League in London that its executive committee had moved to Paris, the heart of the struggle.

The revolution spread from Paris like a fever. In March, mobs brought down governments in Berlin, the capital of Prussia, and Vienna, the seat of the Austrian empire. Metternich, architect of the repressive system that had controlled Europe since the defeat of Napoléon, retired and took refuge in London. The emperor of Austria and the kings of Denmark, the Netherlands, and Prussia saved their thrones by signing democratic constitutions; the king of Bavaria preferred to abdicate. In the patchwork of peoples in eastern Europe, Hungarians and Ukrainians rioted against Austria, Romanians against Russia, and Poles against Prussia. All demanded national rights from the old empires.

In London in April, marchers rallied in Hyde Park with a petition for democratic reform bearing over five million signatures. The Bank of England was barricaded with sandbags. The foreign secretary

Lord Palmerston wedged his office door with bound volumes of *The Times*, and issued cutlasses and muskets to the clerks of empire.

In May, a national assembly met in Frankfurt, intending to unify the numerous German states under a liberal constitution. In Italy, the people of Venice and Milan drove out their Austrian garrisons, the Venetians declaring the return of their ancient republic, the Milanese hoping to unite Italy under Victor Emanuel, king of Lombardy. In Rome, Pope Pius IX prepared to flee to Sicily. In Sicily, the rebel parliament voted to depose their king.

"All that is solid melts into air," Marx and Engels wrote in the *Manifesto*, "all that is holy is profaned, and man is at last compelled to face with sober senses, his real conditions of life, and his relations with his kind." But none of Europe's turmoil had been caused by Karl Marx. The *Communist Manifesto* began the refurbishment of religious communism into scientific socialism, but in 1848 this was a prophecy that went unheard. The locomotive of history had already left the station, and almost all its passengers still believed that, though they must pass the stations of nationhood, politics, and economics, their ultimate destination was religious. "The war against evil and falsehood is a holy war, the crusade of God," the Italian socialist Giuseppe Mazzini informed the pope. The "tremendous crisis of doubts and desires" that was roiling Europe expressed itself in the language of politics and economics, but it was religious at heart. The world was in the grip of "the vices of materialism, of egotism, of reaction" and, Mazzini mourned, the traditional counterweights had lost their strength: "Faith is dead, Catholicism is lost in Despotism; Protestantism is lost in anarchy . . . Nobody *believes*." Society could not exist without religion, and if man no longer believed in the Christian heaven, then he must make a new religion and a new heaven—on Earth: "We shall have these not in the kings, and the privileged classes,—their very condition excludes love, the soul of all religions,—but in the people. The spirit of God descends on many gathered together in his name. The people have suffered for ages on the cross, and God will bless them with a faith."

Metternich despaired. The old order had survived by pomp, illusion, intimidation, and the fear of war, but the spell had been broken. "My most secret thought is that the old Europe is at the beginning of its end. Resolved to founder with it, I will know how to do my duty. The new Europe, on the other hand, is still in the process of becoming; between end and beginning there will be a chaos."

Two weeks after the fall of the Austrian government, the dead began to talk. The spirits were reborn at a one-story house in Hydesville, New York, a humble, wood-framed affair with two bedrooms, an attic, and a root cellar. As in the days of the Sibyl, women did the work of testimony.

John and Margaret Fox had rented the house in December 1847. They slept in one bedroom, their daughters Maggie, fourteen, and Kate, twelve, in the other. From the middle of March, their home shook at night with loud knockings. Maggie and Kate moved into their parents' bed, but the noises continued. On the last two nights of March 1848, the knockings became so regular and insistent that no one could sleep. Finally, around seven in the evening on March 31, Kate Fox formally inaugurated a new phase in Western religion.

"Mr. Splitfoot," she called. "Do as I do."

She clapped once. They heard a single rap in reply. She clapped twice, and they heard two raps. Her older sister, Maggie, clapped four times and got four in return.

Kate, a canny double-bluffer, voiced the obvious suspicion. "Oh, mother, I know what it is. Tomorrow is April-fool day, and it's somebody trying to fool us."

Her mother tested the presence by asking it to give the ages of her children. It duly tapped away, then paused and gave three emphatic raps to describe the age of her youngest daughter, the one who had died.

"Is this a human being that answers my questions so correctly?" Mrs. Fox called.

Silence.

"Is it a spirit? If it is, make two raps."

Knock, knock.

"If it was an injured spirit, make two raps."

The flimsy house shook twice. By this method, Mrs. Fox learned that she was talking to the spirit of a peddler who had been murdered for his money on a Tuesday night about five years previously. His throat had been cut with a butcher's knife, and his body dumped in a creek that ran close to the house. His murderer was still alive.

The neighbors gathered. Their excavation of the creek turned up only the bones of an old horse. The peddler reconsidered. His body was under the cellar, ten feet deep below the apples, potatoes, and turnips. John Fox, a regular Methodist in good standing, had his doubts, but neither his wife nor the rest of Hydesville shared them. The next day, nearly three hundred people gathered at his house, eager to contact the spirit world.

Upstate New York was the seedbed of American spirituality. Evangelists called it the "burned-over district": as in farming, the burning out of one spiritual harvest fertilized the soil for the next one. In the first years of the century this had been the terrain of the Second Great Awakening, where camp meetings had roiled the established churches with the promise of individual salvation. In the 1820s it had produced the revelations of Joseph Smith, who dictated the Book of Mormon after an angel had showed him "Golden Plates" buried in a wood near Palmyra. In the 1830s William Miller of Poultney, Vermont, had convinced his Adventist followers that the world would end in 1844 and later, despite what even Miller admitted had been a "Great Disappointment," continued to insist that the Second Coming was nigh. In the 1840s the "Seer" Andrew Jackson Davis had claimed that his soul took nocturnal flight to commune with the spirits of ancient philosophers in the hills near Poughkeepsie.

This territory of religious innovation was also one of human and economic disruption. The road to the Great Lakes and the West ran across upstate New York. An endless tide of emigrants poured past the Foxes' door and the Perfectionists' dormitory: unsettled people carrying the despair of Europe, dreams of a new life, and the real specter of 1848, Bengal cholera. As commerce and communications created new links between people, including fatal and invisible ones, anxiety, dislocation, and uncertainty spurred new growth.

A hundred miles east of Hydesville, new converts were joining the Putney Perfectionists at Oneida, but not ejaculating or conceiving. The miracles of free love and mutual criticism were making the crooked straight. Beneath the midsummer moon, John Noyes, working by the North Star, staked out the foundations of their new home. Meanwhile, diggers in Hydesville turned up some scraps of bone and hair—probably animal, preferably human. Mrs. Fox sent Maggie and Kate to their elder sister, Leah, in Rochester. Twenty-three years older than Maggie, and with a seven-year-old daughter, Leah had been abandoned by her husband and scraped a living as a piano teacher. She soon discovered that she too had the gift. So did their brother David, who devised an alphabetical board for their mediumship. The board added drama and a whiff of scientific procedure. Like a conjurer who, reaching for his rabbit, flourishes his free hand, the board diverted attention from the medium to the magic.

Spiritualism, the cult that cohered around the Rochester rappings, was the West's first post-Christian faith. Spiritualism was the first faith to articulate divine wisdom through a machine; David Fox's board was the forerunner of the Ouija board and a battery of Spiritualist technology. Like Karl Marx, the Spiritualist lifted the veil on reality. Marx claimed that all was matter, the Spiritualist that all was spirit, and both agreed that modern methods had allowed humanity to understand the unfolding of its destiny in real time.

"Dear friends, you must proclaim this truth to the world," the spirits rapped. "This is the dawning of a new era; you must not try to conceal it any longer. When you do your duty, God will protect you, and good spirits will watch over you."

• • •

"Resolved. *That woman has too long rested satisfied in the circum-*scribed limits which corrupt customs and a perverted application of the Scriptures have marked out for her, and that it is time she should move in the enlarged sphere which her great Creator has assigned for her."

On the bright morning of July 19, 1848, more than three hundred men and women squeezed into the Lutheran chapel in Seneca Falls, New York. Most came from Seneca Falls and the adjoining town of Waterloo, but some had ridden forty miles from Rochester or Syracuse. Although it was the "busy time with the farmers," the chapel was full to the gallery. So nervous that she wanted to run away, Elizabeth Cady Stanton walked to the altar and launched the "greatest rebellion the world has ever seen."

"*Resolved.* That such laws as conflict, in any way, with the true and substantial happiness of woman, are contrary to the great precept of nature, and are of no validity."

"Oh my daughter, I wish that you were a boy!" her father, a Philadelphia lawyer and congressman, had lamented after the death of his last living son. Elizabeth had excelled at a boy's education, but a woman could not enter a university. Instead, she had studied at the Presbyterian seminary in Troy, New York, where the ministers justified slaveholding by the Calvinist doctrine of election. She shed the "gloomy superstitions" of her Christianity. "The old bondage of fear of the visible and the invisible was broken, and, no longer subject to absolute authority, I rejoiced in the dawn of a new day of freedom in thought and action."

Stanton had grown up amid campaigns for abolition, women's education, and "temperance," the reform of manners by renouncing or banning alcohol. Her father's law office was a redoubt of reformers. Her cousin Gerrit Smith of Peterboro, New York, was a prominent abolitionist whose house was a stop on the Underground Railroad, and whose father had given land to the Oneida Indian tribe. She married within the extended family of reform too, meeting her husband, Gerrit Smith's friend Henry B. Stanton, after he had spoken at an antislavery meeting. They honeymooned in London, with the American delegation to the 1840 World Anti-Slavery Convention.

The delegation included eight women. A few months earlier, the American Anti-Slavery Society had ceded to its female members' demand for equality. Nine in every ten British abolitionists voted against admitting the American women to the convention at Freemasons' Hall. They were forced to listen from behind a curtain. William Lloyd Garrison, invited as a guest speaker, refused to take the stage. "After battling so many long years for the liberties of African slaves," Garrison said, "I can take no part in a convention that strikes down the most sacred rights of all women." The talk in the Americans' lodgings was of little else, and so heated that James Birney, the abolitionist candidate for the presidency, moved out.

In London, Cady Stanton and Lucretia Mott, a Quaker from Philadelphia, resolved to form "a society to advocate for the rights of women" and to hold a convention as soon as they got home. Several years passed before the possibility arose. While Mott worked in Philadelphia for abolition and temperance, Cady Stanton followed her husband's career to Boston, where she bore him five children. When the New England winters weakened Henry's chest, they resettled in the small, malaria-prone mill town of Seneca Falls. Henry was absent for long periods, cultivating mind and society in what Elizabeth called a "magnetic circle" of reformers in Boston. Stranded, she experienced the depressing inequality of relations between men and women. She was "wife, mother, housekeeper, physician, and spiritual guide" to an ingrate household. By the time she had dueled with the builders, disciplined the servants, and planned the children's diet, she was desperate for intellectual stimulus but too tired to enjoy reading or company. She was a prisoner. She knew that the suffering of "women in particular" was, like the suffering of slaves, caused by "the wrongs of society in general." But while Henry had joined Martin van Buren's new Free-Soil Party and campaigned against slavery, he did not oppose the "odious" laws that disenfranchised all women, even educated white Protestants, on the day they married.

On July 10, 1848, Cady Stanton took tea in Waterloo at the house of Jane Hunt, a Quaker friend. Two of Hunt's Quaker neighbors, Mary Ann McClintock and Martha Coffin Wright, joined them, as did Wright's sister, visiting from Philadelphia: Lucretia Mott. When Stanton poured out her "long-accumulating discontent," the women decided to announce a public meeting in the *Seneca County Courier* to "discuss the social, civil, and religious condition and rights of women." That meant drafting a declaration of principles. Leafing through the "masculine productions" of abolitionism and temperance, they felt as "helpless and hopeless as if they had been suddenly asked to construct a steam engine." They found the title "Declaration of Rights and Sentiments" in the founding document of the American Anti-Slavery Society. When Cady Stanton read aloud the Declaration of Independence, they found a format.

"The history of mankind is a history of repeated injuries and usurpations on the part of man toward woman, having in direct object the establishment of an absolute tyranny over her," Cady Stanton wrote, substituting all men for George III. She read the final draft aloud to Henry. When she demanded the right to vote, he said he would leave town before the convention. Her father, the judge, visited, to check on her sanity. Even Lucretia Mott had her doubts: "Oh Lizzie! If thou demands that, thou will make us ridiculous! We must go slowly." Cady Stanton persevered, encouraged by Frederick Douglass, who edited the abolitionist *North Star* in Rochester.

None of the women dared to chair the Seneca Falls meeting, so Lucretia's husband, James Mott, presided. All eleven of the resolutions passed unanimously, apart from the ninth, whose claim to "the sacred right to the elective franchise" squeezed through after Douglass spoke in support. Sixty-eight women and thirty-two men signed the Declaration of Principles. A quarter were Quakers. One, Frederick Douglass, was African American. One, Susan Quinn, was of Irish descent. Henry Stanton did not attend.

*To Cady Stanton, the Declaration of Principles was the logical out*come of "republican principles and ethics." It also stemmed from a local peculiarity, the American faith that the "great precept of nature" was individual happiness. That faith was originally Protestant, its happiness the salvation of souls. Cady Stanton's religious faith was dissolving into a "new inspiration," the equality of souls into "new ideas of individual rights," but she believed these were changes of form, not content. The coercive Puritan endured in the temperance campaigner's efforts to deprive the poor and indolent of their unearned consolations. The abolitionists massed in evangelical chapels, and only when their argument for human dignity failed did they turn to the economic case against slavery. The moral principle was eternal, regardless of "corrupt customs" or the "perverted application of the Scriptures." The educated individual was sovereign in reason, and the Inner Light now shone toward the "enlarged sphere" of politics and public life.

By creating the first organized protest against "the injustice which had brooded for ages over the character and destiny of one-half of the race," Cady Stanton changed women's rights from a domestic issue to a political cause. Newspapers from Maine to Texas covered the odd events in New York. The response was vicious enough to force many of the female signatories to withdraw their names from the declaration. But the reformers' press acknowledged the logic of the argument. The headline of William Garrison's *Liberator* read, "Woman's Revolution." In the *New-York Tribune*, Horace Greeley resisted the temptation "to be smart, to be droll, to be facetious" about the "Female Reformers" and endorsed their assertion of a natural right. In the *North Star*, Frederick Douglass repeated his support for giving women the vote. Diplomatically, the *Seneca County Courier* assessed the "spirited and spicey resolutions" as "radical," but praised the women for their "able" speeches and orderly proceedings. Cady Stanton saw an advantage in notoriety: "It will start women thinking, and men, too, and when men and women think about a new question, the first step in progress is taken."

Two weeks later, a woman chaired a second meeting in Rochester, this time with her husband's support. Isaac and Amy Post were Quakers and radical abolitionists. The Inner Light of conscience had already called them to resist the subjugation of slaves and women. Now it called them to join the Fox sisters on the new frontier of spiritual struggle. As the Foxes gave their first public performances in Rochester that summer, their audiences were almost entirely summoned from the networks of reform. Spiritualism, the religion that spoke in a woman's voice, was now a political campaign.

On the road from Amesbury in July 1848, black clouds dimmed the sun. Two men bent before a chill east wind as they traversed the treeless upland, a "vast, green, wavy tract" speckled with silent sheep. Regretting a dinner that had tasted like whale blubber, feeling "dreadfully cold" in a thin summer jacket, and thoroughly tired of his companion's unquenchable cheeriness, Thomas Carlyle led Ralph Waldo Emerson across the fields to Stonehenge.

No one else was there. Ahead, Emerson saw smooth hillocks and a concentric jumble of stones: burial mounds and megaliths, the ruins of a lost civilization. As they walked toward the center of the rings of rock, Emerson climbed onto a giant stone for perspective, then felt its solar warmth and mossy crevices. Carlyle ducked behind one to light a cigar.

A wiry, scathing Scot, Carlyle had lost his Calvinism as a young man. He had been reborn a Romantic, pursuing the divine spirit in the wild places of Nature. The leap into art and imagination landed in new grounds for despair. When Carlyle confronted the life on his Chelsea doorstep without illusion, he saw not lakes and forests but the infernal regions of "Mechanical" civilization. Capital, materialism, and individualism; filth, degradation, and decline. Once, Christians had been "encompassed and overcanopied by a Glory of Heaven" and the old customs had expressed the unity of God and Man. Now the "omnipotence of the Steam-engine," the "fever of Skepticism," and the "barnyard Conflagrations" of economic panic expelled the Godlike from the world. The crowds in the streets of London reminded Carlyle of maggots teeming in cheese. A "Babylonish confusion of tongues" supplanted the Word, and the mob ran wild in the name of liberty.

When Carlyle raised his eyes from the stunning noise he saw not infinity but a cage, "an iron, ignoble circle of Necessity." If he looked down, he would be "crushed under the Juggernaut wheels" of the machine age. If he looked inside himself he saw a hollow empire of doubt. That bewildering and chilling flow of dark air he felt was God in retreat: "The Divinity has withdrawn from the Earth; or veils himself in that wide-wasting Whirlwind of a departing Era."

Wandering among the tombs of extinct nations at Stonehenge, Carlyle sensed his plight and the promise of redemption. The individualist spirit had undone the old unities. Spirit and matter would not cohere again until men accepted the burden of freedom that came with unfettered consciousness. They must either "realize a Worship for themselves, or live unworshipping." And an intuition of a new harmony waited among the ruins. The human soul was immortal, the human imagination infinite and inexhaustible. Like the veiling Divinity withdrawing from the fallen world, the human spirit was sheltering in the domain of the unconscious. From the unseen "abysses of mystery and miracle" a new heroic age would explode.

*"Nay," Carlyle wrote, "in the higher Literature of Germany, there al-*ready lies, for him that can read it, the beginning of a new revelation of the Godlike; as yet unrecognized by the mass of the world; but waiting there for recognition, and sure to find it when the fit hour comes."

From Goethe onward, he believed, German thinkers and poets had faced the modern dilemma more honestly and ably than any others. They had plunged into the tangled forests of philosophy and history, and emerged with new understandings of Man's mind and his place in Nature. In the "cry of their soul's agony," Carlyle heard the struggle to evoke once more the divine presence. The Germans had made religious faith possible again, and even "inevitable" for the scientific mind. On every page, Carlyle sensed new recognitions of the eternal fact that there was "a Godlike in human affairs"; that God "not only made us and beholds us, but is in us and around us; that the Age of Miracles, as ever was, now is."

Kant described a mind both sovereign and moral, grasping the ideal forms behind the sense impressions of material reality. Friedrich Schelling named the "unconscious" as the cauldron of thought and passion, where the intuitions of the *Geist*, the Spirit, bubbled up in art. Poets like Hölderlin and Schlegel hymned its ferment as intimations of that ideal world of perfect forms. Cultural historians like Johann Gottfried Herder and Joachim Fichte traced the emergence of freedom, the German idea, from the tribal depths of the forest to its surfacing in nationalist politics. And the mighty Beethoven expressed all this without a word.

Perhaps most valuably of all, Georg Friedrich Hegel revealed the hidden hand of history as the *Geist*. The *Geist* is the essence of being, the spirit of pure freedom. It surges through time like a baton in a footrace, rushing toward the union of Man and the Absolute. As the *Geist* progresses through the flux of matter, its dialectic sifts out the inessential and the retrograde, shedding superfluous matter like old skin.

The ways of the *Geist* were mysterious. Inscrutably it had marched from east to west, from Sanskrit and India to Latin and the French Revolution. Perplexingly it had brought forth Christianity from the Jews.

Still, the *Geist* always ascended logically, and Hegel believed that his historical promontory afforded the perfect view of its motives in action. When Napoléon humiliated the Germans, he awoke them to historical consciousness. The nineteenth century, Hegel felt, would belong to Germany. After that, Hegel suspected that the twentieth century would belong to the Americas. But all that was too distant in time and space to consider.

Although Hegel did not use the word "evolution," his theory of history is a theory of social evolution in all but name. His peoples and nations form and adapt as they compete to fill a historical niche. Then, their tasks fulfilled, they fall exhausted into decay and fossilization. Hegel, who trained in the Lutheran seminary at Tübingen, identified the Absolute, the source and destination of all life, with the Christian God. He believed that the birth of Christianity had been a historical rebirth, the moment that Man really began to grasp the nature of the *Geist* and his role in its great drive toward freedom. And because Hegel, like other theorists of evolution, identified what was necessary with what was desirable, he found the *Geist* in what seemed to be the necessary forms of modern society: the dictator and the nation-state. Carlyle agreed: only a Napoléon, an ancient hero in modern dress, could keep the democratic hordes in order.

The light was fading and it was starting to rain. Carlyle and Emerson trudged back through the gloom. Amesbury was sunk in silence in the shadow of its stone circle. This road had been the ancient highway to London, but the Great Western Railway had emptied it overnight, taking the business of the world with it. When they reached their inn, there was not enough milk for their tea.

While Carlyle brooded on tumbled altars and fallen civilizations, Emerson noted how almost every stone bore the scars of some "mineralogist's hammer and chisel." These implements seemed heirs to the Neolithic hand axes he had seen in the geological museum at Cambridge. He wondered if the Druids really had built Stonehenge. Perhaps it was the work of wanderers from the Mediterranean, Phoenician or Roman. Or, given its resemblance to "temples of the sun" in India, from even farther east. Perhaps some extinct species had shunted the stones into place—a giant Patagonian sloth, a woolly mammoth?

Then he remembered watching Irish laborers building a house in Boston's Back Bay. With just an ordinary derrick and the sweat of the "Paddies," the masons had swung a large block of granite "of the size of the largest of the Stonehenge columns" without the help of Druid priests or Patagonian sloths. The powers that inspired a capitalist might be metaphysical, but his techniques were practical. And Emerson, though he shared some of Carlyle's alarm about the drift of their practical age, prided himself as a practical man. Man and Nature were partners in invention, with Nature the architect, and Man his navvy. The work was as slow as geological time, but each stroke was a realization that divine sparks fell everywhere in Nature, and in few places more fruitfully than in the mind of Man. In creating, Man concentrated "the radiance of the world" into a single object, and on reflection discovered his original potential. "Thus is Art, a nature passed through the alembic of man. Thus in art, does nature work through the will of a man filled with the beauty of her first works."

Fifty years after Rousseau took to his boat, Emerson had described in "Nature" how, as a solitary walker standing in snow puddles in the woods of Mount Auburn, he looked up at the clouded sky and intuited the unity of Man and Nature. In that merging of the finite and the infinite, he detected a higher unity, the merging of Man and Nature in the divine: "Standing on the bare ground,—my head bathed by the blithe air and uplifted into infinite space,—all mean egotism vanishes. I become a transparent eyeball; I am nothing; I see all; the currents of the Universal Being circulate through me; I am part or particle of God."

The last two words floated away. "Calvinism rushes to be Unitarianism, as Unitarianism rushes to be pure theism," Emerson wrote in a Carlylean meditation called "Character." The Christian God was becoming an elegant synonym for Nature, and Nature was supplanting God as a moral legislator. Man was becoming a part or particle, a "self-reliant" natural form.

As Emerson turned from Unitarianism he rushed to his kind of naturalism, German Romantic in spirit and English liberal in matter. He transcended the contradictions between the two with an idiosyncratic blend of Greek philosophy and Indian religion. His German inspirations had anticipated this turn to the east. The blueprint of his "new revelation" is the "First Systematic Program of German Idealism," a document of 1797 in Hegel's handwriting, possibly copied from his university friend Schelling: "I shall speak of an idea that so far as I know has never occurred to anyone before: we must have a new mythology." The old Christian forms are exhausted, the religious sensibility disenchanted. To speed the making of a new mythology, the "profound, beautiful, and true" elements of the old mythologies must be reawakened.

The sacred origins and actors of myth can shape present behavior. To do this, a myth must address its age and speak a shared language. Only then can it create a perfect and universally comprehensible image. As the Idealists realized, "we are unable to make our ideas aesthetic, which is to say mythological, they can be of no interest to the people." In 1797, the "aesthetic" mythologies of the modern West were still forming. There were many peoples, but few of them lived in a nation-state. If they did, party politics was a novelty, and voting even rarer. An *ideologiste* was a type of French social scientist who mapped private patterns of thought in the human mind, not in the public sphere. The political polarity of left and right referred only to the French division of 1789, when the king's supporters had moved to the right hand of the new National Assembly, and his challengers to the left. Five years later, the revolutionaries had abolished this arrangement, and with it the parties it encouraged; they had not expected either to return. The French republic was sliding into dictatorship and war, like the seventeenth-century English republic before it. The American republic had just survived the election of John Adams, but the failures of the democratic experiments in Britain and France suggested that America's second president might equally be its last.

By the 1840s, the aesthetic mythologies of the nation and democracy had formed. The British Parliament had begun the staged reforms that would enfranchise increasing numbers of male electors. The French had taken a bloodier path but arrived at a similar arrangement. The Germans had still to form a political nation at the heart of Europe. In the earthquake of 1848, the implication of John Stuart Mill's "Age of Change" had disclosed itself by invading "outward objects."

Yet, as after an earthquake, the brief rippling of solid forms was followed by shock, then calm.

Across Europe that summer, declarations of fraternity abounded, and threats of violence extracted promises of reform. Yet the old order did not dissolve as asked. The revolutionaries divided into factions or dithered, or overplayed their hands. The workers accused the middle classes of betraying them by cutting deals with the kings and nobles in return for votes and privileges. The middle classes accused the workers of ignorance, of upsetting the cart in their hunger for apples. The radicals accused both groups of cowardice, and they both accused the radicals of fanaticism. As the wave of revolt broke, the chancellors regained their balance. They tiptoed back into their palaces, backed by the heavier tread of their armies.

The reversal began in Paris. In February the National Assembly had responded to the unrest by giving all men the vote and creating the national workshops to give the poor work and bread. In April the voters had elected an assembly of liberals and conservatives. In May the socialists rejected the vote and stormed the assembly in an insurrection witnessed by Emerson. The liberals in the assembly feared civil war and shifted toward the conservatives. In June the assembly closed the national workshops, which the socialists controlled. Up went the barricades again, and out came the national guard. In three days of rioting and fighting the soldiers killed more than ten thousand Parisians. Afterward the assembly exiled four thousand of its most zealous opponents and jailed their leaders.

Similar repressions followed in Vienna, Berlin, Cologne, and Venice. In Vienna, the Austrian court returned while the provisional government bickered with the elected assembly. In June the Austrian army bombarded Prague. In October it shelled the Viennese themselves into submission. Heartened by the Austrian example, the king of Prussia turned down the offer of heading a constitutional assembly in Frankfurt and, with a sham concession here and there, began stealthily to undo the Prussian revolution. In December the French once more followed a revolution with a Napoléon, by electing the late dictator's nephew, Louis-Napoléon.

The voice of authority remained the same but the revolutions had changed its language. The English, American, and French revolutions had not been aberrations; they had been harbingers of mass democracy and nationalism. The vocabulary of modern politics had arrived: constitutions, parliaments, national rights, and even natural ones. The autocrats recognized the strange children of the revolution: conservatism, dutiful and rigid, the firstborn sitting at the king's right hand; liberalism, cheerful and subversive, splitting the difference like a middle child; and socialism, the prodigal exile whose return threatened to bring down the house. Mass politics, with its parties, rallies, platforms, and voting, would become part of everyone's life. The personal would be political, and the name of the modern catechism was "ideology."

"The main fruit of the revolutionary movement of 1848," Karl Marx concluded on Christmas Eve 1848, "is not that which the people have won, but that which they have lost—the loss of their illusions."

They had also fashioned some new illusions. Apart from meaning "mind" and "spirit," *Geist* also means "ghost."

2

THE STONES OF VENICE

Ruskin and Thoreau
Against the Juggernaut

This world is a place of business. What an infinite bustle!
I am awaked almost every night by the panting of the
locomotive. It interrupts my dreams. There is no Sabbath. —*Thoreau, "Life Without Principle" (1853)*

Religious distress is at the same time the expression of
real distress and a protest against real distress. Religion
is the sigh of the oppressed creature, the heart of a
heartless world, just as it is the spirit of spiritless conditions. It is the opium of the people. —*Marx, "Critique of
Hegel's Philosophy of Right" (1843)*

T he gondola glides down a green canal toward the lagoon. The
English couple tip now to one side, now the other, as the unseen
oar plunges into the sucking water. From inside the humped cabin,
they see the rank grass of the shore, an occasional stunted tree, and
an autumnal flight of birds, briefly framed in black. Far to the west,
the pale afternoon sun colors the Alps purple, like the dead rose leaves
he gave her on their wedding day. Ahead, four or five domes emerge
from the mist and water, a coil of black smoke from a belfry. Then the
mirage dissolves. The brick arches of a railway bridge undulate across

the water like a sea snake in a medieval map. It is November 1849, and the Ruskins have returned to Venice.

John and Effie Ruskin have been married since April 1848 but have yet to consummate their union. After a fumbled, shaming wedding night, John suggested that they wait a few years, and Effie agreed. Venice in winter is damp and foggy, and in 1849 it is emptier than usual. When the Venetians revived their ancient republic in the summer of 1848, the Austrians bombarded and retook the city. The tourists have yet to return. Austrian officers have invested Caffè Florian, on the south side of the Piazza San Marco. Defeated republicans glower from the café on its north side. Effie escapes from her cold suite at the Danieli to flirt with the Austrian officers.

A tall, thin man with thick blond hair, reddish whiskers, and a "delicacy" of manner that was "partly feminine," John Ruskin was the only child of two first cousins. His mother, Margaret Cock, was a publican's daughter who had bowdlerized her surname to Cox and prayed that John would become a clergyman. John's father, John James Ruskin, was a Dickensian striver who had raised himself from a clerk's stool to a partner's desk as a wine importer. He envisioned his son as a gentleman artist. Like little John Stuart Mill, whose father, an official in the India Office, had used his son's nursery as a laboratory for the testing of Utilitarian theories, little John Ruskin grew like a bloom in a walled garden, shielded from harsh influences and other people's children. When John went to Oxford, his mother went too.

Ruskin, reconciling his parents' expectations, became the foremost aesthetic preacher of his time. Art and architecture were spiritual and political testaments. The lines of a church or railway could be read like Holy Writ or a share index. The beautiful was good, and the ugly was not just bad but evil, an inspiration to wickedness. Ruskin found an image of perfect line and life in the Gothic architecture of medieval Europe. Instead of the inhumanely strict Classical line, the curlicues of Gothic masonry elaborated as naturally as leaves from a branch. These organic forms created their social content. The medieval craftsman, secure in his guild, had worked in harmony with his society and created soaring monuments to the Christian ethic. Unlike the egotistical modern artist, he signed his handiwork only with chisel marks. These tiny imperfections were humanity writ in stone, frail proofs of the soul's need for perfection. There were no machine copies in Ruskin's paradise.

Ruskin was a guild socialist for aesthetic reasons. His Christianity was also aesthetic. The dreadful hammers of the archaeologists were pulverizing his faith, and with it the inspirational power of religious art. What remained was the religion of art, the cultivation of organic forms in life as in marble. In *The Stones of Venice*, Ruskin told the modern British a parable of salvation and ruin—a warning of the evils of bad art.

Venice had been a "golden clasp on the girdle of the earth," an imperial clearinghouse connecting northern Europe to the Mediterranean. Its sailors had written history on "the white scrolls of the sea surges." Its palaces had filled with silks and spices and money. Its architects had blended three traditions, the Arabic, Byzantine, and Romanesque. The Doge's Palace, reconciling all three traditions "in exactly equal proportions," had been "the central building of the world." From "the burning heart of her Fortitude and Splendour," Venice had radiated a "world-wide pulsation, the glory of the West and of the East."And now Venice rotted in her lagoon "with the quietness of the Arabian sands."

In the dank basilica of Santi Giovanni e Paolo, Ruskin borrowed a ladder and climbed through dust and cobwebs to the plaster effigy that topped the tomb of Andrea Vendramin, a brief, disastrous doge who had died of "pestilence" in 1478. Vendramin's effigy raised one hand, as though waving from posterity to the pews below. Ruskin wanted to see his other hand.

"At first I thought it had been broken off, but on clearing away the dust, I saw the wretched effigy had only one hand, and was a mere block on the inner side."

The sculptor, Alessandro Leopardi, had betrayed God, traduced Nature, and lied to his fellow man. Ruskin was not surprised to discover that Leopardi had been banished from Venice for forging false coins. Venice, Ruskin believed, had not fallen to the jealousy of popes and princes, or the loss of its import monopolies after the opening of sea routes between Europe and India. Venice had fallen from within, to a plunge in the market of civic virtue: to the egotism, greed, and sensuality of the Renaissance, and to Machiavelli's gift, politics without morality.

Like Edward Gibbon in the forum in Rome, Ruskin read the stones of Venice as runes of Britain's decline: "The foundations of society were never yet shaken as they are at this day." Nothing shook those foundations like a train. Steam technology asserted Man's power over Nature, but this alchemy of water, coal, and steel also imposed Nature's power upon Man. The new lines sliced up the countryside, smashed through city slums, and disturbed the sleeping dead in the cemeteries. The passenger had to submit to regimentation by schedules, to the mobile class system of ticketing, and to a ride that jolted mind and body alike. Dickens found that the train's rhythm complemented his experiments in hypnosis, but nearly died in a train crash. Tolstoy, who would die in a station waiting room, gave Anna Karenina an erotic awakening in one train, but killed her under the wheels of another.

When the train bounded over the lagoon to Venice, Ruskin saw that the "noble" landscape of the ancient approach by sea was reduced to a postcard, a snapshot "seen only by a glance, as the engine slackens its rushing on the iron line." As Venice fell into the mechanized net of trains, timetables, and tourists, even its memory would be erased. This was worse than the bubonic plague, the opening of the sea route to India, or Napoléon's abolition of the Venetian republic: "The last few eventful years, fraught with change to the face of the whole earth, have been more fatal in their influence on Venice than the five hundred that preceded them." Man despoiled his inheritance by intellectual and moral degradation. The locals even defecated in the arcades of the Doge's Palace.

Napoléon had called himself another Attila the Hun, but Ruskin saw that the leader of the modern vandals was Thomas Cook, the pioneer of package tourism. Within a few years, the Baedeker-toting barbarians would overrun Venice. Oddly enough, they would carry pocket editions of *The Stones of Venice* and take Ruskin as their expert, if querulous, guide to the city that stood for everything lost and beautiful.

"Laissez-faire *the only way*," *Emerson wrote in 1848.* "*Meddle, & I see you snap the sinews.*"

If ugliness were evil and the factory ruined everything, then the British were on the road to hell. They paved it with the best of intentions. They had freed the slaves in their empire. They had reformed their electoral system. They had regulated their morals with evangelical faith, and their productions with copyright laws. With native coal and cotton from America and India, they had made the cities of northern England the "workshop of the world." Manchester was "Cottonopolis," the citadel of liberal individualism and its economic double, laissez-faire capitalism. By 1851 Britain was the world's leading industrial and military power, a steam-powered hive of invention and industry that generated a third of global output. Through technical ingenuity, commercial energy, and the equally energetic dispersion of their armed forces and surplus populations across the world, the British had become the first truly global nation.

At home, the English became the first people to escape the ancient pattern of human society. By 1851, more than half of them were living in cities. The rhythm of urban life was a machine pulse, as regular, efficient, and monotonous as the chains of standardized actions that extracted, delivered, processed, and dispersed its products. In December 1847, while Emerson was in England, the British government standardized clocks all over the British Isles to Greenwich

Mean Time, to heighten the efficiency of privately owned telegraph and railway companies.

"It is not, truly speaking, the labour that is divided," Ruskin fumed, "but the men—Divided into mere segments of men—broken into small fragments and crumbs of life." The dumb repetition and "perfectnesses" of the factory were "signs of a slavery in our England a thousand times more bitter and more degrading than that of the scourged African, or helot Greek." The machine stamped the worker like it stamped its products. "You must either make a tool of the creature, or a man of him. You cannot make both."

The Thoreau company's pencils were among America's best, and the proprietor's son was so much their creature that, without looking, he could pick up by feel alone a perfect dozen "at every grasp."

Pensive and awkward, with the hangdog face of a bloodhound that has lost its sense of smell, Henry David Thoreau was manifestly not destined for the life of "quiet desperation," but he knew it well enough. When he found himself unable to survive by writing, he forced himself back to the factory. Adjusting his father's lathes, he sharpened the lines of the Thoreau pencil into a "perfectedness" of New England wood.

The price of that wood was rising. The forests of New England were the raw materials for construction, railway sleepers, and fuel. When Emerson saw that the revolutionaries had cut down the plane trees in Paris, he pondered the loss of value. He knew their price in Concord too. He had already bought and cleared one lot in the woods by Walden Pond when, in 1845, he bought a further fourteen acres. It is unclear whether Emerson wanted to conserve Nature's sacred precincts or speculate on a diminishing resource. A year earlier, Thoreau had contributed to the rise in local wood prices when, cooking fish in a hollow tree stump, he had started a fire that consumed some eight hundred acres of mature woods.

Thoreau was not the woodsman he claimed to be, but he was as rooted in New England as any yeoman of Old England. He refused

the temptations of nostalgia among the stones of Europe, and of amnesia among the settlers rushing westward: "Would it not be more
heroic and faithful to till and redeem this New England soil of the
world?" But Concord was no longer a farmer's town. After Irish nav-
vies had laid the Boston–Fitchburg railway, town occupations and
trade boomed. The businessmen of Concord huddled over their newspapers like pigs with truffles, gorging on the news and prices that
Emerson called their "second breakfast." The commercial network
that Hegel had called the "compact system of civil society" constricted
around Thoreau, and he searched for an escape. Emerson pushed him
onto the train and into the marketplace, bearing introductions to
newspaper editors in New York.

At P. T. Barnum's American Museum on Broadway, Thoreau saw
the precocious dwarf General Tom Thumb, a troupe of Indians doing
war dances, and the Fiji mermaid—a monkey's head sewn onto a
fish's body. At the offices of the *New-York Tribune*, he met Horace
Greeley, the defender of the common man against land speculators,
slaveholders, and monopolists. Greeley accepted Thoreau's essays for
the *Tribune* and offered his services as agent too. But within a few
months Thoreau was back in Concord. "We will not be imposed upon
by this vast application of forces."

Thoreau retreated to the woods. He shed his possessions and reduced his social exchanges and economic needs. Directing his "eye
right inward," he seceded into a one-person state. On Emerson's plot
by the pond, and with Emerson's ideal of self-reliance as his model, he
hacked down some of Emerson's white pines and built the "little
world" of *Walden*: the cabin, the journal, the bean patch, the mystical
botanizing, the meditative union with Nature, the subtle antagonizing of society.

While Marx deferred the natural life of hunting, fishing, and philos-
ophy to a distant and rather vague future, Thoreau jumped the tracks
and lived it. His ascetic vows buffered him from the merchants and

machines. His means of production were his mind and body, and the worker controlled them both. He hoed beans not for the market, but for food. The rhythm of work strengthened his muscles and made them receptacles of sensation. The turn of seasons sharpened his mind like a pencil at the lathe. Whispers of intuition arose from his body like mist on the water. He felt his "awake" self penetrate the surface of things and touch an inner, absolute reality. "Time is but the stream I go fishing in . . . Its thin current slides away, but eternity remains."

Ruskin could conjure an ideal of eternity in stone, but an American mystic had no medieval past, no churches and canals; only the forest and the pathways of its disinherited inhabitants, the calls of birds not gondoliers, the blank slate of the waters. Walden Pond had no tributaries. The melting glaciers had filled its declivities eons ago, and only the rain had sustained it.

Every morning, the steam train clattered past as regularly as sunrise. Meditating on the front step of his cabin, Thoreau integrated the train's pulse with the harmony of the woods and the water. "God Himself culminates in the present moment, and will never be more divine in the lapse of all ages. And we are enabled to apprehend at all what is sublime and noble only by the perpetual instilling and drenching of the reality that surrounds us." Its departure left a deeper silence. He sensed himself merging with Nature, the divine spirit infusing all life. "The yogi absorbed in contemplation, contributes in his degree to creation: he breathes a divine perfume, he hears wonderful things."

The Indian on Emerson's reservation was the first American yogi.

*Sleepless in the sticky July nights, Emerson reached for something hu*mid and sensual: "There was nothing for me but to read the Vedas, the bible of the tropics." He returned to it every three or four years. "It is as sublime as heat and night and a breathless ocean. It contains every religious sentiment, all the grand ethics which visit in turn each noble and poetic mind." Each time he read it, the image of Nature as life's "first legislator" overran his imagination. "It is of no use to put away the book: if I trust myself in the woods or upon a boat in the pond, nature makes a *Bramin* of me presently: eternal necessity, eternal compensation, unfathomable power, unbroken silence,—this is her creed."

Emerson found it easy to sift "primeval inspiration" from the "endless ceremonial nonsense which caricatures and contradicts it." He also found it easy to read. He read his "tropical" bible in English, like his Christian Bible. Over the previous century, the global rivalry of Britain and France had created an arsenal of translations and studies. While traders and soldiers mastered India's resources and markets, the scholars of comparative religion probed its faiths.

In the early 1760s, Jean Calmette, a Jesuit missionary in the French foothold at Pondicherry, obtained Sanskrit copies of all four Vedas; soon, partial French translations appeared. In 1767, a second Pondicherry Jesuit, Gaston-Laurent Coeurdoux, notified the Académie des Sciences in Paris of the parallels between Sanskrit, the language of Hindu holy texts, and Latin, Greek, German, French, and Russian. In 1771, a third missionary, Abraham Anquetil-Duperron, published a translation of the Zoroastrian Avesta; in 1787, Anquetil-Duperron finished the first reliable French version of the Upanishads. By then, however, the British had displaced the French from India.

After the fall of Pondicherry in 1761, the French government had executed the city's governor, Count Lally, and imprisoned its military commander, the Count de Morangies. In 1773 these executions inspired the first use of Indian religion as a weapon in Western polemics, Voltaire's *Fragments Relating to the Late Revolutions in India*. The judges, Voltaire said, had scapegoated the defenders of Pondicherry. The real culprits were the French Enlightenment's usual suspects: an absolutist monarch and the Catholic Church. The new scholarship on India offered new ways of interrogating them. In his *Philosophical Dictionary*, Voltaire pointed out that the ancient Hindu texts predated the Gospels and the Church, and the "declarations of Birma, Brahma and Vishnu" anticipated the parables of Jesus. If, as the Church claimed, eminence rested on tradition, then Hindu wisdom ranked higher than Christian dogma. "Is it not likely that the Brahmins were the first legislators of the earth, the first philosophers, the first theologians?"

This historical perspective was no less harsh on Christian institutions. To explain India's current disarray, Voltaire repeated the theories of early European travelers. The climate of India caused voluptuousness and ease in its people and "effeminacy" in their leaders. Like fruit rotting in the sun, rational faith decayed into superstition, astronomy into astrology, and the rule of the Brahmins into the despotism of the lavish but feeble Mughal emperors. In this light, the power of the decadent court at Versailles was also a chimera.

After the revolution of 1789, this anticlerical, republican use of India's past became government policy. In 1795, the revolutionary regime opened the École Spéciale des Langues Orientales Vivantes, Europe's first secular institution for the study of Eastern languages. Its advocates included the anticlerical polemicist Constantin-François Volney, author of the law by which the revolutionary government had sequestered the lands of the French church. In the sweep of history, Volney decided, Christianity seemed a "relatively insignificant and young" religion. Why should the age of universal reason grant political privileges to "local varieties of solar myth"?

As the Americans were leaving the British Empire with French help, the people of India were passing from French influence to British control. While American lawyers composed their Constitution and French intellectuals used India's past to undermine the legitimacy of their kings and cardinals, British administrators used scholarship to consolidate an empire in the east.

In 1783, the Welsh judge William Jones arrived in Calcutta. Jones, a prodigious amateur linguist and a friend of Benjamin Franklin's, detected a common source behind the resemblances between Sanskrit and the European languages. He also noticed a striking similitude between the Hindu cults and those of pagan Greece. In 1784, Jones founded the Asiatic Society, initiating the formal modern study of India's religions, laws, arts, botany, and geography. In the mornings, he presided over the high court of Bengal. In the hot afternoons, he shuttered himself in his residence and conversed with Brahmins about Hindu poetry and algebra.

"Every accumulation of knowledge," Warren Hastings wrote in his preface to Thomas Wilkins's translation of the Bhagavad Gita, "is useful to the state." Between 1788 and 1839, *Asiatic Researches*, the Asiatic Society's journal, was the West's main source of information on India. Warren Hastings and Thomas Wilkins introduced Emerson and Thoreau to the Bhagavad Gita. William Jones expounded the Laws of Manu in *Institutes of Hindu Law.* Horace Wilson recounted the legends of the *Vishnu Purana.* William Jones's friend Henry Cole-brooke explained the Vedas in *Essays on the Religion and Philosophy of the Hindus.*

The British administrators concurred with the French missionaries. Ancient India had matched Greece in mathematics and philosophy, apparently without direct contact. Modern India would benefit from direct contact with the heirs of Greece, especially their market forces. Jones thought that despotism, the curse of Asian societies, crushed initiative and bred passivity. His friend Quintin Craufurd suggested that India's decline had begun with the Islamic invasions, which had brought bigotry, ignorance, and barbarism. The decline had been accelerated by the caste system, which gave the Brahmins a monopoly on higher knowledge.

Yet if *Asiatic Researches* was one product of the British Empire of the 1780s, its American readers were quite another. Translated to Concord, *Asiatic Researches* seemed less an asset to imperial control than a means to spiritual revolt. If the principles of the American Revolution were to be pursued into the empire of the inner life, this was their legal and spiritual language. In the *Laws of Manu*, Thoreau heard a "volume of sound as it had swept unobstructed over the plains of Hindostan," and smelled "a fragrance wafted down from those old times, and no more to be refuted than the wind." As Thoreau recycled the windows of his hut from the cabin of an Irish navvy, so he built his dream with the intellectual materials of the "compact system" from which he recoiled. Before the yogi breathed and heard, he read.

"Im Orient müssen wir das höchste Romantische suchen," Friedrich Schlegel had advised in 1800. "We must seek the Romantic supreme in the Orient." But the Orient, or at least a digestible version of it, came to the seekers. For Emerson and Thoreau, India was a library specializing in comparative social criticism and the tablets of the Romantic soul. Thoreau's experiment at Walden tested these established methods in a new laboratory. Orienting by Emerson's compass, the "expert in home-cosmography" sailed "eastward and backward" on "a loftier course through a purer stratum—free from particulars, simple, universal." He found there a familiar, exotic India of the mind, a realm of the spirit drenched with sensuality. But his mind, like his cabin, was still furnished with the detritus of the "compact system." Apart from meditating on the face of Walden Pond, Thoreau felt compelled to plumb its depths. The pond's spiritual import was infinite, but its physical profundity was just over one hundred feet. The mentality of the road builder and tracklayer had sailed with him; a more quotidian universal had penetrated his most sacred recess.

Marching "confidently in the direction of his dreams," the noble savage disappears into the trees. In his meditations, Thoreau passes an "invisible boundary." The man who crosses this frontier could "create his own laws" and "live with the license of a higher order of beings." Others will follow him, and "new, universal, and more liberal laws will begin to establish themselves around and within him; or the old laws be expanded, and interpreted in his favor in a more liberal sense." His microscopic eye penetrates to the cellular level, where all matter resembles itself and regains its unity of purpose. Aligning his eye to the lens, he aligns himself with the truth of Nature.

On the farms of the Deccan plateau, laborers pack fresh cotton and load the swollen bales onto carts. Hauled by bullocks at a stately ten miles a day, the bales bump down mud roads toward Bombay, where—

their number and value eroded by wind, rain, theft, and accident—they take ship for the mills of northern England.

Far to the northeast at Raniganj, women and children dig coal from the face of India's largest mine. Steam pumps raise the coal to the surface, where it is loaded into hundreds of small boats. Ferried down the Damodar River, the coal is unloaded at Amta and reloaded for shipment to Calcutta. The passage to Amta is navigable only at the peak of the rainy season, so each year's production must be shipped in ten days. Often the boatmen go on strike when the rains come. If they run aground, or if the water level drops, they tip their coal into the river.

The merchants and "influentials" of Bombay, Calcutta, Manchester, and London examined the columns of profit, wastage, and shipping costs and calculated how much more money could be made with a railway. "If we could draw a larger supply of cotton from India, it would be a great national object," mused Charles Wood, president of the Board of Trade. "It is not a comfortable thing to be so dependent on the United States."

The new governor-general in Calcutta was a technocrat. James Broun-Ramsay, the Marquess of Dalhousie, saw India as a testing ground for the utilitarianism of Jeremy Bentham and the free trade ethos of liberals like John Bright and Richard Cobden. Dalhousie lined up the technical arsenal that the "sagacity and science of recent times had previously given to the Western nations—I mean Railways, uniform Postage, and the Electric Telegraph." He used real artillery too. Exploiting division among the Sikh rulers of the Punjab, he annexed their kingdom as the North-West Frontier Province. The mapmakers of the Great Trigonometrical Survey pushed into Kashmir and set their sights on the inaccessible Himalayan peaks. In 1856 they named "Peak XV" after the recently retired surveyor-general Sir Andrew Everest.

"How much more admirable the *Bhagvat-Geeta* than all the ruins of the East!" Thoreau had enthused in 1844. But India now meant more than ruins and religion. The modern Juggernaut was driving deeper into Indian life. In 1839, five years before Samuel Morse sent his metaphysical inquiry from Baltimore to Washington, William O'Shaughnessy, an amateur scientist in the pay of the East India Company, had created a telegraph circuit in Calcutta. As water transmitted electricity more cheaply than copper wire, the circuit included a two-mile stretch of the Hooghly River.

The *Handbook of British India* described the visible part of the new Indian landscape: "On approaching Calcutta, the smoking chimneys of steam-engines are now seen in every direction, on either side of the river, presenting the gratifying appearance of a seat of numerous extensive manufactories, vying with many British cities." The coal smoke over Calcutta raised the specter of a second Lancashire on the bank of the Ganges, and a political economy that covered the globe.

On May 1, 1851, the new world was condensed into a giant greenhouse in London's Hyde Park. Backed by a two-hundred-member orchestra and the world's largest pipe organ, six hundred choristers belted out the "Hallelujah" chorus, and twenty-five thousand guests responded. Their song echoed through the Crystal Palace, a transparent cathedral built from nearly three hundred thousand hand-blown panes of glass and forty-five hundred tons of structural iron. Shaded by tropical palms, a native elm, and the frozen waters of a glass fountain, Queen Victoria declared the opening of the "Great Exhibition of the Works of Industry of All Nations." A further twenty-five thousand visitors flooded in, past the world's largest sheet of plate glass and a twenty-four-ton block of coal.

The Palace of Peace was a cacophony of people and machines. As with the exhibits, the sheer quantity of city life gave a new quality to social experiences. Dazed crowds wandered amid the modern cornucopia in partial bewilderment. The human mind had not been made for this. Older visitors to the exhibition had been born in the days of highwaymen. People no longer knew themselves. When the geologist Thomas Henry Huxley returned to London that year after a forty-thousand-mile voyage, he felt more alone in the "waves of people silently surging" around him in Waterloo station than he had felt in the empty oceans. Loneliness in the crowd, he noticed, "seems a greater threat than the wilds I have been used to."

"Truly it was astonishing, a fairy scene," Queen Victoria wrote to her uncle Leopold, known to his subjects as King of the Belgians. "Many cried, and all felt touched and impressed with devotional feelings."

Earlier that year, the English journalist Harriet Martineau had wept with similar wonder as she translated Auguste Comte's *The Positive Philosophy*. Comte reckoned he had solved the "revolutionary crisis" of unmoored hopes and violent passions that was tormenting the "civilized nations of the world." Positivism applied scientific principles to all aspects of Nature. Its findings massed like cells into a single, universal system of knowledge. This, the Religion of Humanity, would organize the most complex organism of all, human society. "The Principle, Love; the Base, Order: the End, Progress."

Comte took his base, his principles, and his ends from his late employer, Claude de Rouvroy, the Count of Saint-Simon. The child of an ancient family brought low after 1789, Saint-Simon was an apostle of the Enlightenment's faith in progress. Imprisoned during the Terror, he had received a visit from the ghost of his illustrious ancestor Charlemagne, who told him, "Your success as a philosopher will equal mine as a soldier and politician."

Returning the compliment, Saint-Simon created a theory of history in the medieval image. In Charlemagne's time, knowledge had been the province of the clergy, and power that of the feudal nobility. Their balance created what Saint-Simon called an "organic" stability, a term he derived from chemistry. The rise of science had upset the balance between Man and Nature. An obscurantist church had responded by pitting God against gravity, and the result had been war and chaos. To reunite knowledge and power, theology had to catch up with science. If this was Newton's universe, who better to formulate a modern faith than the scientists, the new priesthood of knowledge?

In 1803, Saint-Simon launched the "Scientific Religion" with a curia called the Elect of Humanity, the twenty-one cardinals of the Council of Newton. No one seemed to notice. Nor did they notice a revised version, Physicism, the "religion of physical science." Saint-Simon lived on bread and water, and when he could not afford a printer, he sold his clothes to buy paper and copied out his pamphlets by hand. He issued fantastical proposals to dig a canal between the Atlantic and Pacific Oceans; to unite "the various nations of Europe" in a single, federal state; to form a global Parliament of Men that could supervise the peaceful resolution of disagreements, and also manage the spread of "the European race over the whole habitable globe." He warned that the Earth was overheating, that the temperate zones would shortly resemble the deserts of Africa and Asia, and that Man would end up where he had begun, playing in the sand. Saint-Simon may have been the first thinker to imagine a posthuman future, a world without *Homo sapiens*. He suspected that the earth would be inherited by the next most intelligent, industrious, and orderly species: the beaver.

In 1823, Saint-Simon shot himself seven times in the head. Comte found him covered in blood, pondering his pistol. "How can a man who has seven bullets in his head still live and think?" Saint-Simon asked, for he was nothing if not scientific of mind. A doctor removed six of the bullets. The seventh loitered in Saint-Simon's brain as the icons of knowledge and power converged in Saint-Simon's third and final system. In 1825, the Scientific Religion became the "New Christianity," a new method of science that would restore the old harmonies of Christendom. Rational systems would create the ideal "political economy" and also the "social institutions" that could fulfill the Christian ideal, the "physical and moral amelioration of the most numerous and poorest class." The lost ideal of the medieval "organic" would be reborn in the modern routines of technocracy.

"Nature uniformly does one thing at a time," Emerson wrote in 1848. "So now, as she is making railroad & telegraph ages, she starves the *spirituel*, to stuff the *materiel* & *industriel*."

Saint-Simon's visions were projections of real trends. The passage of time gave some of them the appearance of prophecies. The beaver never did launch its coup, but the *industriels* continued to cause political chaos. After Saint-Simon's death, Auguste Comte volunteered to complete the "vast intellectual operation" begun by Bacon, Descartes, and Galileo: to build "the system of general ideas which must henceforth prevail among the human race." He developed Saint-Simon's last blueprint, the New Christianity, into Positivism and the new science that he called "sociology."

For Comte, society rested on the three "general elements" of religion: doctrine, worship, and discipline. Like Ruskin, he saw medieval Europe as the "original theocracy" that had balanced all three. Christendom's doctrine had been the neo-Aristotelian explanation of Nature, which reconciled *scientia*, knowledge, with theology. Its worship had been the rituals of the Church, which explained these ideas to the peasants. Its discipline had been that of the feudal nobility who, by maintaining the "institution of caste," had ensured a stable, hierarchical society. But progress never stopped, and it had severed the ancient links between these three elements. Where Ruskin blamed the individualist villains of the Renaissance, Comte praised the heroes of empirical inquiry. When scientific knowledge had undone doctrine and worship, a new class had arisen, the *industriels*, the creators and masters of technology. There would be no discipline until society accepted their eminence.

Positivism would realign doctrine and worship with the higher discipline of science, and the restive human soul with the institutions of society. As reason freed Man from "supernatural influences," it would liberate the "permanent inspiration of universal love," which Comte named "altruism." Through the seven sacraments of the Positive Catechism, Man would worship his best qualities in the spirit of "universal Humanity."

Meanwhile, the experts would manage the Positive State.

In the Religion of Humanity, politics is the "science of production." The state concentrates power in its hands to "enable it better to fulfill its social function." The deity and society become indistinguishable: a "Great Being, of which each individual may become a perpetual organ." Specialization creates hierarchy, the harmony of natural attributes. Like earlier French revolutionaries, Comte divides the masculine work of knowledge from the feminine work of emotion. While men work in the laboratory, women, those "natural intermediaries," handle the difficulties that arise from the "subjective nature" of the Great Being.

Like Marx, another reader of Saint-Simon, Comte masked religious aspirations in rational planning and dressed the corpse of medieval Christendom in the clothes of modern science. Comte even cast his muse, the tubercular aristocrat Clotilde de Vaux, in the role of the Virgin. And, like Marx, Comte saw the future in industrial Britain. Anglophone liberals returned the compliment, though they differed over Comte's increasingly literal and elaborate religiosity. John Stuart Mill wondered if the cult of Clotilde de Vaux had rotted Comte's mind. But Emerson approved of Comte's religious frisson, and George Eliot became a Comtean because of it. Comte insisted that the Religion of Humanity was nothing more than a philosophy of science, the logic of technology. Shortly before his death in 1857, he attempted to join forces with the Jesuits. With a different plan to recover the medieval unity of Christendom, they declined a merger.

Comte's "theory of the future of man" and the Great Exhibition promised a revolution without tears, mobs, or massacres. The new world of the *industriels* could be both rational and devotional. After the reign of the saints, the age of the technocrats.

In Soho, the Marx family was starving, and six-month-old Guido was sick. Karl and Jenny had rented two miserable rooms in the house of a Jewish lace dealer. Money borrowed from Engels saved them from joining the proletariat, but it could not save Guido. Stateless and penniless, Marx visited the Crystal Palace in the park, and saw the distortions of a fairground mirror. "With this exhibition, the bourgeoisie of the world has erected in the modern Rome its Pantheon where, with self-satisfied pride, it exhibits the gods which it has made for itself."

Capitalism was an optical illusion, creating "a world after its own image." More than half the exhibits came from Britain and its empire. The Chinese, insulted by the forced opening of their economy in the Opium Wars, had refused to send an exhibit, so a group of London collectors invented one, a clichéd tableau of vases, dowry chests, and bamboo trinkets. India was represented by similarly eternal and mundane verities: effigies of washerwomen, spinners, and Thuggee stranglers, along with a selection of traditional textiles and the inevitable elephant. A vogue for Eastern styles ensued, a lurid hybrid of Chinese patterns and Indian cloth mingled, like Thoreau's Indian motifs, for local taste.

Effie Ruskin visited the exhibition on the first day with four gentleman friends. John stayed at home in south London, brooding on Venice. "For the first time in the history of the world, a national museum is formed in which a whole nation is inside a building," Ruskin complained.

The exhibition was the first plausible image of globalization. The "concentrated power" of industry, Marx wrote, was "demolishing national barriers" and "blurring local peculiarities." This logic desecrated taboos and virtues, dressed the whole world in Manchester cotton, and cast whole societies "beneath the wheels of the Juggernaut of capital." Worst of all, people seemed to like these indignities, and even crave them.

Six million visitors passed through the glass halls of the exhibition that summer, most on the "shilling days" when prices dropped to attract the workers. Society divided its leisure like its labor. The workers took over the café, enjoying their first taste of ice cream. The middle classes studied the machines; the exhibition offered unprecedented scope for industrial plagiarism. The rich colonized the heart of the Crystal Palace, where the area around the fountain became a display space like the winners' enclosure on Derby Day. The workers griped about the size of the sandwiches; the aridity of the "sixpenny dollops of pork pie"; the banning of alcohol, dogs, and tobacco; and the closure of the hall on Sunday, their only day off. But the only disorder occurred when a shilling-day crowd rushed to acclaim the Duke of Wellington. Enslaved to the gods of class and property, they clung to their oppressor, raising the duke on their shoulders.

Engels called this "false consciousness." The capitalist sapped his workers' brains with cheap goods, illusory comforts, and mind-numbing labor. This alienated them from self-knowledge; "alienation," having originally referred to the distance between God and Man, now described the split within. Like "primitive" tribes hypnotized by a witch doctor's talisman, the workers venerated the graven images of production, as if these objects could magic them into bourgeois. Marx called this state of mind "commodity fetishism."

Marx's theories about the inner life of capitalism would be more durable than his economic theories. For in 1851, reality failed him. In December, forty-seven years to the day after Napoléon Bonaparte had crowned himself emperor, his nephew Louis-Napoléon launched a coup, supported by the army and his mistress's money. The Bonaparte name promised order and glory. Its bearer, whose only experience of public office had been a stint as a volunteer constable during the 1848 disturbances in London, impersonated a man of the people by calling for universal male suffrage. The voters endorsed his coup in a referendum, then elected him as Emperor Napoléon III.

Marx was "quite bewildered" as the voters hurried to ennoble Louis-Napoléon's "commonplace repulsive features" under his uncle's "iron death mask." But when apocalyptic hope is disappointed, the true believer doubles his avowals of faith. In 1848, the law of nature had become visible. Now Marx scrabbled for proofs in invisibility. The truth was veiled in the fictions of Louis-Napoléon, in the hypnosis of the commodity fetish, in the opiate stupor of false consciousness. The Crystal Palace and its Comtean celebration of "industrial and scientific forces" masked a new "great fact." "In our days, every-thing seems pregnant with its contrary."

*Before Juggernaut became a metaphor for everything wrong with mod-*ern life, he was a god. Jagannath was an aspect of Vishnu, and he dwelled in a temple at Puri by the Bay of Bengal. Each year, Hindu and Buddhist pilgrims massed at Puri, and the priests of Juggernaut rolled his image through the streets on an elaborate chariot. As the pilgrims crowded to acclaim him, some were trampled to death, others crushed beneath his wheels. The first Europeans to observe this rite thought that the dead had offered themselves as sacrifices. This image of ancient religious barbarism went west, where "Jugger-naut" came to mean modern technical barbarism: mechanistic, impla-cable, inhuman.

In 1803, Arthur Wellesley, the future Duke of Wellington, had conquered Puri on behalf of the East India Company. Wellesley placed Jagannath under his "absolute protection." Noting that the priests and Brahmins derived "considerable profits" from Jagannath's pilgrims, he suggested that a reform of their "rapacity" might be deemed advisable. Then again, why "exasperate the persons whom it must be our object to conciliate"?

By this tactful blend of war and conciliation, the East India Com-pany had grown from an Elizabethan joint-stock venture, with a few coastal "factories" at Madras, Bombay, and Calcutta, into the inheritor of the Mughal Empire, and the world's first multinational corpora-tion. "John Company" ruled as he traded, greedily and without scru-ple. He was a sensualist and a cynical conciliator. He adopted the Mughal emperors' debauched habits and exploitative tax system. To keep the money coming in, he banned Christian missionaries and tol-erated Hindu habits of child marriage, slavery, the caste system, and *sati,* the sometimes forcible burning of widows on their husbands' funeral pyres. His rapacity made the priests of Puri look like ama-teurs. Words like *nabob* and *mogul* entered the English language to describe the adventurers who returned to Britain as rich as princes. Meanwhile, the famine of 1770 killed a third of Bengal's population.

The loss of America concentrated British attention on the company's conduct in India. In 1787, Edmund Burke secured the impeachment of Bengal's governor-general, Warren Hastings, for corruption. A seven-year trial led to Hastings's acquittal, but Burke won the moral case. As he had at the time of the American rebellion, he insisted that Britain's rule abroad must reflect the law at home. It was the beginning of liberal imperialism, the paradox by which invaders reform their subjects for the good of all.

By 1815, the Company commanded an army ten times larger than Britain's own, and ruled Bengal, most of the Ganges basin, and large tracts of southern and western India. Although the Company was now a government, its shareholders still expected their dividends, so the Company funded its administration with loans from the Bank of England. The resulting debts allowed the London government to take over the Company's role in a series of parliamentary acts. At home, Britain's middle-class *industriels* were busy reforming their workers' morals. As British rule in India became formal, the Indians came under the same pressures. First, Christian missionaries and schools were permitted. Then, the government attacked Thuggee, the cult whose worship of Kali by robbing and throttling travelers insulted Christian decency and the free movement of goods. Next, *sati* was banned. Then, in 1833, the government turned on the Company.

"Reason is confounded," Thomas Babington Macaulay told the Commons. A "handful of adventurers" from a small Atlantic island had subjugated a vast country on the other side of the world. They now ruled "hundred millions of people" who differed from them both "physically" and "morally." How to frame a good government and "engraft on despotism those blessings which are the natural fruits of liberty"?

As it was at home, Britain in India would be more liberal than democratic. India, Macaulay said, must be educated until it was "competent to govern itself." Britain would give the Indians their first common tongue, the English language. It would teach them about free trade, cricket, and Christ. It would give them a modern government, with a civil service of young Indians "superior either in talents or diligence to the mass."

"No native of our Indian empire," Macaulay promised, "shall, by reason of his colour, his descent, or his religion, be incapable of holding office." At the time, only one in seven British men could vote, and one in six Americans was a slave. This was a remarkable promise, to be honored in the breach. This was not Europe, Macaulay warned. Admitting "natives" to high office was a "most delicate matter." The adventurers should feed them the fruits of liberty by "slow degrees" and in "fullness of time." Meanwhile, the Indians should think themselves lucky to be under history's most enlightened despotism. The despots were lucky too, and their profit would be the world's gain: "It is scarcely possible to calculate the benefits which we might derive from the diffusion of European civilization among the vast population of the East."

In 1845, while Thoreau set up at Walden, the western Juggernaut reached Jagannath's temple. A team of British inspectors judged his cult to be "ignorant and superstitious." His pilgrims spread "immorality" and "disease," and would be better employed in productive labor. He was also behind on his taxes. His lands were undervalued, and his priests, who charged pilgrims as they entered the temple, were not declaring their earnings.

After Macaulay had identified a distant terminus for British rule, Dalhousie laid the track. He linked India's towns with metaled roads and irrigation canals. He built courthouses and treasuries. With Sir Charles Wood, he organized a national system of government schools that began in vernacular languages and ended in three English-speaking universities. He imported British engineers and set up training schools for Indian ones. By an ingenious legal contrivance, the Doctrine of Lapse, he annexed the territory and revenue of any state whose ruler died without leaving a legitimate male heir. Then he bound India in the iron and copper bands of modern communications.

In 1851, Dalhousie hired William O'Shaughnessy to link the British garrisons at Madras, Bombay, and Calcutta by telegraph. In 1853, he planned an Indian railway network. In 1854, he found time to visit the temple of Jagannath while launching a cheap postal system with a flat, universal fee modeled on Britain's "penny post." By 1856, Dalhousie supervised four thousand miles of telegraph cable. Hundreds of miles of railway track were running, and hundreds more were under construction.

Calcutta and Bombay were 1,409 miles apart by train, but only minutes apart by telegraph. The condensation of distance transformed commercial relationships. The *New-York Tribune*'s new Europe correspondent, Karl Marx, predicted the advent of Saint-Simon's connected world. "The day is not far distant," Marx wrote, "when, by a combination of railways and steam vessels, the distance between England and India, measured by time, will be shortened to eight days, and when that once-fabulous country will thus actually be annexed to the Western world."

The railways also changed social and political relationships inside India. Dalhousie had intended his trains to carry goods, but they made money from people. In 1857 the Indian railways carried over two million passengers, many on cheap "fourth-class" tickets of Dalhousie's invention. The trains mixed people divided by language, caste, and religion. The newspapers and letters in the baggage car carried personal and local sentiments across the subcontinent. If Juggernaut was a merciless master, he also created new contacts and possibilities.

The "compact system" altered the horizons of Indians in paradoxical ways. It fostered their common identity as Indians, communicating through liberal institutions in English, but it also allowed them to become more sectarian. Literacy granted a personal encounter with religious texts, but mass communication was a tool for doctrinal standardization. The fourth-class ticket made pilgrimage cheaper and faster, and thus more likely to be compulsory. The railways, *The Friend of India* noted, instantly produced a "social change in the habits of general society far more deep and extensive than any which has been created by the political revolutions of the last twenty centuries."

"What is really desired, under the name of riches," Ruskin wrote in *Unto This Last,* "is, essentially, power over men; in the simplest sense, the power of obtaining for our own advantage the labour of servant, tradesman, and artist; in wider sense, authority of directing large masses of the nation to various ends."

The Stones of Venice led Ruskin from the religion of art to Carlyle's "dismal science," economics. Marx made the same journey in the 1850s, from the aesthetic experiences of commodity fetish and alienation to the number-crunching theories of *Capital.* Comte, and Saint-Simon before him, had already gotten there. The problem, Ruskin realized, was that a society regulated by supply and demand would enrich the diligent and the determined, but also the proud, the covetous, the insensitive, and the ignorant. The same system would impoverish not just the foolish, the reckless, and the wicked, but also "the humble, the thoughtful . . . the imaginative, the sensitive . . . and the entirely merciful, just, and godly person."

The true unit of production, Ruskin concluded, was not the commodity, but the individual, and that required an economy of virtue. Like Marx with *Capital,* Ruskin now committed himself to writing "an exhaustive treatise in Political Economy." Like Marx, he retraced his steps to the period before the capitalist revolution. Unlike Marx, he stopped there. The answer, Ruskin explained in religio-economic tracts like *Unto This Last* and *Time and Tide,* was "an organization of labour akin to the ancient guilds," and the restoration of the hierarchies that had produced and sustained the medieval artisan.

Ruskin became the godfather of Arts and Crafts, the movement to revive local design and artisanal production. In the 1870s, he launched the Guild of Saint George, a network of self-sustaining agrarian communities. The guild practiced communal living, not communism, and art instead of liberty. A worker's income reflected his or her position in a fixed, quasi-feudal hierarchy, and the right to marriage could only be earned by chivalric good conduct. Like the elders of Perfectionism, the vanguard of Marx's revolution, and the technocrats of Saint-Simon, the aristocrats of the guild possessed the power to shape their subjects' lives.

❧ 3 ❧

THE FRENCH REVELATION

Baudelaire, Lévi, and
the Romantic Occult

These are strange chronicles of futurity, pictured as things of the past; they seem to intimate a succession of worlds wherein events are repeated, so that the prevision of things to come is the evocation of shadows already lost in the past. —*Éliphas Lévi*, The History of Magic *(1860)*

The inhabitants of the Île Saint-Louis call themselves *les insulaires,* "the islanders," and they talk of Paris as if it were a foreign country. As the sun sets on a winter afternoon, a sickly scarecrow of a man hurries along the quay and ducks into the courtyard of the Hôtel Pimodan. Catching the scent of stale urine from the tubs in the dyers' basement workshop, he turns right, mounts a staircase with a sphinx at its foot, and knocks at the door of the *bel étage.*

The empty salon feels like a "pendulum clock that has forgotten to wind itself." Every surface is covered in gold, glass, and allegory— plaster vegetables in sooty golden stucco, mirrors in etched gilt frames, and, on the ceiling, nymphs and satyrs showing Love conquering Time. But the musicians' balcony is empty and the visitor's footsteps summon fearful hollows from the parquet. The *bel étage* was built for grand receptions but it has outlived its audience. A small group has retreated to the boudoir like guests refusing to leave a party. Here too the walls are gold and vegetal and paneled with long, narrow mirrors and landscapes. Decorated with birds, flowers, and dancing figures, the ceiling rises on gold ribs into a vault like the beautiful and highly refined cage of a huge bird. On the floor, a debris of art and empire: colored Venetian glasses, chipped plates of Limoges china, and saucers of Japanese porcelain containing *dawamesk*, a thick, green-brown paste of hashish mixed with sugar and spices. Nervous, shabby, and prematurely bald, Charles Baudelaire eats a piece about the size of his thumb.

The Île Saint-Louis is the island of Dr. Moreau. After taking hashish in the Levant in the 1830s, Dr. Jacques Joseph Moreau wondered if its hallucinations and delusions might aid the medical understanding of psychosis. On his return to Paris, Moreau searched for volunteers. The hedonistic writer Théophile Gautier responded, then recruited his Bohemian friends into the Club des Hachichins. The club holds a monthly session in the boudoir, and Baudelaire is a regular. Their fieldwork has supplied material for several studies of narcosis and insanity, including Gautier's "Club des Hachichins" (1843) and Moreau's *Du hachisch et de l'aliénation mentale* (1845). A mind intoxicated with the "extension of personality" loses its footing. First it scrambles to the heavens, then it tumbles into hell. After a stint in the gilded laboratory, Gautier is horrified to see that the stairs continue forever in both directions. Dante's Purgatory becomes a Piranesi dystopia where Classical ruins and prisons multiply and mutate like forest growths.

Baudelaire lives in the Hôtel Pimodan. He will write *Les fleurs du mal* in his squalid and ungilded room on the third floor. Tonight he descends past the sphinx and into the courtyard on weak legs. As he drifts down the Boulevard de Montparnasse toward a table at the Closerie des Lilas, he feels himself melting into the heart of the crowd. He is one flesh with the people, and the sacraments of unity sour his mouth—tannins of red wine, bitter tars of opium and tobacco, and a repulsive taste of sour butter from the fecal chocolate pellets of hashish.

Baudelaire does not muddy his feet in the woods. He is the "botanist of the pavement." As air is to birds and water to fish, the city is his element. He loses himself in an artificial paradise. His mind is a *"machine à penser,"* a thinking machine powered by poisons, conjuring temporary *correspondances* between Spleen, the vile world of matter, and the divine realm of Ideal.

> *Nature is a temple whose living pillars*
> *Sometimes let slip confused words,*
> *Man crosses it through forests of symbols*
> *Who watch him with knowing eyes.*

Sensations rise up like stink from the gutters or the acrid scent of his mistress Jeanne Duval's hair. Impressions bleed into each other, beauty and filth, sound and light, rapture and horror, until their ebb and flow melts into synesthesia, the union of the senses. He is the "artist of modern life," the flâneur: the "gentleman stroller of city streets," a saunterer and idler, a wit, dandy, and cynic, a dreamer seeking *le spiritualisme*, "spirituality," in secret correspondences between the gutter and the stars.

Seventy yards from Baudelaire's seat on the terrace of the Closerie des Lilas, the magus of the Boulevard de Montparnasse lives in a single room. Alphonse-Louis Constant, the weak and dreamy boy who had a vision of the Magdalene during his First Communion and spent fourteen years in a seminary, is now forty, fat, and bald. For photographs, he hides his curves in a magician's robe and props himself up with a silver-topped cane, his gouty fingers swollen like quenelles of pike. He may look like a glutton but he is a man of superior will. He is Éliphas Lévi Zahed, the master of the Magic of Light. He is the self-made creator of *l'occultisme*, the modern occult.

If not for appetite, he could have been a priest. A terrible hunger arose in Constant as he catechized young Adèle Allenbach for her First Communion. The monks noticed, and they expelled him eight days before he was due to take his vows. His mother killed herself shortly afterward. Constant became a socialist and wrote *The Bible of Liberty*, which predicted the "explosion" of a "corrupt" world. The police confiscated every copy and charged him with sedition. He exchanged a monk's cell for a convict's and spent a year in prison.

The night before Easter, an angel appeared at the end of his bed and took him to a mountaintop. Below he saw a dark plain in a tempest of "vapors and shadows." Cities crashed together like ships in a tempest. The waves foamed with human heads, and the empires of the earth fell in flames. Desperate voices rose from the destruction, crying, "Man is free, there is no longer a God!" and "We are gods. Man must serve us!" and "Let us drink the blood of those who have drunk our sweat and tears!" Then Mary Magdalene appeared, bearing the body of Jesus in her arms. She crushed the serpent head of Satan with a twist of her foot. A young girl stepped forward and took Constant's hand. "From now on," she promised, "we shall walk together."

His mind was "flooded with light." The Magdalene of the Gospels blurred into the Marianne of the barricades. Society was ruled by the "dead faith and extinct splendors" of paternal tyranny, and the divine feminine must liberate the divine masculine: "Nature, no longer mysterious to me, was emptied of its antique terrors. Sure of my future because I felt eternity and the omnipotence of God within me, consoled to human suffering because I now understood its cause and purpose, I found nothing vague or uncertain in the dream of life. God's mind came to the aid of my own and explained to me every image and dissipated every shadow."

Uniting with the divine feminine, Constant impregnated first a schoolteacher and then one of her pupils, the beautiful Noémi Cadiot. Her father forced him to choose between marriage and prison. He chose marriage but got prison too, for incitement in a pamphlet called *The Voice of Famine*. Appeals from Noémi, who was by now heavily pregnant, secured his release after six months. They lived the *vie bohème* in Montparnasse with their daughter, Marie. Noémi took the nom de plume Claude Vignon from a Balzac novel and wrote for the *Progressive Review*. Alphonse painted and published poems as "Constant de Baucour." His "Correspondances" anticipated Baudelaire's poem of that name:

> *Nothing in Nature is mute*
> *To who knows how to follow its laws,*
> *The stars have a writing,*
> *The flowers of the field a voice.*

In 1848, the spirit of revolution called Constant to run for the National Assembly. But his neighbors did not elect him. The people's republic mutated into the Second Empire. Noémi eloped with the editor of the *Progressive Review* and set up as a sculptor. Then Constant's cherished Marie died.

Constant realized that he had misread the book of Nature. Socialism was a dream that "began in absurdity and ended in madness." The people were deaf to "absolute truths," the divine feminine an untouchable ideal. Adrift in a dark and pitiless universe, the soul struggled toward the light against gravity and Nature. The "foundation" of life was not love, but the will to survive. Purified in the alembic of suffering, Alphonse-Louis Constant Hebraized his name to Éliphas Lévi Zahed, the man not born of woman.

*In July 1854, Lévi met the novelist and politician Edward Bulwer-*Lytton in London. Today, Bulwer-Lytton's writing survives only in anonymous epigrams. He perpetrated the Romantic banal of "It was a dark and stormy night." He sent the "great unwashed" in "pursuit of the almighty dollar" but promised that "the pen is mightier than the sword." To his public, though, Bulwer-Lytton was a master novelist. When his friend Dickens was stuck for the ending of *A Tale of Two Cities*, Bulwer-Lytton suggested that Sydney Carton should sacrifice himself to the guillotine. He also insisted that Pip should get the girl at the end of *Great Expectations*.

The typical Bulwer-Lytton hero is an idealist martyred at a moment of historic finality: *The Last Days of Pompeii, The Last of the Barons, Harold: Last of the Saxons, Rienzi: Last of the Roman Tribunes.* The public Bulwer-Lytton was a modern tribune, an aristocratic Conservative in the House of Commons. The private Bulwer-Lytton was a member of the Orphic Circle, a group of debauched amateurs experimenting with hypnosis, drugs, and séances. These interests inspired a second, smaller group of stories in which past becomes future. For these, Bulwer-Lytton is now overlooked as a pioneer of science fiction, the missing link between Mary Shelley and Jules Verne or Bram Stoker, whose *Dracula* (1897) bears the influence of Bulwer-Lytton's "A Strange Story."

One dark and stormy night above a department store on Oxford Street, Éliphas Lévi summoned the spirit of the Greek philosopher Apollonius of Tyana for Bulwer-Lytton and a female friend. After incense and incantations before an altar, a lean and melancholy specter appeared, wearing a kind of shroud, which seemed more gray than white. Lévi had only one question: Would Noémi Cadiot come back? The answer sounded in his mind: "*Morte!*"

Noémi filed for divorce, but Lévi refused to believe that she no longer loved him. Nor, when he thought about it, did he believe that he had really evoked, seen, and touched the great Apollonius. The magus knew the mechanics of the séance. He himself had sent tables across the room and summoned ghostly chords from a grand piano. He had forced the spirits to write in a mysterious script that turned out to be Estonian. He had cured sick cows in the Channel Islands by mailing their owners the "sign of the microcosm with the sacred letters of Yehoshua, plus a magnetized photograph." This was magic, but it was not the "supernatural" of scripture and myth, or the hallucinated and "unserious" entertainments of the American Spiritualist. A scientific mind knew that magic was natural, a science governed by fixed "physical laws."

The brain, said Lévi, was printed with images from within and without. The slightest "excitement" jarred it. Like a double exposure on a camera plate, disturbance generated apparitions, visions, and "all the intuitive phenomena peculiar to madness or ecstasy." The magus had mastered these processes and could create them at will. He turned his sight inward, meditating until his mental pathways were "congested" like the traffic on the boulevards or "overcharged" like a battery. Then he released his energies. His "impressions and thoughts" sharpened into corresponding images from the "universal imagination." By juggling these images, the mind controlled matter and created the impressions of magic: "Hence comes sympathy and antipathy, hence dreams, hence the phenomena of second sight and extranatural vision." Hence too that "echo" of Apollonius in modern French.

Lévi called his "occult science" the highest form of knowledge. Its truths were not the reformist platitudes of the Spiritualists. The liberated will fought to save the soul of the universe. As the Kabbalists said, God had retreated from Creation, leaving Man the terrifying task of repairing his relationship to Nature. The magus dared to handle the life force itself, the pure energy that was "astral light." This "natural and divine agent" infused all matter and was "infinitely more powerful than steam." Lévi explained his divine agent in the imagery of the new technology. Like the telegraph, astral light was a "universal plastic mediator" that put "every nervous apparatus" in "secret communication." Like the camera plate and the battery, it was "a common receptacle for vibrations of movement and images of form."

Man too had a dash of this divine spark. Along with his traditional body and soul, he had an eternal "astral body" where spirit met matter. The magus knew his Spleen from his Ideal. He saw that the material world was the lower, confused double of the upper, ideal world. Traversing the pathways of astral light, he rebuilt the correspondences between Man and Nature: the grand polarities of matter and spirit, male and female, divinity and morality, love and hate, good and evil. The play of these forces created evolutionary change in the physical world. It imprinted each organism with an astral image of its "succession of forms" and an aura of "magnetic breath." A man who mastered astral light, who could "adapt or direct" it might, by controlling the doubling of reality and unreality, change "the face of the whole world."

"Scientifically provable hypotheses are one and all the last half-lights or shadows of science; faith begins where reason falls exhausted. Beyond human reason there is that Reason which is Divine—for my weakness a supreme absurdity, but an infinite absurdity which confounds me, and in which I believe."

Lévi probably derived the term occultisme *from Cornelius Agrippa's De Occulta Philosophia* (1553). The first modern occultist posed as the last Renaissance magus: the "man of science" as heir of Prometheus, the alchemists, and the old sorcerers. Yet his magical persona was a science fiction, and his occult a peculiarly modern heresy.

Lévi reworked Neoplatonism, the philosophy of the Renaissance, for an age in which mass society, in Emerson's words, was "everywhere in conspiracy against the manhood of every one of its members."

To reconcile scientific perspectives and Christian tradition, the Neoplatonists had, like the early Christians before them, aligned Plato's idealism with the Christian view of history. Lévi gave modern names to their key ideas. His astral light was an electrical update of the Neoplatonists' *spiritus mundi,* the living "world spirit" that linked the *corpus mundi* and the *anima mundi,* the "world body" and the "world soul." His occult science was a form of intuitive knowledge like the Neoplatonists' *gnosis.* He shared the Neoplatonists' faith that all religions descended from a single, original wisdom. He repeated Neoplatonism's false history too: the faith that, though time and transmission had corrupted the "ancient religion," fragments of its truths survived in the various mystical traditions, from Hermes in Egypt to Zoroaster in Persia, then to Plato and the Jews to Christianity.

The word "hermetic" came to mean "secret" because Renaissance occultists believed that Hermes' tradition had been preserved secretly, and because, fearing prosecution as heretics, they had to work in secret. Their furtive hunt for universal answers to perennial mysteries created the fantasy that perfect secrecy meant perfect transmission. The fictive bearers of this hypothetical tradition became the secret order of Rosicrucians. They floated from Hermetic dreams to Enlightenment conspiracy theories, before entering the realms of popular fiction in Bulwer-Lytton's *Zanoni: Last of the Rosicrucians* (1842).

Lévi advised his magus to "keep silent," but he was, like Bulwer-Lytton, a publicist and vulgarizer of the Hermetic tradition. The forces of Lévi's universe remained "occult," hidden or invisible. But, like *Self-Help* (1859), Samuel Smiles's guide to mortal empowerment, Lévi's book of secrets was available in cheap print, an ideal of individualism marketed to history's first mass readership. This new public had little leisure time, and it wanted quick returns on its literary investments. So Lévi invented a "thinking machine" for all: the modern tarot.

The tarot deck contains four suits of fourteen cards—wands, cups, swords, and coins—and an additional twenty-two trump cards. These depict medieval archetypes like the Fool, the Hanged Man, and the One-Eyed Merchant. Southern Europeans had long added tarot sets to ordinary card games; Rabelais describes this in *Gargantua and Pantagruel* (1532). Lévi acquired from the eighteenth-century mystic Antoine Court de Gébelin the specious notions that the tarot came from ancient Egypt and that the priests in the temple of Thoth had used it for divination. Inspired, Lévi decided to purify the tarot of its historic accretions. He took a set from medieval Marseille, painted over its characters' French costumes with vaguely Egyptian outfits, and decorated the cards with sphinxes. The four suits became the "minor arcana," the trumps the "major arcana." He arranged the trumps in a sequence and fixed the value of the Fool, who had previously worked like a joker. Thus purified, the cards no longer expressed ineluctable fate. Now they were aids to its mastery. They were guideposts on the pathways of astral light, generating inward images that their user could manipulate. These correspondences could express the will, and the will to power.

The modern Faust, the magus of exceptional ability and Promethean will, is a stock protagonist in Gothic novels and science fiction.
"Éliphas Lévi," invented after Mary Shelley's Dr. Frankenstein and
before H. G. Wells's Dr. Moreau, is one of those characters. But Lévi
was not the first claimant to mastery of the vital force or the Rosicrucian mysteries. His tarot was the creation of a failed artist, but his
persona was plagiarized from a successful one: Bulwer-Lytton, the
novelist who, when he took his seat in Parliament, exhaled a distinct
vapor of opium pastilles.

In Bulwer-Lytton's *Zanoni*, Glyndon, a well-bred aesthete, and
Zanoni, an ancient and immortal Zoroastrian, compete for the love of
Viola, a young opera singer. Zanoni has preserved himself by practic-
ing the Rosicrucian mysteries, whose object is the discovery of the
elixir of eternal life, and by avoiding love, the entanglement that makes
all men mortal. By denying desire and compassion, he channels his
impulse to love into sublime egotism. He is a Mesmerist and a mind
controller, a master of the electrical "great fluid" that infuses all life.
Zanoni's program, like that other divine order, absolute monarchy, is
undone by the French Revolution. He falls in love with Viola and becomes fully human. Having lost his head in life, he substitutes himself
for his beloved on the guillotine in a manner that Sydney Carton would
soon emulate.

In the twentieth century, the French named as *existentialiste* the
philosophical individual who, after despairing before a godless universe, fulfills his potential by building a personally authentic system
of values. As historians of literature prefer not to dwell on the novels
of Bulwer-Lytton, so historians of philosophy prefer not to call a
mountebank like Éliphas Lévi a progenitor of existentialism alongside contemporaries such as Schopenhauer, Kierkegaard, Dostoevsky,
and Nietzsche. Yet Lévi's occult science, like Thoreau's mystical "conceiving," shares their Romantic themes: the retreat of the Christian
God, the challenge of absurdity, the need to believe, the spiritual rebellion that, overcoming despair, renews and extends personality.
Kierkegaard wrote under numerous pen names. Dostoevsky spoke

through Yakov Petrovich Golyadkin, his "underground man"; Nietzsche as "Zarathustra"; Baudelaire as the flâneur or the "Artist of Modern Life." The persona of "Éliphas Lévi" was another of these pseudonymous leaps of Faustian faith into the supreme absurdity of the modern spiritual crisis, "an infinite absurdity which confounds me, and in which I believe."

"I have been magnetised again today, and I am sure now that I am better, not much, but still sufficient to convince me that I am *better."*
The voices came and went with the sickness. The spirits tormented Achsa Sprague for seven years. She could not move her hands and legs. Abscesses opened in her flesh and caused her left eye to bulge out of its socket. The family doctor examined her stigmata and diagnosed lovesickness. When he dragged her from her bed, she could not stand up. She gave up teaching in the one-room schoolhouse in Plymouth, Vermont, and lay in bed, reading *Jane Eyre* and waiting for her next session of "magnetic healing" with Dr. Graham. This, the method of the eighteenth-century German doctor Franz Mesmer, attributed illness to imbalances of the "universal fluid," the electrical life force that pervaded all matter with "animal magnetism." The body was polarized between its celestial head and its terrestrial feet. Mesmer rebalanced the body with magnets, hypnosis, and massage. Vigorously rubbing the thighs and torsos of his mostly female patients, he brought them to a "crisis" in a private anteroom.

Just when Achsa Sprague had abandoned "hope and all thought of health," a miracle occurred. The "Spirit Agency" that had persecuted her set her free, and the "chains of disease" fell from her limbs. In 1854, she left Plymouth and became a "Public Speaking Medium." She toured from Maine to Missouri, campaigning for the rights of women, slaves, and prisoners, crossing from the world of poverty, sickness, and the Fugitive Slave Act to the "Summer-Land" of the spirits, returning with balm for the needy. When the fever returned, her "Spirit Guides" gave her poems, visions of the coming time of universal peace. The "ruined church" would be renewed, but now "Spirit

Agency" would unite all—"Jew, Christian, Heathen, Musselman"—in worship at the "shrine of thought."

After the Hydesville rappings, the phenomena of "spiritism" became a religion called Spiritualism, with a theology and a political platform. From 1850, the Fox sisters gave three séances a day at P. T. Barnum's American Museum on Broadway, admission one dollar. In the half-lit room, their customers felt the spirits stroking them and saw the table move. A party of doctors and "literary celebrities" conducted a private "investigation" and heard posthumously from the Boston divine William Ellery Channing and the Scottish poet Robert Burns. James Fenimore Cooper believed that he had met the spirit of a sister who had died in childhood. Horace Greeley was convinced "beyond the shadow of a doubt." "Our senses are the only witnesses we will consent to trust," he wrote in the *New-York Tribune.* Greeley and his wife, Molly, invited Kate Fox to live in their home so that she could commune daily with their dead son, Pickie. "The piano was sweetly played upon by spirit fingers, and the guitar was played, then taken up and carried around our heads." As the Fox sisters clicked and tapped themselves into exhaustion, they also succumbed to spirits. They began drinking heavily.

By 1854, more than one and a half million Americans were Spiritualists. Hundreds of professional séance mediums toured theaters and private homes, with Spiritualist journals reporting their travels and revelations. American Spiritualists were entertainers and populists, not aristocratic private occultists like Bulwer-Lytton or reactionaries like Éliphas Lévi. They were moralists preaching democracy and social progress. Achsa Sprague was typical of the American mediums; like Elizabeth Cady Stanton and those in her circle, Sprague was a Northeasterner of liberal Protestant stock and frustrated intellect. "Why is it not possible for me to crush out this repining spirit," she had wondered in her sickbed, "this yearning for something higher, better, this insatiate craving for a life of action, this thirsting to drink deep at the fount of Knowledge, all of which are denied me, and find a new strength springing from my weakness?"

In 1854, Congress received a petition with fifteen thousand signatures demanding a "patient, rigid, scientific investigation" into magnetic communication between the upper spheres and the lower. The United States had lately extended itself to the Pacific Ocean and the Rio Grande. Now it must do the same for the unseen world.

The geography of the expanding Union was, Emerson thought, as "sublime" as the inventions that were industrializing its economy, but he was "ashamed" of the leaders and inventors. Congress had effected the "opening of the West" and "the junction of the two Oceans" by "the filthiest selfishness, fraud, & conspiracy," a land grab in the spirit of the European despots. Afterward, the politicians had compromised over America's second original sin, slavery. Abolitionists blocked slaveholding in the new territories, but the slaveholding states secured the Fugitive Slave Act, which compelled non-slaveholding states to assist in capturing and returning escaped slaves. In 1854, the fissure widened with the founding of the Republican Party on an antislavery platform. The defection of abolitionist Democrats to the Republican Party increased the influence of Southern slaveholders within the Democratic Party. The Compromise of 1850 had averted a civil war but clarified the battle lines of the future.

When the living feared that the republic was heading for the rocks, the ancestral spirits steadied the tiller. Six years after collapsing in the House of Representatives during a debate on the Mexican war, John Quincy Adams returned to his old haunts. In August 1854, Adams's ghost appeared to Joseph Stiles, a medium in Quincy, Massachusetts, and described an American afterlife. Heaven resembled a grand hotel where the tariffs reflected spiritual wealth. In the lobby, harps trilled as the "abused Red Man" and the "down-trodden American slave" mingled with their "pale-faced brother" and "inhabitants of other planets." Above, residents lodged in seven ascending spheres, each more lavish than the last. Joseph Warren, Patrick Henry, and Thomas Jefferson welcomed Adams to a celestial function room, the Hall of Brotherhood. Jesus popped down from the penthouse to shake his hand.

The extension of personality led to uniform conclusions. The medium gave democratic blessings in the spirit of Benjamin Franklin. The patriot spirits demanded abolition, equable marriage, progressive education, and female suffrage. Adams called the Fugitive Slave Law a "direct insult to the Divine." Washington promised the "timely assistance of invisible powers" in the coming war with the "enemies of Republican Liberty." When William Lloyd Garrison sat with Leah Fox, she obliged with a message from a deceased abolitionist: "Spiritualism will work miracles in the case of reform."

For the mortals, Oliver Wendell Holmes noted that the Spiritualist public included not just the obvious "large-hearted women" but also "grave judges, shrewd business men, men of science." If the kind of men who ran the country were in "constant intercourse" with spirits, their otherworldly experiences must gradually alter their "whole conception" of society.

"If the spirits would only just make me a trance medium and put the right thing into my mouth," prayed Susan B. Anthony, who had joined Elizabeth Cady Stanton's campaign for women's rights. "You can't think how earnestly I have prayed to be made a spirit medium for a whole week. If they would only come to me thus, I would give them a hearty welcome."

Spiritualism spoke in a woman's voice, and it spoke on behalf of the voiceless, but the apparatus was operated by men. The medium's natural habitat was the front parlor, the public showcase of a private home. There, a medium could be among friends who shared in her political opinions and in the secret arousals of transgression, of crossing the spheres while touching other people in a dark room. Yet in her trance, she spoke in tongues from the male realm of politics, law, and science. This ventriloquism made her presence in the theater and lyceum acceptable. For if she was entranced and ecstatic, she would not know what she was saying. She needed a "controller," invariably male, to interpret her prophecies and project them into the gallery.

The Spiritualist spoke as a natural right, but her controller justified his faith in her message by science. He explained that her body was a machine, a "spiritual telegraph" for conducting electrical impulses. Her spine functioned like the batteries that were essential to telegraph stations. Her vertebrae were the metal plates in the battery, her spinal fluid a conductor like battery acid. Her mind drew on this reserve of energy as if it were one of Gaston Planté's rechargeable batteries. Her fingers rapped out her letters like a Morse code transmitter.

This appeal to science negated the medium as it justified her words. The logic of the battery also suggested that women made the best mediums because they were "negative" receptors, channeling "positive" male voices. The most productive sittings involved equal numbers of men and women, or "persons in whom respectively the positive and negative elements predominate," holding hands alternately. In an uncertain age, the séance promised an image of balance. Fierce declarations translated into deferred rewards; the American Spiritualists trusted in progress.

Spiritualism had entered the "compact system of civil society." The market in séances became crowded with new talent. The political and financial stakes kept rising. Believers demanded more precise messages, and doubters intensified their scrutiny. A medium had to compete like a vaudeville turn, and one whose male partner was stealing the show. Here too, the machine standard offered to liberate her from a private dilemma, only to imprison her in a public one. In 1855, Robert Hare, a chemistry professor at the University of Philadelphia, invented the spiritoscope, a machine that allowed a medium to shed her controller but keep his scientific authority.

The medium attached herself to the spiritoscope by an electrical wire. Her magnetic cogitations spanned a vertical wheel with the letters of the alphabet printed around its rim. At first, she sat at a table, as though working a sewing machine. With time and practice, she learned to play this celestial roulette sitting behind a screen with her back to the wheel. Escaping the cues of her controller, her spiritual chaperon, she could work in a theater without raising her voice—or even speaking at all.

As the factory had brought women into the workforce, so women began speaking in public through machines.

One of Éliphas Lévi's mentors, the Polish mystic Hoenë Wronski, built a prognometer, a thinking machine to tell the future. "There are two metal globes, enclosed one inside the other, and rolling on two cruciform axes in a large immobile circle, full of little cases that open and close, and contain all the principles of science. The synthesis of the same sciences follows the analogies that are engraved on the double glove which rotates around the two axes."

Years later, Lévi saw it in an antique shop. He bought it as a reminder of folly, a feather from the wings of Icarus. The notion of mastery through machines was risible. Any peasant or Protestant could crank the prognometer, but who could decipher its oracles?

The occultist's task was to restore Nature's "law of equilibrium" by polarizing darkness from light, truth from falsehood. A society whose customs and laws were an analogy of this equilibrium would discover Nature's "greatest secrets," from the "science of government" to the sacramental "mysteries of sexual love." Marx used similar imagery when he contrasted medieval ideals and modern vulgarities: all was "grey on grey" in the chaotic, commercial France of the 1850s because the sacred polarities had collapsed. The names of the ruling class replaced the names of the saints, Marx noted, and bankers sat in cabinet positions like the bishops of old.

Browsing a Spiritualist report of a séance at Lyon, Lévi was not surprised to read an excerpt from one of his books attributed to the ghost of Plato. The *spiritistes* were Panglosses and plagiarists, and American Spiritualists were the worst of all. They stole their techniques from French *spiritistes* and promulgated the heresy of democracy. To Lévi their proofs were, as Jeremy Bentham had said of natural rights, "nonsense on stilts." There were no natural rights, only fictions of equality and the struggle of the individual will. Nature's equilibrium derived not from the equality of all but from the "distinction of contraries." Society rested on a disciplined division of labor and authority. The people were a "vast army of inferiors," a "mass which is ruled and not capable of ruling." They would always be weak, and their weakness was the contrary that allowed the triumph of the strong. The same law of opposites made the "radical emancipation of womanhood" as "absurd" as class equality. When a woman passed from "the passive to the active condition," as Noémi Cadiot had done, she became a "sterile and monstrous androgyne." Why else had Nature given her "a soft voice, not to be heard in large assemblies, unless raised to a ridiculously discordant pitch"?

First the Protestants had abolished Purgatory. Now, Lévi believed, the democrats were replacing Hell with the best of all worlds where the weak and the meek would inherit the higher spheres. Their democratic universe was a lie. Man was not born free. He was a slave to desire and habit. Evil was not a kingdom or a separate creation. Evil was everywhere, because darkness and light were entangled in a cosmic flux. Lévi's mind floated in an electric sea, an unbounded, terrifying morass of spectral visions and dark forces. Astral light was pure energy. It was "indifferent" to morality and lent itself "to good as to evil." Its treacherous current could sweep the novice or dabbler into madness. Damnation was now a living hell, the sensation of "falsehood in action." One slip, and Lévi's web of correspondences would collapse, tumbling him into the meaningless terrors of space.

Romanticism, Baudelaire said, was not a matter of subjects or exact truths. It was a "way of feeling." For a Romantic, intuitive feelings are the primary, natural, and most valuable form of knowledge. The conscious mind floats on a deep sea. Sense impressions bubble up from the unconscious depths. In pursuit of these precious intimations, the Romantic dives into the total immersion that Hegel called *absolut Innerlichkeit*, "absolute inwardness." Romanticism began in explorations of these depths: the torments of solitude in Rousseau's *Confessions*, the torments of love in Goethe's *Young Werther*, the ghosts and night-mares of the "Gothick" novel.

When the Romantic surfaced, he assayed his pearls as a philo-sophical Idealist. His trove of sensations and perceptions were images of reality, but these images were partial and inferior. This compelled him to explain the relationship between imperfect perception and perfect form. For Immanuel Kant, the "phenomenal" world of experi-ence reflected the mind that perceived it: we know an object by expe-rience, and can infer some of its attributes by reason, but the world of the "thing-in-itself" remains inaccessible. To Kant, a metaphysical leap beyond the bounds of consciousness seemed futile. He recom-mended that people concentrate on morals instead.

The Transcendentalism of Emerson and his friends did not refer to the transcendence of self or the forms of matter, but to Kant's "transcendental idealism"—or so they believed. Emerson got his Kant secondhand, through a creative misreading by Samuel Taylor Coleridge. Coleridge believed that our sense impressions and our in-tuitions converge in a higher Reason, and that we can know it. At nineteen, Emerson encountered this Reason as the "beauty & power" of Nature. It seemed "impossible that the wind which breathes so ex-pressive a sound amid the leaves—should mean nothing," and in the "majesty of nature" he sensed his "claims to his rights in the uni-verse." As in Lévi's occult science and Baudelaire's "forests of sym-bols," in Emerson's "wood-thoughts" desire corresponds to reality and confirms its hidden, inner nature.

There was an alternative Romantic sublime. Before Kant derived beauty and morality from Nature, Edmund Burke described Nature's "power" as terrifying and amoral. The price of "beauty" perceived is sensations of fear, diminution before natural forces, and annihilation in the primordial *tohu va-vohu*, the formless void. Emerson saw "in-finite Reason" in Nature, but it could also be the sublime terror of cold, dark space. Lévi saw it in the astral "half-lights" or "shadows," Coleridge in the opiated "caves of ice," Baudelaire in the faltering correspondences of *Flowers of Evil* (1857), where the shoots of life contain their *décadence*, their decay and decline. Waking from the horror, the Romantic dreamer agrees with Burke. Only the power of tradition can hold back dissolution and chaos. Like Coleridge after the political Terror of the first French Revolution, Éliphas Lévi turns from a republican poet to a conservative religious philosopher.

In the immeasurable gray on gray of the 1850s, Alphonse-Louis Constant, the socialist cuckolded by the worship of Mary, becomes the fearlessly masculine Éliphas Lévi. He is a spiritual dictator shaping reality by his superior will. He is his own controller, not a feminine vessel invaded by the spirits. His initiates are a male elite, a brotherhood of "exceptional wills and energies." Despising women, weakness, and democracy, he creates a distinctively French occult, Catholic in spirit and authoritarian in politics. Its *correspondances* corset Nature like the boulevards that Baron Haussmann smashed through the poorer neighborhoods of Paris.

With the light of reason at his back, the magus scares himself with his own shadow. While the Spiritualist and the worker couple minds to the machine, the magus flees into the "luminous darkness" of faith. He traverses space and time on the cosmic circuitry formed by "the Absolute in religion, science, and justice." The signals at its junctions are the cards of the tarot pack and the *sefirot* of the Kabbalah. After an eternity of confusion "revolving in the circle of Faust," all spiritual energy now runs in one of two directions. The magus either heads eastward and backward toward the mythical origins of all religion in Zoroastrian fire worship, via the Egyptian and Jewish connections. Or he heads westward and forward on the wires of European science, to his terminus in the arms of "Mary, the Divine Mother, who crushed the head of the infernal serpent." Any philosophical souvenirs can be stowed in the "miraculous and lawful hierarchy of the Catholic church," the preserver of "all traditions of science and faith." All contradiction is resolved, and the Kingdom of God is near. "At this point, we pause, having discovered the secret of human omnipotence and progress, the key of all symbolisms, the first and final doctrine."

In the ancient cult of Trophonius, seekers descended into a cave and experienced unspeakable horrors. As they ran or staggered out in panic, the priests of Trophonius placed them on the Throne of Memory and transcribed their ravings as prophetic oracles.

Prophet and priest, Lévi reflected the horror he saw in the electric shadows in an obscene icon. Baphomet is a satyr with a goat's head and a human body, an angel's wings and a devil's horns, a man's muscular shoulders and a woman's round breasts, a flaming torch on his head and, standing in his groin like a large erect penis, the wand of Hermes with a serpent coiled around it.

Before Lévi donated him to the tattooists and heavy metal bands of the twentieth century, Baphomet was Muhammad, prophet of Islam. "Baphomet" is a medieval French corruption, dating from the Crusades. A chance assonance endowed it with a false link to the ancient Persian fire cult of Zoroaster. In *Sartor Resartus* (1836), Thomas Carlyle referred to his "Spiritual New-birth" as his "Baphometic Fire-baptism," the moment that he "directly thereupon began to be a Man." Lévi elaborated this false pedigree. His Baphomet was the goat of sacrifice, the scapegoat who carried the sins of the ancient Jews into the wilderness.

Lévi saw Baphomet on a throne among the rocks, lit by bonfires of human remains and candles made from human fat. Accepting the homage of his followers, he distributes "gold, secret instructions, occult medicines, and poisons." His priestesses, crowned in laurel, sacrifice infants and prepare "terrible feasts" of flesh. As the bacchanal begins, wine "runs in floods, leaving stains like blood." Dancing in "infernal circles," all are intoxicated with "wine, crime, luxury, and song." Masked men and naked women exchange "obscene offers and insane caresses." Animals take human forms like "phantoms of nightmare," monstrous confusions of Nature. As the candles gutter into smoke, the dancers pair into couples and clamber into the rocks.

Baphomet is neither wholly male nor female. He is animal in body but divine in mind. The cave beyond the throne of Trophonius is not empty, like the Holy of Holies in the Jewish temple. It is a seething sexual morass. When the extension of personality leads to the "unexplored regions of Nature," the correspondences disintegrate amid "Natural Horror." The seeker after Nature's truth finds that the vital force is sexual, and the astral fluid flows indiscriminately.

At Walden, Thoreau described a serpent slipping down his throat as he drank "stagnant waters." The serpent planted "seeds of thought in his stomach," fertilizing and feminizing him, expanding within him. "How many ova have I swallowed?" Thoreau feared that it was too late. His understanding expressed itself in sexual shame, as it had for the first to eat the serpent's seed, Adam and Eve. Thoreau had drunk from the living waters, and now he felt "all nature reborn in him," as if he would "suckle monsters." He agonized about the serpent that possessed him: "Is there not such a thing as getting rid of the snake which you have swallowed when young, when thoughtless you stooped and drank at stagnant waters, which has worried you in your waking hours and in your sleep ever since, and appropriated the life that was yours?" He resolved to free himself by separating himself from it. "I caught him by the throat and drew him out, and had a well day after that."

The horror is decapitated, throttled, repelled by stones and incantations. Its terrors are condemned as evil, irrational, illusory. These sacrifices of renunciation and denial leave a pure body and an ideal character. The heroic persona protects itself with new rituals. "One may discover the root of a Hindoo religion in his own private history," Thoreau realized, "when, in the silent intervals of the day or the night, he does sometimes inflict on himself like austerities with a stern satisfaction."

"I have, as it were, my own sun and moon and stars, and a little world all to myself," he wrote. After two years in the woods, Thoreau moved into Emerson's house and began to work on his Walden journals. He rewrote his notes seven times in seven years, cutting, expanding, and abstracting to create a sacred fiction in which the "material was pure," like literary art. The final version was nearly twice as long as the first draft. The heroic yogi of *Walden* is a creation like "Éliphas Lévi."

Thoreau depicted his life of simple virtue but neglected to mention that his mother and sisters had brought him food, or that their two Irish housemaids had washed his soiled laundry. He lauded Nature for the fish in the pond but did not admit that the townsmen of Concord had fished there for two centuries and improved upon Nature by restocking it with a variety of species. He vaunted his experiment in self-reliant "economy" but economized with the truth that Emerson and other friends kept him afloat by hiring him for carpentry, fence building, and gardening, the odd jobs of suburban Arcadia. If, as he claimed, Thoreau was a hermit, it was in the fashion of the old woman who had built herself a shanty in Hyde Park and was expelled for squatting on the site of the Great Exhibition.

Walden is a hymn to "wildness" contained, not wilderness unbound. Nature is a "great-grandmother," not a monstrous seductress. The woods echo to the ax strokes of Thoreau's neighbor Alek Therien, a muscular Canadian woodsman, but when Thoreau meets Therien, the body and its desires are transcended entirely. "I lay down the book and go to my well for water, and lo! There I meet the servant of the Brahmin, priest of Brahma and Vishnu and Indra, who still sits in his temple on the Ganges reading the Vedas."

The "religion of Hindostan," Marx observed as Thoreau finished *Walden,* was "at once a religion of sensualist exuberance, and a religion of self-torturing asceticism": the "religion of the Lingam," the sacred phallus, and of "the Juggernaut." Like Marx, Thoreau saw in India a "world of voluptuousness and a world of woes." Most of them were sexual. "I want the flower and fruit of a man," Thoreau admitted in his journal, "that some fragrance be wafted over from him to me, and some ripeness flavor our intercourse." He lacked Baudelaire's appetite for a woman's sweat. He accepted loans from male friends but refused the gift of a mat from a woman, because it was "best to avoid the beginnings of evil." Thoreau was a spiritual aristocrat, and he reserved his "purer stratum" for a male elite. Far below, the people of Concord lived "meanly, like ants." Only he was fully conscious. Only he heard the "different drummer." Only he lived "the divine life."

On a bed in a bare room on the third floor of a mansion on an island in a city, Baudelaire bathes in the languor of the *paysage opiacé*, the "opiated landscape." Nature is alive in this "truly spiritual room." Dawn tints the still air pink and blue, like a "sensual delight during an eclipse." The furniture has the "somnambulate life" of vegetables or minerals, and its fabrics speak the mute language of flowers, skies, and sunsets. The walls are bare of images, the clearer to see the "delicious obscurity of harmony" in their empty spaces. Next to him sleeps Jeanne Duval, the queen of dreams. "To what benevolent demon do I owe for being thus surrounded by mystery, silence, peace, and perfumes?" he wonders. "Oh, Beatitude! That which we generally call life, even in its happiest expanses, has nothing in common with this supreme life, which I know now, and which I savor minute by minute, second by second!"

A knock at the door feels like being struck in the stomach by a pickax. The *correspondances* melt like butter, and the unreal dawn reclaims the sinner. Is it a bailiff, a prostitute, a printer's boy who wants unwritten pages?

"Horror! I remember myself!"

This filthy rented room is his creation: the unlit fireplace flecked with bronchitic spit, the windows grimed with rain tracks, the furniture ugly and worn. The "perfume of another world" sours into a fetid mixture of old tobacco and the ammoniac stink that rises from the basement.

"You have strewn your personality in all directions, and now, what difficulty you have in putting it back together again!" Now he realizes that his visions were only "tinsel magic," a projection of the mind's own nervous excitement. The drug extended the imagination's reach and could "confer genius, or at least increase it," but it sapped the will. The man who uses a poison in order to think would become the addict who may soon not be able to think without the poison. Hashish, Baudelaire realized, "reveals to a man nothing but himself." And that was both too much and not enough.

Time's "brutal dictatorship" returns to the Hôtel Pimodan like a "hideous old man," dragging a train of memories, regrets, fears, and anguish. Every second sounds with a solemn accent, the mind falters, and the dream of *décadence* falls away like a musical cadenza. Only one object retains its ideal character: his vial of laudanum, an "old and terrible friend."

"Go, wake up, but do not make the sign of the cross," Éliphas Lévi advises his initiates. "I have returned you to yourself and you are in your bed. You are a little tired, even a little bruised, from your voyage and your night, but you have seen something about which the world talks without knowing. You are initiated into the terrible secrets like those of the cave of Trophonius; you have assisted in a Sabbath! Now it remains to you not to go mad."

✵ 4 ✵

THE DESCENT OF MAN

Darwin, Gobineau,
and the Meaning of Life

And for myself, I am fully convinced that there does exist, in Nature, means of Selection, always in action & of which the perfection cannot be exaggerated. I can see no limit to the perfection of this means of Selection; & I will now discuss this subject,—the most important of all to our work. —*Charles Darwin, draft for "My Big Book"* *(March 1857)*

The vertebrate mammal Charles Darwin had strong teeth for the tearing of animal protein and a long, powerful mandible for its mastication. He was monogastric, digesting nutrients through a single stomach and colonic fermentation. He had the large skull and overgrown frontal cortex of the advanced hominid, and reversible thumbs too. With these attributes of strength and cunning, Darwin's ancestors had competed to survive. They had fought for food, shelter, and physical security. They had overcome their own savagery, and developed languages, laws, morals, and technical arts. They had created the most sophisticated civilization in their species' history and become the first hominid group to conquer and shape the entire human habitat. They were the survivors of selection, the first to rule the world.

Though none of Darwin's ancestors had been kings, priests, or warriors, his kin group had a high social status. His mother's father, Josiah Wedgwood, was a potter who became a mass producer of bone china. His father was a doctor and an industrial investor. His grandfather Erasmus Darwin had been an Enlightenment natural scientist and a friend of Benjamin Franklin's. The Wedgwoods and the Darwins embodied the English upper-middle classes, the higher orders of commerce and intellect. Consolidating and expanding their tribe, they intermarried to form a vast cousinhood. They were an aristocracy of the middle classes, and Charles was a child of one of their arranged marriages. They were Christian moralists for whom private integrity meant public action. They epitomized a liberalism that carried the Protestant ethos into industrial society and, through the crusade against the "heart-sickening atrocities" of slavery, across the world.

The modern dynasties of money and knowledge challenged the ancient dynasties of landholding and chivalry, but Man remained a social animal. Either he fought the superior members of his hierarchy, or he aped them. Charles was raised to pursue the disruptive pieties of the middle class but to honor the traditional virtues of the aristocracy. He was a man of science, the son of a doctor, the grandson of nonconformists and abolitionists; he was a gentleman of leisure, fond of the dinner ritual and his daily constitutional. Finding medical studies too arduous at Cambridge, he turned to theology. Like many of the wealthy younger sons who idled through the university, he expected to become an employee of the state church, a country parson keeping the peace between the classes as between God and Man. Instead his scientific skepticism waylaid him, but gently.

"If only the Geologists would let me alone, I could do very well," Ruskin lamented in 1851, the year Darwin stopped going to church, "but those dreadful Hammers! I hear the clink of them at the end of every cadence of the Bible verses."

Already a watery Unitarian, Darwin claimed not to mourn the loss of a faith lightly worn. Yet he shared Ruskin's fear that science, by eroding the rock of the church, would undermine the foundations of social morality. When Darwin, age twenty-two, sailed for South America on the *Beagle*, it was as a "gentleman naturalist." He paid his own expenses, and was engaged not just to gather data but to be a companion to the *Beagle*'s other gentleman. Etiquette forbade the *Beagle*'s captain, Robert FitzRoy, from dining with his social inferiors, and the loneliness of the oceans was enough to drive captains to drink, madness, or suicide. Darwin was on board to further knowledge but also to help keep society afloat by sharing FitzRoy's quarters and table. Nevertheless, when Darwin returned to Britain, he began the work that would strike the sacred hierarchies of religion and society with a dreadful hammer of his own.

"I find the noddle & the stomach are antagonistic powers," the gentleman naturalist noted, "and that it is a great deal more easy to think too much in a day, than to think too little—What thought has to do with digesting roast beef,—I cannot say."

Darwin's digestion was the barometer of his thoughts. The weightier their implications, the greater his gastric turbulence. Headaches and palpitations at his desk, reflux and nausea in the garden, cramps and flatulence at the dining table, constipation and diarrhea in his private outdoor privy. His problems may well have been caused by an untreated tropical parasite, an invisible animalcule ingested on the *Beagle*'s South American voyage, and were probably compounded by emotional stress. As a child, Darwin had seen his mother die slowly from stomach cancer; the bowels, the Hebrew prophets had written, were the seat of compassion. His condition flared whenever he worked on an article or prepared for a lecture, or had visitors in the house, or when one of his children became ill. "Wherefore my bowels shall sound like an harp for Moab," Isaiah had lamented, "and mine inward parts for Kirharesh."

Along with his digestive souvenir, Darwin returned from the Southern Hemisphere brimming with speculations on the origins of his species. Like his grandfather Erasmus, he was determined to define the "mysterious law" behind "development." In 1838, he found it close to home, in the work of a clergyman friend of the Wedgwoods'. In his *Essay on the Principle of Population* (1798), Robert Malthus had theorized that societies developed by competing violently for resources. A society's population grew until it outstripped its food supply. Either famine ensued and population growth stopped, or the overpopulated society fought to secure its neighbors' resources.

Translated from demography to biology, Malthusian competition became the spring in the mechanism of Darwin's universe. Hunger tightened it, and sexual attraction released it. In all life-forms, "development" was selection by competition. Life was an unending war of all against all. It conscripted every individual, and all its battles ended in extermination. "The varieties of man seem to act on each other in the same way as different species of animals—the stronger always extirpating the weaker."

Darwin discovered Malthus just as he was selecting his breeding partner through competition with his older brother, Erasmus. Mimicking the aristocracy they displaced, the Wedgwoods and Darwins acted on each other with increasing familiarity. Josiah Wedgwood had married his first cousin. Charles further shortened the biological odds by marrying Emma Wedgwood, his first cousin. They would not lack company. Charles's sister Caroline had just married Emma's brother Josiah, and the vicar at Charles and Emma's wedding was John Wedgwood, first cousin to both bride and groom. The newlyweds drew their pet names from their shared family history of science and abolitionism. Charles called Emma the "most interesting specimen in the whole series of vertebrate animals" and himself a "happy slave." She called him her "own dear Nigger."

In 1853, the Royal Society awarded Darwin its gold medal for his Geology of the Voyage of the Beagle, as well as his remarkably detailed work on barnacles. Now living like a reclusive parson in the Kentish village of Downe, he felt ready to begin his "Big Book," the "species book."

Darwin did not invent evolution, any more than Marx invented socialism or Lévi magic. If these figures loom tall, it is because they stood on the shoulders of eighteenth-century giants. Each pursued the Enlightenment dream of universal knowledge into the altered landscape of the Age of Change. Each harmonized a babble of inquiry into a single "scientific" system. Like Malthus, each explained all historical development by a single mechanism, and declared its logic to be its morality. Darwin inherited more than a century of work on "development" theory. This heresy raised four questions, all of them damaging to a literal reading of the Bible, and each of them transformative of human self-understanding.

The first question was one of category. Did Man occupy, as Genesis claimed, a unique place in the hierarchy of life? In 1735, the Swedish naturalist Carl Linnaeus had placed Man atop the tree of life but in the same taxonomic class as the apes. Yet Linnaeus, who renamed his species *Homo sapiens* in 1758, had not believed that he had monkeys in his family tree. Nor had Hermann Schaaffhausen, who would discover the Neanderthal skull in 1857.

The second question was one of process. Did current flora and fauna reflect their fixed, original design, or had they developed? The Comte de Buffon's *Natural History*, the greatest of Enlightenment catalogs, suggested that environment and descent altered a species over time, and the fossil record seemed to prove it. As Buffon recognized when he noted the resemblance between humans and orangutans, the question of process was inseparable from that of category. How had Africans, Europeans, and monkeys come to occupy the same class? Was there a single human species, its races sharing common descent, or a diversity of different species? If they had a common descent, they must have multiplied by mixing—much of it incestuous—and developed by variation. If they had diverse origins, then pure descent was possible, and hybridity would be against Nature.

The third question was one of time. How old was the Earth? In 1648, Archbishop James Ussher, the primate of all Ireland, had dated the Creation to the evening of Saturday, October 22, 4004 BCE.

Ussher had used the genealogical tables in the Hebrew Bible and Kepler's astronomical tables; Newton, using similar materials, had arrived at a similar date. The fossil record suggested otherwise, and so, Darwin knew, did geology. In *Principles of Geology* (1830–1833), the Scottish geologist and canal digger Charles Lyell theorized the geological processes that had formed Earth's surface. One of the *Beagle*'s tasks had been to gather information on erratic boulders for Lyell.

The fourth and most important question was that of value. Did development theory change the meaning of life? In the last years of the eighteenth century, the French biologist Jean-Baptiste Lamarck assembled the first comprehensive theory of biological change according to natural laws. Lamarck was a biological mystic. He explained the future of science by analogy to its discredited past and called development "transmutation." Nature transmutes impure forms into pure ones like an alchemist transmuting base metals into gold. Biological and moral development align in this process. A mysterious *pouvoir de la vie*, a "life force," compels species to climb the ladder of development. The life force has a governing idea. It strives for perfection through complexity and also through order. Environment determines which characteristics become emphasized by use and which wither through disuse. Organisms learn these lessons and pass them to their progeny. This use-disuse scenario leads to the differentiation of species, and their ascent by transmutation up the ladder to perfection.

In 1852, a self-taught English railway clerk named Herbert Spencer published "The Development Hypothesis," a Lamarckian transmutation theory. A liberal optimist and an admirer of Comte, Spencer called development "evolution" and directed it toward social progress. Darwin was no mystic. As he began his "Big Book" in 1853, he determined to study not the ascent of the spirit toward moral perfection but rather the material facts of the "descent of man." So in the same year did Arthur de Gobineau, who advanced a different theory of heredity and descent.

• • •

The blood of kings and counts ran in Gobineau's veins. His grand-
father had been guillotined in the same year as Louis XVI and
Marie Antoinette. His mother was the illegitimate granddaughter of
Louis XV; when queried, she wordlessly turned her head to show her
Bourbon profile. Arthur was born in his father's mansion in Bor-
deaux, heir to an ancient family and a title despoiled by the revolution.
His aunt died young because Napoléon Bonaparte broke her heart.

Arthur believed all of this, but none of it was true. His grandfather died in bed, not on the scaffold. If his aunt had an affair with
Napoléon, she survived. His father's family had bought a title just
before 1789 but had sold their house in Bordeaux to an actress. Arthur was born on an army base near Paris, the son of two chronic
fantasists. His father was an antiquarian, obsessed with the family
trees of the French aristocracy, and a *légitimiste*, a Bourbon loyalist.
His mother, who called herself a woman of "passionate character" and
"romantic imagination," was almost certainly not descended from
Louis XV. She was an adulteress and a fraudster, and Arthur was her
accomplice.

While Arthur's father was in Spain with his regiment, his mother
became pregnant by a young officer named Charles de la Coindière.
Confined to an asylum for lunatics and unwed mothers, she shinnied
down a rope from the third floor and fled. She and Coindière took
Arthur and his illegitimate sister from city to city. She posed as an
impoverished aristocratic widow, Coindière as her nephew, and Arthur as a fatherless child. They infiltrated the homes of rich men with
marriageable daughters. When Coindière had seduced one of the
daughters and the marriage had been agreed, the impostors "borrowed" money from their new friends. Then they disappeared, pursued by the police.

By his early twenties, Arthur was fluent in Greek, Latin, Persian,
and Sanskrit, and his mother was in prison. Arthur retreated from
one type of fiction into another. The historical charades of Walter
Scott's novels and *One Thousand and One Nights* seemed no less real,
and much more dignified, than his mother's shameful pretenses: "All

his aspirations were turned towards the Orient; he dreamed only of mosques and minarets, calling himself a Muslim ready to make his pilgrimage to Mecca."

Through his short stories and journalism, Gobineau attracted the patronage of Alexis de Tocqueville. As Tocqueville's protégé in the foreign ministry, Gobineau served France in Switzerland, Brazil, and Persia. Travel broadened his horizons, but it narrowed his mind. A furious disgust was brewing beneath the diplomat's manners.

Having seen the world, Gobineau concluded that it was falling apart. Humanity was not improving its abilities or ascending toward perfection. It was falling into chaos and weakness. Man, he believed, had begun as a single species, the Aryans—the term derived from the Sanskrit *arya* (noble)—but had developed into three distinct and unequal species: white, yellow, and black. Their mixing produced democratic flashes of novelty and vigor, but over time, bad blood had driven out good. All three species seemed doomed to a spiral of cultural decay and political violence. The whites, the only race capable of advanced culture, were now an endangered species; like the French aristocracy, they had mixed with their inferiors. As in Maxwell's theory of entropy, development meant decline to Gobineau, a fatal loss of energy. It meant degeneration.

Where Darwin applied Malthus on population, Gobineau applied Tocqueville on democracy. In the 1830s, Tocqueville had seen Europe's future in the United States. He returned brooding on decline. The middle classes had come to power by displacing and suborning the old orders of throne and nobility. They had replaced the rule of the *aristoi,* "the best," with the consensus of what the English called the "middling sort." The middling values were humane but mediocre. When private citizens cultivated individuality through trade, private property, and religious liberty, they neglected the public virtues. If a man became an exceptional individual and attempted to extend his private success into public life, he would be outvoted by the "tyranny of the majority." There could never be a middle-class Athens or Florence.

When Tocqueville read Gobineau's *Essay on the Inequality of the Races*, he thought his young friend had gone mad. Tocqueville's *Democracy in America* described the mixing of ethics, not blood, and in a nation, not a race or species. Tocqueville agreed that the democratic revolt of the middle classes had broken the ancient compact between the nobleman and the serf, and the ancient barrier between the strong and the weak. Yet if Tocqueville feared for the future, he was resigned to it. He was a rational skeptic, and he diagnosed the democratic condition without writing a prescription or selling a cure. Gobineau rebelled against that condition in disgust and panic.

In its mystical egotism, Gobineau's racial science resembled Éliphas Lévi's "occult science." The vital essence at the heart of human existence dissolved in a fluid, polluted society. Besieged by equalizing pressures, the superior man drew new moral boundaries. He established new proofs for the legitimacy of his feelings and the purity of their descent. Although hierarchy and order returned, he could not escape entirely. More Caliban than Prospero, he still spoke his tormentor's language. He rebelled against rationality in the language of science because only science had the objective authority that could protect his private fantasy. He mimicked his equalizing age as he resisted it, for anyone with a white skin was now an aristocrat of race. After writing the *Essay*, Gobineau ennobled himself with a hereditary title. If race were Nature's class system, then the "Comte de Gobineau" would be one of its aristocrats.

He found a willing accomplice in Clémence Monnerot. She was a planter's daughter from Martinique, impoverished by the death of her father and the "democratic inanities" of 1848. The annulment of slavery in France's colonies brought financial ruin to *petits blancs* like the Monnerots. After one of Clémence's brothers had married a "mulatto," her mother took her to Paris, to restore the family fortune and avoid further miscegenation. If Arthur had his father's despairing interest in genealogy, Clémence had his mother's taste for fantasy. As the Comtesse de Gobineau, Clémence filled their Paris apartment with antiques, found them a country château, and ran up appropriately aristocratic debts. Arthur worried about money like a bourgeois.

Synonymous with "nation" and "people," the word "race" had floated around for centuries. The ancient Greeks believed that their love of freedom and the barbarians' acceptance of slavery were hereditary. In the Mahabharata, their Hindu contemporaries had attributed skin color and caste divisions to the distribution of ability. Yet if biological determinism was never absent, it did not dominate until the modern era.

The nation-state was the laboratory in which science redefined the human essence from religion to race, soul to body. In Spain, creating a Catholic state required the expulsion or forced conversion of large Jewish and Muslim populations. The "New Christians" were eligible for previously reserved positions; the "Old Christians" doubted the converts' sincerity. The doctrine of *limpieza de sangre,* "clarity of blood," emerged from genealogists among the Spanish aristocracy and spread to trade guilds and clergymen. In 1496, the "most Catholic" monarchs Ferdinand and Isabella forced Pope Alexander VI to revise the Christian equality of souls and make *limpieza de sangre* a Christian doctrine. Conversion no longer annulled the sins of heredity.

Spain's Protestant enemies continued the merging of race and religion. The national community of the Dutch or the English was an extended family, bound by kinship and experience, praying in its own language, dwelling on its own territory. To legitimize their revolt against Rome, the new nations needed origins that predated papal decrees and even Christianity itself. Using the "New Science" of history, they created new pasts, new family trees. In the national epic, political history developed from natural history. National rights sprang from natural rights, modern statehood from ancient kinship, modern laws from ancient customs. Just as family and tribal ties assured physical continuity and resemblance, so cultural forms preserved the national essence. Dialect and folktales, once despised as provincial and vulgar, became priceless deeds of title, "natural" and "organic" proofs of ownership. The modern mythology of secular progress was established, with the vital spirit of heredity as the carrier of memory.

The discovery of Nature as a political legislator inverted European understanding of civilization and barbarism, city and forest, south and north. Medieval Europeans had understood their civilization as a Mediterranean import, spread among the barbarians by Roman soldiers and Christian missionaries. For Shakespeare's contemporaries, the first king of England was Brutus of Troy, a mythological descendant of Aeneas. In the eighteenth century, northern Europe's ancestors changed. As historians and anthropologists coaxed the *Völker*, the "natural peoples," out of their pre-Christian obscurity, Europeans realized that their forebears had not been ignorant and brutish latecomers, but founding fathers, wise with primitive wildness.

Cinema would turn Jacob and Wilhelm Grimm's compendium of peasant cruelty into the world's nursery tales, but the brothers saw their work as political, the deeds to a future German state. In Britain, King Brutus was overthrown when the archaeologist William Stukeley and his friends gathered in a Soho pub to invent a lost Druidic religion that sacralized their catalog of Neolithic stone circles. In France, Montesquieu explained Europe's political development by climate alone. The Romans were now unreliable southerners, depraved by "inordinate desires." The modern French "race" inherited the hearty, proto-republican virtues of the forest-dwelling tribes in Tacitus' *Germania*.

Gobineau's Aryans and Caucasians appeared by the same method, and amid similar errors. In 1813, a year after the Grimm brothers published *Children's and Household Tales*, the English scientist Thomas Young named Sanskrit's linguistic progeny the "Indo-European" family. Three years later, the German linguist Franz Bopp began his life's work, the *Comparative Grammar* of Indo-European languages, with an article on Sanskrit. The European scholars took the resemblance between Sanskrit and the European languages as proof of direct descent. Compounding the error, they placed Sanskrit at the root of the family tree, as Man's original language. In fact, the "Indo-Aryan" or "Indo-Iranian" branch of languages, which includes Vedic Sanskrit, broke off from the proto-Indo-European language *after* the Hellenic branch, which includes Greek and Latin: Sanskrit acquired its classical grammar in the fifth century BCE, around the same time as Attic Greek emerged in the works of Thucydides and Sophocles.

The Indo-Iranian branch has two major limbs. The word *arya* appears in both. In Old Persian and Avestan, *arya* denotes a kinship group; hence the modern "Iranian." In the Indic languages of northern India, which include Vedic Sanskrit, *arya* is an honorific denoting "noble" deeds or status. The Romantic confusion of culture and blood joins the two senses: in Gobineau's original Aryan, acquired and inherited qualities merge. The new origin myth looked backward in order to look forward. The Aryan virtues were not those of animal husbandry, where mixing makes vigor, but of aristocratic pedigree: undiluted stock, unpolluted blood, selective inbreeding. As democracy eroded the hereditary principle, the dream of Aryan origins offered a vision of perfection lost and a future redeemed.

In 1795, the German anthropologist Johann Friedrich Blumenbach divided the human species into five races by skull type. He believed that four of them—the black "Ethiopian," the red "American," the yellow "Mongolian," and the brown "Malayan"—had developed to fit their environments, and degenerated accordingly. The original and best race was "Caucasian," which was named for Mount Caucasus in Georgia, the mountain to which Zeus had chained Prometheus. Blumenbach did not define Caucasians by their paleness: like the Georgians and many southern Europeans, Caucasians could have tanned, olive skin and thick, wavy dark hair. But Blumenbach knew a Caucasian when he saw one. The villagers who lived on the southern slopes of Mount Caucasus were "the most beautiful race of men."

Their shapely skulls, small mouths, narrow nasal apertures, receding cheekbones, and strong but not protruding jaws matched the ideal proportions of Greek statuary. Blumenbach wondered if the "degenerate" races might be restored to Greek shapeliness by selective breeding. His Neoclassical science went into Gobineau's system for unchaining the Prometheus of race.

The Caucasians were so busy with democratic degeneration that they barely noticed the *Essay*. Only in his old age would Gobineau begin to be acclaimed as the philosopher of racial science. Gobineau found his first audience in the United States, among the most degenerate Caucasians of all. In the 1860s, they would return Gobineau's ideas to Europe.

Gobineau's first American admirer was Josiah Clark Nott, a doctor in Mobile, Alabama. Nott shared Gobineau's interest in the contamination of the blood. Where Gobineau examined the fluid conditions of democratic society, Nott looked into the fever swamp.

In 1848, Nott had suggested that yellow fever was a different kind of "Marsh Fever" from malaria and that it spread through invisible water-dwelling "insects." Nott called them "infusoria" and "animalcules." The latter was a seventeenth-century term, originally applied to spermatozoa; Nott praised the "distinguished naturalist Chas. Darwin" for collecting so many useful animalcules on the *Beagle*. Also in 1848, the German physician Johann Heinrich Meckel noted black and brown structures in the blood and spleen of a dead lunatic. Although ancient observers had linked brain and spleen discoloration with malaria, Meckel attributed it to melanin. A year later, the London scientist John Snow posited that cholera was caused by an invisible animalcule in drinking water. A new understanding of disease transmission was forming.

In the previous world of the miasma, pollution had been detectable to the senses. Hygiene meant avoiding bad odors and stagnant water, or retreating from an epidemic like the raconteurs of Boccaccio's *Decameron*. In the new world of viruses and bacteria, pollution was invisible, and unavoidable. The human body was constantly penetrated by animalcules, yet it could not sense its violation. When the female mosquito pierced the skin and unloaded the invisible virus from her gut, black blood mingled with white, the blood of the Nott family with that of their nine African slaves. The skin and senses no longer protected. As the boundary between health and sickness moved into the body, so did the division on which religions are made, the boundary between purity and impurity. There was now no escape: even a vaccination was a controlled contamination. The religious category of "pollution" took scientific and industrial form. Pollution and purity were now "environmental."

The race scientists looked at fever, but they were looking for melanin. While Nott was studying yellow fever, he worked with George Robins Gliddon on a global inventory of race, *Types of Mankind* (1854). Gliddon, the erstwhile U.S. consul in Cairo, was a showman Egyptologist who attracted crowds by unwrapping mummies over the course of several days. Local academics lectured on Egyptian history and embalming techniques while Gliddon was at work. At Gliddon's 1850 unveiling in Boston, the Harvard professor Louis Agassiz was one of the expert assistants. He persuaded Agassiz to write the introduction to *Types of Mankind.*

Nott and Gliddon took most of their data from the bible of U.S. race science, Samuel Morton's *Crania Americana* (1839–1849). A professor of anatomy at the University of Pennsylvania, Morton collected skulls from all over the Americas, stuffed their orifices with cotton, and filled them with peppercorns. He found that the average European skull contained a mighty eighty-seven cubic inches of peppercorns, the average African a pea-brained seventy-eight cubic inches. Like Morton, Nott and Gliddon took this to prove racial "diversity." Their comparison of ancient Egyptian and Greek art confirmed their belief in fixed differences between African and European skulls. The "Negroes" remained "substantially in that same benighted state wherein Nature has placed them, and in which they have stood, according to Egyptian monuments, for at least 5,000 years." Morton's moral of Nature was that Africans were born slaves, to the pharaoh in Egypt as to the planter in the South.

"I have a friend, a Swiss, Mr. Hotze, now at work translating the first book of your work," Nott wrote to Gobineau in March 1855. Pale, nearsighted, and baby-faced, Henry Hotze had found in Gobineau a "ray of light" that clarified the "transient gleam" of his feelings about race. He had arrived in Alabama believing in "original diversity" and skeptical about democracy and "boundless progress." Affluent slaveholders welcomed his convictions and "suavity." When Nott found him, Hotze was tutoring the children of planters near Montgomery.

Hotze nudged Gobineau's thought toward an American target, the "fanaticism of two-thirds of the American people on the subject of the slavery institution in the South."

To turn Gobineau's *Essay* into a slaveholder's manifesto, Hotze traduced its central concepts. Gobineau was a monogenist and an evolutionist: he believed that the current races had developed from an original, singular race. His American admirers were polygenists: they believed in "multiple origins" and fixed racial differences. Hotze's translation excised crucial passages—notably Gobineau's criticisms of "American decay"—and twisted others. The "inequality" of Gobineau's title rejected the centerpiece of the revolutionary trinity: *liberté, egalité, fraternité*. Hotze translated *inegalité* as "moral and intellectual diversity"—the language of polygenesis. In his introduction, Hotze implied that Gobineau's monogenesis was irrelevant. Let the scientists argue whether each race was a "distinct species"; the permanent effects of diversity were "scientific fact." The reviewer from *The Mobile Register* understood: "No change of circumstance can ever make the Negro look, think, or act like a white man."

Hotze wanted to go further, but that would have offended Christian supporters of slavery. To the Federation of United Protestant Churches, and especially to Presbyterians, original diversity contradicted the "Calvinistic dogma of original sin" and the "authority of the Bible."

Gobineau was appalled by Hotze's conclusions. A lifelong Catholic, Gobineau had cited the biblical genealogy. He disapproved of slavery, if only because proximity brought temptation, and "intermixture" would give birth to the monster of "ethnic disorder." The Americans had confirmed his theory that the United States was a repository of degenerate types. In their descent into America, his ideas had degenerated.

When the young Darwin met the "poor wretches" of Tierra del Fuego, Argentina, he recoiled from their "hideous faces bedaubed with white paint," their "filthy and greasy" skin, and their "violent" gestures. But he did not doubt that they were of his species. He felt sure that when "white conquerors" modernized this "miserable country," its "savages" would advance to the "same degree of civilization." He welcomed Africans into the family of *Homo sapiens.* He had never met people more intelligent than the Cape Verdeans, especially the impish "Negro or Mulatto children," so fascinated by his silver pencil case and his percussion gun.

Darwin's grandfather, Josiah Wedgwood, had been a sainted light in the Society for the Abolition of the African Slave Trade. Young Charles had been raised to believe that humanity was one species, and he wanted to keep it in the family. Though the Christian faith fell away with the Christian chronology, the moral message endured. Darwin believed that the advance of knowledge meant ethical and social progress. To learn more about the human being was to become more humane: "common descent" proved common humanity. As the society's Christian, monogenist motto had asked, "Am I not a man and a brother?"

Yet human *fraternité* was not the only fact of Nature. To Darwin's scientific mind, there was a hereditary *inegalité* of ability and strength within the races, and society must distribute *liberté* according to capacity. In the Hungry Forties, striking workers had massed outside one of his Wedgwood cousins' homes. The mob had burned down a clergyman's house and would have destroyed two churches had not soldiers fired at them, killing three.

The *inegalité* of racial aptitude seemed no less of a fact of Nature. Darwin watched how the hungry emigrants who poured out of Europe destroyed the peoples in their path. Competition, he felt, was Nature's license to dismiss the stragglers who could not keep up and trample the squatters in the path of progress. Progress and murder went hand in hand. Elimination was a universal truth, the biological editing that Emerson called the "grand style of nature."

"Our planet, before the age of written history, had its races of savages, like the generations of sour paste, or the animalcules that wriggle and bite in a drop of putrid water," Emerson reminded himself. "Who cares for these or for their wars?"

In August 1844, Emerson marked the seventh anniversary of Britain's emancipation of its Caribbean slaves in an address at the Concord courthouse. Nature, he explained, practiced the method of Malthus for the moral of Hegel. If men generated a "new principle" or new ideas, they survived. "If they are rude and foolish, down they must go." The fate of America's slaves depended on their fitness for the struggle: "If the black man is feeble, and not important to the existing races, not on a parity with the best race, the black man must serve and be exterminated."

Fortunately for the black man, Emerson judged that he carried "in his bosom an indispensable element of the new & coming civilization." Toussaint L'Ouverture of Haiti and the leaders of the freed slaves of Barbados and Jamaica had made the "proud discovery" that black ideas could survive in the United States too. "It now appears that the negro race is, more than any other, susceptible of rapid civilization." But sentiment, and "songs, and newspapers, and money-subscriptions, and vituperation" would not suffice. Slavishness, he feared, was a universal tendency.

"I say to you, you must save yourself, black or white, man or woman; other help is none." Like the preacher he nearly became, Emerson exhorted the enslaved soul to test itself against the market forces of the spirit. Only the slave could help himself and become the "anti-slave": the independent man whose color was an "insignificance." The logic of elimination would dispose of those who would not save themselves.

Emerson's journey into the scientific literature of the 1850s confirmed his views. In Nature as in politics, massive, impersonal forces dwarf the individual. Most people think only of "the sex & the digestion." Most men are "mere bulls," and most women "cows." Occasionally, all the "bulling and milking" produces a "superior individual" with "some stray taste or talent." The herd, busy with "gross instincts," is oblivious to his qualities. Nevertheless, as soon as he emerges from the breeding pool, "all the ancestors become guano."

Guano is the dried feces of seabirds and sea lions; huana *means "dung"* in Quechua, a Peruvian language. It was an Atlantic commodity, vital to both food production and war. The Incas had spread guano on their crops, the Spanish on their vineyards. The British now dominated its export.

Apart from its value as a fertilizer, guano had preservative powers. In the early 1800s, Londoners marveled at human bodies found "mummified" in guano at Possession Island, off the coast of southern Africa. In Liverpool, shops sold guano bird "mummies" as curios. When the *Beagle* crossed the Atlantic, Darwin inspected the massive guano deposits that caked the cliffs and inlets of Ascension Island. The ossified rocks held priceless proofs of geological history: "Below some small masses of guano at Ascension, and on the Albrolhos Islets, I found certain stalactitic branching bodies."

As scientists unlocked plant chemistry, guano gave further value. Its nitrates made excellent fertilizer, and its saltpeter was a reliable detonator of gunpowder. In London, the Foreign Office maintained a register of guano deposits, reported by British merchantmen in the southern oceans. In 1858, Gibbs and Sons, holders of a government monopoly, carried three hundred thousand tons of Peruvian guano to Britain. Most of it was lavished on the turnip crop. By extending the growing season and sustaining population increase, guano staved off the Malthusian apocalypse.

Apart from being an affront to the Monroe Doctrine, Britain's appetite for guano hampered the American economy. The federal artillery and the Southern plantation both needed guano. In his State of the Union address of 1850, President Millard Fillmore had declared the price of guano to be a national interest. In 1853, amid rumors of massive guano deposits in the Galápagos Islands, President Franklin Pierce had pondered forcing Ecuador to surrender the islands "for a long term of years, or in perpetuity, with an unrestricted right to take away the guano." Three years later, Congress passed the Guano Islands Act, awarding the United States the right to any unoccupied or unclaimed "island, rock, or key." Some sixty guano-caked islands were annexed.

Even fecal waste had value in the comprehensive cycles of empire and economy. As Emerson updated his vocabulary, "guano" replaced "alchemy" as his metaphor of transmutation, the fertilizer of the soil from which the "superior individual" would grow in its American habitat. In 1845, Emerson compared America to a crucible, mixing its populations like the "melting & intermixture of silver & gold & other metals" in the burning temple of Corinth. A "new compound" would form in the "asylum of all nations": the energy of "Irish, Germans, Swedes, Poles, & the Cossacks, & all European tribes,—of Africans, & of Polynesians, will construct a new race, a new religion, a new State, a new literature, which will be as vigorous as the new Europe which came out of the smelting pot of the Dark Ages." By 1851, the immigration of Europeans lacking in "Saxon" qualities elicited images of human beings as waste products: "Too much guano. The German & Irish nations, like the Negro, have a deal of guano in their destiny. They are ferried over the Atlantic, & carted over America to ditch & to drudge, to make the land fertile, & corn cheap, & then to lie down prematurely to make a spot of greener grass on the prairie." As individuals, they were mere "drones." Their historical task was collectively to manure God's plantation, America. "Of course, the more of these drones that perish, the better for the hive."

Two years later, reading a report in his *New-York Tribune* on the "unprecedented wave of emigration" from Europe to America, Emerson paused and copied a reflection from the article into his journal.

Fate. "The classes and races too weak to master the new conditions of life must give way."—KARL MARX

The Jews, Marx wrote in 1843, a few months before Emerson's "Emancipatory Address," were a parasite in Europe's gut. "Out of its own entrails, bourgeois society continually creates the Jew." Money was "the jealous god of Israel," and the products of capitalism were the Jew's waste. The revolution would defecate him from history like guano from a seagull. Marx and Engels envisaged this as the first in a series of historic purges.

"The next world war," Engels promised in 1849, "will result in the disappearance from the face of the earth not only of reactionary classes, but also of entire reactionary peoples. And that, too, is a step forward."

The historical spirit, Hegel had said, passed through peoples, then expelled the unnecessary in its wake. The Jews were not the only impurity in Europe. In the coming "general war," the "standard-bearers of progress" would purify Europe of all its unhistorical races. The advanced "Austrian Germans" would erase the Slavs of southern and eastern Europe "down to their very names." Like the Moswetusets, who in 1869 would be dissolved by law into the Commonwealth of Massachusetts, the "relics" and "residual fragments" of Europe's minorities had a choice: either be absorbed by the winners and accept "loss of their national character," or resist and suffer "complete extirpation."

As his enemies frequently reminded him, Marx carried residual fragments of his own Jewishness. He longed to expel them and dissolve in Nature's universal solvent. The "social emancipation of the Jew," he said, meant "the emancipation of society from Judaism." Like the "removal" of the Indian from the American woods, the expunging of the Jew and his idea were sacrifices to the logic of development.

In Marx's dream, the Europeans of the future slip the shackles of an alien religion and recover their original nature. Posted to Tehran in 1855, Gobineau imagined a similar revolution, but for him the shackles were those of Islam. Unlike most of his future admirers, Gobineau praised Jews and despised Muslims. The ancient Jews, he thought, had mastered an arid, hostile environment, and had been a "free, strong, and intelligent" people, much given to genealogy. Admittedly they appeared to have sullied their bloodline in exile, but they remained recognizably Jewish. "Whoever saw a well-marked Jewish head where there was not Jewish blood?" Josiah Nott added, expressing Marx's nightmare.

Although Samuel Morton's *Crania Aegyptiaca* (1844) had made the Jewish skull an exemplary "Semitic" type, Nott and Gobineau placed the Jews among the Caucasians. So did Disraeli, whose racial reflections in *Tancred* may have influenced Gobineau's *Essay*.

Gobineau's Jesus was an Aryan noble, his Muhammad a Semitic degenerate. In Aryan Persia, Islam was an alien tyrant. The Persians, Gobineau said, were "a most ancient nation," perhaps the "most ancient in the world to have had regular government." Their original religion, the cult of Zoroaster, was "incomparably more dignified, more moral, more elevated" than the "vague, inconsistent" precepts of Islam.

The Persians had resisted "ancient Semitism" through Sufi mysticism and the Shiite heresy. Now, with these movements exhausted, their unquenched essence was surfacing in a religious revolt. Persia was caught between the empires of Britain and Russia, and crumbling from within. Too weak to collect taxes, its shahs stayed afloat by selling government posts. Meanwhile the *faranji*, named for the Franks of the Crusades, sent Christian armies to their borders, Christian goods into their bazaars, and arrogant Christian consuls to their cities.

Led by Ali Muhammad Shirazi, the Babi movement began in 1844 as a protest of faith against the failure of reality. The Babis believed that the twelfth and final Shia imam, Muhammad al-Mahdi, was about to emerge from his *ghaybah*, the "occultation" into which he had disappeared in 874 CE; as the *bab*, Ali Muhammad Shirazi was "the gate" for the imam's arrival. By 1848, the Babis had declared that theirs was a period of *fatra*, an interregnum between messengers. The old obligations of sharia no longer applied. If inspiration defined duty, each person must think out their faith for themselves: "revelation is unsuspended," the Babis declared, "and therefore the [Perfect] Man will have [further] revelations." The shahs and their clerical allies killed and imprisoned thousands of Babis. The cult was forced underground and into exile.

The only attractive beams in Gobineau's gloomy world were those of racial regeneration. He despaired of Europe and America, but the Babi revolt seemed to him a survival of the original Aryan spirit. Islam, he decided, had been a "comfortable blanket" for the ancient Aryan faith. Insulated like plants under rotting leaves, the Shia had raised the "hybrid ideas that bud every day in a soil which contains so many things in a state of putrefaction." Now, he informed his European readers, their pre-Islamic faith was emerging intact.

Instead, a post-Islamic faith emerged from the Babi revolt. In 1850, Ali Muhammad Shirazi died in a Persian prison. In 1863, his follower Mirza Husayn-Ali Nuri declared himself to be "He Whom God Shall Make Manifest," the messianic figure foretold by the *bab*. As Baha'ullah, Nuri went on to found a universal and syncretic creed, Bahaism.

Darwin takes a three-mile constitutional to the chalk escarpment of the North Downs. From this promontory, he detects "ancient sea-bays" in the green declivities of the South Downs and imagines the "great dome of rocks" that must once have covered these gentle hills. He reckons that they once stood a thousand feet tall and that they took three hundred million years to erode away.

Thirty miles to the south at Lewes, the fossil of a giant iguanodon was found in a quarry. In 1841, the naturalist Richard Owen named its group the dinosaurs, the "terrible lizards." Darwin's mind boggles at the iguanodon, chewing tropical ferns in the primordial swamp somewhere near the London–Brighton line. He finds that the effort to imagine the "incomprehensibly vast" sweep of geological time resembles the "vain endeavour to grapple with the idea of eternity."

Ten miles to the northwest, on the fields where John Ruskin had walked as a child, the Crystal Palace has been moved and reassembled in a park at Sydenham. To assist the public in its efforts to imagine geological time, Richard Owen and the sculptor Benjamin Waterhouse Hawkins have planted thirty-three life-size dinosaurs in the shrubbery. The monsters are made of concrete poured over a brick-and-steel frame.

On New Year's Eve 1853, Owen and Hawkins host a dinner for twenty guests inside the mold for the iguanodon. Owen, the host, sits inside the head. He has built his dinosaurs for science but believes that they were created by God. Darwin does not. The long view across geological time raises questions to churn the hardiest of stomachs. If the law of Nature is development, then nothing is fixed. What then of the fixed aspects and essences, the moral law and the soul? What of God?

Darwin's usual walk was in his garden. Instead of crossing the fields, he went up and down a straight gravel path lined with elms. A shorter perspective concentrated the mind and kept him close to the outdoor privy.

He was a scientist, not a metaphysician. His "Big Book" must advance a big theory but avoid the big questions. Malthus had been accused of atheism, Robert Chambers of heresy. Darwin decided to argue for natural selection by analogy, using the commonplaces of artificial selection. He subscribed to *The Poultry Chronicle*, consulted local farmers on the vitality of their hybrid cattle, and collected a small mountain of facts on dog breeding. "I do not discuss origin of man," he warned his publisher, John Murray. "I do not bring in any discussion about Genesis."

It was slow work. Diligent and cautious, Darwin sounded out each new idea on a network of supporters and correspondents. As the great theme emerged from the tessellation of details, the working title of the "Species Book" became "Natural Selection." It might have remained unfinished like Marx's *Capital* but for a sudden environmental pressure.

In June 1858, Darwin received a letter from one of his correspondents, the young Welsh naturalist Alfred Russel Wallace. It contained a twenty-page theory of evolution, almost identical to Darwin's in its use of Malthus, but lacking the "selection" mechanism. Wallace intended to publish. Darwin faced the negation of his labors, the extinction of his original matter. The mechanism of competition engaged. Having planned an epic, he reduced it to a single volume, covering a third of his original plan. He rallied his supporters and organized a public reading. He would neutralize Wallace by presenting their theories in tandem.

The closer Darwin came to declaring his beliefs, the worse he felt. "I have been extra bad of late, with the old severe vomiting rather often & much distressing swimming of the head." Illness prevented him from attending the reading of his paper. "My abstract is the cause, I believe, of the main part of the ills to which my flesh is heir to."

In April 1859, Darwin finished his abbreviated *Natural Selection*. When John Murray rejected the title, Darwin compromised and suggested two titles in one: *On the Origin of Species by Means of Natural Selection, or the Preservation of Favoured Races in the Struggle for Life*.

The manuscript did not fully describe either of its titles. Darwin gave plentiful details of selection and the struggle for life, yet he omitted the specifics of his own species' origins and the development of its favored races. Although the controversy over *Origin of Species* would provoke cartoons of Darwin as an ape-man, the word "evolution" appeared nowhere in the book. In contrast to Robert Chambers's reckless claim that man had descended from apes, Darwin only hinted: "Much light will be thrown on the origin of man and his history." He did not describe the simian shadow cast by that light. Nor did he mention that his *Beagle* notebooks included the idea that the descent of man had included an intermediate, monkey-man stage.

Wallace had forced him to stop procrastinating and publish. Now his caution would be obviated by its context. The political and religious implications loomed like the Sydenham dinosaurs. *Origin of Species* appeared on November 23, 1859, little more than a month after John Brown raided the armory at Harpers Ferry, and nine days before Brown was hanged. The phrase "preservation of favoured races" could not fail to remind Darwin's readers that the debate on human origins and "diversity" would shape perceptions of social and moral justice. When Darwin proved the farmer's commonplace that mixed breeds could be fitter than their parents, he disproved the racists' claim that "hybridity" meant degeneration. When he insisted on the common origin of all species, he rejected polygenist theory as a false science. In this much, Darwin honored the Wedgwood-Darwin tribe. He moved to solid, scientific grounds the abolitionist's conviction: "Am I not a man and a brother?"

Coyness could not avoid the religious implications. As the Chambers controversy showed, the time was ripe for a debate on evolution. Darwin was not ready for it and nor, he believed, was his society. Mrs. Darwin had her doubts too. To soften the blow to Christianity and domestic harmony, he resorted to an eighteenth-century dodge and couched the ultimate source of life in what Richard Owen called a "creative power" and "designed laws." He hoped this would secure the support of Christian scientists like Owen, and Asa Gray of Harvard. But when Charles Lyell asked Darwin to include an explicitly "prophetic germ" and retain the Christian "dignity of man," he was cornered. As a scientist, he had to refuse.

"I am sorry to say I have no 'consolatory view' on the dignity of man," Darwin admitted. "I am content that man will probably advance, and care not much whether we are looked at as mere savages in a remotely distant future."

Darwin's life-forms have a common origin. They develop and form new species through "descent with modification." At the individual level, modification proceeds by "natural selection." The "preservation of races in the struggle for life" is common to all species, including Darwin's.

Darwin's contemporaries tended toward two views of human development. Both placed the human animal in a cosmic moral drama. For optimists, the descent of man was a spiritual ascent to perfection. For pessimists, it was degeneration and spiritual collapse. In his cautious way, Darwin implies a third, more radical position. Once the "creative power" has lit the fuse, evolution proceeds amorally. The mind searches for meaning in the "contented face of a bright landscape" or a "tropical forest glowing with life." But there is no higher purpose than survival. An increase in the complexity of an organism is progress in the technical sense, not the spiritual or moral. The purpose of development is more development. The meaning of life in a specialized age is more specialization. All destiny leads to redundancy.

The future of *Homo sapiens* is neither Lamarck's mystical ascent nor Gobineau's tragic fall. As the Russian nihilists will conclude in the 1860s, Man has no providential purpose. *Homo sapiens* is as embedded in the realm of Nature as a fruit fly. He is subject to the same imperatives, and about as important. Darwin does not fully reject Lamarck's transmutation theory, but he makes no room for its metaphysics of moral perfection and the soul. His account of development is purely materialistic. Man claws and bites his way up the ladder of complexity; eventually, like all other life-forms, he will fall off and fall away. The only consolations are those of euphemism. The "natural" part of natural selection is its relentless, remorseless violence. The "selection" part is the elimination of one race or species at the teeth or hands of a stronger, more favored one. Darwin's argument tiptoes through pigpens, kennels, and tropical forests, until, analogy and implication exhausted, it expels its explosive last word: *"evolved."*

The editing, and the fear that he would be "execrated as an atheist," left Darwin "weak as a child." Vomiting, stomach pains, an eczema rash that swelled his face and one leg like elephantiasis, an eruption of "fiery Boils"—"it was like being in Hell." He retreated to a spa in Surrey for the water cure. Beneath wet sheets, he feared the worst.

⚔ 5 ⚔

THE NEW CHRONOLOGY

Whitman, Huxley, and the War for the Soul

> No matter how far or how high science explores, it adopts
> the method of the universe as fast as it appears; and this
> discloses that the mind as it opens, the mind as it shall be,
> comprehends and works thus; that is to say, the Intellect
> builds the universe and is the key to all it contains . . .
>
> I believe in the existence of the material world as the
> expression of the spiritual or the real, and in the impen-
> etrable mystery which hides (and hides through abso-
> lute transparency) the mental nature, I await the insight
> which our advancing knowledge of material laws shall
> furnish. —*Emerson, "The Natural History of the Intel-
> lect" (1870)*

November 10, 1856. The poet shares his attic room and bed with his brother the simpleton. Books are piled on the mantelpiece and framed pictures of naked, muscled figures are pasted to the walls—Hercules, Bacchus, a satyr. The visitors smell the unmade bed and the unemptied chamber pot. The house has a parlor, but the poet has led his visitors up two narrow flights, to display his privacy. They are in their Sunday best, and he is in his.

Walt Whitman wears a workingman's red flannel shirt, cowhide boots, his patent "man-Bloomer"—a pair of baggy, loose trousers like those worn by his friend, the women's rights advocate Abby Price—and a loose jacket with a Byronic collar to frame his brawny laborer's neck. Atop this ensemble: a slouched hat, unkempt gray hair and beard, a pair of "cautious yet sagacious" gray eyes, and thick, graying eyebrows whose centers curve upward, as if inquiring as to the effect.

Whitman's guests are the Concord hermit Henry Thoreau, the Transcendentalist educator Amos Bronson Alcott, and Sarah Tyndale, a women's rights advocate and friend of Lucretia Mott's. This trio have come from Plymouth Church, where they heard a sermon by Henry Ward Beecher, whose sister Harriet is the author of *Uncle Tom's Cabin*. Alcott thinks Henry Beecher is as much an actor as a preacher, and Thoreau finds him too pagan. This is their second visit to Whitman's ramshackle fringe of Brooklyn. They came yesterday, but he was not home. Like Flaubert, and Baudelaire too when the money runs out, Whitman lives with his mother. She fed cake to the visitors and exposited proudly on her son the great man.

Alcott visited Whitman for the first time a few weeks ago. With his bent arm for a pillow, Whitman reclined languidly in his Bohemian outfit, admitting "naively" how "slow" and lazy he is. To Alcott, the father of the author of *Little Women*, Whitman embodies Young America—the loose grouping of reformers, artists, and political journalists who seek to create a national culture, and also a metaphysical ideal. Whitman agrees. "I too, following many and follow'd by many, inaugurate a religion."

Emerson, the first to make the pilgrimage to Whitman, has praised *Leaves of Grass* as the "most extraordinary piece of wit & wisdom that America has yet contributed." Thoreau has reservations. He finds Whitman's "pomes" exhilarating. They speak, Thoreau feels, "more truth than any American or modern I know," and Whitman may be "the greatest democrat the world has seen." But Thoreau finds their sensuality "disagreeable" and "strange."

The Transcendentalists are adept at transcending the body. "If you would obtain insight," Thoreau advised, "avoid anatomy." In the woods, Thoreau found a stinkhorn fungus, *Phallus impudicus.* He took it home, and as he watched it decompose into "fetid, olivaceous, semi-liquid matter," he wondered how Nature could delight in such "disgusting" creations. Whitman seems to revel in Nature's obscenity: "It is as if the beasts spoke." Thoreau hopes that Whitman's readers will be "pure" enough to read him "without understanding him." In five years' time, Whitman will augment *Leaves of Grass* with a sequence of poems on "manly love," named "Calamus," for another phallic flower.

After exhibiting his slovenly den, Whitman takes his guests back downstairs to the parlor. Whitman and Thoreau exchange "cold compliments." Thoreau notes Whitman's "coarse nature." Whitman senses Thoreau's snobbish "disdain" for ordinary people. Alcott watches as Emerson's would-be heirs eye each other "like two beasts, each wondering what the other would do."

In 1842, Whitman, then twenty-two, heard Emerson deliver his lecture "The Poetry of Our Times" in New York City. Emerson called for a poet who would write the "great American poem on the nature of American things: "our log-rolling, our stumps and their politics, our fisheries, our Negroes and Indians, our boasts and our repudiations." That poet's "possessed and conscious intellect" would summon "new energy" by "abandonment to the nature of things."

"I was simmering, simmering, simmering," Whitman recalled, "and Emerson brought me to the boil." Ingesting self-help and lyceum lectures, Whitman wrote a weak novel about temperance. He worked as a schoolteacher, a printer's typesetter, and a housebuilder and then became a radical journalist and editor. He advocated for women's rights and abolition, praised the European revolutions of 1848, and called Franklin Pierce a president who "eats dirt and excrement for his daily meals, likes it, and tries to force it on The States."

Whitman's father, Walter Whitman, Sr., was a political dreamer, a failed farmer and struggling carpenter, and an angry, unjust bully to his children. One of Whitman's brothers was a syphilitic who died in an insane asylum. Another was a tubercular drunkard who married a prostitute. A third was born feebleminded, a congenital condition then attributed to the influence of syphilis or masturbation. One sister endured nervous disorders and sexual frustration, another beatings from an alcoholic husband. *Leaves of Grass* is the revolt of Walter Whitman, Jr., against the ugly heredities of culture, morals, and history.

"Sex," Walt Whitman declared, "contains all, bodies, souls, Meanings, proofs, purities, delicacies, results, promulgations, Songs, commands, health, pride, the maternal mystery, the seminal milk." The divine "afflatus," the hot wind of desire, fills the mind and body. Imitations of Emerson and the Bible sprout into free verse, its rolling cadence as open and infinite as the western plains. The borders of consciousness and flesh melt as the moral merges with the biological, the species with the universe. Sex is as natural as Mesmer's electrical fluid, and the sparks of the divine fall where they must. Compassion, love, and human "adhesiveness" are waves in the "measureless ocean of love." Sex is the democratic liberator of "forbidden voices": "voices of sexes and lust, voices veil'd and I remove the veil."

His revolt incubated for years in his notebooks and was born fully formed. In "The Song of Myself," Whitman introduces a new spiritual type: the comprehensive man who contains all and accepts all. "I resist anything better than my own diversity," Whitman admits, becoming the first to translate "diversity" from racial science to sexuality, and providing the template for Oscar Wilde's joke about resisting all temptation apart from temptation. The human essence is not a taint in the blood, but an inner spring of vitality, pure and clean. "Divine I am inside and out, and I make holy whatever I touch or am touch'd from; / The scent of these arm-pits is aroma finer than prayer / This head is more than churches or bibles or creeds."

The triumphant individual expands to inherit the cosmos. Emerson is his father and Nature his mother. He is the modern heir to the Renaissance *uomo universale*, with the brutish power of Caliban and the delicate self-love of Narcissus. Nothing human is alien to him because everything is now human, and all that is human is natural—the night soil in the chamber pot, the sweat in the bedsheets, the feces in the president's mouth, the poet's fruity armpits. He contains the sacred and the profane as proofs that the universe is finally known, accepted, and mastered.

The old morality is overcome, the New World democracy unleashed.

*There has never been a civilization healthier than Whitman's Amer-*ica. Democracy is the natural state of the body politic, the gymnasium for "freedom's athletes," and faith is the "antiseptic of the soul." The moral athletes renew their bodies by physical labor, until all are sunburnt and sinewy, prime "naked meat." Unlike President Pierce, their bowels are "sweet and clean." All is one healthy flow, as though life is one long water cure. Everywhere, the wholesome toilers haul, lift, dig, and hammer, incarnating "spirituality the translatress . . . the finale of visible forms." There is plenty of hard and dangerous manual work, but the only trade union is the fraternity of "manly love."

Whitman was a consciously American innovator, pragmatic and promiscuous in his mixing of art and commerce. Forerunners like Poe and Emerson showed how the writer must help himself, and Whitman's years in the print shop and the newspaper office had inculcated the practical virtues. When Whitman took his poems to the Rome brothers' printshop on the corner of Cranberry and Fulton Streets in Brooklyn, he helped with the typesetting. He explained his greatness in the preface to *Leaves of Grass* and included a photograph of himself in disheveled working clothes. Struggling to find a publisher willing to associate itself with *Leaves of Grass*, he found a distributor in Fowler & Wells, a company that was run by phrenologists and specialized in books on health fads. Then he sent a copy to Emerson. Flattered by Whitman's unsolicited but "wonderful gift," Emerson wrote back, saluting *Leaves of Grass* as the "beginning of a great career." Whitman bound this private encomium into review copies, advertised it in the *New-York Tribune*, and placed it in gold letters on the spine of the second edition.

Wheeling in the skies, Whitman eyes the vast scope of "Democracy's lands." Far below, the workers are indistinguishable from their tasks, like Ruskin's medieval urbanites. "See, ploughmen ploughing farms—see, miner digging mines—see, the numberless factories . . . See, lounging through the shops and fields of the States, me, well-belov'd, close-held by day and night."

Whitman has great power, Emerson says, and "great power makes us happy." The future is a golden age, not a gilded one. The endless swarms of alert, turbulent, and good-natured citizens in Whitman's America are not Carlyle's mites in cheese. Their material power is a spiritual power, and each production is a proof of individual "diversity." Man not only retains his soul amid the machines and crowds; he discovers and develops it. In Whitman's America, the free body shapes its own evolution toward a happy ending. As Hegel suspected and Emerson hopes, universal truth will speak in an American accent.

On the morning after the prayers and roast geese of Christmas 1859, Britain's ruling class sat down to breakfast, opened *The Times,* and read Thomas Henry Huxley's review of *Origin of Species.*

Mr. Darwin, Huxley explained, already stood in the "front ranks" of British philosophers, but that did not preclude his remaining a sensible Englishman. Any sheep farmer could explain artificial selection. Darwin merely applied its "familiar but well-nigh forgotten facts" to the wild world. His hypothesis was perfectly simple and comprehensible: "There is in nature some power which takes the place of man." Then Huxley led the reader to Darwin's tableau of slaughter.

"Who, for instance, has duly reflected upon all the consequences of the marvelous struggle for existence which is daily and hourly going on among living beings? Not only does every animal live at the expense of some other animal or plant, but the very plants are at war." The seeds in the ground robbed each other of light and water. Animals dismembered each other for food. Only "robbers" and killers survived.

A square-jawed, dark-haired, self-taught Welshman, Huxley was an eighteenth-century *philosophe* in Victorian sideburns. Voltaire had blamed the mischief and mystification of religion on "women, Jews, and priests" but had granted religion the saving virtue of restraining the masses. Huxley wanted to liberate the masses from holy ignorance and domesticate them through scientific education. He was a slayer of hereditary privilege, the Oliver Cromwell of evolution. And Cromwell, many Britons now felt, had not been a religious dictator but a democrat, a defender of ancient liberties who deserved a statue outside the Westminster Parliament.

Huxley admitted that Darwin had inferred natural selection without proving its workings. He also admitted his "indifference" as to whether Darwin's doctrine of evolution would prove to be final or not. Still, this "rigorously scientific hypothesis" was a perfect vehicle for the progress of science, and for that related vehicle, the Huxley career.

Huxley had known that Darwin's "noble" theory would attract "abuse and misrepresentation." Three days after its publication, he had volunteered as Darwin's champion: "I am sharpening up my claws and beak in readiness." When *The Times* had lost track of its reviewer in the busy days before Christmas, Huxley had pounced, for *The Times* was the "Jupiter Olympus" of Britain's public opinion.

Stepping where Darwin feared to tread, Huxley explained natural selection in a human metaphor: "The individuals of a species are like the crew of a foundered ship, and none but good swimmers have a chance of reaching the land." As in the laissez-faire economy, people must sink or swim.

Immediately, **Origin of Species** *was drawn into the kind of struggle* that Bismarck would call a *Kulturkampf,* a "culture war." In the Britain of the 1860s, as in the Germany of the 1870s, the particular question—the official status of Christianity—stood for larger, more general questions. What were the sources of political legitimacy in this new, man-made world of markets, states, and sciences? Were democracy and liberal individualism rooted in the biology of *Homo sapiens* or artificial creations? Who should be invited to exercise in the moral gymnasium, and who should administer the antiseptic of faith?

A political order legitimizes itself by its origins: the gift of a divine right, the discovery of a natural right, a royal lineage, a founding document. Anchored in time, such origins unfold historically as a moral and legal narrative: a Great Chain of Being; a corpus of customary tradition or natural law or religious dogma; a hierarchy of caste, class, or race. Darwin implied different origins for human society, and with them a different kind of historical narrative. Despite himself, he depicted Nature as the most powerful lawgiver of all, and identified its rulings with the free play of natural forces.

Darwin hoped to pass unnoticed on the middle ground but he landed between the lines of battle. The war of the "apes and angels" was already under way, and the reviewers of *Origin of Species* took up familiar positions. The "angels" were the defenders of tradition. The Church of England was a constitutional pillar of the state. Its primate, the archbishop of Canterbury, was the nation's moral tutor, and its bishops voted in the House of Lords. Their brothers and cousins dominated the benches of Westminster, the officer class of the armed services, and the intellectual citadels of Oxford and Cambridge. The heirs and beneficiaries of past struggles, they criticized the social Malthusians for reducing life to an amoral struggle. Was life a free-for-all?

The Athenaeum, clubland's cultural journal, advised that such questions be left to the theologians: "If a monkey has become a man—what may not a man become?" Adam Sedgwick, Darwin's Cambridge geology tutor, warned his pupil that he had gone off the rails. There was no telling where Darwin would end up: "You have *deserted*—after a start in that tram-road of all solid physical truth—the true method of induction—& started up a machinery as wild, I think, as Bishop Wilkin's locomotive that was to sail us to the moon." In a long, anonymous article in *The Edinburgh Review*, Richard Owen mocked Darwin for raising "the supreme question in biology" but failing to answer it with "conviction." Worse, Darwin had made a "fundamental mistake":

he had taken the effect, the localized variation of species, for its cause, a "creative law." None of Darwin's "common stock of facts, of coincidences, correlations and analogies" proved that Man was a "transmuted ape." Robert FitzRoy, captain of the *Beagle*, wrote to his "dear old friend," then advertised his disappointment in a pseudonymous letter to *The Times*: "I, at least, *cannot* find anything 'Ennobling' in the thought of being a descendant of even the *most* ancient *Ape*."

The "apes" were the crusaders of science and social rationalization. Their leaders were self-made autodidacts of modest origins, like Herbert Spencer, the railway clerk, and Thomas Henry Huxley, the schoolteacher botanist. They launched their assault from the redoubts of the commercial, scientific middle classes: the journal, the newspaper, the laboratory, the public meeting. Their most ardent followers were fellow strugglers on the Malthusian battlefield, the expanding, educated middle classes. They were liberal in politics, laissez-faire in economics, and evangelical in religion. The "scientist" was one of their newest recruits, his title a recognition that a new professional class had developed.

Huxley knew that the churchmen had lost their medieval monopoly on knowledge. Yet they still clung to hereditary monopolies on moral virtue and political influence. Why should an economist propose the nation's budget but hereditary aristocrats vote on it? Why should a bishop pontificate on the fossil record more freely than a geologist? As Herbert Spencer would shortly say, in the free market of ability, justice should reflect "the survival of the fittest."

The Darwin controversy was the third round of this battle. In the 1840s, the angels won two Pyrrhic victories but depleted their moral reserves accordingly.

In 1842, George Holyoake, an admirer of Comte and Robert Owen, gave a lecture at the Cheltenham Mechanics' Institute. Asked about "our duty towards God," Holyoake replied that God did not exist. Holyoake was arrested, charged with blasphemy, and sentenced to six months in prison. Few educated Britons agreed with Holyoake's opinion, but many of them sensed the judicial affront to their freedom of conscience. This was not papal Rome. A modern, liberal state should not persecute law-abiding people as heretics. Even the home secretary felt that the Cheltenham police should not have marched Holyoake to their station in chains. The bishops had overplayed their hand. After Holyoake, there were no more convictions for blasphemy under English law.

Two years later, in 1844, the controversy over Robert Chambers's *Vestiges of Creation* clarified the schism between old and new hierarchies, and proved the limit of traditional authority. Reformers, radicals, and adherents of "rational religion" supported Chambers's right of expression. The scientists of Oxford and Cambridge defended public morality against the implications of geological time; though most of them were scientists by inclination, they tended to be clergymen by training and gentlemen by birth. Again, tradition intimidated the pretenders but could not silence them. Chambers would not dare admit to writing *Vestiges of Creation* until 1884. Nevertheless, his book went into many editions and would outsell *Origin of Species* for the rest of the century.

In modern democracy the power struggle of science and religion would remain a matter of public interest. The public and the interest were growing rapidly. Most liberals wanted to expand the voting franchise, and some wanted to include the skilled upper crust of the working classes. For Huxley, Darwin proved that history, Comte, and human nature were on his side: the evolution of literacy and market forces would succeed where all the French revolutions had failed. As the Darwin debate spilled into the drawing room and the public street, Mudie's Circulating Library added *Origin of Species* to its roster. John Murray printed a second edition. "What a book it is!" Comte's translator Harriet Martineau enthused, "overthrowing (if true) revealed Religion on the one hand, & Natural (as far as Final Causes & Design are concerned) on the other. The range & mass of knowledge take away one's breath."

When readers experienced intellectual and spiritual confusion,

Darwin's praetorian guard explained and consoled. In *The Gardener's Chronicle*, the botanist Joseph Hooker compared natural selection to a gardener favoring the healthiest varieties of strawberry. While Huxley goaded his betters with the brutality of natural selection, he flattered his readers, walking them through the "ABC of the great biological problem" as equals. Once natural selection was discovered, Huxley implied, it was quite obvious. The Darwin business was only the latest battle against the hereditary sentimentalists. Those who denied Darwin would lose, like the deniers of Galileo and Copernicus did.

In June 1860, the British Association for the Advancement of Science held its annual meeting at the newly built Museum of Natural History in Oxford. On its stage Huxley took his most famous scalp, Samuel Wilberforce, bishop of Oxford. The bishop, the son of William Wilberforce, the abolitionist, was a sly, oleaginous debater; Disraeli called him "Soapy Sam." Coached by Richard Owen, Wilberforce had already given Darwin an anonymous savaging in *The Quarterly Review*. This, though, was a public and direct confrontation. "Well, Sam Oxon got up and spouted for half an hour with inimitable spirit, ugliness, & emptiness, & unfairness," Joseph Hooker wrote. Finally, Wilberforce asked Huxley if he claimed descent from an ape on his mother's side or his father's.

"I would sooner claim kindred with an ape than with a man like the Bishop," Huxley replied. On questions of physical science, "authority" had always been "bowled out" by scientific investigation, "as witness astronomy and geology." It was not cricket for Wilberforce to abuse his "wondrous speaking powers" and his nonscientific "authority." The time had passed when a bishop might intimidate "a free discussion on what was, or was not, a matter of truth."

The Oxford debate made Huxley's reputation as "Darwin's bulldog." Huxley, by fighting for natural selection as a political issue, assured Darwin's fame. As Engels would become for Marx, Huxley became for Darwin: the defender and simplifier, the loyal traducer who coined "Darwinism," the extension of a scientific hypothesis into a comprehensive philosophy. Huxley's gladiatorial style did not reflect Darwin's desire for a bloodless victory. But naturally an antagonism of noddle and stomach had prevented Darwin from speaking for himself at Oxford.

Huxley declared the Oxford *disputatio* to be the triumph of science over superstition. Yet this outcome was not clear at the time. Wilberforce also claimed victory. Many of the audience could not decide who had won. It had been hard to hear the speakers—and were religion and science really as antagonistic as Huxley and Wilberforce claimed?

The greatest intellectual scandal of 1860 was not *Origin of Species* but *Essays and Reviews,* a collection of articles by seven Anglican rationalists. The most controversial of the essays was by the Reverend Baden Powell, an Oxford mathematician. Baden Powell praised Darwin's theory as a "masterly" and "undeniable" proof of Nature's divine design. Miracles, Baden Powell wrote, were physically impossible. Darwin had revealed the "grand principle of the self-evolving powers of nature." This represented a "revolution of opinion" to which Christians must adjust. As after all revolutions, there would be a new division of powers. The model of a truce had been proposed by Francis Bacon in the first age of warfare between religion and science. Scientific induction and religious intuition, Bacon suggested, produced different kinds of knowledge. Each ruled its own *mysterium,* like monarchs of adjoining kingdoms. Their particular wisdoms converged in the higher universal where reason was divine. As Baden Powell saw, only a similar division of powers could preserve the Christian ideal after Darwin.

Castigated by Wilberforce, Baden Powell died of a heart attack two weeks before the Oxford debate. His son Robert Baden-Powell became the father of the scouting movement, whose knots and rites were intended to preserve Christian morality in the wilderness of Nature.

"It seemed to me," George Holyoake recalled, "that doing good was being good—that it was good to do good, and that if a God of Good-

ness existed he would count goodness as a merit; and if no such God did exist, goodness was the best thing men could do in this world."

The martyr of Cheltenham had wrestled with "theologic hopes and fears" and won. Now he sought a purely social philosophy, a "simple theory of ethical duty," independent of "theistical or other doctrine." In 1851, Holyoake named it "secularism."

The "secularist" lives in the *saeculum*, "this age." The province of human duty is that which "belongs to this life." The Protestant conscience has long dispensed with the intermediaries between Man and Nature. Magnanimous in victory, it allows the bishops to keep their "mischief" and robes and illusions but not their political spoils. Like Marx's revolutionary, Holyoake's secularist compresses spiritual longings into this world while denying the existence of another world. He annuls the poetry of God and eternity by bringing heaven down to earth by prose. Here on the ground, reason and materialism supply the grammar of life: "Clearly science is the only Providence which can be depended upon." With no other path open, politics becomes the secularist's only hope. "It was not less plain that there was no mode of doing good open to us so certain as by *material* means." The religious impulse must speak the language of a political program.

Huxley also identified moral good with the new Providence of science, but he rejected Holyoake's secularist as an atheist under another name. Like a divorcé who assumes an alias, remarries, and then commits adultery, the secularist was repeating his favorite errors while trying to dodge the scandal. Huxley had no time for Christianity, but he accepted Pascal's argument that, absent proof of God's existence, it was in Man's interest to live as if God did exist. Nor did Huxley like the whiff of radical politics that came with the secularist's philosophical finality. Scientific knowledge was a process, not an end state. An empirical scientist worked from what he knew to what he did not know, like a man assembling an infinite jigsaw puzzle. To advance a hypothesis, he had to identify some aspect of the missing piece. There was nothing wrong with not knowing. It was the premise of discovery.

Annexing the territory of the secularists, Huxley advanced into the old *mysterium* of faith. Beyond the frontier of the known lay the soon-to-be known, the zone of inference and analogy, of absurd facts whose sense escaped like night before the early rays of the sun. The question of God's existence, expelled from the *mysterium* of science, dwelled in this realm. Huxley believed that scientific truth was the higher knowledge; like the further regions of the United States, the *mysterium* of religion was not an independent and equal sphere, but a realm soon to be settled by science. For now, though, science could not be certain whether God existed or not. Huxley called his condition of not knowing "agnostic."

Holyoake realized he had been somewhat hasty. The secularist, he decided, was not an atheist. He was an agnostic too.

Huxley believed that the experts would inherit the earth. The scientist, not the pope, the emperor, or the poet, was now the "unacknowledged legislator of the world," because only the scientist understood Nature's laws. Agnosticism was part of Huxley's campaign to spread the rule of scientific expertise. He depicted religious intuitions as forms of partial knowledge, awaiting their development as scientific facts. As this evolution of knowledge enfolded religious ideas and institutions, the old interpreters would retire and the new language develop. The generals of science would rename the monuments and citadels without sacking the city, for they came from within it. They would not need to frighten the horses, only the riders.

This, at least, was what Huxley expected when he claimed the borderlands of faith for science. There was, however, another possibility. As Americans knew, the frontier was unpredictable, a magnet for undesirable elements, and a settler staked his claim to the land by working it, whether well or badly. Huxley had lowered the standard of proof in the new territories of knowledge. Until science regulated these borderlands, any agnostic could settle there and erect a shrine to a new cult. His faith need only clear the lowest fences of scientific possibility. If its dogma could not be proved, neither could it be disproved under current conditions of knowledge. Under pseudonyms of scientific spirituality, the old categories—divinity, the soul, Providence—all thrived in the agnostic land of not knowing.

"There will soon be no more priests," Whitman prophesies. *"Their* work is done. They may wait awhile . . . perhaps a generation or two . . . dropping off by degrees. A superior breed shall take their place . . . the gangs of kosmos and prophets en masse shall take their place. A new order shall arise and they shall be the priests of man, and every man shall be his own priest."

Whitman says that 1861 will be the "year of the struggle." War will turn the pale and lisping "poetling" into a marching soldier, erect and strong, with a "well-gristled body" and a sunburned face and "masculine voice." In July 1861, two unprepared armies meet at Bull Run. Hundreds are killed. The Union army panics and flees; Whitman sees their disordered arrival in Washington, D.C. Lincoln authorizes the enlistment of five hundred thousand soldiers for up to three years. Whitman's brother George becomes one of them.

In Alabama, Henry Hotze volunteers as an officer in the Mobile Cadets. Josiah Nott enlists as a surgeon. So does J. Goodwin Scott, who married Thomas Huxley's sister Liz and emigrated to Montgomery. Their fifteen-year-old son, Thomas, named for his famous uncle, joins his father in the field hospitals.

"My heart goes with the south, and my head with the north," Huxley admits in a letter to Liz. "I have not the smallest sentimental sympathy with the negro . . . But it is clear to me that slavery means, for the white man, bad political economy; bad social morality; bad internal political organization, and a bad influence on free labour and freedom all over the world." In the war for reason and progress, Darwin's *Origin of Species* will be a "Whitworth gun," a British-made repeating rifle, in the armory of liberalism.

Meanwhile, Confederate agents in Britain buy crates of Whitworth rifles for export. At Cammell Laird's dockyard in Liverpool, a British sympathizer orders the construction of what appears to be a private navy. The British government recognizes the Confederacy as a belligerent, a status that allows it to raise money and buy weapons in neutral countries. Its president, Jefferson Davis, wants to drag Britain into the war. He has blocked the export of Confederate cotton. Southern slaves pick three-quarters of the raw cotton spun in the mills of Lancashire, and half of the finished textiles are sold in India and the Far East. The embargo causes a collapse in the price of tea, a boom in the price of cotton, and disturbances and hunger in Lancashire. Davis hopes that Britain will find neutrality too expensive. As part of this "King Cotton Diplomacy," the Confederate secret service sends Hotze to London. His orders are to help with the purchase of military equipment and to convince the British public to support the Confederate States of America.

At Down House, Darwin's morning cup of tea becomes cheaper, but *The Times* abounds with bad news. The Americans are at one another's throats. Tea is down, cotton is up, and his stomach is all over the place. In Lancashire, six in every ten weavers are unemployed. The "cotton famine" causes riots in the mill towns. The weavers support Lincoln, but they do not have the vote. In 1832, Darwin, following family tradition, favored expanding the franchise. These days, he prefers not to enfranchise the lower orders.

"I have managed to skim the newspaper, but had not the heart to read all the bloody details," Darwin writes to Asa Gray after Bull Run. "Good God! What will the end be?"

Gray believes in both God and Darwin. In May 1859, he launched the Darwin hypothesis in America at a meeting of the Cambridge Scientific Club, with Louis Agassiz among the dissenters in the audience. In 1860, Gray defended *Origin of Species* in three long articles in *The Atlantic* and tried to "baptize" Darwinism as compatible with Christianity. Now, Gray believes that Providence and the facts of life favor the Union. The North has the manpower and the industrial means. Like Whitman, he sees Lincoln as "a second Washington." Gray reminds Darwin that his theory has no limits. "Natural selection quickly crushes out weak nations."

After breakfast, Darwin resumes where Wallace forced him to leave off: the question of human development and the matter of racial difference. He begins with plant reproduction. He has found that orchids are capable of self-pollination but that this method causes their stock to degenerate. The healthiest blooms cast their reproductive fate to the winds and experiment in crossbreeding. The taboo on incest seems to have empirical grounds. If this bodes poorly for Darwin's sickly children, it augurs well for the species: morality, grounded in science, may survive the withering of Christian tradition. If this is a rejoinder to the polygenists, the inference is lost in the storms that rage beyond Darwin's private Eden. But on these matters, Darwin has already said enough.

"Nevertheless, the doctrine that all nature is at war is most true," he wrote in *Natural Selection.* "The struggle very often falls on the egg & seed, or on the seedling, larva & young: but fall it must sometime in the life of each individual, or more commonly at intervals on successive generations & then with extreme severity."

Digestive difficulties render Darwin hors de combat for most of 1862. He emerges with a convalescent's beard, a fluffy white muffler that gives him the aspect of a dolorous orangutan. A member of the first generation to be photographed, he is never comfortable before the camera. The beard becomes a fence against fame but a gift to cartoonists and photographers. Darwin is turning into the face of "Darwinism." In photographs, he resembles a geriatric gardener who, having nibbled forbidden fruit, hobbles round the house toward his master's privy.

"Yesterday, I was influenced with the rottenness of human relations," Thoreau wrote. "They appeared full of death and decay, and offended the nostrils. In the night I dreamed of delving amid the graves of the dead, and soiled my fingers with their rank mould. It was *sanitarily, morally,* and *physically* true."

Thoreau's last, unfinished project was a "Natural History" of plant life, a vegetal apocalypse on the themes of Malthus. The spiritual warrior who had breathed in his own fashion was dying of tuberculosis in his sister Sophia's house. Death became him. He seemed exalted as the boundary between Thoreau and Nature dissolved for the last time. Children brought him flowers from the woods. He died in May 1862, his last words "moose" and "Indian."

At the funeral in Sleepy Hollow, New York, Emerson eulogized Thoreau as the American Adam. The complete woodsman had slipped the bonds of civilization and mastered himself by ascetic discipline: "He never married; he lived alone; he never went to church; he never voted; he refused to pay a tax to the state; he ate no flesh, he drank no wine, he never knew the use of tobacco; and though a naturalist, he used neither trap nor gun." Yet Emerson also buried as he praised. Thoreau's virtuous negations had masked cruelty and aggression. He had enjoyed conflict and "a little sense of victory." He had held ordinary life in "contempt." Thoreau, Emerson implied, had not fulfilled his promise. In disentangling himself from civilization, he had lost his humanity.

In London, Henry Hotze rented an office in Fleet Street and contrived a newspaper, *The Index*, to explain the "mild, humane, and Christian" slave system of the South. The Confederates, *The Index* said, were sons of English liberty. Like their Cromwellian ancestors, they had divine rights to form a nation and natural rights to determine their rights of property. Hotze distributed books and pamphlets, and blurred the loyalties of British journalists with gifts of whiskey and cigars. To emphasize ties of blood, he placed posters in streets and railway stations that blended the Confederate flag with the Union Jack.

British opinion remained unanimously divided, its only consensus a wariness of direct involvement. The Lancashire cotton merchants turned to Egypt and India for imports of raw cotton. The Lincoln administration warned the British government to keep a closer watch on its subjects' involvement in weapons smuggling. Yet Hotze's money and gifts were not entirely wasted. Though he lost the battle for public opinion, he did better among the experts—so much so that they elected him one of them.

Darwin's hypothesis about "common descent" had divided the Ethnological Society of Britain. After the Emancipation Proclamation of January 1863, the society split. The anti-Darwinian wing broke away and formed the Anthropological Society of London. Led by Dr. James Hunt, previously engaged in curing stammerers in the seaside town of Hastings, they elected Josiah Nott as an honorary member and Hotze to their council. Three other Confederates joined him: George Witt of *The Index*, the Confederate diplomat Albert Taylor Bledsoe, and George McHenry, who, given £300 by Hotze, wrote pro-slavery articles in the *Anthropological Society Journal*.

The Anthropological Society glorified in polygenist "diversity." Hunt praised Confederate laws against racial intermarriage. The mace with which he called meetings to order was decorated with the carved head of an African chewing a human thighbone. After Hunt's members hung the skeleton of a "savage" in the window of their meeting hall, they became known as the Cannibal Club.

"Mr. de Gobineau and Mr. Hotze," *The Index* reported, "were wise enough to avoid the rock on which Mr. Darwin made shipwreck."

"The Cannon will not suffer any other sound to be heard for miles & for years around it. Our chronology has lost all old distinctions in one date."

Thoughts of war kept Emerson awake at night. For two years, he and his wife, Lidian, had refrained from endorsing Lincoln's war if it were fought only to contain slaveholding and not to extirpate it. On these grounds they had forbidden their only son, Edward, from enlisting. Lincoln's slow maneuvers against the great evil left Emerson in "a chronic puzzle, & incapacity to move." When Lincoln at last unleashed the power of the state in the Emancipation Proclamation, Emerson greeted it as the inauguration of a "New Chronology." Just as John Brown's martyrdom had made "the gallows as sacred as the cross," so the war might be a sacred rebirth, reordering history like the birth of Jesus.

War, Emerson now wrote, is natural, for it enforces Nature's law, the court of life and death: "The world is ever equal to itself, & centripetence makes centrifugence." War "searches character, & acquits those whom I acquit, whom life acquits, those whose reality & spontaneous honesty & singleness appear." The false, the dishonest, and the weak would be purged, and the "hurried and slipshod lives" of otherwise unrepresentative men enlarged, by "a moment of grandeur." Instead of softening by Southern manners, American society would be cured by "wholesome disinfectants" and toughened by "Saxon" health.

In Europe, relics of history littered a landscape long deforested and tamed. Emerson's American man returned to his origins. War offered the original, essential American experience, the shedding of habit and history. He struggled against Nature to claim his private plot from the forests, insects, snow, and tribes. Like pioneer life, warfare was austere, attritional, and masculine. "Sometimes," he admitted, "gunpowder smells good."

In 1863, Emerson was sixty, a decorous old gentleman with weak eyes, an erratic memory, and the greatest reputation in American letters. There were no new poems, and his obituary for Thoreau would be his last major essay. The war rekindled a memory of ardor, the poet's burning purpose. "It is a potent alternative, tonic, magnetizer, reinforces manly power a hundred times and a thousand times. I see it come as a frosty October, which shall restore intellectual and moral power to these languid and dissipated populations."

Emerson was far enough from the field to romanticize the death of young men he did not know, and old enough to imagine his youthful strength in theirs. In June 1863, his duties as a public figure took him to West Point as the literary ornament on a committee of inspection. In the dormitory, each cadet had rolled up his mattress like a scroll. Each made his own bed, fetched the water he washed in, and blacked his own boots. This, Emerson felt, was "Self-help" in action, a prelude to unrolling of the scroll on the battlefield. Two weeks later, the tide of the war turned at Gettysburg. The bodies of some fifty thousand Americans tested Emerson's assertion that the human mind "cannot be burned, nor bayonetted, nor wounded, nor missing."

One of Emerson's staple lectures was "The Natural History of the Intellect." In it, he describes his doubts about science. No "completeness of system" can reduce the inner life to a "science of the mind." As far or how high science explores, it "adopts the method of the universe as fast as it appears." New knowledge reveals new capacities and experiences. The mind unfolds in perception and "the Intellect builds the universe." The lengthening of perspective diminishes every sacred abstraction. "What is life but an angle of vision? A man is measured by the angle at which he looks at objects."

Emerson called this the "analogy of spatial distance & qualitative difference." The science of modern war proved it, for technology changed the reach of death. At sea, the age of wooden ships ended in 1862 with the clash of the ironclad leviathans *Monitor* and *Merrimack*. The range of the *Monitor*'s cannon and the mobility of its steam-powered turret gave notice that fighting at close quarters would soon be too dangerous to attempt. As warships retreated to the horizon, air balloons and artillery turned the flat battlefield into a wider, three-dimensional space, and a much more dangerous one.

In April 1862, nearly twenty-four thousand of America's fathers, sons, and brothers died at Shiloh. One in every four combatants was killed, wounded, or missing. In two days, the Civil War had exceeded the combined battlefield losses of the American Revolution, the War of 1812, and the Mexican-American War. The rifled barrel spun a bullet, sending it faster and straighter than a musket ball. The repeating rifle reloaded mechanically, accelerating the rate of fire. The Gardiner bullet contained an explosive charge, timed to detonate one and a quarter seconds after impact. Richard Gatling's multibarrel machine gun fired a hundred rounds a minute, and was operated by tipping bullets into a hopper like grain and turning a crank. The canister shell was packed with metal balls or scrap and allowed artillery to stop a regiment of infantry in its tracks.

Soldiers had always shaped the environment of war: castles, ditches, palisades, stacks of bushes. Now, technology controlled the terrain, and its grasp reached beyond the borders of contact and visibility. Attacking Fort Sanders in November 1863, Confederate infantry foundered on wire obstacles. The Union general Ambrose Burnside had strung telegraph cable at knee height; the attackers were fortunate that barbed wire, patented in France in 1860 as a way to control cattle, had yet to be applied to corral men into a killing field. As the landscape became hostile to humanity, the experience of war changed. To survive, soldiers had to hide and melt into the environment and endure an endless psychological battle. They donned green or brown and dug into the ground to avoid shrapnel and snipers. At the siege of Petersburg, Virginia, the armies lived in trenches for nine months while they fought for control of the railway line to Richmond. The detonation of a giant mine left a huge crater into which Union soldiers blundered like ants in a jar. The chivalric ideal could not survive in this hostile environment; in Europe, the battle of Solferino in 1859 was the last time that two monarchs commanded the armies in the field.

The modern army was the industrial state on the move, a complex hierarchy of specialization. At its head were the planners and strategists of the general staff, trained in national schools like West Point, and the Prussian Military Academy, where the *kriegspiel*, the "war game," was invented. Next came the technicians who, like the civilian middle classes, gained prestige from their expertise: the artillerymen, engineers, telegraphists, and doctors. Then came the worker ants: the clerks, transport crews, cooks, and quartermasters who sustained a force too numerous to live off the land. That force did the fighting and dying. The infantry were mostly "three months' men," civilians drilled in basic procedures, interchangeable and expendable. After the Emancipation Proclamation, the Emersons allowed a family friend to dissuade Edward from volunteering.

"I believe," Emerson wrote in "The Natural History of the Intellect," "in the existence of the material world as the expression of the spiri-

tual or the real, and in the impenetrable mystery which hides (and hides through absolute transparency) the mental nature, I await the insight which our advancing knowledge of material laws shall furnish."

In a photograph saloon at Washington Street in Boston, Helen Stuart wove "mourning jewelry" from the hair of the dead as William H. Mumler merged the images of the dead and the living for "spirit photographs." The bereaved sat stiffly in black as their dead hovered overhead, conjured in clouds of silver gelatin. In 1861, Mumler had discovered his method, and Spiritualism its next technical frontier, through an accidental double exposure. His business rose on a tide of grief, with an undertow of criminality. Some of the dim, indistinct wraiths in his pictures were still alive, and he obtained his sharpest images by breaking into customers' homes to steal photographs of their dead. Like Mathew Brady and Walt Whitman, Mumler would find that his most popular image would be that of Abraham Lincoln. Mumler summoned him leaning posthumously over the shoulder of a bereft Mary Todd Lincoln.

All of society was subject to Emerson's law of "spatial distance & qualitative difference." The postal service, newspaper, telegraph, and photograph all brought home the material facts of war. As imaginative proximity stimulated civilians to empathy, intellect built its own universe, a gallery of heroic, redemptive, and unreliable images. Soldiers seemed more human—Henry Dunant's account of wounded French and Austrian soldiers abandoned on the field of Solferino inspired the creation in 1863 of the International Committee of the Red Cross—but civilians became more military.

In Crimea in 1854, the first "war correspondent," William Russell of the London *Times*, had telegraphed battle reports to the breakfast table. Russell described folly and ineptitude, frostbite and dysentery, the Light Brigade slaughtered, soldiers dying without winter uniforms or doctors. Yet the icons that arose from the wreck of ideals were the saintly, prickly volunteer nurse Florence Nightingale and the galloping glory of Tennyson's "Charge of the Light Brigade."

The improvisations of a Crimean winter became a bloodless civilian uniform: the Raglan overcoat, the cardigan, the balaclava, and the beards that would remain in fashion until the advent of the gas mask.

When Mathew Brady exhibited his Antietam photographs in New York, *The New York Times* praised him for bringing home "the terrible reality and earnestness" of war. "If he has not brought bodies and laid them in our dooryards and along the streets, he has done something very like it." But the camera, by offering a higher standard of realism, perjured itself more plausibly. The first documentary photographs of war were taken in the Mexican-American War. The Crimean War elicited the first staged war photograph: for *The Valley of the Shadow of Death* (1854), Roger Fenton rearranged cannonballs on the battlefield, the better to express the Light Brigade's martyrdom. After the battle of Antietam in 1862, Brady's assistant Alexander Gardner moved corpses around, to complement a church in the background.

"Were you ever Daguerrotyped, O immortal man?" Emerson asked. "And did you look with all vigor at the lens of the camera, or rather, by the direction of the operator, at the brass peg a little below it, to give the picture the full benefit of your expanded and flashing eye?" Nature, he knew, was a "rushing stream" that "will not stop to be observed." He disliked his photographic portrait: the unnatural stillness, the clenching of muscles. His gaze seemed fixed as in "a fit, in madness, or in death."

"This Image is altogether unsatisfactory, illusive, and even in some measure tragical to me!" Carlyle complained on receiving Emerson's daguerreotype. His friend seemed "imprisoned in baleful shadows, as of the Valley of Death."

When Whitman viewed his portraits in sequence, he could not decide if the transition from image to image was a bridge or a break. The life they described did not flow; it juddered in a series of unnatural suspensions. "It is hard to extract a man's real self—any man—from such a chaotic mass—from such historic debris."

Whitman remade himself amid the new chronology. When Rufus Griswold reviewed *Leaves of Grass* in 1855, he alluded to Whitman's sexuality through a Latin legal description of sodomy, *Peccatum illud horribile, inter Christianos non nominandum*: "The horrible sin not to be named among Christians." Ten years later, Whitman was a wholesome public man, the "Good Gray Poet" whose "O Captain! My Captain!" lamented Lincoln for a fatherless nation. The war, Whitman admitted, "set up my hope for all time."

In December 1862, Whitman was reading a casualty list in the *New-York Tribune* when he saw the name "G. W. Whitmore." Whitman took this for a report of his brother George's death or wounding. He hurried south to Washington and searched the military hospitals. He found George only lightly wounded but found himself unable to leave the wards. In *Leaves of Grass*, Whitman had dreamed up strong-limbed Adamic youths. In Washington he found them, "noble, sturdy, loyal boys," terribly wounded, stoical and alone in "long rows of cots": the refuse pails filled with "clotted rags and blood," the weeping wounds and septic stumps, the death agony and the "dying kiss." He found work in the Department of Indian Affairs and visited the wards every night, talking, consoling, advising, and kissing. The fulcrum of a new humanity, Whitman realized, was not Emerson's battlefield but its broken aftermath: "The days in the hospitals . . . the social being-ness of the soldiers—the revelation of an exquisite courtesy—man to man—rubbing up there together . . . the doing of necessary unnameable things, always done with exquisite delicacy." These were the "specimen days" of the human capacity for compassion.

Whitman had never sought to deny desire, the snake in Thoreau's throat, or to euphemize it like Emerson. He was a sensualist and an embracer, his soul "reflected in Nature" as through a gauze of "inexpressible completeness, sanity, beauty." The military emergency suspended morality and medical terminology, as the chronology of ordinary movement suspended itself before the camera: "I will lift what has too long kept down those smouldering fires, I will give them complete abandonment."

Whitman published his first hospital reports in the *New York Leader* as "Velsor Brush," an amalgam of his mother and grandmother's maiden names. In this feminine guise, Whitman universalized himself. He merged his cryptic culture war for sexual freedom into the official culture war that Lincoln called the "struggle for the life of the nation" and "the government and institutions of our fathers." Whitman venerated Lincoln and saw him several times in Washington, D.C.: once as the people's Caesar, addressing a crowd from a balcony; again as the nation's husband, out in his carriage with Mrs. Lincoln, but exchanging what Whitman felt were meaningful looks with Whitman, his Everyman.

Whitman insists that the "damned war business" is "nine hundred ninety nine parts diarrhea to one part glory." Expertly he alchemizes that glorious part from the gore and waste. Like a pagan priest feeding a "burning flame," Whitman picks through the guts of the dead and finds democratic auguries in blood, bone, and sinew. Renewed forever, the land "entire is saturated, perfumed with their impalpable ashes," an "exhalation in Nature's chemistry distill'd" in "every future grain of wheat and ear of corn, and every flower that grows, and every breath we draw."

The roots of the sexual revolution lie in eighteenth-century libertinism, where free thought in religion first justified free expression in sexuality. In Whitman, these roots sprout in the marketplace as spiritual qualities: instead of the closeted debauches and anticlerical heresies of Sade and Casanova, the patriotic hygiene and soulful bodies of *Specimen Days*. Science had placed sex, the mechanism of natural selection, at the center of human purpose. Science had also weakened Christian morality, and the biblical insistence on heterosexual marriage and procreation.

Science, Mallarmé wrote in 1867, now defined the human as "Nature thinking," a body "decomposed" into biological components and impulses. Yet the lumps of "fabricated gelatin," Mallarmé wrote, also sustain the "divine impressions" and "glorious lies" that have "amassed in us since our earliest years." The definition of "sexuality" is fundamental to religious and social values. Its redefinition would become fundamental to the spiritual revaluations of the modern age. In 1869, Karl-Maria Kertbeny, in an anonymously published appeal for the repeal of Prussia's anti-sodomy laws, became the first person to use the term "homosexual" in public.

In Whitman's new chronology, development, whether political or sexual, is not just for development's sake. Natural impulses are right because they are natural, and sacred because they reunify mind and body, the individual soul with the soul of the world. Sex has always carried "Meanings, proofs, purities, delicacies, results, promulgations" of the divine. Whitman marks the debut of the modern sexual persona.

"It was a religion with me. A religion? Well—every man has a religion: has something in heaven or earth which he will give up everything else for—something which absorbs him, possesses itself of him, makes him over into his image . . . it is his dream, it is his lodestar, it is his master."

On Good Friday 1865, Whitman's god is sacrificed as he watches the play *Our American Cousin.* In the image of the killing in Ford's Theatre, the "involved, baffling, multiform whirl of the secession period comes to a head, and is gather'd in one brief flash of lightning-illumination." An actor of "statuesque beauty" jumps onto the stage. A phantasmagoria that makes "not the slightest call on the moral, emotional, esthetic, or spiritual nature" becomes "one of those climax-moments on the stage of universal Time." Lincoln's murder is "the highest poetic, single, central, pictorial denouement" of Whitman's century. The lifeblood of America's "first great Martyr Chief" will become the "cement to the whole people, subtler, more underlying, than any thing in written constitution, or courts, or armies."

A secular crime, as monstrously natural as "the bursting of a bud, or pod," denatures to reveal a religious end. The Greeks would have placed Lincoln's form in their pantheon, where "men vitalize gods, and gods divinify men." Whitman keeps Lincoln, his times, and his death "altogether to our own," an immortal of the modern *saeculum*.

The same "radiation" confuses religious spirit and secular time in Lincoln's first obituary. The audience at the deathbed cannot hear Edwin Stanton clearly. Does Lincoln now belong "to the angels" or "to the ages"? As in Whitman's verse, the secular tableau stands for the sacred conception.

❧ 6 ❧

THE ORIGIN OF THE WORLD

Wagner, Jesus,
and the Racial Spirit

Two peoples only are there henceforth—the one that follows me, the other that withstands me. The one I lead to happiness; over the other grinds my path. For I am the Revolution, I am the ever-fashioning Life, I am the only God, to whom each creature testifies, who spans and gives both life and happiness to all . . .

Nearer and nearer rolls the storm, and on its wings Revolution; the quickened hearts of those awakened to life open wide, and the conquering Revolution pours into their minds, their bones, their flesh, filling them through and through . . .

Inspiration shines from their ennobled faces, a radiant light streams from their eyes, and with the heaven-shaking cry "I am a Man!," the millions, the embodied Revolution, the God become Man, rush down to the valleys and plains, and proclaim to all the world the new gospel of Happiness. —*Richard Wagner, "The Revolution" (1848)*

The new harmony is born from the chaos of primordial sound. Indistinct tones evolve into a suspended chord, an unresolved cry of anguish, defiance, need, and desire. This suspension implies an original harmony but its key is lost in time, in the prehistory before sounds and objects were named and ordered. The chord expresses the inner logic of its dissolution and falls forward into the region of A minor. Suddenly it fractures chromatically, one line sliding upward, the other down. Then, as a weaker body is drawn into the orbit of the more powerful, the lines reunite in a higher key. But their reunion restates their dissonance. This unresolved tension grows until the harmonic center collapses again, initiating a further cycle of decay and creation.

It is June 10, 1865, nearly two months after Lincoln's murder. In the National Theater in Munich, Hans von Bülow conducts the opening of Richard Wagner's *Tristan and Isolde*. A married couple play the doomed lovers: the precociously talented and fat Ludwig Schnorr von Carolsfeld and his older, thinner wife, Malvina. In the second act, their duet is interrupted before its climax. In the third, they find consummation, but love's ecstasy will be life's end.

Isolde dies as her consciousness flowers in the fullness of orgasm. Later her love potion will become Tristan's poison. The most intimate of experiences leads to the loss of sensation and personality; the impulse to love is fulfilled in the impulse to death. Like Bernini's Saint Teresa, caught in her marmoreal swoon as an angel thrusts a fire-tipped spear into her heart and innards, *Tristan and Isolde* preserves love's sacrifice to eternity. The fleeting *petit mort* is a foretaste of a final reunion with Nature: the transfiguring, transcendent unification of the *Liebestod*, the "love-death."

Life does not impersonate art but is consumed by its passion. After four performances, Ludwig Schnorr von Carolsfeld suffers an involuntary *Liebestod* of his own when he picks up a chest infection, then dies from an apoplexy. The production closes. Wagner's admirers claim that Schnorr burst his veins in willing sacrifice to the master's art. Malvina also finds redemption in death. Grieving, she turns to Spiritualism and becomes convinced that she will replace Cosima von Bülow, the conductor's wife, as Wagner's muse.

The creator of the "Tristan chord" and other Romantic tensions is short and nervous, with a bird's bony face and an actor's fondness for the silks and ribbons of the costume trunk. Wagner feels himself to be a "different kind of organism," a genius with "hyper-sensitive nerves." He has heard the "music of the future" and must create the Gesamtkunstwerk, the "total work of art." The unity of art forms—music, poetry, dance, visual arts—has been lost since the days of ancient Greece. Wagner's destiny is to reintegrate the arts into a modern synthesis. To experience it will be a spiritual rebirth. A "glinting, overbrimming stream of sound" surges up through the hollowness of modern life like an "unending melody" from the origin of the world. Minds and bodies melt with sounds and sensations, and vision is cleansed with "radiant light." The confusion of matter becomes pure spirit. A new consciousness is born.

Wagner's artistic license is unlimited. His performance never stops. History is his backdrop, ordinary mortals his chorus. The hero summons favored voices in counterpoint to his quest but he plays every role: composer, poet, businessman, philosopher, seducer, courtier, revolutionary, royalist, anarchist, ascetic, sensualist, fantasist, truth-teller. To stage the revolution in art he needs money, lots of it. He needs patrons, donors, supporters, creditors, secretaries, copyists, conductors, an opera house that can accommodate his vision, a villa that does not offend his delicate taste, a chef who panders to it, a wife who understands it, a lover who excites it.

There is a torrent of music in Wagner, but without a constant flow of money, it will die silent within him. Money is "the curse that annihilates everything noble." Wagner is an artist, but he must promote himself through an unending flood of words. He feels his superiority to the masses, but he must entertain them like a "carnival barker." Wagner hates commerce, but he has a peculiar genius for commodifying himself. He dreams of cornering the market in art, of creating the largest and loudest music that anyone has ever heard, of building a theater devoted only to his work, of keeping all the profits. His life is a one-man show, an endless conscription series called "Richard Wagner." He is a prisoner of what Thomas Carlyle calls the "cash nexus," the binding of humanity by commerce.

• • •

Wagner adapted The Flying Dutchman *from a short story by Hein-*rich Heine. A blaspheming sea captain becomes an Ahasuerus, a Wandering Jew of the waves. For his faithlessness he is damned to sail the oceans until he is redeemed by a woman's love.

Wagner's "wandering years" began with a traveling opera company. He married one of its actresses, Minna Planer, but love did not redeem either of them. They argued on the way to the church and continued arguing when they moved to Paris, the capital of opera. Richard struggled to turn Edward Bulwer-Lytton's *Rienzi* into an opera about a people's revolution that ends in blood and fire. Minna cheated on him, and he on her. They pawned their wedding rings and Minna's costumes. The German Jewish composer Giacomo Meyerbeer saved them from starvation, by pointing Wagner toward a pot of gold at Dresden.

As court conductor to the king of Saxony, Wagner was able to stage *Rienzi* and *The Flying Dutchman*, and write *Tannhäuser*, as well as a parable of Christian communism, *The Love Feast of the Apostles*. Then he turned on his patron. In 1849, the German revolution reached Dresden. Wagner hosted revolutionary cells in his garden, helped distribute weapons, and relished the spectacle when the rebels set fire to the opera house in which he had conducted Beethoven's Ninth. Wanted by the Prussian police, he retreated to Zurich and then Geneva.

Brooding by the lakes, Wagner dredged "darkling things" into the light of consciousness. Politics was a surface phenomenon. A "radically transformed world" required a revolution in consciousness, a spiritual rebirth. Once, Christianity had transformed the world. Now, only art could make the consciousness aware of its revolutionary potential. For only art could awaken the power of myth, which called the individual into the community.

Wagner imagines the listener walking alone into the living forest on a summer evening. He hears an "infinite diversity" of voices in the songs of birds and leaves, yet he also hears how each unique bird and tree existed for its species, and for the entirety of Nature. He realizes that his singularity, the "strange distinctiveness" of his individual life, was his experience of a greater biological singularity. In the "great forest melody," he hears the song of the *Volk*, the community of blood, the lineage of the collective soul. Like the pope's staff sprouting green buds at the end of *Tannhäuser*, Myth is Nature's hidden truth, Man's origins resurgent.

Wagner knew the legend of the medieval hero Siegfried from Jacob Grimm's *German Mythology*. Modernizing the myth, he conceived a musical poem cycle in which Siegfried was a "socialist redeemer come down to earth to abolish the reign of Capital." This, the germ of the *Ring of the Nibelung* saga, would obsess Wagner for twenty-four years. Siegfried, he wrote, is "the man we wait and wish for—the future man whom we cannot create but who will create himself by our annihilation—the most perfect man I can imagine." The wanderings of this suffering son will lead him blindly to his final battle, the revolutionary liberation that is the *Götterdämmerung*, the "Twilight of the Gods."

"I know now the future of this world."

"I have no money," Wagner told Franz Liszt, "but what I do have is an enormous desire to commit acts of artistic terrorism." In his wandering years, Wagner was better known as a philosopher than as a composer. It is as though Darwin had advanced the case for natural selection by opening a taxidermist's shop, or if Marx had exposited the labor theory of value in sonata form.

All art, said the English aesthete Walter Pater, aspires to the condition of music. Wagner's prose aspires to the condition of Wagner's music. Fluent and violent, it labors like the Flying Dutchman in a storm. Beneath thick clouds of rhetoric, lightning illuminates the furious waves. Brilliance duets with folly on the plunging deck, and reason slides overboard. The Jews are driving the good ship *Deutschland* onto the rocks of commerce.

German Jews are politically emancipated and dress like other Germans. They mix with other Germans in dining rooms, boardrooms, and bedrooms. Yet Wagner, in the fashion of his day, is convinced that they remain Jews: every *Volk* has its "essence" of blood, and art and politics are its spiritual expressions. The Jewish essence cannot be altered by declarations of equality, changes of dress and name, or strategic conversions to Christianity. Nor, Wagner believes, can the German essence deny its own voice in the blood. If German society were a healthy organism, it would reject the Jews as an "entirely foreign element." Instead, the Germans have invited the Jews to share in unnatural cohabitations and "liberal utopias." The German consciousness is fevered with Jewish materialism, inflamed by Jewish capitalism, and crippled by the "slave mentality" of Jewish morals.

Wagner reckons that he knows sickness when he hears it: Jewishness in music. The counterfeit "synagogue-song" of Meyerbeer and Mendelssohn defiles the heritage of Beethoven. While the ear is seduced with "sensational effects," someone profits by the "confusion of musical taste." To "rout the demon," the Germans must follow Jesus. They must fight for spiritual liberation and free their natural and health-giving urges. Until they accept their innate loathing for the nature and character of the Jews, they will remain *luftmenschen*, dreamers "floating in the air and fighting clouds." To become the Wagnerian man of the future, each German must win his private war of unification and overthrow his inner Jew: "Judaism is the evil conscience of our modern civilization."

Lohengrin arrives at the castle in a boat drawn by a swan and marries the beautiful Elsa. Tricked by a witch, Elsa asks Lohengrin the question he has sworn never to answer: Who is he? Lohengrin is in love, so he tells Elsa his secret. He is the son of King Parsifal and is pursuing the Holy Grail. For breaking his oath, Lohengrin must leave. He sails for the castle of the Holy Grail, his swan turns into a dove, and Elsa dies a *Liebestod*. Lohengrin's secret paternity is the seed of his fate.

Schoenberg will call the Tristan chord a "wandering chord," an ambiguous sonic Ahasuerus that could come from anywhere. Wagner believed that art ran in his blood but feared this was not all. His mother, Johanna, affected not to know her maiden name. Born in a Leipzig bakery, she had been placed in private education by an anonymous friend of the family. Wagner suspected that her biological father was Prince Friedrich Ferdinand Constantin, the rakish and musical brother of the Grand Duke of Weimar. Nor did Wagner believe himself to be the biological son of Carl Wagner, a police clerk and amateur actor who had died of typhus shortly after his son's birth. He believed that his real father was his parents' friend Ludwig Geyer, an actor, painter, and playwright who had known Goethe. Within a year of Carl Wagner's death, Geyer had moved into the Wagner home in Leipzig's Jewish quarter; a *geyer* is a vulture. He called himself Richard's stepfather, and Richard took Geyer's surname. Further blurring real and imaginary roles, Geyer directed Johanna's children in elaborate pantomimes: Hamlet's tragedy, repeated as farce with Claudius as the director.

In Wagner's mind as in Hamlet's, fantasies of royal inheritance mingled with phantasms of corruption. Wagner suspected that Geyer had Jewish blood, because Geyer's grandfather, Gottfried Benjamin, had a Jewish-sounding name. But Wagner wasn't certain. The modern whirl threw together the prince and the baker's wife, the Jewish actor and the Christian clerk, good blood with bad. Money broke the social order that made the nation, and the symbolic order through which Myth spoke. The modern system was against Nature; the nuclear family, as Marx wrote, had developed from the medieval extended household as a resource of capitalist production. The father ruled that extended household in the name of the Heavenly Father. Now, the father's name was uncertain even in the nuclear family, and the son was unsure of his heredity and family relationships.

Early Romantics adopted the myth of Prometheus, the defiant son who steals technical knowledge from his father, Zeus, and is punished by having his liver pecked out by an eagle. Later Romantics found their mythic image in Oedipus, the prince whose efforts to escape the curse of heredity lead to its fulfillment in love and death. In 1851, more than half a century before Freud placed Oedipus at the heart of the nuclear family, Wagner identified Oedipal conflict as the motor of human history.

"To-day we need only to expound faithfully the myth of Oedipus according to its most innermost essence, and we gain an intelligible picture of the whole history of mankind, from the beginnings of society to the inevitable downfall of the state."

Before that state could fall, it had to rise. The Germans dwelled in the heart of Europe, but there was no single German state. Medieval German speakers had lived in the Holy Roman Empire's mosaic of *Kleinstaaterei*, "little states." Some, like Saxony and Bavaria, were kingdoms ruled by hereditary houses. Others, like Hamburg and Bremen, were merchant states ruled by wealthy families. Still more were sleepy Ruritanias where a prince-bishop or a local lord ruled a hinterland of farms. By marriage and war, the little states grew into a family of over three hundred members, with more than 1,800 customs barriers, and no common standards for weights, measures, or currency.

In 1806, Napoléon Bonaparte smashed this charming but obstructive system and compressed sixteen western states into a confederation of the Rhineland. After his fall, the Congress of Vienna resuscitated this union as the thirty-nine-member German Confederation. The victors designed the confederation to be economically vigorous—it had a single *zollverein*, or customs' union—but politically weak. The two most powerful German-speaking states, Austria and Prussia, were not members of the confederation. Their capitals, Vienna and Berlin, lay outside the confederation, but both held territory inside it. "My constitution," Heinrich Heine quipped on his deathbed in 1856, "is even worse than the constitution of Prussia."

The revolutions of 1848 birthed the *deutsch Frage*, the "German question," the conundrum at the heart of central Europe. The German speakers had common origins of language, history, and kinship: the cultural and biological patrimony of modern statehood. But their territorial patrimony was divided. Should they coalesce into a *Klein-deutschland*, a "Little Germany" led by Prussia, an emerging industrial power with a Protestant monarch? Or should they form a looser, more complex *Grossdeutschland*, a "Big Germany" under the Catholic emperor of Austria, with more Germans, more non-Germans too, and fewer factories?

And if the state created a *zollverein* around a nation's patrimony, should minorities be included or excluded? In this age of biological essences, spiritual attributes ran in the blood. Even Heine had not believed in his conversion to Christianity. The *Judenfrage*, the "Jewish question," emerged at the heart of the German question. Wagner's answer was not one of class but of race. The German revolution began with the "recognition that the only God dwells within us, and that we are one with Nature, undivided." When Man and Nature reunite, the bourgeois state will fall, and the "millions, the embodied Revolution, the God become Man," will flood the "valleys and plains, and proclaim to all the world the new gospel of Happiness."

From the philosophy of Arthur Schopenhauer, Wagner discovers that Europe has misunderstood its spiritual heredity. Schopenhauer was versed in the new Indology and saw the parallels between Platonic idealism and Hindu or Buddhist thought. The Greek philosopher's knowledge of nature was the Vedantic self-knowledge of *Tat tvam asi*, "That thou art." A shared ideal of renunciation, Schopenhauer believed, was the "true spirit and kernel of Christianity, as of Brahmanism and Buddhism." Thus when the Romantic recognizes himself in Nature, he also dissolves in *Brahma*, the transcendent unity of life. The hermit becomes a saint and unites with God. The bodhisattva, the "enlightened being," attains Buddhahood.

How, Schopenhauer asks, could this spiritual ideal have descended through the Jews, a "sneaking, dirty race afflicted with filthy diseases"? The Jews seem foreign, oriental, and parasitic. Instead of teaching acceptance of blind fate, Judaism is ignobly optimistic. Jewish ideals of free will, human uniqueness, and a moral universe, Schopenhauer concludes, are not the true Christian morality. The European conscience is a prisoner of a false genealogy. The true Christian spirit is closer to "atheistic Buddhism" than to "optimistic Judaism and its variety, Islam." Like the "idea of god become man," Jesus cannot have come from the Jews. "Christ's teaching, sprung from Indian wisdom, has covered the old and quite different trunk of Judaism." Jesus was an Aryan, not a Semite.

Like dogs and dreams, the Aryan Jesus resembles his owners. Always, the Aryan Jesus follows his masters. The lapsed Catholics of the French Enlightenment inferred his existence; the skeptical Anglicans of British India produced the evidence of his origins; the lapsed Protestants of German Romanticism named him as their racial god. To Voltaire, the ancient Indians had been naked vegetarians, inventing the first religion, the pure doctrine of reason, on the banks of the Ganges; Judaism and Christianity were, as Wagner would conclude about Jewish composers, amoral imitators. As Voltaire sketched this false genealogy, he introduced a forged Veda, the *Ezour Veidam*, as the first true book of religion.

In German Romanticism, the dream of reason took the path of unreason. Friedrich Schlegel called the Orient the font of mythology; the Occident, lacking its own myths, must draw from India's well. In 1808, the philosopher Johann Fichte used the new vocabulary of "Semites" and "Aryans" to disinherit the Jewish Jesus. In *Addresses to the German Nation*, Fichte identified the latest of the four Gospels, that of John, as the earliest. John had provided no Jewish genealogy for Jesus because, Fichte said, there was none. Fichte blamed Saint Paul for projecting his Jewish origins onto Jesus and suggested that the image of the Aryan Jesus would help Germans in purging Jewish traits from their unborn nation-state. It would be best, Fichte wrote, to decapitate the Jews, then place healthier heads and minds on their bodies.

Schopenhauer traced this false trail almost to the origin of the world. After the flood, God gave Noah and his descendants dominion over all life: "Every moving thing that liveth shall be meat for you."

Although God also required Noah to ritually abjure "the flesh with the life thereof, which is the blood thereof," Schopenhauer believed that eating any kind of meat denies the "eternal essence that exists in every living thing." That essence is not molecular but spiritual. Meat-eating deprives the soul of its patrimony, union with Nature through *Mitleid*, universal compassion. Schopenhauer decided that the "revoltingly crude" habit of meat-eating, the "barbarism of the West," had originated with the Jews. Like Marx's capitalist and Wagner's critic, Schopenhauer's carnivore follows a false god through a false consciousness created by Jews.

Schopenhauer was the first militant vegetarian. Like his ideological ancestor, the Protestant, the Western vegetarian lives in spiritual hypertension. When God is within, the standard of perfection is raised because it is internalized. To save his soul and purify his body, he must expel the contaminants by new rituals of purity.

"Out of all your gifts," God told the Israelites in the desert, "you shall present every offering due to the Lord, from all the best of them, the sacred part from them." The burnt offering, the *holocaustos*, is the Lord's portion, for to dismember, burn, discard, or expel an object is to annul its worldly value and obtain its supreme spiritual value. Like the *Liebestod* or the wine and the wafer, this rite gives a taste of comprehensive meaning, a glimpse of totality.

On February 20, 1866, Karl Marx took a sharp razor to his chest. He pressed the blade into the heart of the monster, a red carbuncle as big as an egg, oozing yellow yolk. As he cut into the infected follicles, the "bad blood" and pus "spurted, or rather, leapt, right up into the air."

Three more monsters swelled in his groin. The biggest was where the back of his thigh met the cleft of his right buttock. He palpated it with his fingers but dared not attack it blindly with the razor. He feared he would have to present himself to a doctor. "I cannot abide doctors meddling with my private parts or their vicinity."

Man invented the world, Marx knew, and he invented his hell too.

Every day for fifteen years, Marx had chained himself to desk O, seat 7 in the library of the British Museum. He pursued the origins of the bourgeois cosmos into the mines of economy, staggering out with a dust of fool's gold, plunging back into the blind tunnels, never quite finding the seam from which he could smelt the "iron laws of history." The labor was crushing and endless. His lungs rattled, his liver swelled, his stomach ached, and his head throbbed. He had chalk in his urine, bile in his vomit, and boils on his penis.

The carbuncles were worse. They hatched on his chest, neck, and back, and converged on his most secret parts. They were his "perfidious Christian illness," the stigmata that proved his faith in the unwashed. The one on his right buttock was the most painful yet. Like his economic data, it was beyond his reach and control. Unable to sit, walk, sleep, or work in comfort, he numbed himself with red wine and opium. He scratched his perineum until it was bleeding and raw. He began to sign his letters with pseudonyms. One night, to Jenny's alarm, he recited excerpts from *Capital* in a trance.

"With this delay you are simply destroying yourself," Engels warned. "No one can endure such a history of carbuncles in the long run." Sooner or later, they would poison Marx's blood. "And then where will your family be, and your book?" Engels advised Norwegian cod liver oil for the digestion and arsenic for the boils. Engels's doctor prescribed a liver tonic, then spa water and sea air at Margate.

"My illness always comes from my head," Marx admitted. Tracing every fold and line of the monster called Capital, he had fallen in love with his horror. Capital is a demoniac machine, grinding the workers like wood chips. The old dream of liberty is deferred, the aftermath of music and philosophy forgotten. The violent intermission between the death of the old and the birth of the new lasts forever: an eternal present of purges, relocations, indoctrinations, and industrial armies. The revolution is permanent; the revolution is deferred. Marx, the German socialist Eduard Bernstein complained, described capitalism in "a metaphysical image of which we have no example in reality."

"If progress is the aim, then for whom are we working?" asked Alexander Herzen, the disillusioned Russian anarchist. Progress, Herzen realized, was a modern Moloch, a god propitiated by the sacrifice of children to an ever-retreating future. "Progress is infinite. This alone should serve as a warning to people."

"Man in his arrogance thinks himself a great work worthy of the inter- position of the deity," Darwin had written in 1838. "More humble, & I believe true, to consider him created from animals."

More than two decades later, Darwin had still to clarify the "grand and awful question" of human origins. He feared that the answer would "horrify the world." After *Origin of Species*, he let Huxley and Alfred Russel Wallace fight the cannibals on his behalf, and pushed Charles Lyell to "go the whole orang" on the "relations of men & other animals." It was someone else's turn to take the blame. "How I should be abused if I were to publish such an essay!"

Lyell and Wallace disappointed him. In *Origin of Species*, Darwin included an instigating "Creator" who, like God in Genesis, "originally breathed" life into his handiwork. This concession was a kind of original sin, a slip from pure materialism to natural theology. Although Darwin saw evolution as self-sustaining, he had evoked the power that created life by its Christian name. If this Creator had breathed once, he could do it again. Both Wallace and Lyell believed that he had. In *The Antiquity of Man* (1863), Lyell invited the *deus* to tinker with his *machina* in midjourney. God had tweaked the evolutionary process by separating the "moral and intellectual supremacy" from those of the lower animals. Human origins, Lyell wrote, lay in a "distinct Kingdom of Nature."

Wallace believed that the current human races had a single, "homogenous" origin, but that natural selection had created fixed "higher" and "lower" races, differing in physical appearance, moral attributes, and mental capacity. Their homogenous ancestor had been more ape than human. His crucial asset, a brain large enough for "moral faculties," had developed after the racial split. Wallace located the split as far back as possible, just after the extinction of the dinosaurs. In Wallace's world, it was possible to be human but also to lack the most important human attribute, conscience. Darwinism was turning against Darwin.

Wallace, unlike Darwin and Lyell, was a self-educated socialist. His humble class origins and a stint among the cannibals of Borneo had confirmed his faith in noble savagery. Wallace had developed the idea of applying Malthusian competition to Lamarckian transmutation during a bout of fever in the Malay Archipelago, and his theories retained a dreamlike aspect. Where Darwin saw selection as refinement for its own sake, Wallace saw a higher purpose. The "lower races" would die out like primordial ape-men. The vital "Power" would unite the "higher races" into a new and superior race.

In 1866, Wallace announced a unified theory of race, socialism, and spirituality in George Holyoake's *English Leader*. The "Power" behind evolution was also the "spirit" in the séance room. This life force was an "essential part of all sensitive beings," and their biological development reflected their spiritual destiny. When members of the higher races dimmed the lights and held hands, the selective principle revealed itself in a "visible (and in some instances, tangible) body." Spirit photographers captured this "ectoplasm" floating above the table. Wallace claimed that the ectoplasm proved not just the "reality of another world" but also the destiny of this world in an "ever-progressive future state." Countering Herbert Spencer's free-market "survival of the fittest," Wallace called this the "progression of the fittest." Skeptics noted that the ectoplasm resembled a handkerchief hung from a stick.

"It is remarkable," Marx complained after reading Origin of Species, "how Darwin recognises among beasts and plants his English society, with its division of labour, competition, opening up of new markets, 'inventions' and the Malthusian 'struggle for existence' . . . in Darwin, the animal kingdom appears as bourgeois."

Darwin trusted that natural selection would reward individual "Divergence of Character" like the market rewarding hard work. But this was the 1860s. In the decade of the new chronology, once-eccentric prophecies were becoming governing principles: the organization of society by the state, the maximization of efficiency by machines, the birth of a global system, the advent of biological spirituality. In 1848, Marx had fantasized an international alliance of revolutionary socialists. In 1864, the First International convened in London, with Marx on the committee. In 1848, only the Perfectionists of Oneida dreamed of breeding a better human. In 1863, this ideal appeared in Darwin's own family. His cousin Francis Galton read Darwin's chapters on artificial selection and suggested applying it to human society. In 1848, only obscure German philosophers thought that Jesus had been an Aryan, born in a Semitic manger. In 1863, this idea shaped a bestseller, Ernest Renan's *Vie de Jesus*.

Across the world, the prophecies of Hegel and Adam Smith appeared to be coming true as ancient hierarchies crumbled before the allied powers of the state and the market. In China, British and French troops marched on Peking and sacked the Old Summer Palace. The Qing emperor, losing his grip on the Mandate of Heaven, ceded to his earthly conquerors ten "treaty ports," the gates to China's imports and exports. In Japan, the emperor accepted foreign imports and influence to avoid being shelled by American gunboats. In India the British, having defeated a revolt in 1857, imported a Western bureaucracy, the Indian Civil Service, to accompany the expansion of India's infrastructure. In autocratic Russia, Alexander II broke the feudal nobility by decree, emancipating more than twenty million serfs into a market economy. In the southern states of democratic America, a savage civil war achieved similar ends. And in Germany, Otto von Bismarck created a Prussian-led *Kleindeutschland*.

"The great questions of the time," said Bismarck, "will not be resolved by speeches and majority decisions—that was the great mistake of 1848 and 1849—but by blood and iron."

"Our success sure," Emerson had written as Sherman marched to the sea, "its roots in poverty, Calvinism, schools, farms, thrift, snow & east wind." He omitted another environmental pressure. The agent of liberation was not prayer or virtue, but the Juggernaut and the mechanics of blood and iron: industrial capacity, marshaled by the centralizing power of the state, and standardized by the sciences of the new chronology. Was the individual, the little giant who stood atop Emerson's imperial "I," just an eighteenth-century fossil?

Power seems to be everywhere in the life of the state, Tolstoy wrote in *War and Peace* (1869), but it remains "a word the meaning of which we do not understand." For all his misgivings, Emerson could not resist the temptation to identify power with his desires and to speak in its name. The Civil War, he decided, had confirmed the predictions of Hegel and Napoléon. A unified America could be a world power, a "fist that will knock down an empire." By their sacrifice, the war dead had initiated a "new era" of America's revolution in ethics. Like Bonaparte, the Americans must export their revolution, a moral Monroe Doctrine to cover the planet.

"And they are to establish the pure religion, Asceticism, self-devotion, Bounty. They will lead their language round the globe, & they will lead out religion and freedom with them."

Emerson checked himself. He had forgotten something. He inserted "Justice" before "Asceticism."

Wagner felt that the Schopenhauer mind-cure had purged him of "Hebrew superstition." At last he understood the "full measure of freedom that is possible to mankind." Yet lasting peace eluded him. To float in the warm, primordial lake of *Mitleid*, a man must renounce the vanity of earthly happiness, must kill his lust for money, flesh, and eminence. But Wagner was a man of appetites. At dinner he lectured his guests on Schopenhauer, then ate chops—on doctor's orders. Writing *Tannhäuser*, he had felt himself consumed by sensual excitement. He called it an erotic cure that would assure its punishment.

"I must have beauty, splendor, light! The world ought to give me what I need! I cannot live the wretched life of a town organist, like your Meister Bach! Is it such a shocking demand, if I believe that I am due the little bit of luxury I enjoy? I, who have so much enjoyment to give to the world, and to thousands of people!"

He was secretly in love with Hans von Bülow's wife, Cosima. And though Wagner hoped that the revolution would begin with the burning down of Paris, he felt compelled to conquer it by seduction. To raise the funds that would allow him to stage *Tannhäuser*, Wagner organized a series of concerts in the capital of *civilisation* and artifice. Baudelaire attended one and called it the "most joyous musical experience" of his life. But the revolution did not pay.

The concerts left Wagner in debt. Though he had sold *Das Rheingold* to his patron, the silk merchant Otto Wesendonck, he now sold it again to a German publisher and convinced Wesendonck to transfer his investment to the *Götterdämmerung*, the "Twilight of the Gods," which was not yet written; as Schopenhauer said, life repeats the same thing under a different name and under a different cloak. Meanwhile, Wagner cultivated new friends among the forces of reaction. Princess Pauline von Metternich was the wife of the Austrian ambassador and the granddaughter of the diplomat against whom Wagner's generation had rebelled. She was also an ardent Wagnerian. Through her influence, Louis-Napoléon invited Wagner to stage *Tannhäuser* at the Paris Opéra.

The Tristan chord is also known as a "French sixth." At the Opéra, Wagner shed his artistic principles along with his political ones. The Opéra wanted a French text, so he hired a translator to prepare one. When the Opéra rejected it because it was in blank verse, he paid someone to make it rhyme. The Opéra expected a ballet, so he added one. The first two nights went well, but the third was a disaster. During the second act, the aristocratic philistines of the Jockey Club turned up late. They enjoyed a good dinner and were looking forward to the ballet dancers. But Wagner placed the ballet in the first act. He was also a German interloper who pandered to Louis-Napoléon's pro-Austrian policies. The aristocrats heckled until the performance collapsed. Ambushed by the union of art and politics, Wagner left Paris like Tannhäuser from the Wartburg. *Exeunt, pursued by creditors.*

Ludwig II of Bavaria grew up in the Wagnerian dream of Schloss Hohenschwangau, High Swan Castle, a Gothic fantasy in the mountains, its decor themed after the legend of Lohengrin. At fifteen, Ludwig saw Wagner's *Lohengrin* in Munich and burst into tears. The next year, he dissolved at *Tannhäuser.* Soon, he was quoting Wagner's essays in his conversation and letters. He also obtained a manuscript of the poem for the *Ring* cycle. The poem ends with the impresario's eternal question: When would Wagner's prince come and bring the German myth to life?

Handsome, passionate, and pious Ludwig became king of Bavaria at the age of eighteen. Determined to build a new opera theater in Munich, he sent a secretary to find Wagner. The wanderer was staying in Stuttgart. When a servant presented the secretary's visiting card, Wagner suspected him for a debt collector and refused to receive him. The next morning, the secretary cornered Wagner and gave him a ring, not a writ, along with Ludwig's promise of unlimited funds in Munich. Wagner paid his hotel bill with a snuff box, borrowed money for a first-class ticket to Munich, and plighted himself to the wondrous king who would free him from money.

"My trust in our strength is boundless," Ludwig replied. "We have finally found each other."

In the 1860s, a middling Bavarian family could get by on 320 florins a year. In Wagner's first year in Munich, he received 83,000 florins from the Bavarian treasury and Ludwig's private purse, and another 75,000 florins for furniture and domestic expenses. Ludwig also cleared Wagner's debts, gave him a house in Munich, and bought the performance rights to his unwritten operas. He accepted Wagner's choice of architect for the Munich opera house, Gottfried Semper, a friend whose early works, circa 1849, had included street barricades.

Wagner planned the rest of his life. First, *Tristan* and *Die Meistersinger*, then revised versions of *Tannhäuser* and *Lohengrin*. In 1867 or 1868, a "grand performance" of the *Ring*. Then *The Victors*, an adaptation of a Buddhist legend of a love affair between a servant girl and a monk. Finally, *Parsifal*. By 1873, Wagner's work would be done. Other artists could retire. He would undergo the "final beautiful death and redemption of the votary."

Ludwig's Bavaria was not part of Prussia. Wagner hoped that Bavaria could be the alternative German state, driven by art and spirituality. He mocked Wilhelm I of Prussia as weak and derided his capital, Berlin, as corrupted by French and Jewish influences. Wilhelm's chief minister Bismarck was a minor aristocrat, floated to power on loans from a Jewish banker, Gerson Bleichroeder. If Ludwig led the people in politics, and Wagner led them in spirit, then the trinity of Wilhelm I, Bismarck, and Prussia could be replaced by that of Ludwig II, Wagner, and Bavaria, and a compromised *Kleindeutschland* with a powerful and pure *Grossdeutschland*. Wagner gave Ludwig an essay, "On State and Religion," in defense of the monarchic principle. The boy king must put away his purple Lohengrin costume, Wagner advised, and make Bavaria a shining example to all Germans. Ludwig, invited to join his hero in an artistic-political double act, prepared for his debut. "Let us present this wonderful work to the German nation," he replied, "and show both them and the other nations what 'German art' is capable of!"

Before Wagner's arrival in Munich, Ludwig had shown little interest in politics. His ministers feared that he would end up like his brother Otto, a fully fledged lunatic. While the ministers had steered Bavaria between Austria and Prussia, Ludwig had played at knights and swans with his best friend, Prince Paul von Thurn und Taxis, and a selection of handsome valets and cavalrymen. When Wagner incited Ludwig to pursue his reckless enchantments into politics, the Munich press denounced Wagner's political and financial appetites. In December 1865, he retreated to Switzerland.

Cosima von Bülow joined him there. She arrived with Isolde and

Eva, Wagner's illegitimate daughters, named for Tristan's lover and the heroine of *The Mastersingers.* Hans von Bülow continued working with Wagner. An emissary from Bismarck arrived. If Prussia and Austria went to war, could Wagner persuade Ludwig to support Prussia? Wagner declined, claiming that Ludwig's ministers prevented their direct communication. Secretly, Wagner expected Austria to win. When Austria defeated the Prussian-led *Kleindeutschland,* Ludwig's Bavaria could become the *Schutzgeiste Deutschlands,* the "Guardian Spirit of Germany."

Instead, Prussia won the war of 1866. When Bismarck used that victory to bind Bavaria to Prussia, Wagner was obliged to revise his ideals. His destiny was to unite the Germans by art. Politics was only the means to that end, and Prussia was now the only means to hand. And did not Bismarck also see France as Germany's greatest obstacle? Wagner's next philosophical emission, "German Art and German Politics," advised Ludwig to ally Bavaria with Prussia against a common enemy, French civilization.

"Honour your German masters!" he wrote in *Die Meistersinger.* "Though the Holy Roman Empire should depart, / There still remains with us Holy German Art." Wagner continued to cultivate Ludwig, but he also tried to send Bismarck a copy of "German Art and German Politics."

"I do so hate controversy."

Disabled for most of 1865 by his digestion, in 1866 Darwin accepted fate and included man among the animals that had undergone domestication. Once again he massed reports from correspondents across the globe and strained to align his work with that of his supporters. As in *Origin of Species,* he framed simple and alarming ideas in a mesh of observations and evidence. There was one human species. It shared "common descent" with all other life-forms. It had developed its traits and racial variety by sexual selection: "Among savages the most powerful men will have the pick of the women & they will generally leave the most descendants."

Natural selection worked like Zeus upon Europa, by the imposition of power upon beauty. Hence the distinct races reflected the strength and taste of their most powerful males. This, Darwin had told an incredulous Wallace, was why British aristocrats were "handsomer" than the lower orders: the nobility had once had the "pick of the women." Unfortunately, new money was impeding selection and reversing noble evolution. As Darwin's cousin Francis Galton claimed in *Hereditary Genius* (1869), when "noble families" cleared their debts by marrying with the rising middle class, they polluted their blood. The parvenus had no breeding and lacked "superiority of any kind." Meanwhile in the slums, the "careless, squalid, unaspiring" Irish immigrants bred "like rabbits."

Darwin was now answerable to Darwinism. He had married Malthus to evolution. Less delicate minds were closing the circle and returning his theory of origins to society. His most ardent defenders agreed that Britain needed a dose of Malthusian struggle. Herbert Spencer had always wanted to sift the wheat from the chaff. Spencer advised "pulling off the coloured glasses of prejudice." Instead of letting the do-gooders breed a "sad population of imbeciles," the "laws of nature" should be allowed to "purify" society of its "faulty" members.

Darwin's friend W. R. Greg, the source of his information on Irish immigrants, suspected racial degeneration in the big cities. Natural selection favored the "sounder and stronger specimens," but modern Europe kept alive those who, "looking at the physical perfection of the race alone, had better have been left to die." Humanitarian ethics were against Nature: "Thousands with tainted constitutions, with frames weakened by malady or waste, with brains bearing subtle and hereditary mischief in their recesses, are suffered to transmit their terrible inheritance of evil to other generations, and to spread it through a whole community."

"We are living in a sort of intellectual anarchy, for the want of master minds," Cousin Galton lamented. Charity allowed the unfit to dodge the scythe of selection, and money allowed the sickly to buy healthy brides. To preserve the national stock, a planned program of selection must weed out "the minority of weakly and incapable men" before they could reproduce. Galton called this "eugenics."

The Origin of the World *is a portrait from 1866 by Gustave Courbet.* A nameless, headless white woman lies on an unmade bed. Her right breast and midriff are exposed. Her legs are open, exposing her genitals to the viewer. She is a portrait of her species and her race, not an individual. While Darwin identified beauty with natural selection and Wagner premiered *Tristan and Isolde*, Courbet placed sex, beauty, and violence at the origin of existence and the core of inner life. The body is a biological machine, driven by determinist forces of production. Beauty is form, and form is function.

Courbet was a Comtean in philosophy, an anarchist in politics, and a *réaliste*—a stripper of artifice—in paint. He painted *The Origin of the World* for Khalil Bey, an Ottoman diplomat. Khalil, *L'Artiste* reported, kept a magnificent gallery in his Paris apartment, despite the "law of the Prophet, which forbids the representation of figures." The gallery included the massed nudes of Ingres's *Turkish Bath* and also Courbet's *Sleep*, in which two young women, swooning under the hypocrisy of the Second Empire, are entangled less chastely than the "sisters" who lie "lovingly side by side" in Whitman's "Sleepers."

The Origin of the World was not on display. As the photographer Maxime du Camp noted, Khalil hid it twice over. Du Camp, who had toured Egypt with Flaubert, wrote that the "Moslem who paid for his whims in gold" kept the painting in his private dressing room under a green veil. When Khalil lifted it, du Camp thought the torso seemed extraordinarily "convulsed": a *Liebestod* in paint. Du Camp read the image of the body correctly. Courbet had painted his model, Joanna Hiffernan, intact, but had severed the canvas at the neck. In his depiction of her head, Hiffernan's eyes are wide and unseeing, in the shock of death or orgasm.

"For the world is my representation," Schopenhauer had written. Beauty was a creation of the will, the force that drove reproduction in art as in life. Like a Thoreau sunrise, a naturalistic image is also an ideal one. At Courbet's 1855 exhibition, Baudelaire had seen that while a *réaliste* claimed to "represent things just as they are," he also depicted them as he desired them to be. The *réaliste*, Baudelaire thought, was one of Comte's *positivistes* in disguise, a spiritual optimist whose images tended toward perfection. Baudelaire's contemporary, the philosopher Félix Ravaisson-Mollien agreed. Realist art, Ravaisson-Mollien wrote, proved that "the spirit has an existence of its own" and had survived the transition into modern life. It would be more accurate to call it *positivisme spiritualiste*, spiritual positivism. "In the beauty of poems," Whitman said, "are the tuft and final applause of science."

Scientific knowledge now touched the origins of human life, and technology now covered the world. In 1839, "network," denoting the knots of a fishing net, had gained a new meaning: the fixed web of connections that carries people, goods, and information, and contains them all. By the late 1860s, the knots and fibers of the modern network were tightened across the globe. Technical civilization does not build its shrines as the old religions did, stacking a Mughal mosque over the Hindu temple at Ayodhya, or the Dome of the Rock over a Christian church, itself built on the ruins of the Jewish temples and the rock of the *omphalos*. Technical civilization incorporates with the fluid, subversive quality that Marx could not help but admire in capitalism. The relics of the old are enveloped, like the medieval kernel in the heart of a modern metropolis; or bypassed, like the rural wastes seen from a moving train. At Greenwich, the Royal Observatory sits in a public park that was once a royal hunting ground.

Whitman called this inspiring, world-conquering materialism a "New Theology." Surplus production, cheap shipping, and enforceable contracts created the first global commodity market, in wheat. In May 1869, the Union Pacific and Central Pacific railroads met under a golden spike at Promontory Summit, Utah. As Whitman wrote in "Passage to India," the linking of San Francisco to the eastern rail network at Council Bluffs, Iowa, connected East and West, the Atlantic Seaboard to the Pacific. A new westward vista opened, of the United States as a Pacific power: "Joyous we too launch out on trackless seas." In November 1869, the Suez Canal opened, linking the Mediterranean to the Red Sea: another passage to India, another contraction of distance, another Positivist vision realized. "All these separations and gaps shall be taken up and hook'd and link'd together."

"The earth to be spann'd, connected by network," Whitman sang. "The races, neighbors, to marry and be given in marriage, / The oceans to be cross'd, the distant brought near, / The lands to be welded together." The world of "freetrade" and "intertravel by land and sea" unites all humanity: "nothing too close, nothing too far off . . . the stars not too far off."

*While Whitman imagined riding to Promontory Summit and wander*ing in the strange sands of Egypt, in Berlin the philosopher Eduard von Hartmann proposed a similar welding together of consciousness. Like Alfred Russel Wallace, Hartmann sought to reconcile religion and philosophy with the new biology. His *Philosophy of the Unconscious* (1869) became the nineteenth century's most widely read work of philosophy, and a foundation of psychoanalysis.

Hartmann saved the soul for science by completing the shift from the poetic "unconscious" of Schelling and the early German Romantics to a biological one, the racial soul. "The key to an understanding of the conscious life of the soul lies in the sphere of the unconscious," the polymath doctor-artist Carl Gustav Carus had written in *Psyche* (1846). "The first task of a science of the soul is to state how the spirit of Man is able to descend to these depths."

Carus, a student of Schelling, proposed a three-layered concept of mental life. The deepest waters are the "absolute unconscious," where unknowable currents sweep individuality into the cosmos. But the upper two layers can be described. The middle layer is that of physiology. There, the vital organs act on the mind, and the mind acts on the organs; this, said Carus, is why a face and body reflect their owner's personality. The uppermost layer is a tidal flow of memory and repression, with an undertow that drags conscious materials back down into unconsciousness. Carus described his theory in an image from a new technology. Somehow, "something in our soul unconsciously produces a copy of the *Urbild*" in our minds: the primordial image, the first picture.

Hartmann used Darwinian evolution as the diving bell that lowered science into the "Absolute unconscious." Waiting for him on the ground of all life, he found Schopenhauer's pessimistic Will and Hegel's optimistic Spirit. The Will created the world and its suffering; the Spirit, which Hartmann called "the Idea," creates consciousness and order. The Absolute, being infinite, can accommodate both, and directs biological and spiritual evolution to the same purpose. Like the Aryan Jesus, Man has a clear, pure line of origin.

Clarifying the Absolute transforms the upper layers of Hartmann's mind. The "physiological unconscious" is now the layer of species consciousness: an area of experiment where life-forms organize and develop. For the individual soul, these are confusing waters. In its crosscurrents, the irrational, species-driven impulses meet rational, individual controls. Life is not much easier on the upper layer, the "relative" or "psychological unconscious" where spiritual-biological impulses collide with social pressures. Man is a donkey, whipped on by the stick of Will, reaching for the inedible carrot of Idea. The individual exists to propagate the species. His ideals of glory and perfection are illusions, necessary for his arousal. His soul is the "sum of the activities of the Unconscious directed at any moment on its organism."

Since the beginning of the Scientific Revolution, Western mystics had sought to master different intellectual systems under a single spiritual rubric. Hartmann marks a double watershed: the shift from religious and philosophical concepts of the mind to medical and biological ones; and the identification of that biology with racial types. The metaphysics of the modern soul were now welded to the biological "form of Science."

"The whole theory of the special and supernatural and all that was twined with it or educed out of it departs as a dream," Whitman observed. "What has ever happened . . . what happens and whatever may or shall happen, the vital laws enclose all . . . they are sufficient for any case and for all cases."

Darwin had snagged his sleeve on Juggernaut's chariot. He had to keep up or go under. Between 1859 and 1872, *Origin of Species* went through six editions. In the fifth edition of 1869, Darwin surrendered his idea, natural selection, to Herbert Spencer's definition.

"This preservation of favourable variations and the rejection of injurious variations, I call Natural Selection," Darwin had written in 1859.

In 1869, this sentence read, "This preservation of favourable variations and the destruction of injurious variations, I call Natural Selection, or the Survival of the Fittest."

In 1865, after a Jewish reader complained to Dickens about Fagin, the malign Jew in *Oliver Twist,* Dickens apologized by creating Mr. Riah, the saintly moneylender of *Our Mutual Friend.* When an Irish reader asked Darwin to retract his insult to the Irish, he refused. A scientist did not have the luxury of a novelist. Darwin had no scientific reason to doubt that an English lord was biologically superior to an Irish navvy. He was a humanitarian, so he also believed that superiority was moral as well as physical. It was the strong man's burden to carry the weak without complaining. Culling the "helpless" would weaken the "noblest part of our nature," the altruism unique to "civilized men." Still, the social dangers could not be denied. Perhaps the "weaker and inferior" might be induced to marry less often?

Darwin did not suggest how they might be persuaded. This delicacy applied only to his own race. In 1859, *Origin of Species* suggested that the global expansion of the "higher races" would accelerate the "extinction of less-improved forms." Now, in *The Descent of Man, and Selection in Relation to Sex,* he explained why this was happening.

When all life was ranked on "an ascending organic scale," the "culti-vated men" came out on top of the market in biology. Among his own species, Darwin found a perfect gradation of mental ability, from the mind of an "utter idiot, lower than that of an animal" to the mind of a Newton. The higher abilities were unique to the upper echelons of Newton's race. The lower classes and all non-Europeans fell into the categories of idiocy.

Darwin insisted on an "immense" difference between the minds of "the lowest man" and "the highest animal," but he described the inner life of "savages" as often identical to that of animals. As the plumes of male birds and the feathers in European women's hats showed, beauty was essential for selection. All humans have a "sense of the beautiful," even the "lowest savages," but so do the animals. Sometimes, the ani-mals have more "sense." The "hideous ornaments" and "equally hideous music" of the savages suggest that their aesthetic faculty is less devel-oped than that of the birds. Nor are the birdbrained natives capable of "admiring such scenes as the heavens at night, a beautiful landscape, or refined music." Only "cultivated men" can develop a taste for the beautiful. Only in the cultivated mind do sensations become "inti-mately associated with complex ideas and trains of thought." These "high tastes" are acquired slowly through culture. They cannot be appreciated by "barbarians" or "uneducated persons," whether pyg-mies in the forests or Irish in the cities.

Darwin grants all humans the potential for a "moral sense" and "spiritual powers." But in practice, these too are a hierarchy topped by the "higher races." If by "religion" we mean a "belief in unseen or spiritual agencies," then religion, Darwin allows, is universal among the "less civilized races." But an "ennobling belief in the existence of an Omnipotent God" requires a "moderately high level" of intellec-tual and moral development. The descent of man becomes the history of the ascent of Christian religion, from animism to fetishism, poly-theism, and "ultimately" monotheism. A savage's experience of "spir-itual agencies" must not be confused with the evolved and "highly complex" feeling of "religious devotion." This requires "love, complete submission to an exalted and mysterious superior, a strong sense of dependence, fear, reverence, gratitude, hope for the future, and perhaps other elements" that the savage mind struggles to imagine and contain. The savage races have "no words in their languages" to express the idea of "one or more gods." Even those savages who do find the words cannot distinguish between "subjective and objective impressions."

Darwin believes that Man's "spiritual powers" are beyond the naturalist's method, but he claims to demonstrate that spirituality develops from mental power. Dogs, Darwin believes, show "distant" signs of the sentiments that underlie primitive "religious devotion." The savages of Tierra del Fuego, he recalls, seemed to be in a similar "intermediate condition": they understood the "simplest form of justice" and feared the retribution of their master spirits. But he never could discover if they "believed in what we should call a God" or practiced any religious rites. The savage mind, whether canine or human, believes that "natural objects and agencies are animated by spiritual or living essences." Darwin had observed this process on his lawn at Down House. When a slight breeze ruffled an open parasol, Polly, his white terrier, "growled fiercely and barked." Darwin mentions that Wilhelm Braubach, one of his German admirers, believes that "a dog looks upon his master as a god."

If Braubach is right, Polly the terrier may have an evolutionary advantage over the Fuegians in matters of the spirit. Loyally, she and her moral sense trot along as Darwin perambulates down his "thinking path." He has taught her to "catch biscuits off her nose" too.

"The master," Whitman had said, "knows he is unspeakably great."

Readers of The Descent of Man *would be told that they had evolved* by impressive but blind chance. They had no "God-implanted conscience," and no innate or instinctive faith in God. There was no "special purpose" in their family trees, no greater meaning to "the union of each pair in marriage" and "the dissemination of each seed." Darwin allowed that the mind refuses to accept such ideas and "revolts at such a conclusion."

Yet if God was not a Protestant Englishman, the Protestant Englishman remained closest to God. Darwin reassured the reader that his discoveries did not threaten the "immortality of the soul." Clearly, the "barbarous" races lacked this belief, but their opinion was, as on all matters, of little or no significance. We cannot know "at what precise period in the development of the individual, from the first race of a minute germinal vesicle, man becomes an immortal being." Nor can we know when in the "ascending organic scale" of life the soul appears.

Reaching the borders of his jurisdiction as a scientist and a gentleman, Darwin stopped at the crucial question of whether dogs had a soul, and safely short of a grander matter: "The question is of course wholly distinct from that higher one, whether there exists a Creator and Ruler of the universe; and this has been answered in the affirmative by some of the highest intellects that have ever existed."

Darwin remained a creature of the English liberal consensus. The secret of his popularity, George Bernard Shaw observed, was that he never puzzled anybody. He never went deeper beneath his facts, like a German Idealist, or higher above them, like a French *spiritualiste*. The obfuscations and compromises of *The Descent of Man* reflect the domestic consensus of the 1860s. In *Greater Britain* (1869), the Liberal politician Charles Dilke predicts the rise of a global Anglo-American civilization, Anglo-Saxon by blood, free-trading by culture. In *The Descent of Man*, conquest is the biological right of "civilized men." The distribution of mental and spiritual qualities reflects the "organic scale" of development. Darwin's "lower races" have "superstition," but his "higher races" have a unique capacity for "spiritual" ideas. Their religious ethics are "knowledge," comparable to empirical science. Like Whitman's new American, they are the "spectacle of matter aware," with a soul rooted in this biological consciousness.

Darwin's future blurs with the Manifest Destiny of the spiritual whites. He quotes Foster Barham Zincke, who was not a scientist but a cleric and travel writer: The future of *Homo sapiens* lies in "the great stream of Anglo-Saxon emigration to the west." The human spirit emerges from the layer of species consciousness that Hartmann called the "physiological unconscious." Just as Whitman's "New Theology" puts a poetic "tuft" on Manifest Destiny and technical civilization, so Darwin's *Descent of Man* offers scientific proofs for the triumph of Dilke's race.

Darwin does not dilate further on the mind's revolt against the biology of blind chance. Nor does he speculate on a recent evolution among some of the "highest intellects" of his race: the fact that the universal truths of science are fostering a resurgence of ancient, even "savage" belief at the heart of technical civilization. Many of the "most sophisticated intellects," he notes, feel that "natural objects and agencies are animated by spiritual or living essences." Not just Emerson or Hartmann: even Newton, Darwin's model mind, had felt that way. Plenty of less sophisticated ones—Wagner, Whitman, the armies of table-tappers—agree with them. They see spiritual sense hovering over the disorder of blind chance, a soul working in the species consciousness. As technical civilization becomes the first truly global civilization, this revolt will accompany it as an intimation, a shadow of the imagination. Like Polly the terrier, the religious revolution will be a loyal creature of habit.

In June 1870, as Wagner rehearsed Die Walküre, *the second part of* the *Ring* cycle, for its debut in Munich, Bismarck prepared to complete the unification of Germany by diplomacy and war. As Wotan says in *Die Walküre*, "Where bold spirits are moving, I stir them ever to strife."

The Franco-Prussian War was the first conflict in which both sides cited Darwin to justify their aggression. It was also the first major conflict to have been sparked by manipulation of the press. In 1868, the Spanish government had offered Spain's vacant throne to Prince Leopold of Prussia. Bismarck encouraged Leopold to accept. As Bismarck expected, Louis-Napoléon and his ministers demanded that Leopold forgo his promotion, and avowed their willingness to fight. In early July 1870, Leopold complied, but the French wanted further guarantees.

Meanwhile, Wilhelm I was taking a water cure at the spa resort of Bad Ems. One morning, Count Vincent Benedetti, the French ambassador to Prussia, accosted the kaiser as he was taking his morning constitutional. Benedetti told Wilhelm that the French foreign ministry wanted Wilhelm to promise never to place any of his relatives on the Spanish throne. The kaiser demurred politely, then sent a report to Bismarck by telegram. Before Bismarck forwarded the "Ems telegram" to his ministers, he rewrote it, emphasizing the ambassador's aggression and deleting Wilhelm's conciliatory response. This aroused patriots on both sides. Bavaria and the south German states rallied to Prussia. Crowds massed in Paris, and Louis-Napoléon mobilized his army. Six days after the exchange at Bad Ems, France declared war.

On that day, Wagner was at his villa by Lake Lucerne. He and Cosima were hosting a party of French Wagnerites, including Théophile Gautier and Camille Saint-Saëns, who had just attended the Munich premiere of *Die Walküre*. Wagner made no attempt to hide his joy about the outbreak of war. Although he was fifty-seven, with poor eyesight and recurrent headaches, he spoke of enlisting. As ever, Germany's glory was Wagner's glory. Émile Ollivier, the French prime minister, was married to Cosima von Bülow's sister Blandine. The day before, a Berlin court had granted Cosima her divorce. Hans von Bülow had long known he was in a peculiar situation, but he admired Wagner almost as much as Cosima did. Only after she had borne Wagner a third child, a boy named Siegfried, did Hans concede defeat. He had to accept that Cosima preferred to consecrate her mind and body to a higher being.

The war developed in pleasant counterpoint to Wagner's love life and Darwin's career. In mid-August, Darwin's manuscript went to the printers. He thought the war was a "misfortune for science," and likely to kill his French and German translators too, but he rejoiced at Prussia's "wonderful success." A week later, Wagner and Cosima married in an ostentatiously simple ceremony. On September 1, the Prussians defeated the French at Sedan, Louis-Napoléon surrendered, and the Second Empire collapsed. Wagner heard the news at little Siegfried's christening.

In Paris, republicans led by Léon Gambetta declared that France would fight on as the Third Republic. When the Prussians surrounded Paris, Gambetta escaped by air balloon. Meanwhile, Bismarck eased Louis-Napoléon and Empress Eugénie onto a train and into exile. The journalist Edward Diccy had last seen Eugénie at the opening festivities for the Suez Canal, where she had waltzed with the khedive of Egypt on a dance floor in the desert. Now he saw her stranded amid a "dense crowd of holiday folk" at Charing Cross station, searching for a connection to carry her to suburban Chislehurst.

On Christmas Day, while Wagner played his gift to Cosima, the "Siegfried Idyll," on the piano, Darwin toiled over the "accursed" proofs of his book. In Paris, his French and Russian translators Victor Moulinié and Vladimir Kovalevsky were working through the siege. His German translator Victor Carus, writing from Leipzig, regretted that the "Romanic and Teutonic races" could not settle their struggle "in a form more appropriate to their cultures and civilization." Three weeks later, as Darwin finished editing, a unified German state was born in the Hall of Mirrors at Versailles. Prussia, Bavaria, and twenty-five other territories were now the German empire. Wilhelm I was an emperor, and Bismarck the master of Europe. The "German revolution," Benjamin Disraeli observed, was "a greater political event than the French revolution of the last century."

In the first week of February 1871, Wagner completed *Siegfried*, the third episode of the *Ring* cycle. A week later, the British edition of *The Descent of Man* appeared. The book, to Darwin's delight, was soon selling in large quantities.

"Wonderful progress is being made to establish the new Reich!" Cosima Wagner wrote in her diary. In his dreams, Wagner strategized with Bismarck and Field Marshal von Moltke. He wrote a poem, "On the German Army at Paris," dedicated it to Bismarck, and sent it to him. Bismarck replied politely but did not invite Wagner to consult in his warrior's tent. Undeterred, Wagner began composing the *Kaisermarch*, an anthem for the new empire. "My aim is to call into existence a national German undertaking, the direction of which may be placed entirely in my hands alone."

The war over, there began what Maxime du Camp called the "convulsions of Paris."

Three days after Wagner finished the *Kaisermarch*, the people of Paris rebelled. To defend the city, thousands of them had enlisted in the National Guard. The new republican government of Adolphe Thiers had consented to a Prussian demand for a victory parade through Paris, but the government was based outside the city. The officers of the National Guard, rebelling against a double humiliation, now formed the Central Committee. When the government sent troops to disarm Paris by withdrawing its cannon, the guards and the citizenry resisted, then executed two officers. The troops joined the Parisians, and the rebellion spread to other army units in the city. By the end of the day, Paris was in the hands of its citizens. The Central Committee organized elections. On March 28, it declared the "festive wedding day of the Idea and the Revolution."

The Paris Commune began. The repressed dreams of 1789 and 1848 returned. The revolutionary calendar was revived. Guards and workers fortified the city, erecting barricades across the boulevards. The committee canceled debts and declared the divorce of church and state. Each *quartier* organized its affairs democratically, through endless debates and votes. There was a multiplication of militias and canteens, newspapers and free schools, feminist groups and workers' circles. Gustave Courbet supervised the museums and Camille Pissarro drew propaganda for the papers. For a week, Paris lived in a dream world. For its members, and the socialists who would claim its memory, the Commune proved that true democracy sprang from Man's better nature. For its enemies, it was the triumph of anarchy. Either way, it was also a civil war.

Thiers, aided by the Prussians, had surrounded Paris with French troops, to stop the revolt from spreading. In the first week of April, the army edged into the outlying suburbs, skirmishing with Communard militias and executing prisoners and suspected Communards in the streets. The militias had no central command. Each *arrondissement* fought in its own way and was defeated in the same way. By late April, as Wagner rehearsed the *Kaisermarch* at Leipzig, the French army held the affluent western half of Paris and the Commune only the poorer eastern half.

In late May, the *semaine sanglante*, "bloody week," began. The army cleared the boulevards with American-made machine guns, demolished houses with cannon, and conducted mass executions. The Communards also took hostages and executed them, including the archbishop of Paris. Defeated, they burned their city, setting fire to the Tuileries Palace, the Palais-Royal, the courts of justice, and the Hôtel de Ville. Across Europe, newspapers reported that the Louvre had gone up in flames, the Venus de Milo sacrificed to the fury of the mob. Fortunately, Courbet, the anarchist who boasted that he honored no law but "the *régime* of liberty," saved the museums. The number of dead was impossible to count: some claimed that thirty thousand bodies lay in common graves. Thousands more were exiled to New Caledonia in mass trials.

Sustained by fees for correspondence courses in occultism, Éliphas Lévi survived the Prussian shells and the end of the Commune in blood and fire. The fall of the Second Empire, the interlude of impossible hopes, and the barbarous scenes beneath his window all reminded Lévi of the fall of the Roman Empire. First, Rome had weakened itself by civil wars. Then Attila and his hordes, strengthened by contact with Roman civilization, had grown strong enough to conquer it. But

Attila's sons had been unable to hold together his empire. As Edward Gibbon put it in *The Decline and Fall*, they were "soon overwhelmed by a torrent of new Barbarians, who followed the same road which their ancestors had formerly discovered."

Gibbon had also called the French rebels of the 1790s the "new barbarians," savages who rose up from within civilization. Lévi agreed that barbarism began at home. Yet, he thought, the Communards were not the Huns. Their barbarism was closer to that of the early Christians. The crude socialist improvisations of the Commune were not "the Church of the Antichrist" in Paris but "simply a Christianity separated from God," a confusion of religious impulses and fanatic methods. The early Christians, Lévi allowed, could "pass for the ancestors of the *pétroleurs* who set fire to the temples and broke the antique marbles." They too had defied authority and set "children over their parents." Their morals too had been "far from pure," their tastes more *décadent* than those of the most ardent Bohemian. Some had turned the *agape*, the love feast, into a drunken orgy. Others had "soaked themselves in masturbation" or "castrated themselves like Origen and wanted to castrate the children."

But the modern revolutionaries, Lévi saw, did not aspire like the early Christians to "the glories of the final sacrifice in devoting a celibate human race to withering and sterility." They waged war on "civilization and capital" but not on nature, and they glorified the vitality of "the proletarians, who are the opposite of eunuchs." They wanted power, and when they shot priests, it was to demonstrate "the marvels of the musket." The war and the Commune, like the hordes of Attila before them, only "revealed" the road down which the new barbarians would march.

"Incidentally," Wagner told Cosima, *"the fact that the Communists* really wanted to set fire to the whole of Paris is their one impressive feature."

In early May, Wagner finally met Bismarck. Their brief but, Wagner thought, "very precious" exchange left him "utterly enchanted" and Bismarck largely bemused. Two days later at Berlin, Wagner conducted the premiere of the *Kaisermarch* before his emperor.

Like Beethoven's Ninth, the *Kaisermarch* culminates with human voices. In Berlin, Wagner hid his singers among the audience, camouflaged in evening dress. When the moment came, the song of victory burst out as an apparently spontaneous revelation of the racial soul that united audience and performers, German art and German politics. It was Wagner's gift to his people, to his emperor, to his new state, and, above all, to his imperial self, the "Kaiser of the new German music."

PART II

The New Age

><×<<

1871–1898

Then there will be a new man, then everything will be
new. Then history will be divided into two parts: from
the gorilla to the death of God, and from the death of
God to the change of the earth and man physically.

—*Dostoevsky*, Demons *(1872)*

✻ 7 ✻

PASSAGE TO INDIA

Madame Blavatsky's Empire of Theosophy

> Ideals and faith have been lost almost everywhere. Pseudo-science has destroyed them. People in our century demand a scientific bulwark, scientific proofs of the spirit's immortality. Ancient esoteric science will give it to them.
> —*Helena Blavatsky*

On the morning of July 4, 1871, the steam packet *Eumonia* left Piraeus, the port of Athens, and began its crawl around the eastern Mediterranean, loading and unloading goods, mails, and the polyglot horde of tourists, traders, diplomats, and fugitives along the seam between Europe and Asia. Round the Peloponnese, across the Ionian Sea to the heel of Italy, through the Strait of Messina and into the Tyrrhenian Sea for Naples. Then south to Alexandria, gateway to the Suez Canal and points east, before turning northward up the Levantine coast for Beirut, Cyprus, and Constantinople.

The passengers, searching for shade and breeze, gathered on deck. To port, the ancient blue Aegean; to starboard, the rocks and pines of the Peloponnese. That afternoon, as they rounded the island of Spetsai, the *Eumonia* exploded. In the hold, crates of fireworks; in the magazine, gunpowder, in case of pirates; somewhere below, an unseen spark. Afterward, one of the passengers recalled how, as she had contemplated the coast of Spetsai, she had been blown off the deck and into the water. Though she could not swim, she did not drown. Pockets of air were trapped in the layers of her skirts, and the cinching around her waist prevented the air from bubbling up. Her skirts spreading around her, she floated like a crinoline jellyfish amid "limbs, heads and trunks." The survivors hauled her into a boat and rowed for the nearby island.

She was short and broad, with curly black hair, fluted nostrils, and a full mouth but, she felt, a potato nose. At forty, her eyes were pouched with fat and tobacco. She was the daughter of a soldier and a novelist, and her life was a campaign of conquest and self-invention. The larger she got, the more extravagant her stories became, until she and they covered the globe. She had studied with monks in Tibet, magicians in Egypt, and voodoo priests in New Orleans. She crossed the Great Divide in a wagon, climbed Mayan ruins in Mexico, and slept in the Great Pyramid. She had cured an abscess on her leg by sleeping with a white dog and had played piano duets with Clara Schumann. She had advised Empress Eugénie of France on decor, been wounded five times while fighting alongside Garibaldi, and conducted the orchestra at the king of Serbia's court. She kept a stuffed baboon in the corner of her sitting room and wedged a copy of *Origin of Species* under his arm because she had translated Darwin into Russian while traveling up the Nile.

Mark Twain called Mary Baker Eddy the most successful evangelist since Muhammad. He forgot about Helena Petrovna Blavatsky, prophetess of Theosophy, the first global faith of the New Age.

After the sinking of the Eumonia, *Blavatsky washed up in Alexandria* with no money and no possessions. Egypt was booming: a megalomaniac prince, Khedive Ismail, was determined to restore its pharaonic glory on a tide of cotton exports, foreign credit, and ambitious public works. While Cairo prepared for the premiere of Verdi's *Aïda* in its new opera house, Alexandria pastiched its Greco-Roman days as the cosmopolitan junction of the world. Its governors were Turkish, its workers Arab, its slaves Sudanese, and its businessmen Armenian, Greek, Jewish, Coptic, and Italian. There were British lawyers in the ministries, French advisers in the banks, and Confederate veterans in the army. In the cafés, intellectuals of all faiths, juggling hereditary religious ideas and imported political ones, conjured a modern romance of Egypt, the first Arab nationalism.

At the Hôtel d'Orient, Blavatsky mingled among the potted palms with speculators, con men, prostitutes, scoundrels, British officers on their way to India, and the "fishing fleet" of single women who followed them like gulls after a trawler. She befriended a young Englishwoman, also stranded. Emma Cutting had come to Alexandria to retrieve her alcoholic brother. When he died, she had stayed on as a nanny. Now she was working as a medium. Her controller was her mesmerizing boyfriend Alexis Coulomb, whose father owned the Hôtel d'Orient.

By 1871, Blavatsky had lived in this shifting, seamy international world for two decades. Born Helena Andreyevna von Hahn, at eighteen she had fled her arranged marriage to Nikofor Blavatsky, the vice governor of Yerevan in Armenia, and a family friend twenty years her senior. Carrying only her new surname, she had taken ship for Constantinople disguised, she said, as a cabin boy. She became a lady's maid to Russian aristocrats, a dealer in ostrich feathers, the mistress of an aging opera singer, and even, her family suspected, a stunt rider in a circus. The disgraced Georgian princess Catherine Bagration had taken her to the Great Exhibition. The American artist Albert Rawson had dressed her as a young Arab man and taken her down the alleys of old Cairo to study "astrological formulas, magical incantations and horoscopes" with the khedive's astrologer, the Coptic magus Paulos Metamon. Countess Sophie Kissileff, the wife of the Russian ambassador in Paris, had taken her to the spa at Homburg. A roulette addict, the countess had lost so much at the tables that the grateful Homburgers named a street after her and Dostoevsky put her in *The Gambler* (1867). The countess, who also liked to dress Blavatsky as a man—"a gentleman student, she said"—traveled with a set of "medium apparatuses, writing tables, and tarots." She taught her gentleman maid the medium's art.

The past was ghosts and disgraces, the present a fiction to be rewritten. In Alexandria, Blavatsky persuaded Emma Cutting and Alexis Coulomb to launch a *société spiritiste*. Alexis built a séance "closet" in Blavatsky's apartment. He lined the walls and ceiling with red velvet, left a three-inch space between the walls and the cloth, and strung lengths of twine in the space for the manipulation of phenomena. Blavatsky hired cheap French mediums, most of them "beggarly tramps" and "adventuresses," the camp followers of the army of engineers and workmen who had built the Suez Canal.

One night, a customer noticed that the hand floating over the table was a glove stuffed with cotton. There were "disagreeable scenes" in the half-light. A Greek sitter, feeling himself possessed, drew a pistol and tried to shoot Blavatsky. It was time to leave Alexandria.

In June 1873, Blavatsky sailed to New York City in steerage. She rented a room on the Lower East Side, in a forty-room women's cooperative run by admirers of the French utopian Fourier. As the daughter of a princess, she had no formal schooling and only domestic skills. She made paper flowers for a "kind-hearted Hebrew shopkeeper," painted advertising cards for a shirt and collar factory, took in sewing, and extracted small change from her neighbors at séances. When her father died, she received a small legacy and bought a share in a chicken farm on Long Island. She wanted to retire and settle at last, but the chickens let her down. She returned to the spirits.

In October 1874, Blavatsky attended a series of séances at a farmhouse in Chittenden, Vermont. The mediums, the brothers William and Horatio Eddy, claimed to have inherited their talent from a great-great-great-great-grandmother who had been condemned for witchcraft at Salem in 1692. Reporting for the *Daily Graphic* was another well-bred Yankee, Colonel Henry Steel Olcott.

"Good gracious!" Olcott whispered when Blavatsky sat down at the Eddys' kitchen table. "Look at that specimen, will you!"

Her hair, Olcott recalled, was cut and bleached into a thick blond mop. She wore a red vest like one of Garibaldi's soldiers, rolled her own cigarettes, and spoke French. When she stepped out for a smoke, Olcott followed.

"*Permettez-moi, madame?*" He struck a match.

Blavatsky leaned forward and inhaled. Olcott was forty-two, a year younger. He had a law practice, a wife, three children, the oblong beard of an ancient king of Nineveh, and a boundless credulity. He was, though, respectable. He held degrees in scientific agriculture and insurance law. He had been promoted to colonel for his campaign against corruption in military procurement. He had been one of the three commissioners who inquired into Lincoln's assassination. His law office was now representing the City of New York in a case concerning faulty water meters. But Olcott was more interested in etheric forms than in underground flows. In quiet moments, he read *The Banner of Light*, a Spiritualist journal, at his desk—and not without discomfort.

If Spiritualism was a church, Olcott was a Luther. He loathed Spiritualism's frissons of free love and the fortune-teller's tent. Spiritualists, he thought, should pursue "the instruction of their minds and the purification of their souls," not "the filling of their pockets or their bellies, the nutrition of their vanity, or the exercise of their phallus." Olcott found that this strange, mannish blonde agreed with him. American Spiritualism, Blavatsky pronounced, was a "debauch," a "materialistic" and ignorant circus, and altogether rather provincial.

That night, she showed Olcott what he was missing. The Eddy brothers were semiliterate farmers, and so far their séances had manifested the usual suspects: Americans, native or otherwise, and Europeans. With Blavatsky at the table, and the room so dark that it was impossible to distinguish faces, William Eddy was inspired to produce "spooks of other nationalities." Exotic visitors arrived from central Asia. a Georgian servant boy, the merchant Hassan Aga from Tiflis, a Russian peasant woman. The next night brought Safar Ali Bek, the "Kurdish cavalier with scimitar, pistols, and lance"; an African witch doctor; and a dignified "European gentleman wearing the cross and collar of St. Anne," who turned out to be Blavatsky's uncle.

A few days later, she became ill. She carried a scar near her heart, a wound that, she told her sister Eva, dated from her "solitary travels in the steppes of Asia" in the 1850s. It reopened frequently, often causing "intense agony," even "convulsions and a death-like trance." This time, it only kept her in bed.

Blavatsky invited Olcott to her room, to consult about the wound. She had acquired it, she told him, fighting the Austrians with Garibaldi's patriots in 1867: she had been wounded five times at the Battle of Mentana and left for dead in a ditch. She asked Olcott to feel her scars. She bared the pale skin of her left arm, showing where, she said, an Austrian saber stroke had broken the bone in two places. She told him to squeeze her bare shoulder and feel for a musket bullet that was still embedded in the muscle, and then to probe for another bullet, deep in the flesh of her leg. Then she exposed the scar just below her heart where, she said, she had been stabbed with a stiletto knife. Afterward, she showed him frayed letters of introduction from her noble relatives and described her travels, which now extended to "witnessing the mysteries of Hindoo temples" and pushing with an armed escort "far into the interior of Africa." It was, Olcott thought, one of the most romantic stories ever told.

Mrs. Olcott filed for divorce.

Blavatsky's arrival in the United States was as timely as her departure from Egypt. Twenty-five years after the Rochester rappings, spiritual demand remained high, but the supply no longer satisfied. Professional mediums continued to adopt new technologies, such as the commercial typewriter of 1870, but for the amateur masses, Spiritualism lived in its first habitat. It was a parlor game, its "talking boards" sold as cheap mail-order toys. The Kennard Novelty Company's Ouija board of 1890 would be the last and most famous of these.

While Spiritualism sank into commercial platitudes, Transcendentalism headed for the museum and the curriculum. The next phenomenon from New England would not be another Thoreau. While Olcott was communing with the Eddy brothers, a charismatic healer named Mary Baker Eddy was writing *Science and Health* in Lynn, Massachusetts. It would become the bible of Christian Science, a doctrine with little Christianity and less science.

A few weeks after the Chittenden séances, Spiritualism suffered its worst crisis yet. In Philadelphia, the husband-and-wife team of Jennie and Nelson Holmes had won fame by producing the spirit of "Katie King," who also doubled as a celebrated haunter of the séance rooms of London. In late 1874, one of their assistants confessed to the newspapers that she was Katie. Colonel Olcott traveled to Philadelphia like a bishop investigating heresy in a neighboring diocese. After two weeks in the séance room, Jennie Holmes managed to squeeze out a "Katie" for him. Relieved, Olcott pronounced both medium and spirit to be genuine. Privately, however, the episode left him shaken. To recover the Spiritualist gospel from the counterfeiters, he underwrote a journal in Boston, *The Spiritual Scientist*.

The time had come for Blavatsky to cast off the dead skin of Spiritualism, that "crazy delusion of epileptic monomaniacs," and move from medium to controller. In January 1875, shortly after contracting a bigamous marriage to a Georgian immigrant, Blavatsky injured her leg by falling, she said, as she was moving a heavy bedstead. Her knee became violently inflamed and "partial mortification of the leg" set in, possibly at the site of her old wound. She was in agony, and her doctor warned that only amputation would prevent gangrene. Fevered and despairing, she experienced one of her "breaks."

Helena Petrovna Blavatsky becomes Yakov Petrovich Golyadkin, the weak and unimportant government clerk in Dostoevsky's *Double*

(1846). Golyadkin's second self, his "noxious twin," emerges when he is in bed, between sleep and wakefulness, unsure what is real and what is fantasy. His doctor recommends a complete break in routine. No more solitary walks around Saint Petersburg: the climate is bad and industrial society ruins the view.

The rest cure only makes Golyadkin's condition worse. He suffers persecution fantasies and believes that a fellow clerk has usurped his identity. His double is assertive and strong, yet shares Golyadkin's "despicable meanness of soul" and seems to enjoy inflicting that recognition on his conscious mind. His personality disintegrating, Golyadkin starts to see Golyadkins everywhere. In the end, he becomes insane. Now his double seems "by no means noxious, and not even to be his twin at all, but a person very agreeable in himself, and in no way connected with him." His mind has shaped its despicable and mean elements into a new persona.

The double is the child of the inadmissible elements of inner life. The lodger within leers over the conscious self like a gargoyle, artificial and potent on the threshold of consciousness. Blavatsky first sensed the presence of a double in the early 1860s, after her wounds forced her to recuperate with her family in Russia: "Whenever I was called by name, I opened my eyes upon hearing it and was myself, in every particular. As soon as I was left alone, I relapsed into my usual half-dreamy condition and became somebody else." After the death of her young son Yuri in 1865, she suffered a second "break." This one relieved her of the Orthodox Christianity in which she had been raised and allowed her to put names to this other self.

"In the night, when I am alone in my bed, the whole life of my No. 2 passes before my eyes, and I do not see myself at all, but quite a different person—different in race and different in feelings." Her "other me" took many forms, but he was always male. "Sometimes, it seems to me that he overshadows the whole of me, simply entering into me like a kind of volatile essence penetrating my pores and dissolving in me." He was Seraphis Bey, the priest of Egypt, or Tuitit Bey, the ancient Copt. Soon, he would be Koot Hoomi, a tall and transparent Hindu who on occasion might turn into Koot Hoomi Singh the Sikh. In his final incarnation, he would be Master Morya, a Tibetan lama.

Galvanized by the threat of amputation, Blavatsky cured herself by her "best will power," two days of cold-water poultices, and a white pup "laid by night across the leg" by an "old Negro" servant who, in time, would turn into an Hindu, Master Koot Hoomi.

This time, her double did not disappear with the pain. She began to feel a "very strange duality." Several times a day, she felt that "beside me, there is someone else, quite separable from me, present in my body." Unlike the Spiritualist trance medium or the Pentecostalist speaking in tongues, she remained aware. "I never lose consciousness of my personality; what I feel is as if I were keeping silent and the other one—the lodger who is in me—were speaking with my tongue." She named the part of her mind that contacted her double by an androgynous acronym, HPB.

She told Colonel Olcott that she had hurt her knee slipping on an icy sidewalk in New York. When she got back on her feet in the summer of 1875, Blavatsky's "wonderful psycho-physiological change" converted Olcott from Spiritualism to Egyptian magic. He resisted at first; as he admitted, he had yet to understand "the plastic nature of the human Double."

Séance spirits, Blavatsky told him, were not the eternal souls of the dead, summoned intact. They were composites of ignoble spiritual "dregs," the proletariat of the spirit world. At death, a liberated soul and spirit left the "terrestrial atmosphere" and returned to the astral plane. It left behind the husks of mental life, a seamy accumulation of "terrestrial passions, vices, and worldly thoughts." Like the villagers in Gogol's *Dead Souls* (1842), who remain on the property register after the death of the body, this "residuum of personality" remained in earthly limbo, where it created the "lower order" of spiritual manifestations. It was "ghastly" for Blavatsky to see these "disgusting" and "soulless creatures" feeding parasitically on the energy of the séance.

The way the sitters "wept and rejoiced" around William Eddy had made her want to vomit. The sitters were the other kind of "dead souls" in Gogol's novel. Their spirits were numb with *poshlost*, middle-class philistinism; their minds, Blavatsky complained, full of "platitudes and common talk."

Nor, Olcott learned, did spirits take "intelligent control" of the medium. The Chittenden apparitions had come from Blavatsky's mind: the Georgian servant boy was still alive. When Eddy's "astral body" had floated into the room, Blavatsky had used her double to project a mental "picture," as though her double were a magic lantern. But the real value of the double did not lie in the dangerous and vulgar transmissions of the séance room. A medium trained in the "philosophy of the Occult" could use her double as a receiver: as a "channel" for "truly wonderful phenomena of the higher order, in which undeniable intelligence and knowledge are exhibited"—for contacting the highest spirits, the masters.

"Everything is double in nature," she said, "magnetism is positive and negative, active and passive, male and female." Blavatsky reversed the polarities. She would not be a passive female medium, ravished by active male spirits; her double was the dominant partner, consciously searching out the spirits. While the passive medium received as a "spiritual telegraph," Blavatsky was a conversationalist, using the spiritual equivalent of the telephone, a device invented the previous year by Elisha Gray and patented the following year by Alexander Graham Bell.

Blavatsky wanted to corner the market by annexing Spiritualism to the older, elitist traditions of European occultism. She did not tell Olcott that Éliphas Lévi had already dreamed her visions in French. Lévi was barely known outside France; *Dogme et rituel de la haute magie* would not be translated into English until 1910. Nor did Blavatsky describe the double's roots in Russian folklore and literature, in the *volkh* and the *starets*, the peasant shaman and the mystic monk.

"Her mediumship," Olcott announced, "is totally different from that of any other person I ever met; for, instead of being controlled by spirits to do their will, it is she who seems to control them to do her bidding."

On the evening of September 7, 1875, Blavatsky hosted a lecture on "geometrical figures of the Egyptian Kabbalah" in her rooms at 46 Irving Place. The speaker was George Henry Felt. An inventor of rockets and telegraphic devices, and a student of sacred geometry, Felt believed that the temples of ancient Egypt were a form of religious technology. The Egyptians, he claimed, had built them by "God's Law of Proportion," to generate the same "elemental spirits" that now hovered in the séance room.

The guests were the cream of New York's metaphysicians, skimmed from Henry Olcott's address book. Four were lawyers, including William Q. Judge, the future president of the American Theosophical Society; and Charles Carleton Massey, the future founder of the British Theosophical Society. Three were men of letters: William Livingston Alden wrote editorials for *The New York Times*. John Storer Cobb had edited *The New Era*, a journal of Reform Judaism. Charles Sotheran, publisher of *The American Bibliopolist*, was a prominent Swedenborgian and Freemason, and the biographer of the eighteenth-century mountebank Count Cagliostro. Four were Spiritualists: Henry J. Newton was the president of the New York Society of Spiritualists and an admirer of spirit photography. Lizzie Doten and Emma Hardinge Britten were celebrated trance mediums. Emma's husband, Dr. William Britten, was a Mesmerist, expert in "electrical therapeutics." Another physician, Blavatsky's doctor Seth Pancoast, owned America's largest library of Kabbalah books and manuscripts.

After the lecture, Olcott suggested that the group form a "society for this kind of study." In October, when a smaller group met at the Brittens' home on Thirty-Eighth Street, Olcott suggested they call themselves the Miracle Club. One "sharp-witted savant," probably Blavatsky, offered "La Société des Malcontents du Spiritisme." Then Charles Sotheran, leafing through the *Webster*, found "Theosophy," from the Greek *theos* (god) and *sophia* (wisdom). The word had a

Hermetic pedigree: Renaissance Neoplatonists had used it to refer to the universal and ultimate wisdom of all religions. And was this not the common object of all the spiritual factions on the committee?

Theosophy, Blavatsky told her fellow seekers, must be "a science and a thing of mathematical certitude." She wanted to gather "learned occultists and cabalists, Hermetic philosophers," and "passionate anti-quaries and Egyptologists," and lead them up Éliphas Lévi's path to Thebes, via Paulos Metamon's library in Cairo. Olcott did not know the itinerary but had received an astral letter from Tuitit Bey, a resident of the "Observatory of Luxor," so he knew he was heading to Egypt.

For Olcott, spiritual enlightenment meant social reform. He had cleansed the stables at the War Department and the Navy Department. Now he would purify the procurement of the sacred. There must be no more hedonism and sleaze. The tablets of Theosophy would be temperance for the soul. If the Society shared American goals, it merited American liberties. While Blavatsky, an immigrant from the conspiracies of European occultism, had in mind a "secret Society like the Rosicrucian Lodge," Olcott worked by American methods. He wrote bylaws, created subcommittees, and booked Mott Memorial Hall on Madison Avenue for the society's first public meeting.

Blavatsky was not the first importer of European occult fashions to the United States. Two other malcontents of Spiritualism preceded her. One was Paschal Beverly Randolph, an American sex magician who had died in the summer of 1875, possibly by his own hand. The other was Emma Britten. She was not only alive but on the Theosophical committee.

In 1855, Randolph, a mixed-race Spiritualist and abolitionist, had visited occultists in London and Paris. In London, he acquired Bulwer-Lytton's Rosicrucian idea. In Paris, he found Mesmerists, magic mirrors, Éliphas Lévi's astral light, and a "beatific vision" from a generous dose of *dawamesk*. Hashish, Randolph concluded, was the "Elixir of

Life," the "universal solvent," the "Secret of Perpetual Youth," the royal road to clairvoyance. In 1857, he experimented further with hashish in Egypt. Renouncing Spiritualism, Randolph returned to Boston with 350 cases of liquid *dawamesk* and formed a Rosicrucian fraternity to explore their contents. He sold his "genuine Oriental article" through small advertisements in the *Banner of Light*, at "$four a bottle, with full directions how to secure the celestial."

Blavatsky had also learned to use hashish to elicit visions. "It is a wonderful drug, and it clears up a profound mystery," she told Albert Rawson. Her hallucinations gave "a recollection of my former existences, my previous incarnations." But she recoiled from the next step of Randolph's experiment.

Randolph's Egyptian experiences had convinced him that, as Lévi hinted, the celestial could be secured by sexual magic. In 1861, Randolph returned to the Near East. Somewhere in the hills near Jerusalem, he was initiated into a sex cult; possibly the Nusa'iri sect, long persecuted by Muslims for their alleged pagan or gnostic orgies. In the "mighty moment" of the "orgasmal instant," Randolph reported, the "mystic forces of the SOUL OPEN TO THE SPACES." Mastery of "Sex-passion" was "the key to all possible Knowledge." Its benefits included success in business, and also "Oriental Breast-Love."

Blavatsky wanted to get away from this kind of thing. So did Emma Britten. A former child actress from London, Britten had supported her family from the age of twelve by working as a "somnambulist" for a group of high-born occultists, Bulwer-Lytton among them; later, she implied that she had been sexually abused by some members of this "vicious aristocracy." In the 1850s, while Blavatsky was struggling as a lady's maid, Britten had found success as a medium and speaker. Her *Six Lectures on Theology and Nature* (1860) sketched out what would become the Theosophical synthesis. She mixed Hermeticism and evolutionary theory with comparative religion, topped off with the new Indology. In America, Britten became famous for her Spiritualism, her lectures, and her lament for Abraham

Lincoln. And now she and her husband were working on a grand theory, using Hermeticism not to overthrow Spiritualism, but to revitalize it.

The Theosophical Society was still only an idea without a theology. Blavatsky realized that if she did not write it, Britten would. While Olcott organized, Blavatsky retreated to the house of Hiram Corson, a professor of literature at Cornell University who had taken to Spiritualism after the sudden death of his sixteen-year-old daughter. He asked Blavatsky to conduct a séance, but she was "decidedly opposed to anything of the kind." Instead she sat at a table in Corson's library, smoking and writing furiously. Once more, she was making a new start, outrunning the obscene mysteries of the past. Egypt and Luxor were not far enough. The world was wider now, and she much wiser. Like Phileas Fogg in *Around the World in Eighty Days* (1873), she placed her bets, then hurried east for Suez.

The Theosophical Society, Olcott announced from the stage of Mott Memorial Hall, would recover "the primeval source of all religions, the books of Hermes and the *Vedas*—of Egypt and India respectively."

As Blavatsky sat at her desk in his library, Professor Corson watched as a "slim, brown Indian hand" rose from under the table, pencil at the ready.

Madame Blavatsky gave her daily matinee in the front room of an apartment on the corner of Forty-Seventh Street and Eighth Avenue, overlooking the new street railway and the eastern frontier of Hell's Kitchen. The apartment walls were painted with a jungle mural. In the foliage, an elephant, a leopard, and a snake mingled with photographic portraits of two Hindu gentlemen Olcott had met in 1870 on the Atlantic crossing. A stuffed bat was pinned over the door, and the stuffed owl in the corner blinked. The tea was strong, and the teaspoons prone to dematerialize in Madame's hands. From the hallway, an unseen maid added "astral music and bells" to the tinkle of cup on saucer.

Priests, rabbis, and doctors attended Madame, and also, *The New York World* reported, "secret Bohemians" like Linda Dietz, then starring at the Union Square Theater; "occasional Asiatics" like the journalist Wong Chin Foo, who was the first person to call himself a Chinese American; and "Indian philosophers" like Krishna Varma, a Punjabi Hindu who stayed for several weeks. There were wayward aristocrats like the occultist Baron de Palma; Countess Pashkov, who had first met Blavatsky over a campfire somewhere between Baalbek and the Orontes River; and Helene von Racowitz, the Bavarian princess whose husband had killed her lover, the German socialist Ferdinand Lassalle, in a duel. It was, Olcott thought, "the most attractive *salon* in the metropolis." With aristocratic wit and ease, Blavatsky massaged personal information from her guests like a medium before a séance.

Toward midnight, when the guests had gone, the maid had cleared away dinner, and the trains and drunks were asleep, the dining table became a desk. Blavatsky and Olcott faced each other. Six months after its launch, the Theosophical Society had contracted into their small apartment. The Spiritualists on its committee, realizing that Blavatsky would crush them in her embrace, had withdrawn; twenty blocks south of Blavatsky's desk, the ghost of a spectral European nobleman dictated to Emma Britten while Charles Britten transcribed. Olcott no longer rented Mott Memorial Hall or collected membership dues. Night after night, they worked alone.

Olcott's clearest indication of Blavatsky's direction was, as with the Indian heads on the walls, visual. Tuitit Bey's letter from Luxor contained a design for the society's icon: a Mediterranean mélange of Hebrew letters, Gnostic symbols, a Maltese cross, and a pentangular star. A year later, Blavatsky expanded the icon.

At its core, there is an Egyptian crucifix within a Jewish star. These are surrounded by the ouroboros of the Gnostics and alchemists, a snake eating its own tail. This is a traditional Hermetic image, ordering Greek, Egyptian, and Hebraic elements by Christian philosophy, but Blavatsky gave it an oriental frame. The ouroboros is wrapped in a motto taken from Sanskrit, "There is no religion higher than truth." On the horizontal plane, the eye is led toward the Egyptian cross and the origins of Christianity. But vertically, the eye is guided upward to the higher, original truths of Buddhists and Hindus. A swastika in a circle symbolizes the solar energy of the world, the flux of destruction and creation. Atop the swastika and highest of all, three Sanskrit letters rest like the crown on a pineapple and form the eternal and absolute *Om.*

Olcott did not find it easy to capture the fugitive HPB on paper. She thought in a unique language, neither Russian nor French. Olcott suspected it was the "Pythagorean numbers" or even some dead language employed by "races who had attained to a civilization of which the present phonograph may have been but the nearest commonplace to them." Soon, he hoped, archaeologists in Egypt might find an ancient "sheet of tinfoil," like those Edison, an early recruit to the Theosophical Society, used for his phonographic recordings, so that this pharaonic disc would talk to Madame in "the very language of her thoughts." Until then, she wrote in English and Olcott repaired the damage. Sometimes he corrected her almost undecipherable drafts and she recopied them. When her handwriting was beyond mortal correction, he read aloud and she transcribed.

She was a font of revelations. First, Olcott had believed the Rosicrucians to be the "Unknown Superiors" who had preserved the mystic traditions of the "neo-Platonists and the last theurgists of Alexandria." Then, Tuitit Bey had confessed that the Rosicrucians were merely a European outpost of the Brotherhood of Luxor. Next, it had emerged that the Brotherhood did not dwell in Luxor or anywhere else in Egypt, but on the astral plane. Then Tuitit admitted that the Luxor group was only the "Egyptian section" of a global freemasonry of spirits, the Universal Mystic Brotherhood, which also had an Indian section. Luxor, Blavatsky revealed, was an orthographic and geographical deviation from "the ancient Baloochistan city of Looksur, which lies between Bela and Kedgee."

When the astral masters were on form, Olcott noted, Blavatsky could produce ten or twenty pages in perfect English. The first contributors to Blavatsky's spectral internationale were Tuitit Bey and Serapis Bey, whom Olcott revered as "my first Guru." Then came Henry More, the seventeenth-century English Neoplatonist, and Polydorus Isurenus, an expert in Hebrew *gematria*, number magic, from ancient Alexandria. After them came a Rajput master who twirled an etheric mustache; Nârâyana, a landed proprietor from Thiruvallam in southern India; and Koot Hoomi Singh, who, though his astral form resided in British India, spelled "skeptic" in the American style. These masters held invisible books before Blavatsky for her to copy. They did not insist that she cite her sources, or quibble with her erratic translations, or thank Éliphas Lévi, a copy of whose *Dogme et rituel* Blavatsky had borrowed from the journalist William L. Alden, and which all of them seemed to have read.

Olcott and Blavatsky worked until four in the morning before they went to bed, separately. If Olcott had ever exercised his phallus with Blavatsky, that was in the past. He now felt thoroughly "psychologized" by her, but chastely. His nicknames for her were relentlessly fraternal: Jack, Mulligan, Latchkey, Old Horse. The reporter from *The New York World* compared their home to a "lamasery," a Tibetan monastery. This was a spiritual union, and its child would be "The Veil of Isis."

Or rather, until Charles Sotheran, their publisher, discovered that a book called *The Veil of Isis*, a speculative account of the "mysteries of the Druids," had been printed in England in 1861. To avoid copyright problems, Sotheran retitled Blavatsky's book *Isis Unveiled*.

Isis Unveiled *is an epitaph to the Renaissance Hermetic tradition that* found the roots of religion in the ancient Mediterranean. It is the first major work of the New Age tradition: a fantasy of evolutionary mysticism, projecting modern science and psychology onto India.

Isis unveils herself like a fan dancer. She has a substantial pair of volumes, one *Science*, the other *Theology*, but she never quite bares as much as she promises. The purpose of the dance is not the unveiling but the skill with which she defers it. In *Science*, Isis defends the Hermetic tradition against its historical double, scientific materialism. Modern science, Blavatsky argues, thinks itself superior to the "philosophies and sciences of antiquity," yet its discoveries and terminologies are antique truths under new names. The new definitions are necessarily incomplete, for they describe only matter.

Isis is still a Neoplatonist. She knows that material forms are the inferior shadows of their ideal, spiritual forms. Truth is always eternal and universal, an emanation of a perfect consciousness, and Man has always perceived it partially from the narrow perspective of his terrestrial plane. Like all Man's handiwork, the truths of modern science are crooked, cockeyed impressions: not so much wrong as childish. If the theory of evolution is aligned correctly with its ancient forebears, Darwin cowers like a slave in the shadow of the pyramids, dwarfed and dispensable. To Isis, the pyramids, like all significant human productions, are an Aryan work. Plato was the "world's interpreter," but his philosophy merely echoes the "spiritualism of the Vedic philosophers" who had lived "thousands of years" before him. The astral light is "identical with the Hindu akâsa."

After the new chronology of *Science*, the new *Theology* of race: Isis's second volume reunites religion and science under the motif of evolution. Just as races have multiplied and diverged from common ancestors into "branch nations," so religions have developed and declined from a "primitive stock." The deep roots of knowledge are not severed, only hidden as fossil memories. For a century, the tinkling hammers of comparative religion and linguistics have chipped away the dead rock: a revival of true and complete knowledge becomes possible.

Isis digs down to the original Aryan roots. She knows her Gobineau, but her ideas have evolved. Her Jesus is not the Semitic magus of Éliphas Lévi, but the Aryan Jesus of Ernest Renan. Christianity chose for its guidance "the national records and scriptures of a people perhaps the least spiritual of the human family—the Semitic." Blavatsky's

Semites are "purely sensual and terrestrial" peoples and have never developed a language capable of embodying "moral and intellectual" ideas. Their literature contains nothing original and is borrowed from "Aryan thought." Their science and philosophy lack the "noble features" of the "highly spiritual and metaphysical systems of the Indo-European races." The Bible is merely a "local allegory." As science corrects the historic errors of theology, it restores the primal unity of spirit and biology.

As the net of communications, exchange, and knowledge expanded across the globe, Blavatsky created its spiritual counterpart, the first truly global religion. Theosophy was an empire of the spirit, advancing on the paths of the modern networks. In the age of cheap intercontinental travel, Blavatsky was the first spiritual impresario to claim to have found her insights in fieldwork, not an occultist's library or an alchemist's laboratory. In the age of the global market, she was a spiritual circumnavigator, passing through "far-away countries where they still believe in magic, where wonders are performed daily by the native priesthood, and where the cold materialism of science has never yet reached—in one word, the East." She processed the raw materials of the Hindu and Buddhist spirit in the mills of Western science, and planted Western materialism in the temples of the East.

It is almost certain that Blavatsky had never been east of Suez. But the best lies have the ring of plausibility. She laid her skein of falsehoods on the real network, the web of trains, steamers, hotels, and telegraphs. She had no witnesses or proofs, but her story seemed technically plausible. Always, she ran just ahead of the traffic. In 1879, the English journalist Edwin Arnold, coiner of the phrase "Cape to Cairo" to describe British ambitions in Africa, would write *The Light of Asia*, a verse biography of the Buddha. In the same year, the first volume of *The Sacred Books of the East* would appear. Conceived and edited by the German-born philologist Max Müller, the series would run to fifty volumes.

The age of esoteric mysteries was also the age of prosaic exchanges; the age of the fictional circumnavigator Phileas Fogg was also the age of the genuine circumnavigator Nellie Bly, who would test the modern networks in 1889 for *The New York World*. Bly found that truth was faster than fiction, and returned her to New York in seventy-two days. The imaginable becomes the possible, the possible the ordinary. Queen Victoria had never been east of Suez either, but she was now empress of India.

In December 1878, Olcott and Blavatsky visited Thomas Edison at the world's first research laboratory in Menlo Park, New Jersey. One of his ideas, he told Olcott, was to try whether "a pendulum, suspended on the wall" could be made to move by "will-force" and wires attached to his forehead. Another idea, the electric light bulb, was about to undergo its first public test.

Olcott and Blavatsky returned to New York with one of Edison's recording phonographs, and its operator, Mr. Johnson. On December 15, the lamasery heard its last burst of disembodied voices. With Johnson at the controls of the hundred-pound electrical beast, Olcott, Blavatsky, and the society's inner circle spoke in turn into the "voice-receiver," recording a series of messages to their "known and unknown brothers in India."

"CONSUMMATUM EST," Olcott wrote in his diary the next day, reprising Jesus' last words in the Gospel of John. "It is finished." He sold their furniture and entrusted American Theosophy to Major-General Abner Doubleday, a soldier and engineer whose monuments include a statue at Gettysburg and the grip and cable car system of San Francisco. He was back at the apartment by 7:00 p.m., bearing tickets for the British steamboat *Canada*. They left the lamasery for the last time just before midnight. "What next?" Blavatsky wondered. "All dark, but tranquil."

"Have you seen the lighthouse?" they call. "There it is at last, the Bombay lighthouse!"

Thirty-two days out of Liverpool, and having been delayed by boiler trouble in the Arabian Sea, the S.S. *Speke Hall* sights its destination just after dinner. Blavatsky has never trusted sea travel since the sinking of the *Eumonia*, and she has found it a rough voyage. The ship is filthy, the food terrible, and after banging her leg during a storm in the Bay of Biscay, she has been obliged to cross the Mediterranean lying down.

The passengers abandon their books, music, and card games. They rush outside, and Blavatsky limps after them. At dawn on the morning of February 16, 1879, the *Speke Hall* glides past the caves of Elephanta and through the rocks and coconut-forested islands of the blue bay. As they drop anchor, Blavatsky explains to Olcott that Bombay is named not for the Portuguese *bom bahia*, "good bay," but for "the goddess Mamba, in Mahrati Mahima, or Amba, Mama, and Amma, according to the dialect, a word meaning, literally, the Great Mother."

The pilgrims disembark into wet heat, white light, dark skins, strange odors. When Olcott's soles touch "sacred soil," he falls to his knees in his tropical suit, and kisses the granite steps of the dock: "my instinctive act of *pooja!*"

The New Age has begun.

❧ 8 ❧

THE REVOLT OF ZARATHUSTRA

Nietzsche in Urania

> I gradually came to realize what all great philosophy had hitherto consisted of—namely, the confessions of its author, a collection of involuntary, unpremeditated memoirs. Thus, in every philosophy, the author's moral (or immoral) intentions have constituted the real seed from which the whole plant has grown . . .
>
> The degree and kind of a man's sexuality reach up into the absolute pinnacle of his spirit. —*Nietzsche*, Beyond Good and Evil *(1885)*

Wearing swimming trunks, Panama hat, glasses, and mustache, Friedrich Wilhelm Nietzsche basks on the sand like a lizard. The seabirds cry, the fishermen sing, the sun alchemizes sickly northern flesh into golden muscle, and his unusually sensitive nostrils breathe a Homeric essence of salt, ozone, sweat, and old fish.

"What a glorious time!" He alighted in Genoa a friendless invalid with just a few clothes and books, but these are the days of the "great health." He perches in attic rooms, writes in cafés, and subsists on offal and scraps of fish. Evading his old life, he flits into telegraph offices and lays false trails by directing letters to old lodgings. If anyone asks, he tells his mother, say I am in San Remo.

Early each morning, the free bird peregrinates alone into the hills, exploring the coasts from which, nearly four centuries ago, Columbus cast off for the New World. One day he is overtaken by an onrush of joy on the heights. "Never have I been so happy. The flood of life swept over me as waves of happiness cast their previous seashell towards me, the purple melancholy. I was ready for anything!"

In a hundred years' time, he feels, they will erect a little column to commemorate the dawn when the idea of a voyage to a new world struck like lightning. The inscription will read "Columbus-Nietzsche: 1481–1882. Liberators of the Human Race."

Columbus conceived his great voyage in 1481, eleven years before he sailed. Now Nietzsche prepares for the new world of beautiful monsters. He will explore the golden continent, the human body, and its ultimate terra incognita, the self within. The old Jewish god is dead, and Christian morals are dying. Biology, the body's truth, is coming out. Nietzsche cannot bring himself to name this truth, the love that Whitman and Wilde speak of indirectly. Nevertheless, Nietzsche will be the first to construct a theory of mind, body, and soul around the liberation of male sexuality. As Christian civilization expires by senescence and suicide, pagan Greece returns as homoerotic spirituality, and Nietzsche becomes the founding philosopher of identity politics.

His parents named their little prince Friedrich Wilhelm, for the king of Prussia, who shared his birthday. His father was a village pastor at Röcken, near Leipzig, his mother a pastor's daughter. When Friedrich was four, his father began to stutter and babble, to fall and forget who he was. He went blind and died within the year. An autopsy revealed softening of the brain. Expelled from the rectory, Friedrich's mother took the "little pastor" and his sister, Elisabeth, to live with his grandmother and aunts. The women tortured him with cold baths, mockery, beatings for imagined errors, and short rations of food and love.

His mother also taught him word games and piano duets. He became an ardent reader, admiring kings, dukes, knights, and other lost patriarchs. He called himself "Prince Squirrel," a secret hoarder, agile against gravity, but he was powerless in sleep's dark labyrinth. Phantasmal animals clawed him, avalanches crushed him, and his father stepped from his grave, then returned to the earth with a child in his arms. Friedrich awoke to the damp shame of the bed wetter. On a nearby hill, he and Elisabeth piled stones and fragments of bone to build an altar to Wotan, the thunder god. They lit the fire and circled it, chanting, "Wotan, hear us!"

At fourteen, he went to a boarding school in a converted monastery at Pforta in the Thuringian countryside. The school pitied the widow and charged no fees, but it showed no mercy to her son. Its brutal regime was designed, Nietzsche recalled, to create warriors, young men to be used and misused by the state. He was constantly ill with head pains, rheumatism, catarrh, congestions of the lungs and bowels, and diarrhea. The school doctor attributed Nietzsche's ailments to hereditary weakness. Biology was against him.

Fritz retreated into the secret mysteries of art and friendship with other sensitive youths. He formed an arts society called Germania and won prizes for his verse. Losing faith in Lutheran pieties, he admired Hölderlin, who, deriding his fellow Germans as barbarous and philistine, had dreamed of the ancient Mediterranean; Byron, one of the last aristocratic libertines and first modern celebrities; and Emerson, the aphoristic American pagan.

Byron's *Manfred* was a particular favorite. Manfred, alone in the Alps after an unspecified transgression, breathes a mixed air of "degradation and pride." He hears a Faustian promise in the song of the shepherd's pipe and the "bells of the sauntering herd," the old patriarchal melodies. In an 1861 essay, Fritz called Manfred an *Übermensch*, a "superman," for summoning the spirits and projecting his mind across time. Later, Nietzsche would compose a *Manfred Overture*.

At Leipzig University, the Classics professor Friedrich Wilhelm Ritschl spotted a prodigy in the squinting, staring theology student with the powerful skull. Turning from theology to philology, religion to science, Nietzsche took "Papa" Ritschl first as his mentor and then as his *doktorvater*, the "doctor-father" who directed him toward the new standard of secular expertise, the specialized research degree.

In 1864, Leipzig was yet to join Prussia, the motor of the new Germany, but signs of economic and social transformation were everywhere. No Europeans industrialized and urbanized as rapidly as the Germans did in these years of the *Gründerzeit*, the "foundation time." Steel-framed apartment buildings appeared on the axial roads around Leipzig's medieval center, and dense, airless tenements around its new mills. The city was equidistant between Prague and Berlin, and it became a transport hub. A few months before Nietzsche arrived, Ferdinand Lassalle had founded the first German socialist party at Leipzig; the constituents gathered by rail.

German universities had always been fortresses of nationalism, and Nietzsche shared the students' patriotism. With another of Ritschl's students, the handsome Erwin Rohde, he pursued the aristocratic, martial pursuits of pistol practice and riding. The pair often strode into Ritschl's seminars in their riding boots, crops in hand. One student nicknamed them Castor and Pollux, after the mythological brothers who were usually depicted in equestrian attitudes.

When Nietzsche was alone, the ghosts returned. One night in his lodgings over Rohn's bookshop, he heard a voice from behind him, speaking in a "terrifyingly inarticulate and inhuman tone." When his landlord died and was laid out in the next room, his ghost manifested in Nietzsche's bedroom in a nightshirt and sleeping cap. One day in a bookshop, Nietzsche's inner "daimon" told him to buy Schopenhauer's *World as Will and Idea*.

To read Schopenhauer, he felt, was to be penetrated by the spirit of a "vigorous, mysterious genius." It was a "magical transference," like a son being taught by his father. Transfixed by the "vast, disinterested solar eye of art," Nietzsche saw his flaws and shame as in a mirror. He saw the "horrific grandeur" of the universe, its fields of sickness and health, exile and sanctuary. He punished himself with contempt, mortification, and four hours' sleep a night. "Who knows to what degree of foolishness I would have goaded myself had not life's delectable decoys, the seductions of vanity, and the compulsion to regularity in my studies worked against it?"

In 1868, Papa Ritschl secured his protégé a professorship at Basel in Switzerland, with subsidiary teaching duties at the gymnasium. Nietzsche was twenty-four, unusually young, and had not formally completed his doctorate. His sister, Elisabeth, joined him to manage his household and maintain his fastidious habits of dress. When they went to lunch, they clung to each other as they navigated the uneven cobbles.

In the gymnasium, Nietzsche shuttered the classroom and asked his youths to meditate on heroic warriors and philosophers; on the Maenads, the intoxicated women who dismembered Dionysus, their idol in Euripides' *Bacchae*; on Achilles' lament for Patrocles in the *Iliad*. Plato's *Symposium* was his favorite.

Reclining at an Athenian drinking party, Pausanias argues that Eros takes no single form and that love, like all activities, is "simply in itself neither good nor bad." He reminds the group of the varying accounts of the birth of Aphrodite, goddess of love. In Homer's version, Aphrodite is the daughter of Zeus and Dione. As Aphrodite Pandemos, the Aphrodite of the "man in the street," she represents the lower form of Eros. This common male desire for the body, not the soul, is usually felt for a woman or a boy. In Hesiod's version, Uranus, the god of the heavens, creates Aphrodite Urania, the "heavenly Aphrodite," from his own genitals. This love is a male creation. It symbolizes the highest form of love, the union of male minds, and is known through the pederastic love of the mentor for his pupil, the youth who has not yet grown a beard. Although Athenians despise slavishness, an older man is not demeaned by voluntarily enslaving himself to a boy, providing he does not suborn him with "financial or political inducements." Nor is the boy demeaned, providing he chooses a mentor through whose influence he will "improve in wisdom in some way, or some other form of goodness."

Later, after Socrates has discussed the Platonic ideal of love, the young and handsome Alcibiades arrives drunk, with ribbons in his hair. He tells the group what Socrates is really like. They think of Socrates as a satyr, seducing boys with his pipe music. True, when Socrates opens his mouth, the divine power of his speech transports the hearer and "reveals those who have a desire for the gods and their rites." But Socrates has also mastered his mortal passions. He rejects wealth and status. When Alcibiades sought to seduce him, he was a "model of restraint." Socrates exercised, wrestled, and dined with Alcibiades, and even slept under the same cloak with him, but he did not take him as a lover. To Alcibiades, this proves that the real Socrates, "the figure inside," is "utterly godlike and golden and beautiful and wonderful." Socrates reminds him of one of those figures of Silenus the centaur that sculptors keep for luck. "You can open them up, and when you do, you find little figures of the gods inside."

Nietzsche invited favored pupils to drink beer and converse at his lodgings, shutters drawn. One drew a heart on his desk in chalk; another gave him violets. Walking arm in arm with a third, he proposed a holiday in Italy. Rebuffed, he withdrew his arm sharply, and stared silently, his face a "lifeless mask." Jacob Mähly, an older colleague, feared that Nietzsche's appointment had been a miscalculation. He seemed too close to his boys, too distant to women. He dressed too well and smelled of scent, like a man raised by women. His huge mustache was a shield against the imputation of femininity. Nietzsche's colleague Jacob Burckhardt agreed: "Nietzsche cannot even let out a fart like a natural young man."

In 1858, William Gladstone, liberal politician, Christian moralist, and amateur Classicist, had decided that the ancient Greeks had been partially color-blind. Few of Homer's adjectives for color, Gladstone pointed out, seemed to match the modern spectrum. The ancients had been able to see only black, white, and red: hence the *Iliad*'s description of the sea as *oínos pónton,* "wine-faced" or "wine-dark." Writing as Darwin finished *Origin of Species,* Gladstone attributed the ability to perceive other colors to "development."

Nietzsche's contemporaries faced other perceptual difficulties when it came to the Greeks. It was an article of educational faith that ancient Greece had been the political precursor of Rome and a spiritual precursor of Christianity. As the eighteenth-century archaeologist and art historian Johann Winckelmann showed, Classical art had anticipated this future. Statues of heroic male nudes depicted "noble simplicity" and "quiet grandeur." They subordinated physical impulses to intellectual forms and embodied the moral restraint that stabilized society. In his letters, Winckelmann privately admitted that sex and beauty coexisted in the male form. Life's imitations of art tending to fatal irony, he was murdered by a youth in a bedroom at a roadside inn.

A century later, the British liberal Matthew Arnold repeated Winckelmann's image of Hellas as an ideal of restraint in *Culture and Anarchy* (1869). Arnold addressed not a small caste of aesthetes and antiquaries but the new, mass-educated middle classes, the whip-holders of democracy. The state and the industrial economy now conjoined the fates of all. If the future was not to be a Ruskinian hell of "Philistines" and "Barbarians," then all must rise together. True uplift required the heightening of individual feeling, especially in a world where machines blunted sensitive minds. But the middle classes were divided by a culture war between "Hebraists and Hellenizers."

The Hebraist majority were religious moralists, demanding perfect conduct and obedience. The Hellenizers were an aesthetic minority, desiring perfect experience in order to see life in its totality and things "as they really are." The Hebrew quarreled with the body and its desires because they hindered "right action"; the Greek because they hindered "right thinking." But both Hebrew and Hellenist shared a common spiritual purpose, human "perfection or salvation."

Arnold identified the Hellenizer's beauty as the "master-impulse" of life, and the Hebraist's harmony as the organizing principle of society. In a democratic age when every man contained a potential Socrates, it was necessary that the Hebraist should unbridle his inner Hellenizer and overcome his philistine tendencies by cultivating a "disinterested play of consciousness upon his stock notions and habits." And Hebraist morality, Arnold reckoned, could withstand the Hellenizer's critique because Christianity braced society's moral fiber: "He who works for sweetness and light, works to make reason and the will of God to prevail."

Arnold, who described the "long, melancholy, withdrawing roar" of Christian faith in the poem "Dover Beach," argued for the social utility of Christian ethics. He believed that the Hellenistic temperament was Christian in spirit and morals. Nietzsche knew that it could not be. Historical evidence was accumulating, scientific views gaining ground, and Christian taboos loosening; his own faith had been one of the casualties. The Greek temperament, Nietzsche saw, had encompassed "all manifestations of the terrible, from a tigerish passion for destruction, to the unnatural urges released when men are charged with the education of youths."

*This recognition did not spring whole from Nietzsche alone, like Dio*nysus from the thigh of Zeus. As science conquered the old theology, it reclassified sexuality and created new medical disciplines like psychology and sexology. The first new theories of sexual identity appeared in Germany in the 1860s.

Karl Heinrich Ulrichs worked at a provincial court in Hanover. He had always felt himself to be different. As a child, he had enjoyed wearing girls' clothes. Later, after an adolescent experience with his riding instructor, he sought sex with men. In *Researches on the Riddle of Man-Man Love* (1864–1880), Ulrichs adapted Pausanias' reflections in the *Symposium* to a scientific typology. Men who loved women, followers of Aphrodite Dione's "common" love, were *Dionings*. Men who followed Aphrodite Urania, and created a love object without a woman, were *Urnings*—in English, "Uranians." The Uranian was effectively a third sex, with female sexual impulses in a male body.

Uranian impulses, arising from the body, had natural rights. In 1867, when Ulrichs was pleading in Munich against the sodomy laws of Ludwig II's Bavaria, he became the first man to declare himself a Uranian. He lost his job, became an advocate for sexual tolerance, and expanded his typology of sexual drives and attractions. He identified female Uranians, and bisexuals, or *Uranodionings* too, but he concentrated on males. His final system contained four types of men (Dioning, Uranian, Uranodioning, and Hermaphrodite) and four subcategories of Uranian. In 1870, he published *Uranus*, a journal that folded after its first issue and was subtitled "Prometheus."

While Ulrichs mapped a spectrum of sexual identity, the Austrian novelist Karl-Maria Kertbeny proposed a binary model. The words "heterosexual" and "homosexual" first appeared in print in 1869, in a pamphlet in which Kertbeny opposed extending Prussia's anti-sodomy law of 1851 to the new North German Federation. Kertbeny rejected the medical orthodoxy that moral weakness and masturbation led to sexual acts between men. Like Ulrichs, he insisted that sexual orientation was innate. To criminalize homosexuality as a moral crime was to deny biological destiny, and also to expose "homosexuals" to contempt and blackmail.

The prescriptive biblical vocabulary was on its way out. An alternative and morally neutral vocabulary began to replace the pejoratives "sodomite" and "pederast." The sin of Onan would become the stress-relief reflex of masturbation. The venerable Sodomite would have his last, misspelled rally in 1895, when the Marquess of Queensberry would accuse Oscar Wilde of "posing as a Somdomite" and seducing his son, Lord Alfred Douglas. But the descriptive scientific vocabulary would take decades to settle. The founding work of modern sexology, Richard von Krafft-Ebing's *Psychopathia Sexualis* (1886), would use both Ulrichs's Greek allusions and Kertbeny's medical descriptives. In court, Wilde, a husband and father, would defend himself as a Uranian, not a homosexual or a bisexual. The

Uranian defense would predominate in aristocratic and aesthetic apologia well into the twentieth century.

"How could I think of betraying you!" Nietzsche wrote of his fellow pagans. "I know your kind! You and I—are we not of one kind? You and I—do we not have one secret?"

Nietzsche would boast that he was a moral outlaw, but without naming his crime. Instead, he foresaw a future in which the law and sentence were annulled. After Christian morality, the body would become a "new human flora and fauna," and love neither right nor wrong. A free and expansive sexuality would crash upon the soul in waves, oceanic and overwhelming, with an "infinite white mane of foam and spray."

This erotic overthrow would give birth to a new spirituality. He would gather a brotherhood of the *Unzeitgemässe*, the souls born in the wrong time, into a monastery, a "new Greek academy." The free and noble spirit was male; woman was a "dangerous, creeping, subterranean little beast of prey." High among the rocks, far from the common gaze, he would train an army of erotic scholars, masters of the all-male world.

Perhaps Nietzsche was a bisexual *Uranodioning* with a pedophilic *Zwischen-urning* twist; perhaps he was a *Virilisierte Mannlinge*, a Uranian forced by society to wear a *Dioning*'s mask. His colleagues and students recognized his sexual dilemma. So did the idol for whom Nietzsche, enacting Alcibiades' seduction of Socrates, would create the Greek world anew.

*Nietzsche had discovered Wagner's music and philosophy as a school-*boy at Pforta. His mentor Papa Ritschl's wife was a friend of Wagner's sister's, and Ritschl arranged the introduction. In November 1868, Nietzsche and Wagner met in Leipzig and agreed that Wagner was the Schopenhauerian genius of the age. Wagner invited Nietzsche to join him by the lake at Tribschen, Switzerland, where they might "make music and discuss philosophy."

At Tribschen, Cosima presided in the salon while the master

toiled at his piano like, he joked, a rat playing the flute, and young volunteers transcribed his compositions. In the evening ritual, the household gathered to hear the master reading from choice works, most of them written by him. Nietzsche addressed Wagner as "Master" and Cosima as "Mistress," but both bestowed secret intimacies upon this useful acolyte.

Cosima was a keen occultist. She asked Nietzsche to join her as she tried to levitate tables and summon musical "oracles." She sat him on the sofa and read the libretto of *Parsifal* to him. She allowed Nietzsche to play the master's piano while Wagner took his constitutional by the lake. Nietzsche segued from the preludes to *Tristan* and *Die Meistersinger* into his own compositions, merging the master's sacred harmonies with what sounded to Cosima like impersonations of Schumann. Nietzsche was entranced. Cosima felt a touch of Kierkegaard's "fear and trembling" at his "inner turmoil." Richard pottered unseen along the lake path.

Nietzsche visited Tribschen forty-two times in the next four years, so frequently that Cosima reserved two rooms for him, and Richard, who happened to have been born in the same year as Nietzsche's father, promised to take Nietzsche into his family. The harmonies grew stranger, the dynamics more violent, the improvisation more reckless. After Christmas at Tribschen, Nietzsche wrote a Wagnerian essay, "Socrates and Tragedy." The "progressive enervation of modern man," Nietzsche explained, was the fault of the "optimistic, liberal *Weltanschauung*" of the Jews, the controllers of the world's economy and, worse, its opera houses. These "homeless usurers" and "stateless nomads" must be purged by "war, war, and war again." There must be a slaughter of "purification and consecration" until "everywhere corpses are smoldering on the funeral pyres."

The Wagners were planning a shrine at Bayreuth, a Bavarian resort with good railway links. They thought the professor from Basel could add some academic polish to Wagner's name. When Nietzsche played the piano, Wagner laughed. Nietzsche became their willing servant. He cut out newspaper clippings about the master and tidied the library shelves. He went to Leipzig to fetch a portrait of Wagner's uncle Adolf, to Dresden to collect a lamp from Jews with whom Wagner would not deal directly. The Wagners sent him back to Basel with shopping lists: caviar and caramels, children's toys, the master's favorite silk underwear. He improved the drafts of Wagner's autobiography and took it to the printers. But when he returned with the galleys, the master exploded. The coat of arms on the title page was wrong: the eagle was missing its symbolic ruff. Without it, Wagner complained, an eagle might be mistaken for a *geyer*, a vulture. Perhaps he was thinking of his stepfather.

Nietzsche believed that Germany must be liberated by cultural war, that the Jews were the enemy within, and the French the enemy without. His task was to expound how Wagner's art would liberate the spirit of history. He had written four essays for Wagner and planned a book, to be called "Socrates and Instinct," but then the Franco-Prussian War broke out. He volunteered as a medical orderly; an old injury sustained while recklessly mounting a horse prevented him from bearing arms. Amid the gore and reek of death on the battlefield of Metz, Nietzsche contracted dysentery and diphtheria. His bowels leaking, his ears ringing with a high, screaming sound, he was invalided back to Basel. Recuperating, he wrote a *pneumatische Ausgelung*, a "spiritual" or "soulful explanation" of the horrors. The Prussians were the modern Achaeans, besieging Paris as Achilles and his warriors had besieged Troy. They were fighting to liberate a "second Helen," the Venus de Milo who languished in the Louvre.

As in ancient Greece, death and desire mingled in the abyss of war. "We were giving chloroform to a Frenchman whose hand had been shot to pieces, to put his arm in plaster," Nietzsche noted, "when suddenly he cried out from under the anesthetic, 'My God, my God—I'm coming!'"

*The masked dancers cavort in goat and deer skins. In the rite of delir-*ium, the reborn god Dionysus appears. He rides a chariot drawn by tigers, and he holds in his hand a *thyrsus*, an ivy-wrapped stalk of fennel dripping honey. The audience becomes the dancers, the dancers become their masks. Every man is a goatish satyr, every woman a savage Maenad.

Nietzsche realized that in the minds of the Athenians in the audience, the spectacle had opened a "gulf of oblivion" between the orderly surface of society and the depths revealed by the collective orgies of religion. A new rite was needed to bridge the abyss and its "nausea of the absurd," to ease the *tristesse* of return to lonely consciousness. In the East, where Dionysus was born, this bridge had led to Buddhism, whose passing ecstasies lead to a "longing for the nothing." In the Roman West, this *angst* had undergone "extreme secularization" and been answered in politics, in the Roman ideal of stoical perseverance. Only the Greeks were capable of inventing a third response. Between India and Rome, they had been strong in both Dionysian and political instincts. They had exhausted and consoled themselves neither in "ecstatic brooding" nor in a "consuming scramble for empire and worldly honor." Instead, they had blended a noble wine, the tragic drama.

The sun sets and the rite of consolation begins. The revelers, lethargic and glowing, sit on the warm stones. The music and the song of the satyr chorus begin. On the stage, protagonists die for their individual hubris, resolving their dissonant desires into the cosmic harmony. Dionysus was the first and greatest of the tragic protagonists: the rest, from Prometheus to Oedipus, are "mere masks" of this original hero. All Greek art begins in the inchoate, obscene sounds of his rite, but it ends in order and catharsis. As the chorus comments, the band plays on. A divine dispensation of wisdom and solace is born.

The audience sympathizes intensely with the protagonists' suffering, but this tragic art consoles and calms. The drama cools the insights and ecstasy of the Dionysiac frenzy with the balm of Apollonian rationality. In the "spiritualized introspective eye," the world expands infinitely from the stage, and all is orderly and clear again. The rite of

Dionysus has immersed the Athenians in the "sexual omnipotence of nature," but the Apollonian order of art now carries them back over the abyss and the "vortex" of being, back across the bridge to their everyday personalities. Athenian society is reborn in "fraternal union": *The Birth of Tragedy from the Spirit of Music.*

Even more tragically, the drama degenerated like any other living form. The Apollonian philosophers, Nietzsche believed, had offered an earthly panacea: the dream of reason. Their cult of rationality reduced myth and spirit to the "higher egoism." A managerial elite reduced the cosmos to a small sphere of solvable problems. Apollonian rationality hardened into rigidity, and Athenian culture into a senile twilight. Music deteriorated into abstraction, drama into the slovenly comedies of Euripides. Protagonists no longer evoked the divine by martyrdom but survived through low cunning and flattered their audiences by resemblance. The Dionysian spirit went underground, surviving only in the "degenerate form of a secret cult." When Art no longer explains Nature, Man suffers a "tragic dissonance."

The villain of this degenerate drama is Socrates. Not the inner Socrates, the one whose music carries people away and reveals a desire for the gods and their rites, the one known to his young intimates; but the outer Socrates, the pedant, the demystifier, the gratuitous rationalist. This Socrates is "the mystagogue of science." The Socratic method grinds art, heroism, and the unfathomable into dialectical dust. It drowns beauty and magic in ever-widening circles of concepts, judgments, and inferences. Myth, the "prerequisite of every religion," is paralyzed under the gaze of Socrates' "great Cyclops eye."

Nietzsche saw that the probings of materialist science had forced reason to its intellectual and spiritual limit. The Apollonian tyranny and its claims of universal validity were exhausted. Christianity was dissolving, the Dionysian spirit reemerging. From the decay of science, there would be a rebirth of tragedy. The secret cult, the life of instinct, would return.

First came the bearers of the Aryan myth, Dionysus, Oedipus, and

Prometheus. Then their inheritors: Hamlet, the first modern Diony-sian, paralyzed by his insight as though by Medusa; and the German sages Kant and Schopenhauer. And now Wagner appears, working the "renovation and purification of the German spirit through the fire magic of music." The old knowledge, orgiastic and terrible, is re-vealed. It is again possible to imagine the inner Socrates, the man of instinct and intuition, waiting in the wings of history, ripe like Silenus with little gods.

When Cosima read The Birth of Tragedy from the Spirit of Music, it changed her mind about Nietzsche. The professor from Basel had grasped the source of Wagner's magic, the Dionysian fury of annihilation through art.

"A more beautiful book I have never read!" said Wagner.

The philologists were appalled. Nietzsche played the German phi-losopher's game of generating heat by rubbing together two abstrac-tions, irrational Dionysus and abstract Apollo. He gathered tinder by the academic rules too; the idea that the Attic drama had developed from the festivals of Dionysus came from Karl Otfried Müller's *History of Greek Tragedy* (1857). But Nietzsche kindled his flame with arson in mind. He wanted to burn down the temple of Western ratio-nalism and erect a shrine to Wagner in the ruins. Papa Ritschl called *The Birth of Tragedy* an "inspired waste of energy," and wondered if Nietzsche was megalomaniacal or merely insane. Ulrich Wilamowitz-Moellendorff, the doyen of Classical philology, attacked Nietzsche as the wrong kind of Socrates, a corrupter of impressionable young men.

"I had discovered the only equivalent and counterpart in history for my own inmost experience—and thus became the first to under-stand the wonderful phenomenon of the Dionysian." He hoped that *The Birth of Tragedy* would carry him to a chair in philosophy. Instead his trickle of students dried up, and he suspected his colleagues were laughing at him. The Wagners left for Bayreuth, to build the master's temple. He offered to follow or become Wagner's roving publicist but

Wagner told him to stay at his academic post. The Wagners invited him to Bayreuth only four times in the next five years. The great sickness began: aches in his eyes, throbbing in his brain, churning in his stomach, vomit in his throat, incontinence in his undergarments. He could not sleep without chloral hydrate, an addictive sedative whose cumulative effects included organ failure and hallucination.

Nietzsche had edited *The Birth of Tragedy* on Wagner's advice and allowed Wagner to pilfer his ideas. He had sacrificed his career and health, only to be cast aside, alone and absurd. The Wagners had seduced him.

Wagner advised Nietzsche to marry: "I have never in my life had the contact with men that you have in Basel in the evening hours."

In June 1876, Nietzsche attended at the first rites of Bayreuth. For the opening of his theater, Wagner had prepared a triumph, *The Ring* in its entirety, before an audience of kings and dukes. Nietzsche stayed in the shadows. The sun was too hot, the town crowded and dusty. His eyes and head hurt so badly that, invited to attend rehearsals for *The Ring*, he could only listen from a darkened room. After two weeks, he retreated to a spa.

Nietzsche's next essay, "Richard Wagner at Bayreuth," purported to be a tribute but was a subtle unmasking. Wagner was the supreme artist of his era, but his era was one of perversion. Wagner built Bayreuth, a marvel of fundraising and publicity, in an age when language was diseased and the soul corrupted by money. Wagner's high-minded triumph was a victory of vulgar instinct.

Wagner's response was to send an unsigned note, ordering Nietzsche to buy him some silk shirts and underwear. They met again at the end of the summer, at Sorrento, a resort near Naples. The Wagners were resting after the Bayreuth Festival. Nietzsche was on sick leave from Basel and traveling with a Uranian friend, the philosopher Paul Rée. When the Wagners realized that Rée was Jewish, they snubbed him. Nietzsche might think he had subjugated Rée, Cosima said, but the clever "Israelite" would outwit him, as it ever was with

"Judah and Germania." After an evening walk alone with Nietzsche, Wagner departed for Rome. They would never see each other again.

The Wagners never left treason unpunished. In October 1877, Nietzsche, his health worsening, was examined by his doctor, Otto Eiser. A founder of the Wagner Society of Frankfurt, Eiser had written an article on *The Ring*. He asked Nietzsche to forward it to Wagner. Nietzsche obliged and also shared a description of his symptoms with Wagner. Wagner wrote to Eiser, professing concern but assassinating Nietzsche's character:

"As I follow the development of N.'s malady, I find myself reminded of identical and similar cases on other occasions with talented young men. These young men fell victim to similar symptoms, and I was made all too clearly aware that these symptoms were the result of masturbation." Eiser showed Wagner's letter to Nietzsche. He was furious: he knew how the Wagners worked through whisperings and "spiteful tricks."

By the second Bayreuth Festival, in 1882, an innuendo would attach itself to Nietzsche. He was a deserter, a degenerate, a criminal. Wagner, Nietzsche complained, "wrote letters—even to my doctors—in order to convey his conviction that my changes of temperament were the result of unnatural perversions, with allusions to paederasty."

In 1879, the year that Blavatsky and Olcott left for India, Karl Heinrich Ulrichs retreated from Germany to L'Aquila in Italy, pursued by prosecutors. In the same year, the Scottish aesthete Horatio Brown moved with his mother to Venice, where they became pillars of Anglo-American expatriate society, and Brown the lover of a muscular gondolier named Antonio Salin. The Mediterranean peoples took a more tolerant view of Uranians, especially discreet travelers with money to spend. Northerners in search of forbidden sex no longer had to rough it in North Africa like Flaubert or the explorer Sir Richard Burton.

As Ruskin had foreseen, modern transportation allowed the middle classes to afford the aristocrat's Grand Tour. The Mediterranean was now Europe's resort, with intersecting train and steamer schedules, and full-board hotels with multilingual menus and guided day trips to the lagoon and the souk. Permanent expatriate communities developed: businessmen and teachers, retirees stretching their pensions, remittance men kept at arm's length by payments from home. Not all the visitors came for the sights. Inadvertently, Thomas Cook and his ilk facilitated a wave of sex tourism. From Tangiers to Capri, Venice to Cairo, the weather was better and the money went further.

In the year that Ulrichs and Brown retired to Italy, a sickly bachelor from Basel went south with a professor's pension. Nietzsche left the barren and petty "house of the scholars" and took off his "socks of the spirit." He left the cults of Germany and Wagner and became a stateless nomad. He declared himself an immoralist, pursuing philosophy as an art, a *décadent* in the French style; among painters, Prussian blue is also known as Paris blue. As his body changed under the sun, so did his style. He became a master aphorist, mingling pellets of insight and paradox with poems and lyric visions.

The true artist, Flaubert said, must find "a bitter undertaste in everything" and be disengaged from religion, motherland, and society. For the next nine years, Nietzsche worked his way up and down the "blessed isles," sometimes with Paul Rée or another close friend, but ultimately alone. In his solitude, Nietzsche cultivated a new and superior kind of universal man.

Marx had named Prometheus as the "foremost saint and martyr in the philosopher's calendar." Nietzsche now stole the divine fire and became the foremost saint and martyr of the New Age: a self-made icon, individual, defiant, and unrepentant. From his revolt the West would receive Zarathustra, its first new god in eighteen centuries. "You shall create a higher body, a first movement, a self-propelled wheel— you shall create a creator."

The God of the Christians was dead. "We have killed him—you and I. All of us are his murderers." Modern science and philosophy had refuted Christian history and annulled the Christian chronology.

Perhaps the Almighty still floated somewhere out there in the empty cosmos, soft-brained and weak-willed like Nietzsche's father, unhearing and unspeaking like the ghost in *Hamlet.* Meanwhile, Christian ethics expired on earth. Western man, the would-be new Prometheus, had lost his bearings. "Whither are we moving? Away from all suns? Are we not plunging continually? Backward, sideward, forward, in all directions? Is there still any up or down? Are we not straying as through an infinite nothing?"

Nietzsche saw himself as the "last man": a witness to the death agonies of the Christian age—and a visionary who saw the dawning rays of the New Age. Man always sacrificed what he most loved. Pagan man had sacrificed other humans to the gods. Christian man, internalizing a cruel morality, had offered up his own strongest instincts, his biological nature. Now the long and onerous age of morality was over. The evolution of faith had reached the top of the "great ladder of religious cruelty." From the top step, the pastor's son contemplated the "oddly painful and equally crude and subtle comedy of European Christianity" with the "mocking and aloof eyes of an Epicurean god." The view amazed and appalled him, so much so that he could not stop laughing.

What Nietzsche saw was the "genealogy of morals," the evolution of Man's spirit and society. Every morality was a "precipitate" of its historical circumstance, a hypothesis "like astrology or alchemy." The ethics of the first civilization, the Aryan, had prized "aristocratic values" and noble blood. In heroic loyalty to their bloodlines, the Aryans had construed the value of actions through not consequences but origins. The ethic of the successor civilization had been a catastrophic moral "reversal." The Jews had countered the Aryan ethic with a "calamitous new superstition," a faith in rational intent. The Christians, misled by their Jewish priests, had raised this into the tyranny of conscience, in which the value of an act derived from good intentions.

Modern man, whether philosopher, psychologist, or immoralist, knew that this morality of good intentions was false. The intentional and conscious belonged only to "the surface and the skin." They were meaningful only as a "sign and symptom" of deeper processes. An intention, Nietzsche observed, is like a buoy marking a hidden shoal in the sea: it "betrays something but *conceals* even more." The "decisive value of an action lies precisely in what is *unintentional* about it." In Nietzsche's biological morality as in Eduard von Hartmann's philosophy and Darwin's evolution, conscious acts emerge from instinctual drives and the snake pit of species life.

"O you dolts, you presumptuous, pitying dolts, what have you done?" The Christian age was a cosmic joke that grew more bitter and hollow as its punch line lost its meaning. The dream of reason led only to the abyss of atheism and nihilism, an almost Buddhist worship of "the stone, stupidity, gravity, fate, the nothing." Yet the "religious instinct" could not be denied. The death of the Christian father-god was a liberation from long repression. It was time for a new self-understanding, another "growth in profundity": a "fundamental shift in values" that would restore Man's center of gravity. Nietzsche remembered the words of Emerson, his "Brother-Soul" in nihilism.

"If I do not discover the alchemist's trick of turning even this— excrement into *gold*, I am lost.—Thus I have the most *beautiful* opportunity to prove that for me 'all experiences are profitable, all days holy, and all men divine'!!!!"

*Stepping off the top of the ladder, he finds himself floating like Pro-*metheus unbound. He sees all, feels all, knows all. "Verily like the sun I love life and all deep seas. And that is what perceptive knowledge means to me: all that is deep shall rise up to my heights."

Nietzsche called this weightless, perfect, godlike intuition by Emerson's name: the "Joyous Science," the *Fröliche Wissenschaft*. In his journal, Emerson had called himself a "professor of the Joyous Science, a detector & delineator of occult harmonies & unpublished beauties . . . an affirmer of the One Law, yet as one who should affirm it in music or dancing, a priest of the Soul, yet one who would better love to celebrate it through the beauty of health and harmonious power." Nietzsche cannot have known this, but he knew Emerson's lectures. "Ascending souls congratulate each other on the admirable harmonies of the world," says a figure called "the Magian" in "Prospects," an Emerson lecture of 1842. "We read another commission in the cipher of nature: we were made for another office, the Joyous Science."

Nietzsche reread Emerson almost yearly. He annotated with furious approval and copied favorite passages into a notebook. When he left his Emerson set on a railway platform, he bought new volumes and annotated them all over again. Emerson had declared his independence, warred against moral complacency, and become a practical, aphoristic philosopher. "Life is a search after power," he wrote, and power the vital force of life, the great will that lives in "the moment of transition from a past to a new state." If we are to accept fate, Emerson advised, we are equally compelled to "affirm liberty, the significance of the individual, the grandeur of duty, the power of character." It was a prescription for Nietzsche's revolt into health.

Nietzsche traced the roots of his personal rebirth to the origins of the European Renaissance in the *gai saber* or *gaia scienzia*, the "joyous science" or "happy knowledge," of the Provençal love poets. Like the German *Wissenschaft*, *scienzia* can also mean the kind of knowledge that constitutes itself as a sensory fact, an aesthetic impression. This is the "science" of the Scottish journalist Eneas Sweetland Dallas's search for the sources of literary pleasure in *The Gay Science* (1866). It was also the science of Walter Pater, the English Uranian who called the *gai saber* a series of beautiful "pulsations." In *The Renaissance* (1873), Pater used the letters of the "pagan" Winckelmann to show that the scholar whom Hegel had praised as initiating "a new organ for the human spirit" had believed that the supreme beauty of Greek art was "rather male than female." Pater had defended Winckelmann's "romantic, fervent friendships with young men" too. They brought Winckelmann "into contact with the pride of the human form" and "perfected his reconciliation to the spirit of Greek sculpture"—a perfection "staining the thoughts with its bloom."

Pater, the London *Quarterly Review* complained, used "the most advanced modern science" to present a world "completely uninfluenced by the moral side of our nature." He talked of science but argued for art and Epicureanism, and against Christianity. "To burn always with this hard, gemlike flame, to maintain this ecstasy, is success in life," Pater wrote in *The Renaissance*. "Not the fruit of experience, but experience itself, is the end. How shall we pass most swiftly from point to point, and be present always at the focus where the greatest number of vital forces unite in their purest energy?"

"With knowledge, the body purifies itself," Nietzsche concurred, "making experiments with knowledge, it elevates itself; in the lover of knowledge all instincts become holy; in the elevated the soul becomes gay."

Nietzsche followed Emerson's cue when he named his god. Zarathustra is Zoroaster, the "Magian" of Emerson's essay, and the Persian fire god that Gobineau had imagined rising from the embers of Islam.

Nietzsche's Zarathustra is a fusion of man and divinity, a little god hatched from the "light and heat" of consciousness. He does not lurk on the margins with the Russian doubles and Socratic spiders. He rises from below, from the body, a force and its master. "It is not enough for me that lightning no longer does any harm. I do not wish to conduct it away: it shall learn to work for me." He reads the runes of his flesh and accepts his intuitions of glory and fate. "Thus alone—thus alone, man grows to the height where lightning strikes and breaks him: lofty enough for lightning." And he laughs, stepping high over the void in philosophical abandon. "Brave is he who knows fear but conquers fear, who sees the abyss, but with pride. Who sees the abyss but with the eyes of an eagle; who grasps the abyss with the talons of an eagle—that man has courage." When everything is alive, all life is holy. Laughing, light, lithe Zarathustra dons his "rose-wreath crown" and dances like David before the Tabernacle.

"Zarathustra the dancer, Zarathustra the light, waves with his wings, ready for flight, waving at all birds, ready and heady, happily light-headed; Zarathustra the soothsayer, Zarathustra the sooth-laugher, not impatient, not unconditional, one who loves leaps and side-leaps: I myself have put on this crown!"

⚘ 9 ⚘

THE ETERNAL RETURN

Colonel Olcott and
the Modern Buddha

> New struggles.—After Buddha was dead, his shadow
> was still shown for centuries in a cave—a tremendous,
> gruesome shadow. God is dead; but given the way of
> men, there may still be caves for thousands of years in
> which his shadow will be shown.—And we—we still
> have to vanquish his shadow, too. —*Nietzsche*, The Gay
> Science *(1882)*

S*adhu! Sadhu!*" The crowd on the dock acclaimed the man on the
ship. "Holy man!"

In May 1880, Colonel Olcott and Madame Blavatsky took a P&O
steamer to Colombo, Ceylon. They descended to a jetty decked in
white cloth and mounted the waiting carriage to the acclaim of their
admirers. They met Buddhist dignitaries and saw the sights, including one of the Buddha's teeth, preserved in a temple at Kandy. On
May 25, they visited the Wijananda monastery in Galle. Kneeling
before a large statue of the Buddha, they "took pansil," reciting in Pali
the precepts of Theravada Buddhism.

Blavatsky and Olcott were the first European and the first American to formally become Buddhists. They understood neither the language nor the full meaning of their vows, but they felt that they were

Buddhists at heart, if not in mind. In New York, Blavatsky had called herself a "benighted Buddhist," even as she steered Theosophy toward Hinduism. Olcott, a seeker easily led, reached a similar conclusion: Buddhism held the answer to the spiritual crisis of the West.

For nearly a century, Westerners had struggled to understand what a "Buddhist" was. Their information came from hostile or partial witnesses: Christian missionaries hunting for converts; Hindu Brahmins seeking to discredit their rivals; British officials searching for the Romantic Orient; and Westernized Buddhists pining for its chimerical twin, the rational Occident. The Hindus admitted the Buddha to their pantheon as the ninth of the ten incarnations of Vishnu, the supreme deity, but as a deceiver who had come to trick them away from the Vedas. To Christians, a creed that seemed to aspire to nothingness could hardly be called a religion. They had a name for belief without God: atheism.

From European reports, Olcott gathered that the Buddha, the "enlightened" Prince Gautama Siddhartha, had been born in Nepal just over five centuries before the birth of Jesus. The Buddha, then, had been a contemporary of the priests of Zoroaster, who held that the divine was an eternal unity, a thought permeating all matter, and that time was an illusion. The historical Buddha, like the historical Jesus, seemed often to have been unsure as to his purpose. Was he an innovator, a heretical son speaking new truths to the priests of Brahma, like the Jesus of the Gospels? Or was he a renovator and restorer like Isaiah, rejecting Hindu temple cults as the degenerate offspring of a purer tradition?

Many of Olcott's sources believed that there had been more than one Buddha. Sir William Jones identified two: first an originator identical with Vishnu, and then Gautama, whom the Hindus had rejected as a heretic. Others thought that Gautama had been the last of four Buddhas. Each had taught the same "noble truths," but because people had been forgetful, they had received each Buddha as the first. This explanation had the virtue of consistency, in that forgetting seemed as important to Buddhists as remembering was to the Jews. This amnesia was essential: Buddhists believed that the soul died with the body but was reincarnated according to the moral value of the body's conduct. The cycle could repeat forever, with personality dissolving and re-forming in each life, or it could end when a soul improved to the point of perfection, nirvana.

Olcott knew that Buddhism, while almost extinct in India, had developed into two schools. The earliest European reports described the southern, Theravada school in Ceylon, Siam, and Burma. In 1799, Francis Buchanan of the Bengal Medical Service had described nirvana as "the most perfect of all states, consisting in a kind of annihilation, in which beings are free from change, misery, death, sickness, or old age." Otherwise, Buchanan surmised, Buddhists were fatalists, and "strictly speaking, atheists." When they spoke of "gods," they meant men who had acquired "supreme happiness" through "virtue." This picture of philosophical atheism was complicated by the discovery in the 1820s of the northern, Mahayana school. The Buddhists encountered by the civil servant B. H. Hodgson in Nepal worshipped a pantheon of gods, like the Hindus did. They followed speculative, mystical doctrines, and their stock of saints, devils, and ghosts exceeded that of the most superstitious Mediterranean villagers. Like the southerners, these northerners claimed to practice the original Buddhism.

For Olcott, only one of the two schools carried the authentic, pure light of Asia. The other must be degenerate, a weakened flame. But which was which?

*The Theosophist, like the professor of Joyous Science, advanced by re*turning to the "root idea" of "knowledge." Olcott, an errant Presbyterian, decided that Buddhism had grown from Hinduism in the way that Protestantism had grown from Catholicism. Gautama had been a Luther in a loincloth, a renovator who unleashed a revolution. Just as Protestants attended to their Bibles while Catholics persisted in fiddling with incense and wafers, so the original Buddhists would cleave to their textual inspirations while the inauthentic ones digressed into ritual and superstition. By this illogic, Olcott guessed—correctly, it turned out—that the southern, Theravada school was older.

Unfortunately, the law of spiritual entropy still applied. In Ceylon, Olcott found not the pure "old religion" of Gautama but its "debased modern" varieties. Upon inspection, Olcott found that the Sinhalese mind was riddled with superstition, dogma, and caste prejudice. Not only had Gautama's wisdom been perverted by the usual tyranny of priests and kings. After the Portuguese conquest in 1509, waves of Christian missionaries washed over the island: Catholics, Dutch Reformers, and Anglicans. In 1815, the British annulled the Sinhalese monarchy in the name of George III. The Sinhalese priests, deprived of their secular muscle, retreated to their monasteries and left their people to be bombarded with Christian tracts. By 1880, British administrators supervised twelve hundred schools in Ceylon. All taught English as the language of government, commerce, and social advancement, and all but four taught Christianity as its spiritual complement.

The response of the Sinhalese priests seemed to confirm Olcott's assumption that the history of Protestantism was a kind of Baedeker's guide to other people's faiths. The Sinhalese priests had launched a Buddhist reformation, using the technology of Luther's people. In 1862, they founded two Buddhist printing presses, one of them acquired from Christian missionaries. After a monk named Migettuwatte Gunananda read one of their magazines, *Buddhist Brotherhood*, he founded the Society for the Propagation of Buddhism, modeled on the missionary arm of the Anglican Church, the Society for the Propagation of the Gospel. In 1873, the war of souls culminated in a two-day public debate at Panadura between Migettuwatte Gunananda and the Wesleyan missionary David de Silva. A home crowd of five thousand awarded a symbolic victory to Gunananda. In the loser's corner, Reginald Copleston, the Anglican bishop of Colombo, attributed the defeat to native resentment of the imperial power.

When Olcott read about the Panadura *disputatio* in J. M. Peebles's *Buddhism and Christianity Face to Face,* he wrote to Gunananda, describing the Theosophical Society and its aims. Gunananda invited him and Blavatsky to Ceylon. In his six-week tour of the island, Olcott met Gunananda's allies Hikkaduwe Sumangala and Sumangala Unase, the high priest of the temple atop Adam's Peak, Ceylon's highest mountain. Olcott realized that their religious revolt was, like the Protestant revolt, inherently political. The Buddhists of Ceylon shared a faith, language, history, and territory. Now they needed an army. The followers of Luther and Calvin showed Olcott how to organize one. Before returning to Bombay, he founded a school and eight lodges of the Buddhist Theosophical Society.

At dinner with the Colombo lodge, Olcott sat beneath a banner depicting two hands, one black, one white, clasped under the slogan "Brotherhood." Another banner wrapped the room in a "condensed statement of the law of Karma." The return to spiritual fundamentals was a new political venture. "The Past you cannot recall," he told the Buddhist Theosophicals, though they probably knew that already. "The Present is yours. The Future will be what you make it."

As Blavatsky began to make her Indian future, she was recalled to her Egyptian past. Within weeks of her arrival in Bombay, two ghosts from Cairo sent her a letter.

Emma Cutting and Alexis Coulomb had left Cairo for Calcutta because of a misunderstanding over an insurance claim. Emma had found work as an English teacher and lady's maid, but her health had collapsed. They had moved to Galle in Ceylon, gambled Emma's earnings on a hotel, and lost. A scheme to grow European vegetables for the local whites left them penniless and exhausted. When Emma read in *The Times of Ceylon* that Blavatsky had landed on her feet in Bombay, she and Alexis took the chance as a "God-send." She wrote to their "old acquaintance" and appealed for help.

Blavatsky knew that the Coulombs intended to blackmail her. She had no choice but to surrender and share the spoils of Theosophy, if only temporarily. In March 1880, the Coulombs came to the Theo-sophical Society's Indian base, a rented villa in a native quarter of Bombay. Blavatsky managed to produce a cry of joy. She appointed Emma as her housekeeper and Alexis as the society's handyman. Now Blavatsky held the Coulombs as they held her: three unwilling accomplices, bound by the honor of thieves. Together, they must work wonders.

Blavatsky installed the Coulombs in a bedroom over Olcott's office. She told Alexis to cut a hole in the floor and gave Emma an envelope containing a photograph. One evening, as the Colonel and Blavatsky conversed in the office with a Hindu guest, Emma reached into the hole and mailed the envelope through a slit in the ceiling cloth of the room below. To Olcott's astonishment, a portrait of a yogi, mislaid during the move from the apartment in New York, now tumbled down through the air before his very eyes.

Blavatsky told Emma not to feel guilty. The Colonel had experi-enced "certain painful occurrences" in America, and he needed his il-lusions. If not for Blavatsky, he "certainly would have destroyed himself." This was not the first time she had defied the laws of physics on his behalf. In their first weeks in Bombay, she had climbed through his window to stop him from shooting himself.

Blavatsky was also in need of a miracle or two. The society's first year in India had not gone as planned. Only a handful of Hindus had joined, and most of them seemed inauthentic, soaked in the hybrid Anglo-Indian civilization that she despised. She blamed that scoun-drel Hurrychund Chintamon.

In New York, Olcott's Hindu friends had told him that as Theos-ophy turned east, India was turning to meet it. A Hindu reformer named Swami Dayananda Saraswati had founded a movement for the "resuscitation of the pure Vedic religion," the Arya Samaj, the Noble or Aryan Society. Correspondence with Chintamon, the president of the Samaj's Bombay chapter, had convinced Olcott that its principles were identical to those of Theosophy. Both groups believed in the im-personality of God, and that all religions reflected a single "Eternal and Omnipresent Principle." Chintamon had suggested that they amalgamate. In May 1878, Olcott and Blavatsky persuaded their committee in New York to agree, and they renamed the group the Theosophical Society of the Arya Samaj. This was history's first formal union of Eastern and Western religions.

A few weeks later, Blavatsky and Olcott had received a "great shock" when an English translation of the Arya Samaj's doctrines arrived in the mail. The Eternal and Omnipresent Principle was still universal, but it now emerged that Swami Saraswati was its "supreme judge" and that he, not Blavatsky, would decide which parts of the Vedas and Shastras were infallible. The two societies believed that they were annexing each other. Fearing their absorption into a Hindu rival, the Theosophicals annulled the alliance but retained a loose affiliation. Interested members could join a subsect, the Theosophical Society of the Arya Samaj of Aryavart.

Despite these losses in translation, Hurrychund Chintamon had met the *Speke Hall* in Bombay with dancing girls, musicians, and a white elephant, onto whose back Blavatsky had been levered by "naked coolies." Chintamon had taken his guests into his home. He had shown them the sculptures of Shiva as half-man, half-woman at Elephanta. He had garlanded them with flowers at a reception for three hundred of his friends. He had even taken them to the theater. Then he had presented his bill, which included repairs to his house and the rental of three hundred chairs. When Blavatsky asked about the six hundred rupees that Olcott had sent as a gift to the Arya Samaj, Chintamon admitted that he had spent it.

In April 1879, Chintamon took Blavatsky and Olcott across India to meet Dayananda Saraswati at Saharanpur in Uttar Pradesh. Saraswati was impressively tall, pleasantly pale, and alarmingly prone to modulate from a "sweet, almost feminine whisper of admonition" to thundering wrath against the "evil doings and falsehoods" of the Brahmins. Blavatsky thought this promising: his attack on the priests and aristocrats suggested that he was a survival of the original Vedic religion, one of "the ancient Gymnosophists mentioned by the Greek and Roman writers." Before his emergence as the scourge of Hindu priestcraft, Saraswati had lived as a hermit in the jungle and studied the occult meaning of the Vedas with "mystics and anchorites." He was, Blavatsky decided, the "Luther of India."

For his part, Saraswati took the Theosophists to be exotic *chelas*, "disciples." Olcott's letters and Chintamon's reports confirmed this assumption, and so did Olcott's behavior when they met. "Look at us, our teacher: tell us what we ought to do," Olcott begged, assuming his habitual posture. "We place ourselves under your instruction."

But the summit meeting of the soul at Saharanpur disappointed both parties. Saraswati shunned Blavatsky as a woman, and possibly mad. He would only address Olcott, and even then he wanted to talk about his career. Disheartened, the Theosophists left for Bombay. They arrived with the monsoon. The Theosophical garden flooded, and the bungalow filled with bedraggled scorpions, lizards, and snakes. The roof leaked, and Blavatsky and Olcott had to sit under umbrellas in the drawing room on rotting furniture. At night Olcott wept over pictures of his sons. Blavatsky stomped around, killing cockroaches the size of small mice and spiders the size of large crabs.

The arranged marriage of Theosophy and the Arya Samaj lasted two years. It ended in claims of mutual infidelity, with both parties naming the same co-respondent. For arranging the union of East and West, Hurrychund Chintamon became the first person to be expelled from both the Theosophical Society and the Arya Samaj. Later, Blavatsky would call Saraswati devious and tyrannical. Saraswati would accuse Blavatsky of willful misinterpretation and deception. In 1882, he would send the Arya Samaj into the streets to denounce her.

Dayananda Saraswati was no fossil. He was a modern fundamentalist and nationalist, a pioneer of *Hindutva*, political "Hindu-ness." Blavatsky was a foreign woman, and Theosophy cosmopolitan in the imperial style; Saraswati was not a good match. But there were, Blavatsky discovered, more congenial Hindu partners.

Dayananda's base of operations was in Calcutta, the epicenter of British influence in Bengal. By the early 1800s, Calcutta's commercial and political role had created a class of affluent Bengali middlemen. They had raised their children to acquire British habits of mind while observing Hindu traditions. The children learned the British lesson that India had been weakened by despotism and barbarism. They absorbed the Protestant definition of religion as a private practice, and they learned the philosophical complement of religious freedom, freedom of inquiry. Then, as adults, they met the political and social barriers of liberal despotism and British bigotry. As they fell back on their own culture, their impulse to revive Hindu culture expressed itself along the European lines of their education. Liberal and utilitarian ideals would release the repressed spiritual energies of Hindu civilization.

With this political-religious kedgeree, the "Bengal Renaissance" began. The first reformers had more in common with the British than with their fellow Hindus. When the "Hindu Unitarian" Ram Mohan Roy founded the Brahmo Samaj, the One God Society, he was acclaimed by the Utilitarian Society in London but reviled in Calcutta. When Debendranath Tagore revitalized the Brahmo Samaj in the 1840s, the group remained upper caste and pro-British. In the 1850s, however, the picture changed, first with the founding of the British Indian Association, which took a skeptical view of the British and claimed to speak for all Indians; and then after the Indian Revolt of 1857.

The British, now wary of meddling with Hindu sensibilities, no longer agreed with the reformers that the caste system was an obstacle to progress; after the Mutiny, caste looked like a source of stability. In the 1860s, the Brahmo Samaj split. The "progressives" under Keshab Chandra Sen seceded, forming a pro-British group, with Sen as its secretary and God as its president. While Sen developed Christian leanings and told Queen Victoria that the Raj was a moral force for India's modernization, Debendranath Tagore steered the rest of the Brahmo Samaj away from universalism and toward Hindu identity. From the late 1860s, the Tagore family underwrote Calcutta's annual

Hindu Mela, a cultural fair with patriotic anthems written by junior members of the family; the anthem of 1875 was written by Tagore's son Rabindranath, a future winner of the Nobel Prize in Literature. In the same year, Dayananda Saraswati founded the Arya Samaj.

As the crowds at the Hindu Mela showed, the reformers now had a public. Nearly fifty years had passed since Thomas Macaulay's education reforms. In 1855, there were 55 English schools in India. In 1882, there were 209; by 1902, there would be 1,481. India's first university opened in Calcutta in 1857. By the end of the century, the eight thousand students at Calcutta University would be the world's largest enrollment. India now had a modern middle class, the group whose rising expectations had been crucial to Europe's revolutions.

To reach these English-speaking Indians, and reconcile Hindu reform with Theosophy, Blavatsky launched a journal, *The Theosophist*. For its editor she chose Damodar Mavalankar, a young Brahmin from Bombay. When it came to recruiting the committee who would manage it, she looked to the bungalows of the British.

In late 1880, Blavatsky and Olcott spent six weeks at the home of Al-fred Percy Sinnett and his wife, Patience, in Allahabad, the capital of the North-Western Provinces.

Alfred Sinnett edited *The Pioneer*, Allahabad's "most influential" English daily. Patience was a charming hostess who lived up to her name. The Sinnetts were keen "mediumistic" dabblers, and they wanted Blavatsky's help in fathoming "the laws of the phenomena." Blavatsky won their trust by betraying the tricks of the Spiritualist's trade and showing them how mediums created their raps. She won their allegiance when Koot Hoomi strewed their house with tiny cards and letters tied in blue silk.

Enchanted, the Sinnetts invited Blavatsky and Olcott to join the annual British migration to Simla, the Raj's summer capital in the Himalayan foothills. At Simla, Koot Hoomi's postal round expanded to include the Sinnetts' friends: Syed Mahmood, the district judge; Alice, the wife of Colonel William Gordon of the Bengal staff corps;

and Allan Hume, a retired civil servant whose hobbies included bird-watching, radical politics, and the afterlife.

Blavatsky formed her Simla circle into the Eclectic Theosophical Society, a research center to rival Olcott's Buddhist Theosophicals at Ceylon. She titillated her Eclectics with parlor tricks. She tore up a cigarette and reproduced it intact. She told Allan Hume that his wife's brooch, which his daughter had lost in Bombay, was waiting for him in a star-shaped flowerbed in his garden. After a "prolonged and careful" night search with lanterns, Patience Sinnett found the brooch among the leaves, wrapped in two cigarette papers. The brooch, Blavatsky explained, had been "transmitted": broken down into "infinitely minute particles," conveyed on the currents of the *akasha*, the magnetic ether, and then "reintegrated at its destination."

When the Eclectics, picnicking on rugs in the woods, found themselves a teacup and saucer short, Madame directed Major Henderson, the chief superintendent of the Simla police, to dig under a nearby cedar tree. There, tangled in the roots, he found the necessary china, matched to the set in the Sinnetts' pantry. Henderson made inquiries among the ladies. Patience Sinnett vouched that her servants would never betray her by abetting a fraud. Blavatsky refused to answer, because Henderson was not a Theosophist. When Henderson asked to join the Society, she told him his membership diploma was waiting on a nearby branch, tied with blue string. The party plunged into the shrubbery once more.

Apart from being a policeman, Major Henderson was a leading light in the Simla Amateur Dramatic Club. As he parted the lower branches of a deodar bush and saw his diploma, he responded like a player in a country house farce.

"I have it!" he cried.

In the spring of 1881, Olcott booked his return to Ceylon. When he told Blavatsky, she locked herself in her room for a week. She told him he could go to "Timbuctoo," for all she cared: she would not be going back to Ceylon with him. The Sinhalese monks had shunned her and refused to shake her hand because a woman was impure. Koot Hoomi, who had already given astral approval to Olcott's plan, now changed his mind. The masters, Hoomi warned, would withdraw their favor from the society if Olcott continued to defy them.

Madame had not expected that the Ceylonese would acclaim pliant Olcott as "the White Buddhist." Nor was she prepared for his response. If the masters were such "vacillating and whimsical creatures," he told Blavatsky, then he would do without them, even if he "never saw the face of a Master again."

Blavatsky lacked Olcott's male privileges. With letters from his contacts in Washington, he had wafted into Bombay "with the Govt. seal on his backside." As a white English-speaking gentleman, he could waft out just as easily and leave her stranded. Blavatsky's only male prerogative was her inner "HPB." With a past like hers, she had no choice: Theosophy must succeed in India. For that, she needed Olcott. She emerged from her room in time to escort Olcott to his boat. The next night, a master confirmed that the whole situation had been an astral misunderstanding.

In Ceylon, Olcott set up the National Education Fund for a network of Buddhist schools, then set off for the villages of the western provinces. He customized a bullock cart into a cross between a preacher's caravan and a pioneer wagon, with compartments for his books and furniture and removable planks for a collapsible dining table. With Gunananda as his interpreter, he preached to the peasants. Most of them, he discovered, watered their Buddhism with "primitive nature-worship," magic, and "devil-dancing."

The children in Olcott's schools would need a primer. Given the "dense popular ignorance" of the parents, only he could write it. Since the Reformation, simple question-and-answer books had worked miracles of indoctrination. The Ceylonese could use something similar as an "antidote" to Christianity. *The Buddhist Catechism,* written on Olcott's collapsible dining table and printed on a Sinhalese press, appeared in English and Sinhalese on July 24, 1881.

1. *Q. Of what religion are you?*
   A. The Buddhist.
2. *Q. What is Buddhism?*
   A. It is the body of teachings given out by a great
   personage known as the Buddha.
3. *Q. Was Buddha a God?*
   A. No.

The respondent in Olcott's script was a child under the inquisition of a particularly sophistic missionary, a tropical Torquemada. After a simple start, the exchanges grew more complex and harsh. The inquisitor jabbed relentlessly, probing for philosophical flabbiness and blind spots of compassion, but the infant Buddhist parried gamely. Crammed with useful facts about Buddhism, he knew a lot about Christianity too, and used it to wrong-foot his tormentor. He called his philosophy a religion, then explained why it was not a religion, but a philosophy. He described the Buddha's life and mission, then said that Buddha was not so much a person as he was an idea.

A Christian might learn a lot from this manly, rational philosophy. The Buddha, it transpired, took a positively Calvinistic line on sex, drink, idol worship, and mixed dancing. A scientific materialist might agree that belief in souls and miracles was ignorant and unscientific. And all would be relieved to learn that Buddhism could survive in a world of science.

70. *Q.* Is this Buddhistical doctrine supported or denied by
    the teachings of modern science?
    A. It is in reconciliation with science, since it is the
    doctrine of cause and effect. Science teaches that
    man is the result of a law of development, from an
    imperfect and lower, to a higher and perfect condition.
71. *Q.* What is this doctrine of science called?
    A. Evolution.

The scientists and Buddhists agreed that some living creatures reached "perfection" faster than others. While the "men of science" attributed an organism's evolved form to "the influences (Environment) that surrounded the previous generation," Buddhists attributed the nature of the reincarnation to karma. Not all men could become Buddhas, but when they did, their knowledge outstripped that of the scientists. Wherever science reached, Buddhism waited, rational and patient, and all under the elastic, ever-expanding rubric of Theosophy.

On some matters, the Buddhists were well ahead of the scientists. Not until 1844 had Baron von Reichenbach identified the *Buddha-ransi*, the divine radiance that shone from the Buddha's body, as the "human aura." Similarly, the modern theory of hypnotic suggestion was a rediscovery of *manomaya iddhi*, the Buddhist's ability to "impress pictures" on other people's minds by "thought and trained willpower." The further recovery of lost knowledge would bring wonders. As Gautama Siddhartha had known, a Buddhist could interact with "races of elemental invisible beings" on planets more perfect than Earth. If he conquered his "baser nature," he could work magic, even master these invisible personages still unknown to science. Reincarnation, Olcott now knew, could place a soul in any of the universe's numberless and inhabited worlds.

"Let us pursue this thought in its most terrible form: existence as it is, without meaning or aim, but inevitably recurring, without ending in nothingness: the eternal recurrence."

In the summer of 1881 Nietzsche retired from the heat to the village of Sils Maria in the Swiss Alps. He would return there every year. Each morning, he set off for the woods and valleys with his red parasol; too much sunlight hurt his eyes. From the hills, the villages seemed tiny like toys, the peasants in the fields as small as ants. He walked for up to eight hours a day. In the evenings, he wrote in a simple, cavelike room with a bed, a writing table and lamp, a washstand, a small sofa, and a view of a damp rock face.

Two weeks after the publication of Olcott's *Buddhist Catechism*, Nietzsche was walking in the woods by the lake of Silvaplana when a revelation struck. Stopping by a "huge, pyramidal boulder," he pulled out his notebook and wrote "Eternal Return." He sensed that all life was an infinite and unconditionally repeated cycle. There was no fixity, only an endless flux, a stream of becoming. Matter and energy formed and diffused, over and over again. Existence had no end: there was no heaven, no nirvana, no finale in nothingness, only implacable, meaningless fate. The individual was tied to the wheel of life, remembering and forgetting, rising and falling from joy to despair.

"This is the most extreme form of nihilism: nothingness (That is, 'meaninglessness') for ever!" It seemed to be the most unbearable of thoughts: a vision of pain without end or sense. It was not, he knew, a novelty. The circularity of life had been a common image in ancient religions and philosophies, Greek and Indian. Nietzsche had just read Hermann Oldenburg's new biography of the Buddha and recognized that Gautama too had known this feeling of straying through an infinite nothing attended only by the consciousness of suffering. Buddhism, Nietzsche surmised, had arisen from an earlier death of God. A loss of belief in Brahma, the highest god, had led to a general loss of meaning, an inability to discern the *brahman*, the reality within and above the physical world. Now, science had carried Christians along the same "evolutionary course."

For two thousand years, Christians had believed that everything good, everything that gave meaning to life, lay outside and beyond their world, in heaven or in a time to come. The Apollonian onslaught of reason had discredited these dreams and broken the Christian faith that time was as sure and straight as an arrow from God's bow. Once, Christians had illustrated the grandeur of man by looking back to a divine origin. After Darwin, this was impossible. If they looked back, they saw not God enthroned but "the ape, together with other gruesome beasts, grinning knowingly as if to say: no further in this direction!" Meanwhile, the positivists and the priests of progress carried the West forward with a mechanical and materialist science that ignored the spirit and constructed cause and effect from mere appearances. Thrown by their excess of knowledge and strength, Christians had become nihilists, believers in nothing. "It is a European form of Buddhism; the energy of matter and force *requires* such a belief. It is the *most scientific* of all possible hypotheses."

The Buddha, Nietzsche felt, had looked into the vortex of nature but drawn the wrong conclusions. The collapse of the old values had led the Buddha to pessimism, to believing that existence had no values at all. He had surrendered to "passive nihilism," the "decline and retrogression of mental power," to the dubious consolations of morality and the illusions of good and evil. The Buddha had resembled a tourist who mistakes a bout of unseasonable weather for a permanent climate. He had forgotten that the wheel of life never stopped turning. The bottom of its arc plunged into biological chaos, but its zenith reached into space, giving precious perspectives on man below and the open sea ahead.

Whether modern Man knew it or not, science had already carried him past the "half-Christian, half-German narrowness" of Schopenhauer, as well as past the Buddha's delusions of morality. It was now necessary to imagine the "elevation and enhancement of man in another direction": to view life with a "super-Asiatic eye," not so much beyond good and evil, as high above it. To imagine a new ethical system for the New Age: the "revaluation of all values."

Before resuming his walk, Nietzsche marked his location vertically: "6000 feet above the ocean, and far higher still above all things human!"

Seven thousand feet above sea level at Simla, Koot Hoomi dashed from house to house like a music hall turn on a Saturday night. His supply of blue thread was infinite, but his repertoire was not. Blavatsky's act was becoming familiar, and her patter no longer distracted her public from her sleights of hand. Reviewing Blavatsky's residency, Sir Edward Buck, a stalwart of the Simla Amateur Dramatic Society, noted that many of Hoomi's mystic phrases "appeared to savour of the Yankee dialect." Sir Edward concluded that Hoomi must have had "considerable intercourse with America."

A showman from his turbaned head to his astral toes, Hoomi stayed in character. He did not so much leave the stage as magic himself away and dissolve like the Cheshire Cat. Confiding in his audience, he admitted that all this time he had been only a warm-up man. The stars were coming straight from the monasteries of Tibet. The Himalayan brothers were now ready for their international debut.

"The inexorable shadow which follows all human innovations moves on," Hoomi told a baffled Alfred Sinnett.

Blavatsky placed faith ahead of the shadow of science's advance. She punted it over the Himalayas, as if a wall of rock would block the advance of rationality. Up there in Tibet lay the bones of the mahatmas, the "great souls" who had drunk from the "mother source" of knowledge. In a monastery on the snow line they had imbibed the "esoteric meaning" of the "grand primitive Scriptures." All subsequent streams of wisdom flowed from that source, and none remained closer to it than the wisdom of the Buddha. Yet even his "most logical" wisdom had been corrupted by time and transmission. As natives defecated into a river then drank from it downstream, so the "wily brahmins" had polluted Gautama's sublime idea. Down in the crowded deltas, the priests channeled the dirty water into the swamps of "popular religion." In a mass culture, true religion was for the elite.

In September 1882, as Nietzsche finished *The Gay Science*, Blavatsky set off for the pure waters and yak milk of Tibet. She met the rest of her party at the hill station of Darjeeling: three Buddhists from Ceylon and Burma, and a "dozen Babu-Theosophists" from Calcutta. Their plan was to climb the Sikkim *himalaya* to the watershed, descend through the passes of Bhutan, and then travel several hundred miles across the Tibetan plateau to Shigatse. There, they would meet the Panchen Lama, believed by his followers to be the reincarnation of the Amitabha Buddha, who had founded the Pure Land school of Mahayana Buddhism.

The whole party fell sick at Darjeeling from the cold weather.

Only three other pilgrims set off with Blavatsky and a Nepalese guide. In the mountains of Sikkim more bad weather forced them to change their route. For eight days they "climbed and crawled" to the border of Bhutan and Tibet, with Blavatsky carried in an armchair. The border was a steep gorge with a rapid stream at its bottom. A bamboo bridge was strung over the abyss, with a military post and a monastery on the other side. Two Englishmen waited for permission to cross, spies disguised as "beggar-monks," as in Kipling's *Kim.*

A Tibetan lama helped Kim in his espionage against the Russians; the lama of Pamionchi, a monastery north of Darjeeling, helped Blavatsky by giving her a letter of introduction. She sent it across the bridge, and a group of yellow-robed monks emerged with their lama, a "dried up skeleton." They offered Blavatsky tea with butter, escorted her into Tibet, and installed her in a wooden hut by the monastery walls.

Inside, the monks glided by, the silence broken only by the resinous crackle of hashish in the lama's "inextinguishable *chelum* pipe" and the etheric whispering of Koot Hoomi in Blavatsky's mind. The lama, she claimed, recognized her as a female incarnation of one of the bodhisattvas. "I spent hours in their library where no woman is allowed to enter—a touching tribute to my beauty and its perfect harmlessness." Then, after only two days, she left.

Meanwhile in Ceylon, Colonel Olcott developed healing powers. He had heard that Catholic missionaries were winning converts at a village near Colombo with some "humbug" about a well with healing waters. Olcott advised the local Buddhist priest to set to work before this "collective hallucination" spread. If the Catholics could sway "ignorant Buddhists," why not send out some monks to "cure people in the name of Lord Buddha"?

"But we can't do it," the priest said, "we know nothing about those things."

Once more it fell to Olcott. His American research had included a few "necessary experiments" in mesmeric healing: it was simply a matter of attuning his "nerve-fluid" to that of the patient. Once the "sympathetic vibration" was established, the "vibratory thrills or pulsations of aura" restored balance and vitality. His first patient was a man with a paralyzed leg and arm who approached him after a lecture. A few passes of his hand over the afflicted limbs, and Olcott had the man worshipping him as "something superhuman." After four days of treatment, the invalid was hopping from foot to foot and waving his arms over his head. He told his friends.

Within a week, Olcott's house was besieged from dawn to the small hours. The sick hobbled and crawled after him from room to room. They gave him no time to eat. They even pestered him in his bedroom while he was dressing. His powers grew with his confidence, so a cure that would have taken days now took only half an hour, but new patients kept coming. When he wanted to go to bed, he had to drive them from his house. When he awoke, he found that paralyzed bodies had been placed on the floor by his bed while he was sleeping. In the mornings he worked for five hours until, his powers drained, he fled for the harbor, where he jumped into the water to recharge his body for the afternoon clinic. He made full use of the chance to prove Lord Buddha's healing powers. Naming the broad veranda that ran around his house "The Cripple's Racecourse," Olcott would pick two or three of the worst cases and "compel them to run against each other."

Word of his miracles spread. When he took a break to visit a temple, he found himself walking for a mile on white cloths, shaded under "a white canopy (*Kodiya*) which enthusiastic Buddhists carried on painted staves," while other admirers held up "two continuous lines of palm-leaf fringes." He knew that the British would see this as an "abasement of the race-dignity." It embarrassed him too. He felt a fool when, half smothered in garlands atop a "decorated elephant," garlands round his neck and thousands of natives cheering him on, he wobbled past a European and registered the sneer on his fellow-white's lip. But it was wise, Olcott decided, to acknowledge reality before trying to change it. He compared himself to an engineer using native labor to replace a rope walkway with an iron bridge. First a "childish show" and a little technical "magic." Then give orders from the blueprint.

"The most difficult lesson for a white man in Asia to learn is, that the customs of his people and those of the dusky races are absolutely different, and that if he dreams of getting on well with the latter he must lay aside all prejudice and hereditary standards of manners, and be one with them, both in spirit and in external forms."

*Olcott's thaumaturgy in Ceylon drew Theosophy southward. In De*cember 1882, the society left Bombay for Madras and settled on a finger of land overlooking the estuary of the Adyar River.

"What air! What nights!" Blavatsky wrote. At night, the sparkling, shoreless water shone under a moon like a giant pearl.

"Happy days are in store for us," Olcott promised Blavatsky. He furnished the house with a library and a shrine room, with a cabinet fixed to the wall for receiving messages from the masters. After the strife and suffering, the sudden departures and sapping fevers, this would be Theosophy's last resting place. And possibly Blavatsky's too. She suffered from backaches, sclerosis, bloating, and blood in her urine. She ate fried eggs swimming in grease every morning and chain-smoked cheap tobacco in roll-ups, probably mixed with hashish. She was so obese and debilitated that she needed crutches to walk. Her doctor warned that her kidneys were inflamed and might not withstand the climate for long. Olcott persuaded her to join the residents in their daily swim in a creek behind the house. He tried to teach her, but she would only "flounder about after a fashion."

As their roles reversed, their pre-Theosophical pasts returned. Olcott, once a Protestant, had chosen Theravada and Ceylon. Blavatsky, a child of the saints and incense of the Orthodox Church, looked to the cosmologies and spirits of Mahayana and Tibet. Olcott was now a public man, healer, lecturer, and political organizer. Blavatsky remained a private woman, restricted by her sex, her garbled and accented English, and the need to keep her past secret. No sooner had

Olcott set up the society in Adyar than he was on a steamer for Calcutta to preach to hundreds.

Blavatsky had "psychologized" him all too well. He had learned the tricks of her trade, and fame was turning him into her controller. She had come so far, but she remained a prisoner of the medium's closet. Under her guidance, Alexis Coulomb turned the house in Adyar into her masterpiece. He worked alone and would become furious if one of the society's Indian employees intruded; to ensure he was undisturbed, Coulomb claimed he liked to perform carpentry in the nude. He drilled a spy hole between the bedroom of Damodar Mavalankar, editor of *The Theosophist,* and the library where the society's board convened. He took down the shrine cabinet from the wall in the shrine room, cut a sliding panel in its back, hid the seams with a mirror, and fitted the cabinet flush with the wall. Then he removed the bricks between the rear of the cabinet and Blavatsky's bedroom, creating a hollow partition. On Blavatsky's side of the wall, he positioned a heavy sideboard, also with a sliding panel at its back. Objects could be placed inside the cabinet by leaning through the sideboard and the partition. To hide the hole on Blavatsky's side, Coulomb lined the wall with teak panels. One of the panels slid aside, so an accomplice could step inside the partition should raps and voices be needed.

In the sitting room Coulomb scraped a thin niche in one of the roof beams. A letter from a mahatma was wrapped in dark cotton, placed in the niche, and tied to a thin thread that ran along the ceiling and out to the veranda. When Blavatsky called for her dog, an accomplice on the veranda yanked the thread, releasing the letter for Madame's guests to marvel at its contents. Similar threads trailed from niches in the ceiling lamp on the veranda and even in the branches of a mango tree in the garden.

"I could be the Buddha of Europe," Nietzsche realized, *"though* frankly, I would be the antipode of the Indian Buddha."

By the end of 1882, Nietzsche felt entirely alone. A series of misunderstandings over Paul Rée's new friend, a striking and brilliant young Russian woman named Lou Andreas-Salomé, had led Nietzsche to fall out with both of them, and then with his mother and sister, who had suspected that Salomé wanted to marry him. The collapse of these relationships left him floundering in Heraclitus' endless stream. He felt like a lunatic.

"This last *bite of life* was the hardest I have chewed yet, and it is still possible that I may *suffocate* on it," he told Franz Overbeck, his old friend from Basel, on Christmas Day. "I am broken on the wheel of my own feelings. If only I could sleep! But the strongest doses of my opiates help me no more than my six- to eight-hour marches."

He would have to erect his bulwark from his own materials, just as he did when he forged his prescriptions for chloral hydrate as "Dr. Nietzsche." The god-making Dionysian spirit within recurred eternally. It was the biological foundation, the physiological and psychological basis of existence, and he divined in its strange, violent music the promise of liberated senses and unsuspected potentials, a new human ideal.

"Could you create a god? Then do not talk to me about any gods. But you could certainly create the *Übermensch*." The *Übermensch* is the future human, the Promethean man beyond the limits of conscience and science, the Superman arising from the fury of unleashed potential. Zarathustra is his prophet, the Dionysian seer. His knowledge overtook Nietzsche, catching him from behind on the lonely hillsides like the terror of Pan. It left him feeling pregnant with wisdom, a feminized man filled with nausea. He felt "ready and ripe in the great noon," like "clouds pregnant with lightning, and swelling milk udders—ready for myself and my most hidden will."

Over ten days in February 1883, Nietzsche expressed this excess of self-knowledge in the first book of *Zarathustra*; the second and third books arrived in similar spurts in the summer and following winter.

When Zarathustra announces the Superman in the marketplace, the people prefer to be entertained by a tightrope walker. So he retreats to a cave in the high places. Ascending the mountain of the human future, he creates himself as a higher man. He climbs from the abyss of nature, filthy with feminine fecundity, to the sun, the summit of masculine power. "I draw circles around me, and sacred boundaries; fewer and fewer men climb with me on ever higher mountains: I am building a mountain range out of ever more sacred mountains."

Only men can enter Zarathustra's sacred cave. Most of them seem to have wandered out of a Wagner plot: a wicked magician, a young shepherd, an old pope, a deceitful dwarf. Far below, the women wait in the fertile valleys like cattle, and serve the warriors with recreational sex. Women are treacherous, cunning creatures, best visited whip in hand. "Is it not better to fall into the hands of murderers than into the dreams of a woman in heat?" High above the nausea of round udders, Zarathustra's hidden will emerges in visions of phallic violence and death in penetration. He is "a bow lusting for its arrow, an arrow lusting for its star—a star ready and ripe in its noon, glowing, pierced, enraptured by annihilating sun arrows—a sun itself and inexorable solar will, ready to annihilate in victory." He is now the antipode of a passive, soft, rounded Buddha: a brutal, hard, muscular warrior.

"I have discovered the Greeks: they believed in eternal recurrence."

Shortly before teatime on March 14, 1883, Karl Marx settled down for a nap in his favorite armchair and died. Since Jenny's death in late 1881, he had ailed with pleurisy and bronchitis. The spas of France and Switzerland had been unable to cure him, and the death from bladder cancer in early 1883 of his favorite daughter, also named Jenny, had accelerated his decline. He died a citizen of no state, without ever having stepped foot in a factory, and reliant to the end on donations from Engels.

Three days later, eleven mourners gathered over a fresh plot amid the damp Gothic stones of Highgate Cemetery. Apart from Engels and the German socialist Karl Liebknecht, there was a pair of scientists whom Marx had lately befriended; a pair of old communists with whom he had omitted to fall out; and a pair of French socialist

sons-in-law that he had delighted in mocking—one of them, Paul La-
fargue, had to attend because he was married to another of Marx's
daughters, Tussy.

Engels, having made the down payments in Marx's life, took possession of his memory. "Just as Darwin discovered the law of development of organic nature," he announced, "so Marx discovered the law
of development of human history: the simple fact, concealed by an
overgrowth of ideology, that mankind must first of all have shelter
and clothing, before it can pursue politics, science, art, religion." This
was not all. Apart from being a second Darwin, Marx had been another Newton. For Marx, science was a "historically dynamic force."
He had discovered "the special law of motion governing the present-
day capitalist mode of production, and the bourgeois society that this
mode of production has created." This was only one of his scientific
achievements. Wherever Marx had spread his intellectual manure,
remarkable crops sprouted. Even in mathematics, Engels claimed,
Marx had made "independent discoveries."

The second French socialist at the funeral, Charles Longuet, read
telegrams from parties representing the workers of Spain, France,
and Russia, the first land to read *Capital*, that "gospel of contemporary socialism," in its own language. Then Karl Liebknecht praised
Marx as a "revolutionary in science, and a revolutionary *through* science." Marx, Liebknecht explained, had found socialism as a religious
sect or a philosophical school, stranded in the melting world of industrial capitalism. He had turned it into a political party, standing in the
paved streets on solid scientific foundations. Instead of mourning
the great man, his friends and followers should continue in his spirit.
"It is a heavy blow that has fallen on us. But we do not mourn. The
deceased is not dead. He lives in the *heart*, he lives in the *head* of the
proletariat."

Marx the man of science was in no state to remind his friends that
the nonexistence of spirit had been one of his great discoveries. But at
least Liebknecht's metaphysics acknowledged his lifelong pretension.
Marx had always claimed that his philosophy was the quintessence of

science. If science never stopped, then Marx's thought, too, must continue to evolve, even posthumously. "Science is the liberator of humanity," Liebknecht explained. "The natural sciences free us from *God.* But God in heaven still lives on although science has killed him."

*"Sexual unions," Olcott concurred, "are perfectly natural for the aver-*age human being, but perfectly unnatural for the evolved ideal man."

The Theosophical Society, he said, did not meddle in mortal matters. It saw no differences of sex, for "the Higher Self has no sex." The society was above the caste system, and differences of color, rank, wealth, and political condition too. It avoided arguments about "diet, intemperance, widow re-marriage, chattel slavery, the social evil, vivisection, and fifty other outlets for philanthropic zeal." Of course, individual members were perfectly free to plunge into the thick of social battles if they so desired. Meanwhile, like a portrait of Queen Victoria above the counter of the most far-flung, fly-blown post office, Theosophy stood over all divisions.

Relishing his ideal life, Olcott spent most of 1883 preaching all over India. In one year he covered seven thousand miles, set up forty-three branches of the society, and treated thousands of people. His magic hands cured paralysis, dysentery, epilepsy, deafness, and blindness. To save time and his vital force, he resorted to handing out "mesmerized water" and used his hand as an "aura meter." If the patient wobbled at its first pass, he continued the treatment.

In a fifty-seven-day tour of Bengal, he traveled two thousand miles by "rail, steamboat, budgerow (canal boat), horse-gharry, elephant, horseback, and palanquin." The daily temperatures topped a hundred degrees Fahrenheit, and he often slept in huts or on a railway-station bench. In addition to daily consultations with hundreds of physically fit and religiously minded men, and recurrent attacks of sciatica and "nervous fever," he cured 557 patients, dispensed the equivalent of 2,255 pint bottles of mesmerized water, established twelve new branches, and gave twenty-seven lectures. In Calcutta, he shared the stage with Debendranath Tagore and healed the eyes of an elderly

Hindu's "comely young wife" by the "hysteric" transfer of sight from his fingertips to hers. He deflected all praise and attributed his outpouring of vital force to the mahatmas. It puzzled him that they said so little while he was working so hard.

In Adyar, Blavatsky noticed that *The Theosophist* was turning into a newsletter on Olcott's triumphs. The mahatmas had never told him to start healing people, but in late 1883 they suddenly ordered him to stop and told him that it was time to return west. He and Blavatsky must go to London. Olcott put away his mesmerized water and packed his trunk.

In a dream Zarathustra is alone on the cliffs in the moonlight. He meets himself as a young shepherd. A "heavy black snake" has crawled into the boy's mouth as he slept and sunk its fangs into his throat. He wakes "writhing, gagging, in spasms, his face distorted," the snake's body hanging out of his mouth. The boy is a human ouroboros, caught in an eternal circle of disgust and shame. Zarathustra has "never seen so much nausea and pale dread" on a human face. He pulls at the snake but cannot remove it. Then a voice cries out from inside him: "Bite! Bite its head off! Bite!"

The boy bites the snake and vomits. "Far away he spewed the head." Purified, he jumps up "radiant" and laughing. No more is he a shepherd, a servant. Separated from all that revolts and endangers him, he can become the "victorious one, the self-conqueror, the master of your sense, the master of your virtues." He is pure and can continue the climb toward divinity. "Once you said God when you looked out onto distant seas; now, however, I have taught you to say: *Übermensch.*" For man is a "polluted stream," and only a sea is great enough to "receive" it without becoming "unclean." The Superman is the great sea: "in him your great contempt can go under."

Later, Nietzsche realized that eighteen months had elapsed between the crushing vision of August 1881, when he had felt the Eternal Return, and the erotic discharge of February 1883, when he wrote the first book of *Zarathustra.* No less significantly, this rebirth, with its expulsion of long-held desires and hatreds, had overtaken him as Wagner had expired at Venice.

"This figure of eighteen months might suggest, at least among Buddhists, that I am really a female elephant."

On February 20, 1884, a month after Nietzsche had "spewed out" the last book of *Zarathustra*, the French steamer *Chandragore* left Bombay, bound for Marseille. On board were Olcott, Blavatsky, and their aide Mohini Chatterjee. After their odyssey east, the Colonel and Madame returned as the first Westerners permitted to accept converts to Buddhism.

The mahatmas gave Mohini Chatterjee strict instructions on his comportment among the Europeans: "One has to impress them externally before a regular, lasting, interior impression is made." When Blavatsky disembarked at Marseille, Chatterjee was to ignore the crowd of foreigners, pretend he did not know her, and "meet and receive her as though you were in India, and she your own mother." If Olcott objected to this theatrical, Chatterjee should say that he was saluting not Blavatsky but her better self, "the interior man, the indweller."

"You have to stun them."

✤ 10 ✤

THE WILL TO POWER

Afghani's Islamic Science
and Other Conspiracies

> The English have now put their hands on every part of
> the world. The English have reached Afghanistan; the
> French have seized Tunisia. In reality, this usurpation,
> aggression, and conquest has not come from the French
> or the English. Rather, it is science that everywhere
> manifests its greatness and power. Ignorance had no
> alternative to prostrating itself humbly before science
> and acknowledging its submission. —*Jamal al-Din
> al-Afghani, "Lecture on Teaching and Learning" (1882)*

On March 12, 1884, the day the *Chandragore* docked at Marseille,
Jamal al-Din al-Afghani went to an attic room above the Rue de
Sèze in Paris, to see the first issue of a new journal. *The Unbreakable
Bond* called for the *umma*, the community of Islam, to unite against
the unbelievers.

Like the wisdom of Allah, Jamal took many forms and paths. In
Herat, he was Said al-Istanbuli, "Said from Istanbul," or ar-Rumi, "the
Greek," the adviser to the emir of Afghanistan who wore European
clothes. In Istanbul, he was al-Afghani, "the Afghan" who wore a reformer's fez and praised the sultan as the caliph, the pope-emperor of
the pan-Islamist dream. In the cafés of Ottoman Cairo, he was still

"the Afghan," but this Afghan was the sultan's enemy, an Egyptian nationalist—and, though he wore a cleric's turban, a French-speaking Freemason. In Paris, this French Afghani ran wild in the way of Voltaire and declared his true faith to be philosophy, not religion. To the British, he was a Russian spy. To the Russians, he was a Persian nationalist or a Turkish provocateur. To the Turks, he was a Shia heretic, but a useful one, a publicist for the Sunni caliphate. To his small but devoted following, he was *hakim al-sharq*, the Sage of the East. And to Helena Blavatsky, ever simplifying without clarifying, he was the Star of the East.

All these Afghanis dwelled behind one bearded visage, its eyes popping as if extruded by inner pressure, and in one portly body, its flesh stretched tight as with the effort of retention. Afghani also carried a sheikh's learning, and a sayyid's dash of the Prophet's blood, with occasional dilutions of tobacco, coffee, and brandy. He was an ascetic, a preacher of purity, but the world, he knew, was a realm of paradox. As an eclipse preceded the first rays of light, so impure means might serve pure ends and apostasy the true faith. This was the philosopher's view, and the scientist's view. It was Afghani's view too, except for when he felt otherwise. He was in two minds. This confusion, he believed, had three causes.

The first cause, which Afghani knew better than to discuss in front of Sunni audiences, was that the twelfth and final Shia imam had disappeared over a thousand years earlier and had yet to reappear. When he did, it would be as the Mahdi, the redeemer who would inaugurate a millennium of divine justice. This messiah should not be confused with the Mahdi of the Sudan, a boatbuilder-cum-messiah who in March 1884 was besieging General Charles Gordon at Khartoum. The Sudanese Mahdi was perhaps a precursor, a portent of redemption like the extraordinary comet that appeared in the eastern sky that spring. He had arisen because of the second cause of Afghani's troubles.

From the Himalayas to the Atlantic, the Christians had violated the house of Islam. They had conquered or corrupted its princes, then seduced their subjects with material goods and materialist doctrines. The philandering British had "entered India and toyed with the minds of her priests and kings," had "penetrated deeply into India's interior" and "seized her lands piece by piece." The foreigners, having deposed the Mughal emperor, were now binding the Ottoman sultan in debts that were denoted in *kafr* currencies and accumulating at *kafr* compound interest. When the Egyptians rebelled in 1882, the British invaded to protect their investments and the Suez Canal, and deported the rebel government to Ceylon. Islam was the final call, God's last thought on the meaning of life. Yet everywhere the pink-faced infidels humiliated the heirs of the Prophet and drowned the words of the holy Koran in a heathen chatter of stock prices and English verse.

This impossible condition had arisen from the third cause: Muslims had failed to keep up with history. Afghani had read Guizot, the French *positiviste* historian. History was change, change was progress, and progress was the evolution of scientific knowledge. The new science endowed its holder with "the strength of ten, one hundred, one thousand, and ten thousand persons." Science was like an emperor who changed capitals as he expanded his realm. First, he had marched from east to west. The Indians, the "inventors of arithmetic and geometry," had passed his wisdom to the Greeks, who had passed it to the Arabs, who had passed it to the Europeans. Now, the emperor of science was marching back, from west to east, and melding his conquests into an "industrial world."

Five times daily, the faithful enacted their submission to Allah, getting down on their knees and pressing their foreheads to the ground. The emperor of science demanded a sixth abasement. His knowledge was his power. Everywhere, it shamed ignorance into "prostrating itself humbly before science and acknowledging its submission."

If Muslims resented this humiliating posture, Afghani maintained, they should blame their leaders and teachers. Living in Egypt in the 1870s, he had absorbed the anticlerical politics of the French Enlightenment. His diagnosis was that of Voltaire or Diderot—or Nietzsche and Blavatsky, who reached similar conclusions in the same decade: the priests had betrayed the believers. The ulama, the religious scholars, had strayed from the path of truth and pandered to despotic rulers. Imitating their masters, the servile scholars had divided knowledge into petty fiefdoms such as "Muslim science" and "European science." They had appointed Aristotle as an honorary Muslim and labeled Galileo, Newton, and Kepler as infidels. This had returned Muslims to an Age of Ignorance resembling that of the Arabs before the coming of Muhammed. The kings and priests had grown fat on taxes, and the minds of the faithful had weakened. Now, as Christian missionaries sidled forward in the shadow of the European empires and "opened their mouths to swallow this religion" alive, the Muslim mind was paralyzed like a mouse before a python.

Coveting the power that he wanted to destroy, Afghani was the first philosopher of Islamism, the application of Islamic principles to modern politics. He judged Muslims through the eyes of European civilization and found them wanting. He saw the world of science through the gauze of an ideal Islam and found it corrupt. This double vision was intolerable. Islam was not the problem; it was the solution. True Islam, Afghani claimed, was "really the closest of religions to science and knowledge." It was more universal than Judaism and more rational than Christianity. It despised the "false beliefs" of the Hindus or the ancient Egyptians, with their "idols, cows, dogs, and cats." If Muslims perused the foundations of Islam as seekers of truth rather than servants of power, they would find that all science was Islamic science. To restore clarity of vision, Muslims must reassess Islam from its foundations and live like *as-salaf as-salim*, the "pious forebears."

In the 1880s, fundamentalism in religion and Islamism in politics were presences yet to be named. The first to call themselves "fundamentalists" would be American Presbyterians. In 1910, after decades of dispute over the historicity of the Bible, the "Fundamentalists" would declare a "Doctrinal Deliverance" from the heretical "Modernists." The Presbyterian fundamentalists would erect their house of faith as Muhammad had done, on five principles.

The modern search for authority and continuity is a response to the world of science, a product stamped in its image. Many popes had considered themselves infallible, but papal infallibility did not become Catholic doctrine until 1870. Many Christians had despised Jews for theological reasons, but the world of science demanded its own formulation. In 1879, the socialist and Prussian nationalist Wilhelm Marr obliged with "antisemitism," a comprehensive theory in the modern argot of race, nation, and economy—a political platform erected on older religious foundations. Similarly, before Afghani's admirers could promote jihad as the "sixth pillar" of Islam, the other five had to weaken.

In March 1883, Afghani debated Ernest Renan on the relations of Islam and science.

At sixty, Renan was as corpulent as a Balzac *maître* whose girth had expanded with his reputation. The Aryan Jesus had cost Renan his academic post, but the Third Republic had adopted him as the nation's philosopher. A facile compounder of fashionable prejudice and patriotic flatulence, Renan sweetened the sour pleasures of anticlerical politics and Aryan theory with a thick syrup of medieval nostalgia and a tear-jerking pinch of Christian sentiment. He presented his readers with a republican cake and permitted them to eat its sickly religious essence. Their appetite was insatiable. Having given them his massive *Origins of Christianity*, Renan had paused to raise a monument to his own origins, *Memories of Childhood and Youth*, and then begun another grand sequence, *The History of Ancient Israel.*

Renan met Afghani through Khalil Ghanim, a Maronite Christian who, like Renan, wrote for the *Journal des débats*, France's leading republican newspaper. Renan liked Afghani: he took the sayyid for one of Gobineau's survivors, an energetic Persian with an "Aryan spirit" beneath his "superficial layer of official Islam." Invited to speak at the Sorbonne, Renan pondered Semites and Aryans, "Islam and Science." To Renan, phrases like "Arab science," "Arab philosophy," "Islamic science," and "Islamic civilization" were misleading. The Arabs, he said, were an "intellectual nullity," incapable like all Semites of original or profound thought. Of the early Arab philosophers, only one, al-Kindi, had been Arab by blood. The rest had been Persian, Turkish, or Spanish, and none had been Arab in spirit. If they were not Parsees, Christians, or Jews, they were Aryan Persians, and frequently Muslims "in interior revolt" against their faith. The only Arab element in the "Arab science" had been its language. The "fecund element" in Islamic science had been the "scientific tradition of Greek antiquity," its fertilizers the Aryans of Persia.

Renan admitted to feeling a "certain regret" at not having been born a Muslim, and he allowed that Islam had been crucial to the evolution of the human spirit. In its early centuries, Islam had linked antiquity to Latin Europe. Islam's highest expression, the Hellenistic rationalism of the Mutazilite philosophers, had resembled a "species of Protestantism." But, Renan judged, in the twelfth century, while Europe found its genius and "created a new *sensorium* for the work of the spirit," Islam had succumbed to its barren Arab blood and declared war on science and reason. The Mutazilites had been persecuted, the Greek legacy repressed among all but the Persian Shiites. To praise this "religious terror and hypocrisy" was like thanking the papacy for Galileo, or the Inquisition for discovering modern science. Islam was essentially "injurious to human reason," and Muslims had an innate "hatred of science."

Renan despised all clerical interference in public life. Here, Islam was particularly guilty. All religions tended to persecute "free thought," but Islam did it more effectively. Its refusal to separate "the spiritual and the temporal" closed societies and minds to "rational cultivation." The "absolute" tyranny of sharia law had "destroyed vast areas of our globe." Islam, Renan concluded, was the "heaviest chain that humanity has ever borne."

When Afghani read a transcript of Renan's lecture that appeared in the *Journal des débats*, he felt compelled to reply—and agree.

"In truth," Afghani admitted, "the Muslim religion has tried to stop science and stop its progress." The alliance between the ulama and the despots had purged the Mutazilites, banned scientific inquiry, and condemned hundreds of millions to "barbarism and ignorance." But none of this, Afghani argued, derived from Islam's Arab origins. Nor, though Afghani was Persian, did he describe his wisdom as Aryan. The problem with Islam was not specific or racial, like the "Jewish question" was in Europe. Islam's flaws were those of degree, not kind: "Religions, by whatever name they are called, all resemble each other."

The resemblance that Afghani detected was not flattering. A new civilization faces the world like a frightened child, incapable of distinguishing good from evil, unable to trace causes or effects. As the dream of "pure reason" dissolves, the mind, failing to obtain "complete satisfaction of its desires," seeks "an unlimited field for its hopes" in the "vast horizons" of religion. These hopes too are unattainable, and that turns faith from "a place of refuge" to a prison. The religious impulse, Afghani agreed, really is one of life's "heaviest and most humiliating yokes." But science, by opening new horizons, restored the fundamental perceptions. Among the Christians, a Renaissance in knowledge had produced the Reformation in spirit and politics. The same logic of cause and effect, Afghani hoped, would force Islam toward a "more advanced civilization."

"What is heavy? Thus asks the weight-bearing spirit; thus it kneels down like the camel and wants to be laden."

In Zarathustra's allegory of the spirit, the resentful camel perceives his complicity in his humiliation. Shedding his load on the sand, the camel becomes a lion, a "master in his own desert," the will personified. His path is blocked by a dragon with "Thou Shalt" written on its scales in gold: the beast of ancient obligations. By slaying this last god, the lion can enter his third and final metamorphosis and become the Superman. Only now can he bear the heaviest weight: not the camel-like servitude of religion, but the lion's recognition that life never was a Christian morality play. It is a biological cycle, and the whirl of its vortex consumes the two extremes of thought, the "mechanistic and the Platonic," the physical presence and the spiritualized ideal. The spiritual warrior must struggle for "hardness" and "cleanliness," embrace the yoke of biology, and celebrate *amor fati*, the "love of fate." Then the "plant called Man" will grow strong and tall, his religious impulse aligned with the truth of existence.

Though biological Man aspires toward the light and the great health, he stunts his growth by an unnatural passion: *ressentiment*, a hatred implacable as love. Nietzsche named it in French because, he said, the Germans cherished resentment with a passion that dared not speak its name. "Countless dark bodies are to be inferred near the sun—and we shall never see them. Among ourselves, this is a parable; and a psychologist of morals reads the whole writing of the stars only as a parable."

For all his modernity, Nietzsche wrote, a Christian retained the moral apparatus of an "Oriental slave," for Christian morals were the Jewish "slave rebellion in morals," diffused through the Roman Empire. A dutiful Christian groveled before God like a slave who sacrifices "all freedom, all pride, all self-confidence of the spirit" for an illusion of paternal protection. The Judaic poisons of conscience and guilt pollute the wells of the Christian spirit, until the gall of resentment and sanctimony tastes strangely sweet.

The "psychologist of morals" marveled at the Jews' slave rebellion. How had this small people achieved this miracle, an "inversion of values" across an entire civilization? How had they replaced the noble and merciless values of the Greek warriors with the slave morality of cunning in weakness, hatred in servility, survival without dignity? How had they replaced the biological imperative of hardness with the consoling monstrosity of "pity," that sentimental fondness for the weak, the feeble, the undeserving, and the womanly that caused "corruption of the instincts"?

His answer explained not only the turn toward disaster and indignity that history had taken after Jesus, but the undignified disaster unfolding around Nietzsche, another suffering son rebelling against the priests. The Jews, Nietzsche believed, had been able to invert the values of the Roman Empire because the Romans themselves had abandoned those values. Aristocratic, martial Rome had decayed into a higher barbarism, civilization without virtue. Modern Europe was similarly decadent, and susceptible to modern forms of slave morality, all of them stamped with the image of a Christianity in which it no longer believed. The only beliefs left to the modern European were his sinister resentments.

Commerce and democracy had inverted the martial and aristocratic virtues. This was the age of the mob and the herd, of leveling by socialism and democracy, of "general uglification" and witless optimism, of instinct perverted and sickliness indulged, of the "ever-spreading morality of pity." The modern age mixed races and classes indiscriminately, filling the body with a "heritage of multiple origins" and the mind with humanitarian fictions. The result made Man a "ludicrous species." The "hybrid European" was an ugly plebeian: a herd animal, sickly, mediocre, and brimming with sentimental cowardice. His consort annulled her female instincts by suppressing her "fear of man," and now claimed her right to be as "obnoxious and ridiculous" as her husband. Only a morality that defied biology and denied instinct could produce such weak specimens.

Zarathustra spoke in parables, but Nietzsche's notebooks described the "upward" evolution of the species in scientific terms. By 1884, he had decided that the New Age would need a new doctrine, an ethic powerful enough to work as a breeding agent. Instead of the democratic "dwarfing of man," the aristocratic breeding of a stronger race through "the strength and the will to *inflict* great suffering." A philosophical eugenics for strengthening the strong and destroying the weak, the womanly, and the world-weary. Only virility and war could draw the species upward from the "sand and slime of present-day civilization and metropolitanism."

The eugenic master would need the eye of an artist and the hard conscience of the warrior: "the body and physiology the starting-point."

Nietzsche realized that Zarathustra's doctrine of the infinitely repeated circular course of life had already been taught by Heraclitus and the Stoics. But the world of science demanded that its highest spiritual insight should also be the deepest biological fact. Nietzsche had to make his Dionysian wisdom the "most scientific of hypotheses"; otherwise, no one would believe him in the future. Through the 1880s, he strove to integrate his spiritual intuitions with the pure materialism of "physiology, medicine, and the natural sciences."

As Engels had said at Marx's grave, that meant a reckoning with Darwin. Yet Nietzsche, despite his scientific objectives, never read Darwin. Nor did Afghani. Instead they knew Darwin through unreliable narrators, philosophical dragomans who domesticated the English materialist to French and German tastes. Like Marx and Engels, they ingested just enough Darwin to nourish their prejudices.

For Afghani, Darwin was the Democritus of development theory. Democritus and the Epicureans had claimed that the universe was composed of "hard particles" that appear in their present form by chance. Darwin's doctrine of "germs" and the evolutionary change in forms was merely the latest iteration of the materialist lie. Misled by pure materialism, this "unfortunate" Englishman had wandered into a "desert of fantasies" and concluded that man descends from a monkey. This materialism, by denying the existence of the spirit, bred all the other civilizational sicknesses: "Religion is the mainstay of Nations and the Source of their Welfare. It is their happiness, and around it is their Pivot," Afghani told Indian Muslims. "Materialism is the root of Corruption and the Source of Foulness. From it comes the ruin of the Land and the Perdition of Man."

Nietzsche's Darwin was not a source of foulness, but a spiritual pivot. The Eternal Return orbits in the flux of Heraclitus, but it is held by the gravitational principle of evolution. The emergence and dissolution of individuals express the fate of their species. The strongest and most creative individuals accept biological fate in its totality. Their Promethean defiance of gravity and mortality is a heroic overcoming.

"Thou shalt not propagate only thyself," Zarathustra says, "but propagate thyself upward."

Nietzsche derived his Darwin from Friedrich Lange's *History of Materialism and Critique of Its Present Importance* (1865) and from Ernst Haeckel, who by the 1880s had become Darwin's leading German interpreter. Lange viewed Darwin through a Romantic mist. He traced the roots of the empirical method to Democritus and called the mind a biological organism with a Kantian sensibility. He also referred to the French socialist Louis Blanqui's *Eternity by the Stars* (1872), whose reflections on recurrence anticipated Nietzsche's on the Eternal Return; and on the nihilism of Max Stirner, a youthful contemporary of Marx and Engels whose influence Nietzsche partially admitted and partially concealed.

Nietzsche did not read Haeckel either, but his Darwin is the German Darwin, more Lamarckian than Darwinian. Darwin had been amused to hear that German socialists quoted him to vindicate their politics, but Haeckel's adaptations had alarmed him. Visiting Down House for tea, Haeckel had argued that Darwin's theories supported a Lamarckian mysticism about the political destiny of the Germans.

Zarathustra's spiritual bestiary resembles Haeckel's recapitulation theory, the idea that "ontogeny recapitulates phylogeny": as the fetus recapitulates the evolutionary history of the species, so the Superman must pass through the stages of camel and lion. The will that drives the struggle for life is the vital force, striving to reunite with the cosmos. Will and environment cause immediate and permanent changes to the individual, and these effects are transmitted to descendants not just as physical traits but also as mental perceptions. In the struggle for life, Darwin's "fittest" becomes Nietzsche's "hardest"; Darwin's "development" and "selection"; Nietzsche's "becoming" and "breeding." The Superman is an evolved species, Nature's aristocrat. A biological theory drifts into spiritual metaphors; as Nietzsche knew, in Greek, *metaphoros* means "moving."

"Intellect alone does not make noble; on the contrary, to *ennoble the* intellect, something is needed beforehand. What then is needed? Blood."

The philologist fantasized a pure genealogy. Dismissing his mother's side as *canaille*, a coarse and dirty "rabble," he conjured a false history from his father's surname. "I am a pure-blooded Polish nobleman without a single drop of bad blood, certainly not German blood."

Nietzsche observed that, while Europe's hereditary Aryan virtues leached away, the Semites preserved their blood. The Jews were now Europe's "strongest, toughest, and purest race"; like the Russian Empire, they changed only when they had to. They certainly seemed stronger than Nietzsche's people. The Germans, as Wilde was to say of the Americans, seemed to be passing from barbarism to decadence without stopping for civilization. Nietzsche was certain that if the Jews wanted "mastery over Europe," they could take it. But he was equally certain that they did not want it.

A growing number of Europeans disagreed. In the 1880s, antisemitism emerged as a political force. In the states of central and western Europe, where Jews only one or two generations out of the ghetto had the impertinence to excel, it became a platform issue in democratic politics. In the Russian Empire, where Jews were debilitated by legal handicaps and corralled into the Pale of Settlement, a strip of land running down the empire's western border, anti-Jewish legislation and riots precipitated the westward flight of millions and made "pogrom" one of the few Russian loan words to enter Western languages. The scale of the exodus was without historical parallel—so great that in the 1890s, west European states began to pass laws limiting "alien" immigration.

For both democrats and autocrats, antisemitism was an ideal greater than loyalties of class and divisions of wealth. In a fractured age, it united nation, family, and personality. A benediction from the church of racial science, it caught the resentments and votes of displaced aristocrats, thwarted businessmen, and exploited workers alike. It explained the intolerable confusion of modern life—its trans-gression of ancient taboos, its collapsing of ancient bonds—not in the waning theology of the church, but in the waxing tongues of science and economy, the imperial masters that everywhere marched over the old ways. "You taught me language," Caliban retorts to Prospero, "and my profit on't is / I know how to curse." The age of scientific reason had birthed a dream of magical malevolence, a conspiracy the-ory that imagined the defilement of the modern icons, the stock ex-change and the national blood, as lasciviously and fantastically as medieval Europeans had imagined Jews mutilating Christian children on church altars and poisoning the wells with the plague.

Antisemitism would become the most popular of all modern doc-trines of revolution, a leap forward that recovers lost unity. It is not just the socialism of fools, but also their conservatism and liberalism, their nationalism and internationalism, their royalism and, as the dead echo of their Christianity, their nihilism too. It is a total system, transcending petty differences of party and nation, predicated on an ineluctable cosmic presence, like the firmament of the medieval scho-lastics, the solid vault that limits and shelters all life beneath. Com-bining ancient resentments with modern fears, it is the most successful of all the replacements of religion by science. The Jews' moral chal-lenge, the biblical burden of conscience, is annulled by the sacred com-mands of instinct: the contest of good and evil becomes a Darwinian "struggle for life." The theological teaching of contempt is replaced by the biological standard of inferiority; the medieval poisoner of wells becomes the modern poisoner of discourse; the torturer of children, the exploiter of the workers; the usurer, the financier. The hands pol-luted with the blood of Jesus become the blood polluted with a deca-dent heredity, somehow mongrel yet pure; the untouchable becomes the decadent. The triune theology of father, son, and spirit reappears in the plan of the czar's minister: a third of the Jews to be excised from the nation, a third to be dissolved by intermarriage, a third to survive.

When Buddha died, his followers worshipped his shadow on the wall of the cave. Nietzsche recognized antisemitism as the shadow of Europe's dying Christianity, *ressentiment*'s attempt to resurrect its lost beloved, the dead father resurrected as a wicked uncle, the last gasp of Christians convinced, lapsing, or lost. He was the detective who traced the sickness, the judge who passed the sentence, the loving executioner who administered the hemlock, the suffering son who ran in the streets to announce the death of the father-god. If he was among the first to "psychologize" antisemitism as a symptom of collapse, an augury of catastrophe, it was because he shared its vocabulary and grammar, and used its language to launch a suicidal attack on Europe's moral foundations.

In 1884, Nietzsche still remained nectar for aesthetes. But already he sensed the tramp of boots coming to meet him: "Something extraordinarily nasty and evil is about to make its debut." With mounting terror, he saw how his high path would lead to the low pass, to the crossroads where the resentful, slavish mob would hail their scourge as a hero, the apparition come to save them from their crisis of belief. "The problem of the value of truth came before us—or was it we who came before the problem? Who of us is Oedipus here? Who the Sphinx? It is a rendezvous, it seems, of questions, and question marks."

The confusion and recognition were not accidental. Nietzsche and the antisemites were blood relatives. His ontogeny, his personal development, recapitulated his phylogeny, the evolutionary past he shared with his species. He recapitulated the racial science that equated "Aryan" with purity and the aristocratic virtues of warlike nobility, and "Semite" with the pollutants of decadence, weakness, and femininity. He recapitulated the antisemite's nostalgia for order and meaning, his resentful desire to transcend the standardizing, homogenizing world of industry and market forces. He longed for the tyrant who oils the chariot's wheel with blood, a Napoléon who would replace the lawyer's contract with the emperor's orders, commercial compromise with military glory.

Nietzsche shared the antisemite's vision of religious history as racial morality, and the antisemite shared his dream of a revolt against

the ignoble modern age, a spiritualization of scientific facts and political principles: the "transvaluation of all values." Asking the same
questions of their time, they differed only in some of their answers.
Human responses, said Nietzsche, are shaped by fear and the avoid-
ance of pain. The priests of antisemitism pandered to the mob because
they feared it; the vulgar appeal to populism allowed them to tame
and direct it. The Christian Social Workers' Party of Adolf Stoecker,
the court chaplain to Kaiser Wilhelm, was "Christian" in the sense
that it excluded Jews from membership, and "social" in its use of welfare programs and protectionism to distract workers from the Marx-
ists of the Social Democratic Party. The growth of the antisemitic
parties, with their false science, fatuous economics, and fake Christian
piety, confirmed Nietzsche's suspicions of the democratic horde. Sentimentality and superstition, the degraded forms of faith, could raise
a mob; even, as Afghani recognized, when their leader did not believe
at all. In the godless world of science, antisemitism was the next best
thing to Christianity: a consolation of nihilism.

Nietzsche had erected symptoms as icons in order to defile them
more thoroughly. But other travelers, less interested in "psychologiz-
ing" a sinister culture than worshipping it, made their own devotions
at his toppled shrines. He approved when the philosophy professor
Georg Brandes, a Jewish Dane, hailed his thought as "aristocratic
radicalism." Isolated from an industrial, urban society he despised,
Nietzsche realized only slowly that the ontogeny of the high places
was ineluctably the phylogeny of the cities of the plain. The secret
sharing of aristocrats and peasants: two permanent castes, once tied
to the land by blood and vows, now cut adrift by revolution and the
market; once bonded by their resentment of the urban economy, with
its merchants and moneylenders; now bonded in resenting its modern
heirs, the self-helping, self-improving, self-satisfied middle classes.

In 1885, Nietzsche's sister, Elisabeth, married Bernhard Förster,
a schoolteacher, Wagnerite, vegetarian, and fanatical antisemite who
had set up the German People's League in 1881 while Nietzsche was
tanning on the rocks at Genoa. The newlyweds left for the rain forests

of Paraguay to found Nueva Germania, a human farm for the breeding of pure Aryans, its breeding stock five families from Saxony. It was too late: the "aristocratic radical" was married to the mob.

"I know my fate. One day my name will be associated with the memory of something tremendous—a crisis without equal on earth, the most profound collision of conscience, a decision that was conjured up against everything that had been believed, demanded, hallowed so far. I am no man, I am dynamite."

As every parish once had its priest, and every culture would soon have its Nietzschean, every nation now had its racial philosopher to translate an arcane theology of the blood for the common tongue, to explain the science of heredity as ancestor worship, to make sacred the quotidian. The Germans had Stoecker, Förster, and, for the intellectuals, Paul Lagarde, who, like Nietzsche, was a philologist by training and a biological mystic by taste. The Austrians were spoiled for choice but settled on the handsome bachelor Karl Lueger, who, as mayor of Vienna, would advance an impeccably modern program: raising the quality of the city's transportation, water supply, parks, and sanitation while lowering its political tone into its well-swept gutters. The British took their race theory like the quinine in their gin, diluting science in the cynical practicalities of rule by division and profit by trade. In India, their task was to remind the Indians of their Aryan roots; in Africa, the Aryan importer of civilization could, as one of Conrad's speculators says, "make no end of coin by trade." The Russians, no less impractically, had Dostoevsky, the unlucky gambler and epileptic visionary, championing Jesus and Mother Russia against the nihilists, the Germans, and the Jews. And the French had Ernest Renan.

Nietzsche read Renan's *Origins of Christianity* with "much spite" and "little profit." With much of both, he would pay Renan the writer's supreme homage and plagiarize the title of the fourth volume of *Origins of Christianity*, "The Antichrist." Renan's Antichrist was Nero, the depraved persecutor of early Christian fanatics. Nietzsche declared himself a modern Antichrist, a righteous tormentor of late-Christian sentimentalists. He loathed Renan intimately enough to appoint him as his "antipode," a voluptuous southerner who doused himself with French perfume to hide the reek of philistine optimism. The centrifugal force of reason had spun Renan and Nietzsche to opposing extremes. They shared the French Enlightenment view of Christian history: the black legend of anticlericalism in which despotism pandered to foolish faith. They shared the intellectual's tic of disparaging priests and aristocrats while affecting the attitudes and privileges of a rival elite. Both saw an Aryan kernel emerging from the flayed husks of Christianity, and sensed biological wisdom in the blood. To Renan this was the true, original Christian ethic. To Nietzsche, who thought that "the last Christian died on the cross," that ethic was Christianity's antipode.

Nietzsche also shared Renan's envy of Islam: The desert bred noble warriors, and their pitiless masculinity was the antipode of the soft, sentimental Europe of women, Jews, and priests. The harsh masters of Islam knew how to control their slavish inferiors: the female bodies imprisoned in the harem; the feminized *dhimmi* spirits of Jews and Christians. In 1881, Nietzsche invited his homosexual school friend Karl Gersdorff to spend a few years in Tunisia. Distance made the heart grow harder, the eye keener, and Europe's decadent sunset more aesthetic.

"I want to live for a while among Muslims, especially at the place where their belief is strongest at the moment: this will sharpen my judgment and vision for all things European."

Cruelly the French spoiled Nietzsche's dream by invading Tunisia. That too seemed to be fate. "In these days," the British historian James Froude explained in *Oceana* (1889), "the world has grown so small, and the arms of the Great Powers are so long."

Destiny manifested as family ties, extending to form political blocs of blood, language, and faith. Russia, the patron of Orthodox Christians, used pan-Slavism to push Turkey out of the Balkans. Liberal

British politicians talked of their empire as a "Greater Britain" and enlisted the United States into a global "Anglo-Saxon" civilization. The pan-Germanists wanted their *Grossdeutschland* in central Europe. Turkish officers who had studied in Germany in the 1870s had returned as pan-Turanists, dreaming of an empire in central Asia.

Islam's unbreakable bond was faith, not blood or language. The new sultan, Abdul Hamid II, kept up with the times. Dusting off his hereditary claim to the caliphate, he adopted pan-Islamism to buffer his throne against European interference, Arab secessionists, and his own pan-Turanist reformers. To Renan, the sultan's turn to pan-Islamism was a historic event: the return of Islam in modern politics, backed by a major power. In his Sorbonne lecture, he used *Islamisme* to describe Islam both as a faith and as a form of modern politics. He predicted massacres.

Afghani agreed that only an appeal to shared piety could stir the masses of Islam. He admired Martin Luther for transforming the inner and outer life of Christianity, and claimed that Muhammad would have approved: "Verily, Allah does not change the state of the people until they change themselves inwardly." And verily, the people were in a terrible state. Ottoman Turkey was the "sick man of Europe," but his ailments affected every limb of the *umma*. The Christians were spreading the European diseases: democracy, communism, nihilism, Darwinism, sexual license.

Afghani advised two treatments, taken simultaneously. The first was regular doses of nationalism. This had worked wonders for the Christians and had already invigorated the Egyptians and Turks. The second was to rub the bruising with the balm of pan-Islamism. This had the appeal of a traditional, indigenous remedy but the potency of a modern synthesis, like cocaine from the coca leaf. The instability of the reaction between nationalism and Islam would not be discovered for several decades.

Afghani's mind was altered by his materials, like a hatter with mercury. "He excelled in the study of religions, until this led him to irreligion, and belief in the eternity of the world," Salim al-Anhuri, editor of the Egyptian journal *Mirror of the East*, recalled of Afghani. "He claimed that vital atoms, found in the atmosphere, formed, by a natural evolution, the stars which we see and which revolve around one another through gravity, and that the belief in an omniscient Prime Mover was a natural delusion that arose when man was in a primitive state of evolution." As Afghani said to Renan, in the age before cause and effect were understood, explanations in the name of the Supreme Being had been the only path to knowledge. Now, science had opened a new path.

Speaking to Muslims, Afghani said the opposite. From Democritus to Darwin, a "sect of *neichiris*," naturalists, had conspired to corrupt religion and collapse the pillars of social order. They denied the existence of the exalted Creator, and claimed that Man was like other animals. They called religious ideals a "meddling of the mind," a priestly conspiracy of "superstitious rules and artificial chimeras," a denial of bodily pleasures that ran contrary to nature. They tricked Muslims into Western education, then poured false opinions into the "pure ears of children." The Western curriculum was a scheme to "seduce the sons of the rich" into slipping the "bonds of the Law of Islam," and pursuing "bestial passions." For only the "habit of shame" and the fear of judgment kept Muslims from the "path of animality" and the "way of bestiality." Like the French after Rousseau, they would slide from "denying divinity and slandering the prophets" into "license and communism." They would hold their goods and women in common, and despoil their mosques and minds, just as the French skeptics had desecrated a church by "bringing in a girl and placing her on the altar."

At least this is what Afghani wrote in 1884 in *The Indissoluble Bond*. In the same year, he told the French socialist Henri Rochefort that Western education was the key to Muslim freedom. "England believes it has made a great political stroke by imposing the English language on the Hindus, Muslims and idolaters," he told Rochefort. "She has made a great mistake. Today, they understand the newspapers published by their conquerors, and make themselves perfectly aware of the state of subjection to which they have been reduced."

Afghani's opinions shaped themselves to resistance like mercury on glass, reflecting and distorting the image he loathed and desired. Believing in a united *umma,* he saw a united Christendom that no longer existed. Dreaming of a spiritual revolt, he saw a materialist crusade. To recover mastery, Muslims must absorb these hateful images, then free their souls from the "vile animal qualities" of matter. They must master the perverse temptations of Democritus and Darwin by *ijtihad,* the struggle to purify the soul through reason and will.

Afghani had the necessary self-mastery. In Paris, a German blonde named Kathi offered herself "body and soul," along with "a thousand kisses" and a stipend from Bismarck's foreign ministry. Afghani, the analyst of Muslim weakness, was impotent with women; like Nietzsche after the birth of Zarathustra, he shunned their company. Rashid Rida, the pupil who would pass Afghani's teachings to Hassan al-Bana, the founder of the Muslim Brotherhood, explained Afghani's impotence as holiness: "Owing to his preoccupation with great things, he had lost the need and capacity for marriage." When Abdul Hamid II offered Afghani a woman from the imperial harem, Afghani refused. He would, he told the sultan, rather "cut the organ of procreation" than contaminate it. The Sage of the East contemplated many heresies in private. Placing a woman on his altar was not one of them.

The essential religious type, Nietzsche believed, is the "ecstatic," the man possessed. He speaks in tongues and fury. He inspires terror, which is where "authority took its origin." As rich in vitality as he is poor in diet, the fanatic is intoxicated with the vapors of a "superabundant life," or its pathological variety, a "morbid nutrition of the brain."

"Wherever on earth the religious neurosis has appeared, we find it tied to three dangerous dietary demands: solitude, fasting, and sexual abstinence." In his monstrous, unnatural denial of his body's needs, the ascetic saint poses as Nature's unconquered enemy, a tyrant of the will. Set high on his platform like Simeon Stylites, he raises his eye from the turd-scattered sand and the swinish mob below, to gaze on an empty heaven. An icon of selfless sacrifice, he is secretly enthralled by *libido dominandi*, his lust for power.

"It was because one was wrong about him, because one misinterpreted the states of his soul and drew as sharp a line as possible between oneself and him, as if he were something utterly incomparable and strangely superhuman—that he gained that extraordinary power with which he could dominate the imagination of whole peoples and ages." The fanatic did not dare look down to consider what was "eccentric and sick in his nature, with its fusion of spiritual poverty, faulty knowledge, spoilt health, and overexcited nerves," any more than those who looked up at him wanted to consider his concealed nature. He was not especially good or especially wise, but he "signified something that exceeded all human measure of goodness and wisdom," to himself as to his followers.

"In the evening splendor of the world-end's sunset that illuminated the Christian peoples, the shadowy figure of the holy man grew into something enormous—indeed, to such a height that even in our own time, which no longer believes in God, there are still thinkers who believe in the holy man."

All in all, Colonel Olcott felt, it had been a delightful voyage. The Chandragore had been comfortable, the passage calm, the chef French. Nor had there been any squalls from Madame.

On the quay at Marseille, Baron Giuseppe Spedalieri, Éliphas Lévi's pupil and executor, acclaimed HPB as Lévi's heir. Along the coast at Nice, Lady Caithness invited "the cream of the nobility" to meet Blavatsky at the Palais Tiranty and donated her Paris home as the office of a new lodge, whose meetings Ernest Renan would attend. Gliding north, Madame and the Colonel were profiled in Victor Hugo's newspaper, *Le rappel*, and interviewed by a man from the *Chicago Tribune*. It was as if Theosophy's return west was ordained in the cosmic timetable.

It was the year of Tolstoy's *Ivan Ilyich*, Ibsen's *Wild Duck*, Lewis Waterman's dripless ink pen, James Ritty's cash register, and Charles Parsons's steam turbine. In Berlin, Bismarck convened Europe's foreign ministers around a dining table to carve up the map of Africa. In Washington, D.C., representatives from twenty-five nations met for the Prime Meridian Conference and proposed the division of the world into twenty-four time zones, with a universal day whose beginning would be registered at Greenwich in London. For Blavatsky and Olcott, these were months of picnics and first-class carriages, of lectures in august halls and parties in lavish mansions, of gullible aristocrats and credulous physicists: the summer that a horde of independent, titled, and thoroughly superior minds all agreed that this was the season of Theosophy. An age of scientific facts and universal prescriptions was ready for a scientific and universal religion.

On March 27, 1884, Blavatsky's party crossed the Seine, rounded the Louvre and the Tuileries Gardens, and made the ascent to Afghani's attic. Blavatsky and Afghani had first met in Cairo in the early 1870s, probably through the Star of the East Masonic lodge. Each had moved to India in 1879, Blavatsky to Bombay after the séance scandal, and Afghani, expelled from Egypt for plotting against the khedive, to Hyderabad. In India, the British had spied on them both, taking Afghani for a Muslim rabble-rouser and Blavatsky for a Russian agent. In India, Afghani fished in the same waters as the Theosophists, and he used the same bait. In a talk at Calcutta University in 1882, he called on Hindus and Muslims to form an Indian nation by reviving their original wisdom and language.

Afghani and Blavatsky were fellow travelers on the road of philosophical religion. They were also heading toward a confrontation with the European empires. When the English radical Wilfrid Scawen Blunt squeezed into the attic, he found Blavatsky and Afghani deep in conversation about the Mahdi of Sudan. The Mahdi had expelled the slave traders and Turkish garrisons from the upper reaches of the Nile and declared a caliphate. If his revolt spread, it would threaten Egypt, the Suez Canal, and the Red Sea ports, and even sever the links between Britain and India. Who, Blavatsky asked, was this man who threatened to choke the sea-lanes and the empire that depended on them? From his hatred of the Turks and British, he seemed to be a "humanitarian." But why did he persist in a troubling "attachment to the slave trade"?

Afghani explained that the Mahdi was a sign of the times, part of a global reaction against the empires. He explained "how much slaves gained among Mohammedans in exchange for their freedom." He contained his amusement as Blavatsky and Olcott nodded sagely.

While Blavatsky worked on the successor to Isis Unveiled, *Olcott pursued Buddhist diplomacy.* At the Hospice de la Salpêtrière in Paris, he met the hypnotizing psychologist Dr. Charcot, with whom Freud would shortly study, and took Charcot's theory that "abnormal" phenomena had physiological causes as a victory for Theosophy. At the Colonial Office in London, Olcott persuaded Lord Derby to make the Buddha's birthday a national holiday in Ceylon. At dinner, Olcott talked Theosophy with Robert Browning and Edwin Arnold. At Oxford, his host was the philosopher John Francis Russell, Bertrand's elder brother. At Edinburgh, Olcott gathered dozens of disillusioned Presbyterians into a Scottish Theosophical lodge. Presbyterians, he thought, resembled Muslims. It was either tolerance and amity or "bigotry and massacre."

Returning to London, Olcott visited the physicist William Crookes and viewed his "Crookes tubes," the glass chambers in which Crookes, using partial vacuums, had discovered cathode rays. In the offices of the *Pall Mall Gazette*, Olcott watched the "thought reader" Stewart Cumberland at work. The other witnesses were the industrialist Andrew Carnegie; the *Gazette* editor W. T. Stead, who was leading the press campaign for Gordon's rescue from the Mahdists at Khartoum; the novelist Edmund Gosse; Ernest Hart, editor of the *British Medical Journal*; and the *Gazette* book critic Oscar Wilde.

After recovering from the "pleuritic cold," which all the best people seemed to catch that spring, Olcott resumed his sociable labors as guest of honor at a private dinner at the Junior Athenaeum Club. His hosts were the committee of the Society for Psychical Research, president Henry Sidgwick, professor of moral philosophy at Cambridge.

"Are the much despised Spiritualists and the Society for Psychical Research to be the chosen instruments of the new era of faith?" William James wondered in March 1884. "It would surely be strange if they were, but if they are not, I see no other agency that can do the work."

The SPR had formed in 1882 as a research group in the Spiritualist Society, but its members soon broke away. Sidgwick and his friends believed that "psychical" phenomena had physiological causes. They wanted to sieve genuine phenomena from the exploitation and fakery of the séance room. The neutral and universal modes of science would supply the proofs. Their leaders were the "intelligences of the elite": the moral philosopher Sidgwick; the physicists Lord Rayleigh and William Crookes; the Classical scholars Frederic Myers and Gerald Balfour; Balfour's brother Arthur, a philosopher and future prime minister; and Edmund Gurney, a lawyer whom William James thought "one of the first-rate minds of the time." The group's only female member, the mathematician Eleanor Balfour Sidgwick, was, as Sidgwick's wife and a Balfour cousin, doubly integrated into this male network. "Truly a brilliant company of scholars and literati!" Olcott said.

The upper echelons of the SPR, the Theosophical Society, and the Spiritualist Society overlapped in the way of aristocratic houses. The London Theosophist George Wyld was a member of all three groups. So was Olcott's friend Charles Carleton Massey, who attended the births of Theosophy in New York and the SPR in London. Sinnett, Crookes, and Myers of the SPR were also Theosophists. The physicist William Fletcher Barrett, who coined "automatic writing," remained a Spiritualist after joining the SPR. So did Frank Podmore, a postal inspector who filled his evenings as an SPR investigator, a Christian

Theosophist, and a member of the socialist group that he named the Fabian Society.

The SPR ruled the anarchy of the spirits with the methods of the governing class. They prepared the national Census of Hallucinations. They created a specialist vocabulary of "automatic writing," "psychography" and "telepathy." Like civil servants assessing sewers or schools, they sent committees to investigate psychical complexities, then issued reports titled "Mediumship," "Apparitions and Haunted Houses," "Mesmerism," and "The Odic Force"; this last being their preferred name for the vital force, named in 1845 by Carl von Reichenbach after the Norse god Odin. The SPR viewed a medium as a judge eyed a habitual offender. Its members would no more pay for a séance than a judge would pay a witness. They trusted completely in what Sidgwick called the "spirit of justice" and the "consensus of experts," as well as the tutelary value of a stiff sentence. So far, the SPR's findings suggested that telepathic communications were "crisis apparitions," etheric messages from the dying or those fearing imminent death.

The summer sensations of 1884 were the slow martyrdom of General Gordon at Khartoum and two images of feminine power, anonymous, mysterious, and dressed in black.

In June, John Singer Sargent shocked Paris with the creamy upper body of *Madame X.* Her right shoulder strap slipped down her arm to suggest the imminent collapse of her corsetry, by gravity or her innate Odic Force. Her anonymity did not last long. She was the young American socialite Virginie Gautreau, and her mother ordered Sargent to remove the portrait from the salon.

In July, Blavatsky made her London debut, corseted to the neck at a reception for over five hundred at Prince's Hall in Piccadilly. Ambassadors and consuls from Russia, France, Holland, and Romania mingled with diplomats, scholars, scientists, a splendid array of titled nobility, and Oscar Wilde, whose mother and wife were fashionably Theosophical that summer.

Blavatsky entered a "mad turmoil" of visitors, meetings, dinners, and evening callers. At Cambridge, the SPR questioned her for two hours in a room "crowded to overflowing." Sidgwick was "favourably impressed with Mmc. B." Some of her answers recalled the worst aspects of *Isis Unveiled*, but she seemed "frank and straightforward." He found it hard to imagine that she was an "elaborate imposter." The next day, he and Myers enjoyed a "Theosophic lunch" with Blavatsky. Sidgwick found Blavatsky to be a "genuine being," a humanitarian with an excellent sense of humor. His objectivity was unimpaired: "She is extremely unattractive—with her flounces full of cigarette ashes—and not prepossessing in manner." At the end of August, Frederic Myers of the SPR interrogated a bedridden Blavatsky for five and a half days. He too found his confidence growing.

*If Europe seemed suddenly Theosophic, it was because Theosophy re-*turned west at a pivotal moment. A different idea of mental cause and effect was emerging, with a different relationship to the cosmos.

In December 1882, Edmund Gurney of the SPR had invited William James to address the Scratch Eight, a London dining club whose members included the Cambridge philosopher George Croom Robertson and Leslie Stephen, a man of letters and the father of Virginia Woolf and Vanessa Bell. James was then forty years old, a slight, dapper assistant professor of philosophy at Harvard whose moods swung from energetic enthusiasm to insomnia and lethargy. The first teacher of psychology at an American university, James had joined the Theosophical Society in 1882, and in 1884 would be instrumental in setting up an American wing of the SPR.

James believed in the reality of what he was to call "religious experience" and in the possibility of contacting the dead. Yet the familiar explanations of mental life disappointed him. He could not believe that the brain was a machine for linguistic logic, its mechanisms rendered opaque by language; as his novelist brother Henry showed so elegantly, language was an unreliable narrator. Nor could he accept the mystical view of the "Platonizing schools" as expounded by his father, Henry James, Sr., a Swedenborgian depressive who, after a lifetime of preaching "supersensible Reason," died while William was in London.

James had come to London to rest his nerves but also to work. The promising but untilled field of psychology, he thought, either overlooked or falsified "immense tracts of our inner life." His experiments with laughing gas had convinced him that "normal waking consciousness, rational consciousness as we call it, is but one special type of consciousness." All around it, parted by "the flimsiest of screens," are "potential forms of consciousness entirely different," each awaiting its stimulus, each with its field of application and adaptation. James wanted to map the borders of rational consciousness and its adjoining territories for science. "No account of the universe in its totality can be final which leaves these other forms of consciousness quite disregarded."

His talk to the Scratch Eight began the work that would become *Principles of Psychology* (1890), a new basis for the science of the mind. Mental life, James told his hosts, was not stable and fixed but endless and fluid. The mind did not proceed by mechanical increments like a clock or an engine. It was a single flow, a "wonderful stream of consciousness." In the words of Nietzsche, another philosopher who now called himself a "psychologist," life was not a state of being but a permanent becoming.

The SPR thought that the "crisis apparition" came from outside the mind, just as exorcists had understood possession by devils. But the new psychologists like Charcot and his rivals Ambroise-Auguste Liébeault and Hippolyte Bernheim believed that "abnormal" mental states had physiological causes. In "What Is an Emotion?," an article from 1883, James also argued for the new "introspective psychology": emotional states are physical experiences, the bodily effects of perception. None of these new theories explained mental states as responses to external actors, ghostly or not. All of them looked within. The "other world" of external spirits was becoming the "inner world" of medical psychology.

Sidgwick described his mission by quoting Walt Whitman: "I have urged you forward, and still urge you, without the slightest idea of our destination." In the summer of 1884, the outlines of that destination emerged. The SPR had been founded by philosophers and Classicists, but its American committee was made up of doctors and scientists. The white coat of the doctor was replacing the stagy silks and velvets of the Mesmerist. The séance room was becoming a consulting room, the theater a laboratory.

For Blavatsky, the summer of 1884 was an extended moment of mastery. The SPR seemed to be on the verge of endorsing Theosophy. When it did, she would be crowned as the empress of the new era of faith, holding East and West in her hand like Zarathustra. She talked of the eternal cycle of forgetting and remembering as the sweep of cosmic time, and of its current movement as the entry into the next Kali Yuga. But the recurrence that now overpowered her was Nietzschean: personal, interior, and physical, a "crisis apparition" from her own past. Like the eruptions at Krakatoa the previous autumn, this sequence of subterranean explosions from the Southern Hemisphere shifted tides in the English Channel, and raised a dust cloud that, rolling slowly around the globe, dampened the hopes of summer, and spoiled the European harvest for years to come.

Before Olcott had sailed for Europe, he had placed the Indian headquarters of the Theosophical Society in the hands of the seven-member Board of Control under Dr. Franz Hartmann. At once, a dispute broke out between Hartmann and Alexis and Emma Coulomb, who also claimed that Blavatsky had left them in charge. The point of dispute was access to the epicenters of Adyar phenomena: Blavatsky's bedroom, the library, and the shrine room.

While Alexis Coulomb was hurriedly plastering over his handiwork, his report of the crisis had reached Blavatsky in Paris. She had decided to denounce the Coulombs before they exposed her. In April, when Olcott had been on the boat train for London, Mohini Chatterjee had slipped him an astral warning: "You have harboured a traitor and an enemy under your roof for years." A conspiracy was afoot and "great domestic annoyances" were coming. Three weeks later, Dr. Hartmann had received a missive from one Mahatma Morya, warning him that Emma Coulomb was negotiating with "enemies of the cause" and was in the habit of falsifying evidence with "trap doors and tricks." At the same time, Emma Coulomb received a forged letter, in which "Dr. Hartmann" promised that he no longer believed in Blavatsky. The handwriting did not look like Hartmann's. "Excuse short letter," the writer apologized. "I am writing in the dark."

Hartmann and the Board of Control removed the shrine cupboard from the wall and found the hidden cavity. They opened the shrine and peered inside. "You see, the back is quite solid," insisted Ananda, one of Blavatsky's Indian aides, striking the back of the cupboard with his hand. At which, to everyone's surprise, the middle panel of the cupboard shot up.

The Board of Control charged the Coulombs with extortion, blackmail, slander, and embezzlement and expelled them from Adyar. The Coulombs refused to go; they worked, they said, for Madame. So the board cabled Blavatsky in Paris. She dropped the Coulombs by telegram, not astral letter: "Sorry you go. Prosper."

The Coulombs had followed Blavatsky's instructions to the letter for five years and they took her last order literally. They cashed in their insurance policy: forty letters containing Blavatsky's instructions for the preparation of phenomena, including the Simla teacup trick. Emma Coulomb gave these souvenirs to Blavatsky's greatest enemy, Reverend Pattison, the principal of Madras Christian College. Less than two weeks after Blavatsky had won Frederic Myers's support, *Christian College Magazine* printed the Coulomb correspondence under the headline "The Collapse of Koot Hoomi." Pattison did the Lord's work and forwarded the story to newspapers all over India. Nine days later, his allegations appeared in the London *Times*.

Blavatsky denied everything. The letters were a "fabrication." The Coulombs had mixed old notes with "interpolations that entirely pervert their meaning." To protect Theosophy from these tawdry accusations, she must resign as the society's secretary while she defended her reputation. Like Madame X's shoulder strap, which Sargent now repainted higher on her arm, Blavatsky retired to a more decorous location: "I am returning to India to prosecute these traducers of my character, these fabricators of my letters."

She sailed for Madras on the last day of October. She stopped in Egypt—where a belated attempt to relieve Gordon at Khartoum was under way—to collect a police file on the Coulombs, then cabled Olcott: "Success complete. Outlaws. Legal proofs."

Olcott remembered his past life as a lawyer. He cabled back: if Blavatsky sued the Coulombs, he would resign from the society.

In November 1884, the SPR's investigator Richard Hodgson landed in Bombay.

Hodgson had been one of Henry Sidgwick's students at Cambridge. He believed in telepathy; later in the decade, as secretary of the American SPR, he would endorse the Boston medium Leonora Piper, with whom William James would sit many times. Hodgson's methods, though, drew on another new discipline at the junction of materialist science and speculative psychology, named that year by the Italian lawyer Raffaele Garofalo as *criminologia*, "criminology." Two years before Sherlock Holmes appeared in print, Hodgson examined Blavatsky with the forensic method. He soon detected a "huge fraudulent system."

At the society's first home in Bombay, Hodgson climbed into the attic through a trapdoor in the ceiling of Blavatsky's bedroom, then crawled over to inspect the ceiling of the adjoining room. Two of the planks had been prized apart, and the gaps "carefully filled in with bits of stick and dust," leaving a niche for the delivery of astral letters. In Adyar, Hodgson peered through the spyhole in Damodar's bedroom wall, reopened the hollow partition behind the shrine, and cross-examined the suspects. Aided by the Coulombs' confessions, he exposed the lies of Blavatsky's Indian aides.

Blavatsky had tailored her phenomena to their recipients. She had given instructions to the Coulombs in coded notes, letters, and telegrams, and they had strewn her path with manifestations and messages from the ether. While Blavatsky had distracted in the drawing room, Emma Coulomb had scurried ahead to place a mahatma note in some distant but specified location. The Simla teacup trick and Major Henderson's diploma had been achieved by Coulomb corrupting Mrs. Sinnett's servants. When Leonora Piper used the same trick against William James, he, like Patience Sinnett, would be unable to imagine treachery behind the baize door.

It transpired that Mrs. Hume's lost brooch had not been retrieved from the *akasha* and "reintegrated" in her shrubbery. Her daughter Minnie had secretly given the brooch to a lover. He had pawned it, then sold the ticket to Blavatsky as he was leaving India on a one-way passage paid for by Colonel Olcott. The ghostly mahatmas were not tall because they were ancient Aryans. They were tall because the Coulombs, who both seemed to have donned the mahatmas' white robes, had finished the ensemble with a plaster "Indian head" like a top hat. Damodar Mavalankar had learned to mimic Blavatsky's handwriting so that he could write mahatma letters in her absence. To obstruct the board's inquiry, he had hidden the shrine cupboard in his bedroom, then broken it up and burned it.

Handwriting analysis showed that, like Blavatsky, Koot Hoomi neglected to close his "o," wrote a German "d," and put a dash over his "m" in the style of a Russian "t." One of his Tibetan missives had reproduced a speech given two months earlier by the Christian Spiritualist Henry Kiddle in Lake Pleasant, New York, which had been printed in the *Banner of Light*.

"For our own part," the SPR committee reflected, "we regard her neither as the mouthpiece of hidden seers, nor as a mere vulgar adventuress; we think she has achieved a title to permanent remembrance as one of the most accomplished, ingenious, and interesting impostors in history."

When the trap in Olcott's bedroom ceiling had jammed, Alexis Coulomb had crawled into the attic and dislodged the letter by hand, releasing a small cloud of dust. Olcott had taken the dust for the astral "vapour" from which the letter had cohered. Hodgson pitied Olcott's "extreme deficiency" of observation, his peculiar lapses of memory, and his "extraordinary credulity." Yet Olcott's honesty of purpose could not be doubted. He seemed entirely devoid of the sharpness and cynicism needed for "wilful deception."

Olcott was determined to remain an innocent abroad. Hodgson, he reckoned, had too much confidence and too little knowledge. The mysteries of the Indian occult would always elude the plodding methods of a Scotland Yard detective. When Hodgson informed him that Blavatsky called him a "psychologized baby," Olcott responded with a Buddha's laugh. He no longer cared whether her images of spiritual perfection were illusory or if the impulses behind them were swinish and voluptuous, the spiritualized lusts of a desert saint. Sure of their ultimate cause, he had perfect faith in their effects. The *Buddhist Catechism* was about to appear in American, French, Burmese, German, and Japanese editions. He had ideas for an international Buddhist flag.

In early January 1885, Olcott was at Rangoon in Burma when a telegraph boy woke him at one in the morning with the news that Blavatsky was dangerously ill. Taking the steamer *Oriental* to Madras, he found her between life and death, her kidneys weak, her heartbeat erratic. When he sat at her bedside, she embraced him and wept.

She recovered so fast that her doctor called it a miracle. So did she. She told Olcott that, as she slipped away, a master had laid his hand on her chest and recalled her to life.

"Wonderful woman!" he sighed.

Blavatsky's heart remained weak. Her doctor, Mary Scharleib, thought her "quite unfit for the constant excitement and worry to which she is exposed in Madras." HPB must go at once to Europe and remain in a temperate and peaceful climate. The Board of Control agreed. The Coulomb scandal had shamed Theosophy before the whole world. Politely the priests drove Isis from her temple and put her on a steamer.

Hippopotamine in a black scarf, stiffly upright in her chair, the gouty empress Blavatsky rose into the air above the ship's deck and, floating ectoplasmically over the rail, drifted over the heads of dock-workers, customs officials, sailors, and passengers to land softly on the quay at Naples, where the stevedores, like magician's assistants, untied the ropes. The cable was winched up, the crane swung back, and Madame's nurse gripped the handles of her hospital chair, a three-wheel sarcophagus with a polished black lid. Forward Blavat-sky wobbled across the cobbles, boxed in from the waist down, her eyes wide in a thyroid bulge, like a corpse who, woken by the wailing of mourners, sits up in surprise.

She settled in the new south London suburb of Sydenham, over whose hills Ruskin had wandered as a child. Each day, she was pro-pelled through its dustless streets for an invalid's constitutional in a park where the Crystal Palace and its dinosaurs moldered in the soft English rain. She never returned to India.

"She is indeed a rare psychological study," Hodgson reflected, "almost as rare as a *Mahatma!*" Hodgson had unveiled Isis, but her motives tormented him. Why had this "strange, wild, passionate, un-conventional woman" devoted twenty years to "a fantastic work of imposture"? Theosophy resembled "an incipient world religion," but Blavatsky, Hodgson thought, did not suffer from religious mania. She showed no inclination to personal sacrifice. Nor were her manners of "the St. Theresa type." Challenged, she had flown into terrible, purple-faced rages and denounced her denouncers with "unique resentment." She seemed more like a criminal. An "accomplished forger" of other people's handwriting, she incited her confederates to impersonations and "dishonorable statements," then betrayed them. Yet she lacked the criminal's desire for pecuniary gain and, Hodgson believed, its amoral twin, a "morbid yearning for notoriety."

Only one hypothesis remained. The rumors must be true. If the Theosophical Society was not a spiritual or financial venture, it must be political. Blavatsky was not a prophet or a philosopher, but a Russian spy, a pawn in the Great Game. She had come to India, Hodgson reported, to scout for the Russian army that would invade through the Khyber Pass and to "foment as widely as possible among the natives a disaffection towards British rule."

Hodgson wanted to believe. His next SPR case would be the Boston medium Leonora Piper; unable to detect her tricks, he would pronounce her genuine. He could not imagine that Blavatsky was driven by the desire for power over others. He thought she seemed too pitiful for that. It took a decaying culture, Nietzsche had written, to produce the ripest and most sinister kind of pity: the self-pity that denied its offenses as it justified them. This was the path of western nihilism, "a European form of Buddhism."

Theosophy was not a political conspiracy from Russia, but it did reflect the politics of a conspiratorial Russian. To Blavatsky, democracy meant mob rule. Radical politics meant *Narodnya Volya,* "The People's Will," the bomb-throwers who in 1881 had murdered Czar Alexander II. The ideal Theosophist was a spiritual aristocrat, like the high-caste Brahmins who gathered in Adyar; the European nobles whose house-guest Blavatsky became; or Pushkin's African great-grandfather, whom Peter the Great had seen as an example for courtiers to emulate in handling their serfs. Theosophy was above the plebeians.

In India, Blavatsky fomented disaffection, but selectively; like Afghani, she wanted to cultivate a small but authoritative group of leaders. Her admirers found a different use for Theosophy's lofty view of life. All of them, British or Indian, were liberal in politics, proud of India's development, optimistic about its *babu* middle class, and frequently alarmed by the ignorance of its unlettered majority. Theosophy appealed to them as the key not just to past glories, but also to the present mystery of India's political development. Theosophy transcended the fissures of language, caste, color, and faith. It was above ordinary politics because it stood not for negotiation and compromise but for inviolable truths. It was a form of spiritual politics, the kind that Nietzsche, an esoteric practitioner, derided as "Petersburg metapolitics."

Theosophy's falsity was the secret of its success. It was a vulgar Platonism, an ideal image unmarred by the imperfections of reality, a reconciler of irreconcilable differences, a shared icon erected on the common ground of the inner life. Fictive or not, conjured from a lust for power not truth, Blavatsky's creation now had a life of its own. Allan Hume, the radical ornithologist of Simla, called Blavatsky "the most marvellous liar he had ever met" and laughed at his own credulity. Nevertheless, it was on the Theosophical Society's common ground that the Indian independence movement first appeared. In 1885, Hume and his Theosophical friends organized the first meeting of the Indian National Congress at Poona.

Two weeks after Blavatsky arose from her deathbed, the Mahdi's horde overran Khartoum and slaughtered almost all its defenders. Speared on the steps of the residency, General Gordon received the posthumous indignities of an early Christian martyr. His mutilated body went into the Nile and his severed head, having been presented to the Mahdi, was jammed into the fork of a tree, where it swelled in the heat like a mustachioed melon.

It turned out that Gordon had not wanted to be rescued. He had gone to Khartoum in search of martyrdom. He was a desert saint following a private, apocalyptic version of Christianity, a soldier who yearned to slip what the Spiritualists called the "sheath" of the body, a virgin bachelor who had picked up street urchins and preached the Gospels to them as he scrubbed them in a horse trough. He was a case of what Nietzsche, no stranger to the condition, called the "religious neurosis," and his kinsmen honored him accordingly. The artist William Joy produced a Victorian icon from the first scene of Gordon's apotheosis: the Christian soldier offers his body to the spear's thrust and does not raise his revolver against the latter-day legionary. This image may mask a different impulse. One of the few survivors claimed that Gordon had died fighting his way to Khartoum's magazine, in an attempt to blow it up, and himself too.

The Mahdi enjoyed a sybaritic interlude in the ruins, then died from typhoid before the year was out. The new caliph, Abdullahi, was no scholar or mystic but merely the strongest of the tribal leaders who had rallied to the Mahdi's call. The Sudan became a private kingdom of tyranny and starvation. Afghani left for Russia at the invitation of Blavatsky's publisher Mikhail Katkov, the editor of the *Moscow News*. He returned to Persia after Katkov's death in 1887 but was expelled in 1891 for agitating against the granting of a monopoly on tobacco exports to a British company. He spent his last years in a gilded cage on the Bosphorus as a propagandist for Abdul Hamid II's version of pan-Islamism. From this perch, Afghani may have inspired the assassination of the shah of Persia in 1896. He died of throat cancer in 1897, more a prisoner than a guest, his capacity for ambivalence undimmed. To the last, the sultan suspected he was a British spy.

"And do you know what I take 'the world' to be? Shall I hold my mirror up to it? This world is a monster of energy, without beginning or end; a fixed and invariable magnitude of energy, no more, no less, which is never expended, merely transformed . . . a space everywhere filled with energy, a play of energy and waves of energy, simultaneously the 'One' and the 'Many,' waxing here and waning there, an ocean of tempestuous and torrential energies, forever changing, forever rolling back, with enormous periods of recurrence . . . this is my beyond good and evil, which has no aim if it does not lie in the happiness of the circle, which has no will, unless a ring must by nature keep goodwill to itself."

The deeper Nietzsche dug into the brazen life of instinct, the less he believed in the materialist doctrine of cause and effect. If the body was an empire, the emperor had no idea what was going on—not just in his barbarian satrapies, but even in the palace of his mind. The conscious mind was a regent, unaware of his subjects' activities until they caused him pleasure or pain by crossing the frontier of his awareness. Beyond that frontier, all was mist and confusion. It was absurd to equate a singular perception with its plural sources in instinct, to reduce uncertainty and ignorance to a single value of truth, to confuse the spume of the waves with the currents at their depth.

He suspected that the emperor of science, in replacing God as the icon of truth, had assumed his predecessor's robes and eminence, like the cunning student who, masking resentment in compliance, covets his mentor's chair. The world of science covered the globe, but its firmament, though it looked opaque, was merely reflective, a fictive concavity, a shield from the truth. There was no "intelligible world" on which to build the "moral" conceit, no materialism capable of gratifying the "metaphysical need" for meaning.

"Do you want a *name* for my world? A *solution* to all its enigmas? A *light* for you who are best concealed, strongest, most intrepid, most Northerly, most midnightly? *This world is the Will to Power—and nothing besides!* And even you yourselves are this will to power—and nothing besides!"

❧ 11 ❧

CULTURE AND ANARCHY

The New Age Education
of Mohandas Gandhi

> Whether it be that I was born mad or a little too sane, my kingdom was not of this world: I was at home only in the realm of my imagination, and at my ease only with the mighty dead. Therefore I had to become an actor, and create for myself a fantastic personality fit and apt for dealing with men, and adaptable to the various parts I had to play as author, journalist, orator, politician, committeeman, man of the world and so forth . . . I was outside society, outside politics, outside sport, outside the Church. If the term had been invented then, I should have been the Complete Outsider. —*George Bernard Shaw, preface to* Immaturity *(1879)*

H is mother and uncle had feared that he would pollute his body, so before leaving Porbandar, his little town by the Arabian Sea, he had procured a Jain monk to administer a vow to avoid meat, alcohol, and sex. Nevertheless in Bombay his caste had expelled him for his determination to cross the black waters. Still, he kept his vow. He spent much of the six-week voyage in his cabin, surviving on the Gujarati sweets and savories that his mother had prepared, emerging to take an Englishman's constitutional around the deck at sunset or

admire the Englishman's handiwork at Aden and Suez, or to decline
an invitation to use a beautiful girl of fourteen in the docks at Brindisi.

The new white suit stayed in its trunk all the way. Now, on the
night of September 29, 1888, he unpacked it. The *Clyde* slid into the
Thames Estuary, the lights in the amphibian villages on the banks
glinting like yellow teeth. It was nearly midnight when he disembarked at Tilbury, a dock with a hinterland of slums and barracks, and
realized his mistake. The English summer was over. The civilized had
already mothballed their white suits. Checking into the Victoria Hotel by Charing Cross station, his shame was almost too much.

After the sunlight, spices, and salted air of Porbandar, the maw of
the metropolis swallowed him up. Gray northern skies and the smells
of sweat, beer, and tobacco. Coal dust on his skin, horse dung on his
boots. London had Indian students, African dockers, and Chinese tai-
lors; every variety of European, including a menagerie of socialist and
anarchist refugees from the Continent's less tolerant regimes; enough
Muslims to merit the building of its first mosque; and as many Jews
in its East End as there were in Warsaw. He rented a room in a house
overlooking the railway tracks of West Kensington. He was alone for
the first time in his life.

Mohandas Gandhi wanted to become a doctor, but his uncles had de-
cided that a lawyer would be more likely to restore the family's for-
tunes. His father, Karamchand, had been *diwan*, prime minister, to the
princes of Porbandar, Rajkot, and Vankaner, only to die suddenly,
leaving nothing to his fourth wife and his seven children. With the
land and jewels sold, Mohandas, the youngest and brightest son, took
up the task of recovering his father's office. Children, Gandhi later
advised, should sacrifice all happiness and pleasure in "devoted service" to their parents. But his offerings seemed paltry. He was shy, and
his ears and nose were too large for his head. He suffered from headaches and constipation, and he had nightmares about ghosts, thieves,
and serpents. Prone to tears and poor at cricket, he drifted through

school, dropping out of his first college after a few months because he could not keep up.

Gandhi blamed his mediocrity on his marriage, and on his parents for prematurely exposing him to the "disasters of lustful love." At seven, Gandhi had been betrothed to Kasturba Kapadia, the beautiful daughter of his father's friend. At thirteen, they married. The new husband was consumed by "devouring passion." Sexual reveries distracted him in the classroom. He woke Kasturba when she was sleeping in order to pleasure himself, then kept her awake afterward with his chatter. Impersonating a patriarch, he jealously accused her of faithlessness and used "severities" and "imprisonment" to bully her into being an ideal wife. "My ambition was to make her live a pure life, learn what I learnt, and identify her life and thought with mine." Impersonating a reformer, he tried to teach her to read and write, but could not keep his hands off her: "Lustful love gave me no time." Kasturba failed to reciprocate his enthusiasm in bed, and she seemed determined to remain illiterate. It was his first experience of passive resistance.

Gandhi believed that his "burning attachment" to filial duty prevented sexual desire from leading to disease and premature death. One night, duty and disaster woke him from the "sleep of lust." The fifteen-year-old Mohandas was a nurse to his ailing father, but each evening, as he massaged his father's legs, his mind remained in the grip of desire. He would hurry straight to the bedroom after "doing obeisance" to his father. One night, Mohandas's uncle relieved him of his duties, and Mohandas retired to his bedroom early. He woke his pregnant wife and, defying "religion, medical science, and commonsense," had perfunctory sex with her. Within five minutes, a servant brought the news that his father had died. He would never efface his conviction that, through sexual desire, he had betrayed his father at the critical hour.

Shortly afterward, Kasturba was delivered of a "poor mite" that lived for only three or four days. Mohandas believed that this too was the price of lust. "Nothing else could be expected. Let all those who are married be warned by my example." Soon, Kasturba was pregnant again. This time she bore him a healthy son, but Mohandas still carried his "double shame." Apart from equipping him for his career, a few years in London would be a "long and healthy spell of separation" from the fertile and infuriating Kasturba. His act of filial piety was also an escape from piety's punishments, the shame of conscience.

The natives were friendly, but they could not cook. The cuisine was barbarically carnivorous. Roast beef was a totem of family ritual, vegetables were boiled to a denatured pulp, and spices and condiments were avoided. Alcohol was taken at all hours. The latest street food was a crude immigrant medley, combining the fried fish of the Jews with the fried potatoes of the Irish. Mohandas's landlady, a widow whose husband had served in India, let him keep a portable stove in his room. He made oatmeal for breakfast, and soup and rice for dinner. He was perpetually hungry.

To qualify for his law degree, a student had to attend a minimum of seventy-two dinners at the Inner Temple. After grace, the gowned students sat in groups of four, sharing a joint of beef or mutton and two bottles of wine. Gandhi refused both. He knew the taste of dead flesh. At school, Sheikh Mahtab, a Muslim friend of his older brother's, had seduced him into the other kind of carnality. Mahtab was a muscular athlete who could "put up with any amount of corporal punishment" and boasted that he could hold live snakes in his hand. This idol attributed his strength, and the strength of India's imperial rulers, to the British diet. The schoolboys repeated a doggerel of the Gujarati poet Narmad:

> *Behold the mighty Englishman,*
> *He rules the Indian small,*
> *Because being a meat-eater,*
> *He is five cubits tall.*

Mohandas wanted to be like Mahtab. When he confided his wish, the older boy took him to a quiet spot by a river and unwrapped a piece of goat flesh. Mohandas felt sick as he chewed it; that night, he dreamed that a live goat was bleating inside him. There were more "meat-feasts," some of them public, before his idol took him to a brothel and paid for him. His desire stirred as he sat on the woman's bed, but he was tongue-tied, almost "dumb and blind." Instead of drawing him into the "jaws of sin," she threw him out. "I then felt as if my manhood had been injured, and wished to sink to the ground for shame." He never told his wife or parents about the double shame of these seductions. But he had confessed to his father a lesser infraction, stealing copper coins from the servants. His father had forgiven him and cried. His tears were "pearl-drops of love," fertilizing love and guilt in the wicked son's covetous heart.

In London, an Indian friend gave Mohandas acetic acid for the ringworm he had acquired on the boat, and also gave him a short course in English etiquette. He must not talk loudly or ask too many questions. It was not done to stare at people or touch their possessions. Only servants addressed people as "sir." The acetic acid stung his skin. He cried for his mother at night.

A few months later, another Indian friend bumped into him in Piccadilly. Mohandas was taking lessons in dancing, elocution, French, and musical appreciation, and reading the *Pall Mall Gazette*. He was a scholar dandy, "playing the English gentleman" in a top hat of brushed silk, a stiff, starched Gladstone collar, a "fine striped silk shirt," patent leather boots, and a silver-tipped cane.

He wrote home to tell them that English life was expensive, but there was no money to send. Penurious and delicate, he walked instead of squeezing into a train or omnibus, then washed the greasy soot of the London Peculiar from his skin as soon as he returned to his room. One day, he came across a vegetarian restaurant in the City of London. He entered, ate his first hearty meal in weeks, and bought a pamphlet, *A Plea for Vegetarianism*. In it, a socialist named Henry Salt masticated the politics of meat and the sinews of cruelty that tied the eater of flesh to imperialists and capitalists, the eaters of men. "God had come to my aid."

Salt said that when a vegetarian renounced the evil of meat, he declared his moral independence. By defining the boundaries of his body, he created himself as a spiritual power and a political force. Nor, Gandhi learned, was the Hindu the natural inferior of the Briton. The vegetarian was not the beefeater's plaything. The man of conviction was stronger than the man of appetite. The great-souled herbivore was more durable than the parvenu materialist, the handmade and human more valuable than the mechanical and technological. The renouncers would inherit the earth.

Mohandas Gandhi began his revaluation of values. He joined the Vegetarian Society, which defended dietary renunciation on the scientific grounds of health and hygiene. Soon, he was writing for the society's newspaper and addressing its meetings. He informed his British readers that the Indian shepherd, sustained by fresh air and vegetables, was "a very fine specimen," almost always free of "deformity," and bursting with "bodily strength." But when some Theosophist vegetarians asked him for his thoughts on the Bhagavad Gita, he had to admit that he had never read it. They gave him Edwin Arnold's translation. He had found the most important book of his life.

*A colonel's son, Henry Salt had taught classics at Eton before retreat-*ing in disgust to a cottage at Tilford in Surrey. Forswearing beef, servants, snobbery, and sex, Salt and his wife, Kate Joynes, subsisted on root vegetables, high principles, a small annuity, and—Kate having an "instinctive repulsion for any physical intimacy with the opposite sex"—celibacy. Their friends were a motley of eccentrics, agitators, lifestyle experimenters, socialists, aesthetes, homosexuals, feminists, anti-imperialists, anti-vivisectionists, and humanitarians: as the name of one of their early organizations had it, a Fellowship of the New Life, united in the search for what would soon be called the New Age.

Edward Carpenter had left a don's chair at Cambridge and, inspired by a gift of a pair of sandals from Kashmir, retrained as a sandal maker. He advocated for the rights of Uranians, the Irish, and Indians, and for a "return to Nature": nudism, handicrafts, and a vegetarian diet. He lived in a "homogenic" union with a working-class man; the Salt circle called him their "Noble Savage."

Henry Hyndman was the "scientific socialist" who in 1881 had founded the Democratic Socialist Party with Karl Marx's daughter Eleanor and the Arts and Crafts designer William Morris. Sidney Webb and his wife, Beatrix Potter, were social scientists and came down from London by train and tricycle. In 1884, the Webbs founded the Fabian Society, the forerunner of the Labour Party, to work for the "gradualist" conversion of Britain to socialism; in 1895, they set up the London School of Economics. The critic Edward Archer, whose translations of Ibsen introduced socialism to the London stage, convinced his fellow critic George Bernard Shaw to write for it. The sexologist Havelock Ellis, demonstrating his case for the complexity of human sexuality, was married to a lesbian, the feminist Edith Lees, and would remain impotent until, at the age of sixty, he watched a woman urinating.

And then there was George Bernard Shaw, the glib Dubliner who, incontinent with ambition and garrulity, inserted himself into every group, then emerged as its spokesman. He was present at the creation of the Fabian Society, the LSE, the Independent Labour Party, the *New Statesman*, and, in 1906, *The New Age* magazine. Playing Wagner duets on the Salts' piano with Edward Carpenter, supplanting Archer as the local Ibsenite, and claiming to be the "only man in the country" who had read Karl Marx, Shaw had Wilde's knack for fatuous cleverness and meaningless paradox, but he avoided Wilde's convictions—aesthetic, sexual, and criminal. The son of an alcoholic and a singing teacher, Shaw was profoundly shallow, a self-promoting flirt. He talked fearlessly about sex, and called his interrogation of women "vivisection," but remained a virgin "devotee of the Uranian Venus" until, aged twenty-nine, a widowed friend of his mother's cornered him on a sofa. Disinclined to repeat this violation, the socialist Don Juan at forty-three entered into an unconsummated marriage with a

Fabian heiress: "We may become celibate through a surfeit of beauty and an excess of voluptuousness. We may end as ascetics, saints, old bachelors." Unlike Nietzsche, Shaw thought this was the height of cleverness.

Soon the educated would take a dose of Shaw like constipated children lining up for their cod liver oil. But in 1889, Shaw was only a socialist lecturer and music critic, the editor of that year's *Fabian Essays in Socialism*. The worst was about to come: *The Perfect Wagnerite*, a Marxist reading of the *Ring* for people without the time to listen to Wagner or the patience to read Marx. *Man and Superman*, with Nietzsche cast as the straight man to Shaw's joker. The Shavian religion, a Nietzschean knock-off in which the dying God and the dogged Darwin ceded to the Life Force of "Creative Evolution." And "Shavian eugenics," the subordination of woman's biological fecundity to man's superior intellect, a twinkle-eyed blend of Lamarck and socialism whose punch line was gassing the "unfit to live."

If it was new or merely a novelty, clever or merely difficult, Shaw was there, never first, but reliably second. Affluence and education had created a society of self-helpers, masochistically enthralled to the bundlers of culture, and Shaw helped himself as he helped them. No simple life was simple enough to be lived without him; nor could the Fabian vision of an industrial caste system be achieved without his help. In Shaw's world, vivisection and inoculation were scientific barbarisms, but reorganizing society by eugenics and authoritarian control was common sense. For Shaw's world held no contradictions or impossibilities, only opportunities for paradoxical wit and self-advertisement.

Shaw was the first person to prepackage his character for public consumption. He dressed for the camera and spoke for the sound bite: the Jaeger suit that let the Shavian pores breathe, the curated beard of Mephistopheles and Don Juan, the sandals and bicycle of the higher man, the claim to be better than Shakespeare, the relentless rigging of the market in taste, the inanely topical commentary on the issues of the day, the fluent evasiveness that, as G. K. Chesterton complained, gave every logical reason for its opinions, and never the actual one.

Shaw's true motive, Chesterton thought, was sentimentality. His compassion for the poor and other animals reflected the shallow pool of his self-love. In Havelock Ellis's terminology, he was a "narcissist." He ranged so confidently because his reflection awaited him wherever he went. When personal photography became fashionable in the 1890s, Shaw bought a camera. In the new culture of images, he was one of the first to dive into the lens. From Shaw, Gandhi learned the arts of paradox and presentation. Only Gandhi would exceed Shaw's celebrity as a sandal wearer. Only Hitler would exceed Shaw's celebrity as a Wagnerite.

*Gandhi arrived in London as the New Age began to accumulate a crit-*ical mass: a consciousness of its growing density and youthful energies. Eighty years had passed since William Blake, coining a phrase, had called on the "young men of the New Age" to arise; sixty years since John Stuart Mill had detected the tremors of a revolutionary spiritual shift in the Age of Change; forty years since the midcentury prophets Thoreau and Ruskin had wept by their waters; twenty years since Blavatsky and Nietzsche had turned east. Throughout, the "compact system" had only intensified. On the infrastructure of railroads and laboratories, steam and electricity, industrialization accelerated into the surge of affluence that Twain called the Gilded Age and Carpenter the "Commercial Age": petrochemicals and telephones, imperial economies and finance capitalism, monopolies and scandals.

In Joaquin Miller's *The Destruction of Gotham* (1886), New York lies "trembling, panting, quivering in her wild, white heat of intoxication, excitement, madness—drunken and devilish pursuits of power, pleasure, and gold." Men have piled "thousands of filthy things" on Manhattan, a pollution that cries "to heaven for purification." Heaven hears, and Gotham goes up in flames of oil, gas, and rum. A river of hot lead runs from the newspaper offices in Franklin Square. Tramps from the Bowery attack the diners in fashionable restaurants. There are no reservations, no restraint.

"This is the era of anarchy," Carpenter wrote in *Civilisation: Its*

Cause and Cure (1889), "the democracy of Carlyle; the rule of the rabble and mob law; caucuses and cackle, competition and universal greed, breaking out in cancerous tyrannies and plutocracies—a mere chaos and confusion of society." The cities of the West produced more filth and luxury than any civilization in history. The revolt of their intelligentsia came from a surplus of production, an excess of good intentions, a waste of injured sentiment. It was, Carpenter insisted, a revolt against material surfeit, not physical starvation. Its search for meaning assumed the satisfaction of the need for food, shelter, and security. The poverty that it denounced was spiritual and emotional. Its outrage was a luxury product of industrial society, like the boredom and cynicism that Wilde reworked as wit and wisdom. Its protest was less a cry of hunger than of existential distress, like the "cry of disgust" that marks the turn from death to resurrection in Mahler's Second Symphony (1894).

In 1969, a century after Gandhi's birth, Theodore Roszak named the spiritual revolt of the New Age the "counter culture," and identified its enemy as the "technocracy." The nineteenth century knew these antagonists by their German names, *Kultur* and *Zivilization*. Civilization was the beef-laden sideboard, the starched collar, the whalebone corset, the corpulent paterfamilias: the Victorian edifice of control and affluence, resting on the backs of the workers. In this smug, brutal realm of mechanization and money, the spirit was strangled in the silk nooses of complexity, duty, and progress, or crushed by political, economic, and social facts as heavy as mahogany bookcases. Empire, the glory of the age, spread this domestic tyranny across the map, leaving a pinkish stain like washed-out blood.

If, as Carpenter wrote in *Civilization*, materialism and capitalism caused diseases of the soul, then culture was the cure. A simple and wholesome diet, planted, watered, grown, and harvested by those who ate it. Meals shaped by the seasons and the science of nutrition, not the cook in the basement and the need to impress. Fresh air, sunlight, and exercise to clean blackened lungs and straighten bent backs. The intoxicants of alcohol, tobacco, and sex in small doses, if at all.

Loose, practical clothes that allowed the body to move and breathe. The conscious embrace of responsibility in friendship and ethics, not the unthinking repetition of hereditary duty to father and class. The conscious acceptance of shared humanity, expressed by socialism on a human scale. The conscious pursuit of beauty and meaning instead of mass production and ignorance. The conscious affirmation of life as art and Man as artisan, a creator not a producer. The conscious creation of a community of equals from the quiet army of Bartlebys: the ranks of dreaming refusers blinking like fugitives from Plato's cave, the traumatized refugees fleeing the industrial Sodom and Gomorrah, the leagues of Isaacs despairing of the angel who would persuade the Abrahams to lower the knife.

William Morris commissioned a suit of armor for a painting, tried on the helmet, and then found he could not remove it. The visor was down, the vision narrowed. In the Manichean perspective of the culture warriors, civilization crushed consciousness. It bred dumbness, falsity, illusion, and insensitivity, a stuntedness of the soul. Culture was the war of liberation, its weapons intellectual conviction, artistic imagination, and religious joy, its rewards authenticity, health, and hygiene. But the cultural revolution was a product of technical civilization: a double or antipode, a secret sharer in its affluence, education, and optimism.

The ranks of rebels were swelled by a population boom: civilization had cheated Malthus with prosperity, medical hygiene, and public sanitation. The emblematic New Age vehicle, John Kemp Starley's safety bicycle (1885), was patented only a few months before Karl Benz's design for an automobile powered by a four-stroke combustion engine. Both of these antipodal transports ran on pneumatic rubber tires (1887) and roads smoothed and hardened with tarmac (1901).

Morris, the quintessential New Age designer, held violence to be essential to the revolution. He was arrested in street battles between socialist marchers and the police, and saw his Arts and Crafts designs as inspirations to revolt. Instead his handmade furniture and the vegetal riot of his block-printed wallpaper became totems of sophisticated consumption, the forerunners of Art Nouveau and the *Jugendstil.* His Ruskinian purging of clutter from Victorian interiors fostered not just Gothic simplicity, and later the workers' paradise of Bauhaus, but also the philistine complacency he reviled. While the New Agers fulminated against the empire over a Morris & Co. dining table, the bourgeois vulgarians massed at the door of Morris's shop on Oxford Street. Morris's wallpaper flattered the tea ceremony in a myriad of middle-class villas, including two of the biggest, St. James's Palace and Balmoral Castle.

In 1889, the revaluation of this surplus of energy and aspiration, long the dream of artists and philosophers, became a public phenomenon. Gandhi's first year in London was the year of *Fabian Essays*; of *A Doll's House,* Ibsen's attack on the conventions of a staid drama and a cruel patriarchy; and of *Seed-Time,* the journal of the Fellowship of the New Life. It was now possible for Oscar Wilde, tiring of journalism, to write *The Picture of Dorian Gray* and expect a readership. Shaw's "Complete Outsiders" were now recognized as political and aesthetic actors. If, like Wilde, they masked the implications of their performance in universalities and allusions, they could even be conditional insiders. For his leaden verse and packaging of medieval nostalgia, William Morris was offered the poet laureateship. He refused on principle, but politely.

In the same year, New Age ideas began to expand from the margins of British life to the edges of the empire. The novelist Olive Schreiner left Salt's fellowship and returned to her native South Africa to work for civil rights and feminism. Edward Carpenter, having privately studied the Bhagavad Gita for the best part of a decade, sailed for Ceylon. There, he communed with the local Theosophists and took "sun-baths" naked in the woods around Adam's Peak. He would return in 1891 as the first, but not the last, Western tourist talking of "cosmic consciousness" and the dissolution of the individual in the mystic eddies of Hindu spirituality and artisanal socialism.

"This is the way back to the lost Eden," Carpenter promised, "or rather forward to the new Eden, of which the old was only a figure."

*"The new aristocracy is in need of an opposing body which it may com-*bat," Nietzsche noted. "It must be driven to extremities in order to maintain itself."

He hoped that his thought would cure mankind of "metaphysical" needs as an ax cures a headache—perhaps "one day, at some future time—1890!" He wrote those words in October 1888, Gandhi's first month in London. In a sense, his prophecy was accurate. In the 1890s, Nietzsche became notorious by association, a synecdoche for spiritual revolt against modernity. The New Age adopted Nietzsche as the prophet of the life aesthetic. At the same time, the nationalists and Jew-baiters adopted Nietzsche as an Aryan warrior, despite his be-lated disavowal of pan-German nationalism, his rejection of antisem-itism as vulgar, and his conclusion that Wagner was not a mythic "redeemer" but part of the problem.

Neither of these interpretations did justice to Nietzsche, but nei-ther traduced him entirely. Nietzsche had recognized these subtle commonalities and his complicity with them. "He has to be the bad conscience of his time," he wrote of Wagner. "For that, he needs to understand it best."

Yet blood and biology, Nietzsche saw, were not the only forces that would shape the society and "spiritualization" of the future. Qual-ity contended with quantity, the individual with the species, aristoc-racy with slavishness. The new century faced two futures. Either Europe would lead mankind along the road to "perfection in being," or it would chase the fool's gold of the Wagnerian quest and founder in *ressentiment*. Either the breeding of the man of the future through personal discipline and the eugenic "annihilation of millions of the ill-constituted," or the dissolution of the aristocrat in the herd and a "levelling" that reduces "most people to mere social functions." Either the breeding of slavishness, perversion, dwarfishness, and degeneracy, or the conscious aloofness and self-development of a spiritual aristocracy in the name of Teutonic obedience and "long legs."

Nietzsche chose the aesthetic future: the eugenic future, the engineering of a "ruling race" of Supermen, the future "lords of the earth," an army of "philosophical authorities and artistic tyrants" that could stamp its will on the pliant masses of democratic Europe. But he feared that the gravity of the masses was already dragging the species downward. Europe had a surfeit of "ill-constituted, sickly, weary, and exhausted" people. Prostrate before "fatality" and false ideals of progress, they reeked of decayed morals and bad blood. Democratic politics placed the "maggot-man" in power, and he sensed a fatal alliance forming between the aristocratic ideal and the misshapen mass.

"Who can say whether modern democracy, even more modern anarchism and especially that inclination for 'commune,' for the most primitive form of society, which is now shared by all the socialists of Europe, does not signify in the main a tremendous counterattack— and that the conqueror and master race, the Aryan, is not succumbing physiologically, too?"

In an age of decline, Nietzsche realized, the public chooses not to expose itself to the healing and horror of Dionysian art. When the masses decide, they raise the collective thumb for illusion and the flattery of gratification. The new era is a golden age for the actors, the "machinists" of the inauthentic. The modern slave revolt will synthesize spiritual combat and mass politics into a "counterfeiting of transcendence." The theater of democracy will be bread and circuses, a "plebiscite against good taste." Actors will pose as gods, and base resentment will bay for noble blood. The emperor will be a slave raised to the purple.

"And when you look long into an abyss, the abyss looks long into you." For four years, Nietzsche had planned his *Götterdämmerung*, a "Twilight of the Gods," his final battle with the metaphysics and morals of the Christian world. In out-of-the-way lodgings and spas out of season, he had filled notebooks under the working title "The Will to Power." This scheme had inflated to ten volumes. The title had changed to "An Attempt at a New Interpretation of the World," then deflated to four volumes and "The Revaluation of All Values." Now he was ready for the duel of "Dionysus versus the Crucified," to "assassinate two thousand years of perversion and human disgrace."

Through the spring and summer of 1888, Nietzsche stared into the abyss of Europe's future. His limbs were numb and tingling, his headaches and eye problems worsening. He had the symptoms of syphilis, and suspected that the spirochete was in his brain. "In a significant sense," he wrote in December 1887, "my life now stands at *high noon.* One door is closing, another opening." He was overwhelmed by melancholy and "violent" mood shifts, and he could not control his emotions when he heard music. "My entire used-to-be is crumbling and falling away from me."

The merciless light of prophecy pulsed into Nietzsche and murderous, lucid visions poured out. Spurred on by "accidental contact" with French translations of the *Laws of Manu* and the novels of Dostoevsky—"the only psychologist from whom I had something to learn"—in the spring of 1888 he launched his last battle with Christianity, *The Antichrist.* "Two thousand years have come and gone—and not a single new god!"

At Sils Maria in June, he paused to disinter and desecrate the paternal cadaver in *The Case of Wagner*: "Through Wagner, modernity speaks most intimately, concealing neither its good nor its evil—having forgotten all sense of shame." Invigorated and disinhibited, Nietzsche resumed the nocturnal heresies of *The Antichrist.* In a single frantic week, he composed a primer to initiate readers into a revelation of heresy. Its title, *Götzendämmerung*, mocked the climacteric of Wagner's *Ring*: this age was a twilight of the *götzen*, false "idols," not true gods. "One has almost completed an account of the value of what is modern once one has gained clarity about what is good and evil in Wagner."

Nietzsche could not rest. The next day, September 4, the preface to *The Antichrist* came in a single burst. Spent, he stepped outside into a transparent, glowing dawn. On September 21, he returned to Turin,

the "aristocratic" city of Cesare Lombroso, the criminologist and author of *Genius and Insanity*. "I took the same apartment I had occupied
in the spring, Via Carlo Alberto 6, iii." Ignoring the view of the Pa-
lazzo Carignano and the hills beyond, he worked furiously on the last
quarter of *The Antichrist* and edited the proofs of *Twilight of the Idols*.
On September 30, Gandhi's first day in London, Nietzsche recorded a
"great victory": *The Antichrist* was complete. Overflowing, he poured
out a preface to *Twilight of the Gods*.

And then the creator, pleased with his work, rested: "Seventh day;
the leisure of a god walking along the River Po." Desire and pain dis-
charged, he drifted through an autumn of "indomitable perfection,"
each day a Claude Lorrain landscape, a perfect allegory "projected
into the infinite." The great transvaluation was complete.

The Antichrist was Nietzsche's oration to a mob that had yet to
assemble. After the neurotic repetitions of "monotono-theism"; after
their antithesis, the procedural fetishes of scientific materialism; at
last, the synthesis: the anti-Christian, a new god from the body of the
dead god. He felt certain that when *The Antichrist* was understood, it
would "split the history of humanity into two halves." Then September 30, 1888, would be celebrated as inaugurating a new chronology,
year one of *Anno Nietzschensis*.

"Good; even very good: since the old God is abolished, I am prepared to *rule the world*."

It was a decade of brutal claims to omniscience. In the 1880s, "imperi-
alism" entered common parlance. Hiram Maxim invented a portable,
automatic machine gun. Belgium, a small, recently confected state,
extracted the rubbery heart of Africa by the distinctively modern
blend of technology and barbarism. Engels revised Marx in *Scientific
Socialism*, in which Darwin and the dialectic converged in a necessary
future of centralized authority and industrial power. *The Antichrist*
shared in this violence and race snobbery, the triumphalism that, as in
Nietzsche's annexing of the Book of Revelation, evoked the past in
order to declare it obsolete, and invoked the future to declare its

mastery over a new age of blood and fire. "You are sanctified by a task like this, you are a type belonging to a higher order of things!"

Nietzsche made no new argument in *The Antichrist.* The content was in the style, the novelty in the power of execution. Having damned Wagner's grand style as a "lie," he now counterfeited himself with a gallery of "ideal" types. Like a tarot reader, Nietzsche promised an individual reading, a masterpiece of the new psychology, but produced mythic generalities. The woman is "a serpent," the source of "every evil in the world." The priest is a "holy parasite" in need of "hygiene": fat with tithes and beefsteaks, a parasite sprung from a "corrupt" soil. The Muslim is a warrior and despises the effeminate Christian: "Islam at least assumes that it is dealing with *men.*" The Jew is two-faced, double-headed like a royal card, split like Zoroaster's world of good and evil.

The Christian has no value unless combined with higher cards or multiplied by mass. Christians are *Chandala*, the "Untouchables" of the West, polluted and smelly like Polish Jews. Jesus is a degenerate "idiot" suffering from delayed puberty, more fool than holy. "It is a pity there was no Dostoevsky living near this most interesting decadent; I mean, someone with an eye for the distinctive charm offered by this sort of mixture of sublimity, sickness, and childishness." The Sermon on the Mount is the dream of a Galilean Buddha, preaching a vapid retreat from the world into an illusory inner kingdom. The Gospels are the work of malicious Jewish priests. Nietzsche is the trump and the joker, a god reborn as a "good European." The only rules are those of caste and war. "Either you *are* Chandala or you are *not* . . . War to the death with Rome! Peace and friendship with Islam!"

His subtitle for *Twilight of the Idols* was *How to Philosophize with a Hammer.* To sound the hollowness of the idols, each blow had to be as subtle as the stroke of a tuning fork. He could still hit the notes, but he had lost his perfect pitch and maestro's touch. He could no longer control the velocity of his stroke, or the recoil that bounced back and struck him like the pebbles that the urchins of Sils Maria threw as he walked along under his parasol. Shattered under the hammer, his brittle categories collapsed into each other, crumpling him inward into the heart of darkness: emptiness, nihilism, *ressentiment.*

After his disavowal of Wagner, the antisemites, and the nationalists, Nietzsche created an elaborate and personal genealogy for the Jews. The Jews were at the heart of his revaluation of values because they were at the heart of European civilization: the core where *ressentiment* met worship.

Nietzsche attacked Christianity with the rhetoric of antisemitism but called antisemitism a symptom of the "scabies of the heart." He also called for a revolution against an omnipresent and pernicious "Jewish" and "Oriental" tyranny of ethics; the revolt of blood against reason and caste against democracy; the spiritual regeneration of Europe by the destruction of unnatural and alien forms created by a metaphysical enemy called Judaism. In achieving exaltation, he became what he loathed. He glamorized hatred and despised compassion as weakness. He elevated contempt as the morality of the "higher man" and defined that man as a racial type. He derided liberalism as the path to degeneration, the modern disease.

Rolling elegantly in the pleasures of the gutter, he insisted on his virtue. He was no demagogue; his revaluation aimed for the stars: "I never speak to masses." Yet he expected that they would acclaim regardless, and even enjoyed the premonition of power that came with declaring an apocalypse. Like an actor after his soliloquy, he knew that the believers would applaud their "man of calamity."

"For when truth enters into a fight with the lies of millennia, we shall have upheavals, a convulsion of earthquakes, a moving of mountain and valleys, the like of which has never been dreamed of. The concept of politics will have merged entirely with a war of the spirits; all power structures of the old society will have been exploded—all of them are based on lies: there will be wars the like of which have never yet been seen on earth. It is only beginning with me that the earth knows metapolitics."

• • •

"Nothing like this," Nietzsche wrote, *"has ever been written, felt,* or *suffered."*

But it had: not as spiritual autobiography, but in the kind of science fiction where the reader did the suffering. Bulwer-Lytton's *Zanoni* had preceded Éliphas Lévi and Blavatsky. While Nietzsche declared himself Caesar and predicted the race war of the future, a Minnesota politician named Ignatius Donnelly wrote *Caesar's Column*, a dystopian "story of the twentieth century."

Donnelly was a utopian antisemite and an agrarian populist. In 1892, he composed the Populist Party's platform, which alleged that a "vast conspiracy" of capital was "taking possession of the world." Tastefully, he issued *Caesar's Column* as "Edmund Boisgilbert, MD": a pseudonym part medieval and part modern, its Norman surname suggesting a nostalgia for good breeding and the society of orders, its appendage scientific expertise. Nietzsche wanted his philosophy to last two centuries. Modestly, Donnelly set *Caesar's Column* only a century ahead.

In 1989 a Ugandan wool merchant arrives in New York. The city is in civil war between the Oligarchy, a cabal of Jewish financiers who rule the city with airships and poison bombs, and the Brotherhood of Destruction, a horde of "brutal and ravenous" slum dwellers. The old aristocracy has intermarried with Jews or been ground down into the "swarming" masses. "Well," one of the Brotherhood explains, "it was the old question of survival of the fittest." The Jews had been strengthened by "the most terrible ordeal of persecution." Now the "wheel of fortune has come full circle," and the Christians are paying for the cruelty of their "bigoted and ignorant ancestors" toward a "noble race."

The masses rise up against the Oligarchy and its middle-class aides. They flood the streets with human waves and slaughter their betters with "dynamite bombs." Their leader, Caesar Lomelli, orders them to stack the bodies in Union Square, for a modern monument like Caesar's column in Rome. Lit by bonfires, gangs of prisoners, some of them prominent merchants and lawyers, tip corpses from carts. Other slaves stack the bodies inside large wooden boxes, "like double lines from a central point" in a "many-rayed sun of death." Concrete is poured in, the wooden frames removed, the box lifted and stacked as the tower rises. The inscription commemorates the "death and burial of modern civilization."

Nietzsche diagnosed his illness as the sickness of his civilization. In declaring the death of the Christian world, he wrote his obituary; in announcing the birth of "metapolitics," he became its messiah. The sickly prophet placed himself as a sacrifice on the highest altar of power. It was as if King Leopold of the Belgians had encouraged his Congolese slaves by cutting off his own hand with a machete, or if Hiram Maxim had demonstrated his weapon by peering down the barrel as he pressed the trigger. It was the nadir of Romanticism, a vision of nihilism: a dead end, the murderer as a suicide.

The "resistance to natural instincts" had been the old morality's "center of gravity." Nietzsche had unseated that morality from the universe within. He had toppled the judge of conscience, purged the ideals of sin and guilt, rooted out the pollutants of pity, altruism, and "selflessness." He had unseated the omniscient eye of reason, the great Cyclops eye of Socrates, from its throne at the center of the universe. Displacing Jesus, he declared himself the "objectivist" who cut through the "world of appearances" to the "eternal core of things," his thoughts like the X-rays that in 1895 William Röntgen would discover beyond ultraviolet.

It was too late to stop. On October 15, his forty-fourth birthday, he began a philosophical autobiography, *Ecce Homo*. Nietzsche finished his gospel in just under three weeks. "This book is about me,— I come forth in it with a world historical mission." It explained the visions of his *Zarathustra*, and was the "first book of all millennia, the bible of the future, the highest outbreak of human genius, in which the fate of humankind is grasped." As he edited the proofs of *Ecce Homo*, he compiled *Nietzsche Contra Wagner*, a jigsaw puzzle of polished fragments taken from his previous monologues. He was taking a bow before posterity, commenting on unpublished works and unsecured fame, condensing his unresolved struggles for the reader of the future.

"Alas . . . no more!" On January 3, 1889, Nietzsche walks in the piazza below his room when he sees a coachman whipping a dying horse. An upsurge of compassion overwhelms him. He throws himself on the animal's neck, shielding it from the blows, sacrificing himself to the driver's anger. Back in his room, he dances naked like Shiva as his landlady peers through the keyhole.

Four days later, Franz Overbeck appears; Jacob Burckhardt urged him to rescue Nietzsche before the police arrest him. Overbeck finds Nietzsche cowering in his room. They embrace tearfully, Nietzsche trembling and groaning. He takes a sedative, then sits at the piano, stroking soft chords as he explains that he is "the Crucified," the son of the dead God. The bromide is not strong enough, and he begins to clown, jumping around, dancing, and shouting, making obscene gestures in the sacred tumult of Dionysus.

Nietzsche refuses to leave Turin. His doctor, a German Jewish dentist, suggests a ruse: Overbeck must tell Nietzsche that he has come to escort him to a grand reception in his honor. Nietzsche accepts the invitation. At Turin station, he offers to address the rabble. The dentist persuades him that he is too august a personage. He agrees and boards the train.

In the summer after Nietzsche's collapse, Gandhi's vegetarian friends gave him a pamphlet, *Why I Became a Theosophist.* The author, Annie Besant, described her apostasy and rebirth. Besant had been a propagandist for the Fabians, the Secular Society, and the Social Democratic Federation, an organizer of strikes and demonstrations, and a friend of Shaw, Carpenter, Hyndman, and the Russian anarchist Prince Peter Kropotkin. Her attempts to organize "bands of unselfish workers" had failed, and she had despaired. She had read A. P. Sinnett's *Occult World* and begun to dabble in Spiritualism. "Where was the material for a nobler Social Order, where the hewn stones for the building of the Temple of Man?" Besant asked. In early 1889 she found them when the *Pall Mall Gazette* asked her to review Madame Blavatsky's latest confabulation. Besant was "dazzled, blinded by the light" of Asia. Intrigued, Gandhi next read Blavatsky's *Key to Theosophy*, a primer for potential recruits written as a dialogue between a seeker who is dissatisfied with materialistic philosophy and a believer who is patronizingly satisfied with his new faith. Civilization, Blavatsky said, meant "the death of art and beauty," the victory of money and machines. Gandhi chose the revolt of culture.

Gandhi was never an intellectual. His grasp of philosophy was parlous, his understanding of science minimal, and his inquiries weak with credulity. In London, he found the Bible and Bentham's utilitarianism beyond comprehension. When, like other ambitious Indian students, Gandhi sat for the London matriculation exam, he passed Latin on the second attempt but failed chemistry because the experiments baffled him. He chose an easier course, Heat and Light. His reading showed his lifelong fondness for the former over the latter. In London, he pronounced "attractive" the ideas of Anna Kingsford, a worshipper of the Aryan Jesus who claimed to have killed two vivisectionists by mind power, and enjoyed Howard Williams's *Ethics of Diet*, which claimed that all true philosophers, from Pythagoras and Jesus to those of the present, were vegetarians.

In November 1889, Gandhi's friends judged him ready to meet Blavatsky and Besant. Blavatsky could still roll a cigarette singlehandedly as though on horseback, but her ailments had worsened and multiplied. Half deaf, she could not mount the stairs unaided, and she leaned on Besant when she moved and spoke. Despite this, she had rebuilt Theosophy after the Coulomb scandal. Her recent acolytes had established a Blavatsky Lodge, with an "inner section" for the choicer mysteries, and a new journal, *Lucifer: The Light-Bringer*, to launder her reputation. Meanwhile Blavatsky regained control of Theosophy by driving it forward, like a shark in the water. She updated its theology in *The Secret Doctrine* and, to control posterity, groomed Besant as her heir.

Blavatsky knew that *The Secret Doctrine* would be her final testament in her current incarnation; like Nietzsche, she wrote it for posterity. *Isis Unveiled* and *The Birth of Tragedy* had been works of unbridled philology, imaginative to the point of fiction and in beyond. *The Secret Doctrine*, like Nietzsche's "Will to Power" notebooks, spoke the scientific truths of the 1880s, and with similar license. Blavatsky's scientist followers kept her up-to-date on their fields, and she remained a bold plagiarist. *The Secret Doctrine* mingles digressions into comparative mythology with speculations on the Ice Age. Electricity is still the astral fluid, and the life force, or "Vril" of Bulwer-Lytton's *The Coming Race* (1871), but now it is also "atomic matter," as James Clerk Maxwell called it. The mythical lost continent of Atlantis was now essential to human origins; probably because of Ignatius Donnelly, who, improving on Plato, had proposed Atlantis as the earliest civilization of all in *Atlantis: The Antediluvian World* (1882). As in Bulwer-Lytton's and Donnelly's novels, Blavatsky's Atlanteans used airships and poisonous bombs.

Gandhi did not record the details of his encounter with Blavatsky's "Kosmic Mind." Nor did he describe the experience of reading *The Key to Theosophy*. But Gandhi did describe how Blavatsky and Theosophy permanently altered his self-understanding. In his autobiography, *My Experiments with Truth*, he wrote that Blavatsky had returned him to the faith that was his inheritance. Blavatsky rated the Hindu past higher than the European present. This, Gandhi recalled, "disabused me of the notion, fostered by the missionaries, that Hinduism was rife with superstition." Her ahistorical fantasies and her fictions of "science" filled him with a "desire to read books on Hinduism" and recover his true self. In March 1891, three months before leaving London, he joined the Blavatsky Lodge.

The New Agers lived inside the dominant culture of their day, but they did not feel part of it. This was Gandhi's dilemma, both in India and London, and he took the New Age path out of it. Gandhi would retain the Theosophical worldview through all his "exfoliations" of personality, through all his changes of address and costume, and through his slow metamorphosis from supporter of the British Empire to its feted antagonist. For the rest of his life, he would repeat Theosophy's mixture of religious tolerance and false science. As late as 1946, he would call Theosophy "Hinduism at its best." He would see Jesus as a Galilean Buddha. He would equate the ancient with the ideal, and the religious with the scientific, without fully understanding either.

In April 1891, Blavatsky caught influenza. Two weeks later, after a last bout of tapping and knocking, she was dead. Laid out in white, and crowned with a wreath of white flowers, she manifested briefly in the drawing room before a Theosophical honor guard accompanied her on the train to the London Necropolis in suburban Woking.

At the Necropolis, William Stewart Ross, the editor of the *Agnostic Journal*, found her admirers "crowded round a boiler-looking object with an anxious but decorous curiosity." An attendant opened a "circular orifice about the size of a crown piece," to show the flames within: Blavatsky would return to the realms of the spirit via Britain's first public crematorium. After some short obsequies in a Gothic-style chapel, her "physical instrument" went into the pyre. Her ashes were divided equally between her societies in London, New York, and Madras.

"H.P.B. stands before us now," the *Indian Mirror* mourned, "all herself, free from disease, and seems to whisper to us the larger faith, which animated her through life, that trust in the infinite purpose, which is both the *karma* and the destiny of the Divine Man."

No one, the *New-York Tribune* observed, had done more to "reopen the long sealed treasures of Eastern thought, wisdom, and philosophy." After Blavatsky, it was no longer possible for an educated Westerner to believe that the East produced only "crudities and puerilities": Blavatsky had elucidated that "profound wisdom-religion wrought by the ever-cogitating Orient." She had been misrepresented, slandered, and defamed but had remained a utopian, opposing all barriers of "race, nationality, caste and class," teaching the "spirit of brotherly love," just as Jesus had done. Already, the *Tribune* detected signs of

Blavatsky's influence: "A broader humanity, a more liberal speculation, a disposition to investigate ancient philosophies from a higher point of view."

Blavatsky, W. T. Stead wrote in the London *Review of Reviews*, had forced a "race of inquirers and economists" to consider whether the material world was only an illusion. Stead thought that her insistence on "the spiritual alone" was closer to the spirit of Jesus than the "pseudo-Christian" teachings of the modern churches. Thanks to Blavatsky, the most "cultivated and skeptical" modern—even Annie Besant—could believe again in the existence of an invisible world and the possibility of astral contact with "intelligences vastly superior to our own knowledge of the truth." Blavatsky might not have been the "oracle of God," but she had worked miracles. Her "new-old religion" brought the "infinite sense of the vast, illimitable mystery" of Oriental religions into the "very heart of Europe."

Blavatsky was a plagiarist and a serial fraud, but she had shifted the boundaries of Western belief. She had condensed modern science with ancient magic. Her recipe was not original, but her sales pitch was perfect. In an age of democratic equality, every reader wanted to discover the aristocrat within, an inner quality to defeat the forces of quantity. She packaged spiritual self-help for her hurried age, a secret doctrine in a single volume. She reformulated relations between life and death, ethics and personality, into a portable, potted reduction, like Bovril, the mass-produced jars of beef extract whose name derived from "Vril" and whose boiled-down contents were alleged to be scientifically nutritious.

Science and skepticism had weakened the Christian theology, imperiling the soul and its afterlife. Blavatsky returned it to them. In *Isis Unveiled*, she had dismissed the survival of personality after physical death, but in *The Secret Doctrine* she revived it. Cremation had been illegal in Britain until 1884: How, when Jesus returned, were the dead to arise if their bodies had been turned to ash? In 1891, the year of Blavatsky's death, fewer than a hundred dared to request a practice associated with Hindus and other aliens. But the Western perception of life and death was changing, the New Age theology emerging. Blavatsky was a catalyst. She was Britain's first celebrity cremation, a burnt offering to Theosophy.

"Reincarnation may or may not be true," Stead wrote in 1894 in *Borderland,* his Spiritualist journal, but it was becoming feasible. Even skeptics had to admit that reincarnation was "a hypothesis explaining many of the mysteries of human life." The "range of popular thought" had widened, and this "great achievement" would ever be associated with Blavatsky, who "bridged the chasm between the materialism of the West and the occultism and metaphysics of the East."

Sir James Frazer did not include Vril in The Golden Bough *(1890).* Still, Vril's passage from magical elixir to scientific tonic confirms the Scottish anthropologist's theory of the evolution of faith.

Belief, Frazer thought, began in the Age of Magic in the effort to control elemental forces. These forces were terrifying, but predictable. The magician's incantations were orders, an effort to coerce supernatural forces and beings to act in a certain way. When Nature disobeyed orders, the magician became the priest and the Age of Religion began. The priest propitiated and conciliated Nature. He cajoled instead of commanded, trying to secure the suspension of Nature's decree with prayers, prostrations, and blood sacrifices. Yet the gods remained wrathful, the believers needy. Persistent and ingenious, men contrived a third way of knowing and controlling the world: the Age of Science.

For Frazer, the Age of Science resembles the ancient Age of Magic more than it does the intervening Age of Religion. The fundamental conception of magic is "identical" to that of modern science. The magician and the scientist both believe in the order and uniformity of nature. For both, the "performance of the proper ceremony" elicits the desired result. Both enact a script of actions whose operations are "foreseen and calculated precisely," and whose outcomes are determined by "immutable laws." The magician errs only in his "total misconception" of the nature of the laws.

Magic and science, Frazer wrote, lure us with "endless promises of the future." This sense of potency and potentiality explains their attraction. It also explained the alarming recrudescence of savagery that Frazier saw everywhere around him. The procedures of science and skepticism had restored an illusory sense of magical power. When modern man drilled down into the bedrock of mental life, he was met by irrationality and his inner primitive. From St. James's to the Australian desert, the surface of human society was split with the "rents and fissures and yawning crevasses" of "religious dissension." Everywhere, a subterranean faith in "sympathetic magic" had survived the rule of the priests; everywhere, it probed for weaknesses in the foundations of society and erupted into the "polite world" above. Belief among the "ignorant and superstitious" classes of Europe was the same as it had been "thousands of years ago in Egypt and India," and as it still was among "the lowest savages surviving in the remotest corners of the world." Man's truly universal faith was in "the efficacy of magic."

"We seem to move on a thin crust which may at any moment be rent by the subterranean forces slumbering below . . . From time to time a hollow murmur underground or a sudden spurt of flame into the air tells of what is going on beneath our feet." A solid layer of savagery endured beneath society's surface, unaffected by superficial changes in manners or custom. It was not Frazier's place to suggest how this peril might affect the future of humanity, but he saw nothing noble in savagery. "The dispassionate observer, whose studies have led him to plumb its depths, can hardly regard it otherwise than as a standing menace to civilization."

The Age of Religion, with its rituals of petition and its admissions of weakness, degrades into superstition, secret fears, and vain boasts of technical perfection. As the new layer of civilization forms, it obscures the old forms, and magical thinking returns as scientific thinking. The past is no longer a mire of disease and ignorance, but a lost home in time, a natural order that needs restoring. The Age of Science procures evidence of original forms: fossils on the beach, tribes in the forest, the first language or faith. The evidence of civilization becomes the proof of barbarism. Civilization domesticates and deforms. The unrefined is authentic, the sophisticated unnatural. The barbarian is no longer ridiculed as inarticulate or despised as vicious. He is envied as honest and admired as strong.

The societies of the New Age rest on technical and commercial ingenuity, and their governments are capable of monumental projects, but they prize everything primitive. The sophisticate of the Age of Science scans the mirror for the lost virtues of the Age of Magic. The age of scientific thinking about magic is an age of magical thinking about science. It is an age of biological mysticism and biological politics.

His studies completed and his seventy-two dinners eaten, in June 1891 Gandhi returned to his mother country. He discovered that his mother had died in his absence. Shattered by the loss, he pushed on, studying Indian law and finding work as an advocate of the Bombay high court. He was on his way to satisfying the family, but he felt divided against himself. In London, he had discovered his Indianness, and had addressed vegetarian audiences confidently. In Bombay, he faltered in cross-examination and fell asleep in court.

He gave up after six months and returned home to Porbandar. He failed to find work. In 1884, Lord Ripon, remembering how a surplus of lawyers had contributed to the French Revolution, had thought it wiser to close India's universities rather than educate ever-increasing numbers of young men whose resentment would rise with their frustration. Ripon's forebodings were accurate. Almost all the Indians in the leadership of the Indian National Congress would be British-trained lawyers, including the crucial trio of Gandhi; Muhammad Jinna, a Gujarati Muslim who had gone to London in 1891 and read law at Lincoln's Inn; and Jawaharlal Nehru, a dapper enthusiast of Fabian socialism and cricket who read natural sciences at Cambridge and, like Gandhi and Jinna, law at the Inner Temple.

At Porbandar, Gandhi imposed English norms in the face of

Kasturba's resistance: European dress, oatmeal porridge, cocoa, sitting at a table instead of squatting to eat. He overrode his "squeamishness and suspiciousness" about Kasturba and fathered a second son, Manilal. Then, thoroughly depressed and glad to escape the choking atmosphere, Gandhi fed himself back into the imperial system.

In April 1893, he took the steamer *Safari* to South Africa. In the Cape Colony the discovery of diamond fields and the imperial ambition of Cecil Rhodes had created a boom in the economy and territory. The British, holding the natives to be idle and incorrigible, imported Indian workers to their African colonies. Most of the Indian immigrants to South Africa were poor Hindus, many of them indentured to sugar plantations, but the region also attracted smaller groups of "Arab" traders: middle-class Indian Muslims as well as Hindu and Parsi clerks. Gandhi joined this exodus of educated Indians, as lawyer to Dada Abdullah, a businessman who had emigrated from Porbandar to Durban.

In the Caribbean, the British habit of globalizing Indian labor would produce the Jamaican patty, the samosa of the West Indies. In South Africa, it complicated an already racialized political system and, by degrees, turned Gandhi into a revolutionary. South Africa was a patchwork of British colonies and Boer republics ruled by European minorities, mostly of British or Dutch origin. By color and class, the Indian immigrants fell between the indigenous Africans and their European rulers. The whites accepted the Indians as an economic necessity but feared their blurring of the color line. For the racial difference was also the political one. The whites could vote; the blacks could not. An intermediate "coloured" group might ask for intermediate political rights too; or even, given the emergence of Indian nationalism, the rights of the white rulers.

As the number of Indians rose with the economy, the Boer republics and the British colonies passed laws to segregate "Asiatics" like Gandhi. The indenture contract between the Indian government and the Natal authorities promised equality of status to Indians when they had served their indenture. But in 1883, Natal denied citizenship to "Asiatics," handicapped their businesses, and restricted their rights of residence for "sanitary purposes." The imperial authorities in London, happy with the growth of their colonies and wary of antagonizing the Boers, approved of these measures.

When Gandhi arrived in his frock coat and turban, he saw the whites' "snobbishness" toward the Indians, even wealthy ones like Dada Abdullah. The British called him a "coolie barrister" who worked for "coolie merchants," as though he were an illiterate, indentured peasant. When Gandhi visited Durban's courthouse, the magistrate ordered him to remove his turban. He refused and was expelled.

Gandhi was outraged. He believed in the blindness of justice and, despite his humiliation in Bombay, still trusted in British law. He believed in racial hierarchy too; being a modern sort, he doubted the Hindu caste system but embraced the Theosophical race system. In London, his British friends had treated him as an equal. The humiliations he had suffered had been the social stumbles of a hick student, not a racial inferior. Britain was a liberal state and increasingly a democratic one too. The empire was a different matter. In India, the Raj was liberal in economy, in government, and in its intentions toward the Indians, especially the lighter-skinned "Aryans." But the Raj was in no way democratic. In South Africa, a territory of racial contempt and massive profits, the British were racial despots. And Gandhi was on the wrong side of the color line.

When he had returned to India from London, Gandhi had seen himself as a subject of the Raj. Fleeing to Durban, he encountered this second-class self in its degraded form. Standing on his rights in law and race, he wrote a letter of complaint to the *Natal Advertiser*. He would not let the British treat him like a coolie, an Untouchable, an African. "Is this Christian-like? . . . Is this civilization?"

The racial system was worse in the independent Boer republics. In the Transvaal, the Boers limited Indian residence by charging a £3 entry fee. "Colored" residents had limited rights of property, no voting rights, and a 9:00 p.m. curfew. In the Orange Free State, the

Boers had expelled the Indian merchants entirely, retaining only waiters and servants.

A few days after the courthouse incident, Gandhi took a train to Pretoria, the capital of the Transvaal. He had a first-class ticket, but at a night stop in Maritzburg, the ticket inspector ordered him to sit in third class. Gandhi refused. A policeman shoved him onto the platform, and the guards dumped his luggage off the train.

After a night shivering in the waiting room, Gandhi went on to Charleston, to board a stagecoach to Johannesburg. At Charleston, he found his ticket had been canceled. As a "coolie," he was not allowed to sit inside the coach: he had to sit on the box with the driver and his "Hottentot servant." The driver ordered him to sit on the dirty footboard. Again, Gandhi refused. The driver attacked him, hitting him around the head and trying to pry him from his seat. After some of the passengers objected, the driver relented. Gandhi kept his seat. The Hottentot lost his.

At the next stop, the town's best hotel refused Gandhi a room. The local Indians warned him that he must travel third class in the Boer territories, regardless of the law: "First- and second-class tickets are never issued to Indians." Gandhi used his best English and bought a first-class ticket for the final leg of the journey. Again an inspector tried to expel him into third class. This time, the only other passenger, an Englishman, defended Gandhi. "If you want to travel with a coolie," the inspector muttered, "what do I care?"

At Pretoria, Gandhi found a room in a European hotel, but he could eat in the dining room only with the permission of the white guests. Shortly afterward, as he walked on the footpath near the house of Paul Kruger, the Transvaal's president, a policeman kicked him into the gutter.

In April 1894, Dada Abdullah's case being resolved, Gandhi left Pretoria for Durban. His South African engagement was over and his family expected his return. By his account, a reason to stay arose at the last minute, at a party thrown to mark his departure.

In 1893, London had granted Natal and Cape Colony self-government. Now, Gandhi read in the *Natal Mercury*, the authorities had announced laws that would totally disenfranchise their Indian populations. "The Asiatic," the *Mercury* explained, "comes of a race impregnated with an effete civilization, with not an atom of knowledge of the principles or traditions of representative government. As regards his instinct and training, he is a political infant of the most backward type."

Gandhi decided to delay his return by a month and to organize the Indian merchants against the law. In one night he gathered four hundred signatures; soon, he had ten thousand, and had sent an appeal to Joseph Chamberlain, the colonial secretary in London. This success obliged him to delay his departure once more. When Chamberlain denied his appeal, he delayed again.

In August 1894, Gandhi founded the Natal Indian Congress, to petition for the moral, social, and political conditions of the Indians in South Africa. He told the Durban merchants that he would not charge for his services but that their lawyer would need to be a man of standing; he asked only that they provide him with enough work to give him £300 a year. A temporary delay had led to a secure career. He placed three portraits on his office wall: Tolstoy, Annie Besant, and Jesus. Africa, he later said, was that "God-forsaken continent where I found my God."

ॐ 12 ॐ

THE PERSPECTIVISTS

Vivekananda and Herzl
Among the Aryans

No one has ever thought of looking for the Promised
Land in the place where it really is—and yet it lies so near.
It is here—within ourselves! —*Theodor Herzl, 1895*

Now, as each individual can only see his <u>own</u> universe,
that universe is created with his bondage and goes away
with his liberation, although it remains for others who
are in bondage. —*Swami Vivekananda, 1896*

While Gandhi pondered race hierarchy in Pretoria, the crowds
poured into the World's Columbian Exposition in Chicago. Held
in the summer of 1893, the exposition celebrated the four hundredth
anniversary of Columbus's arrival in the New World. Unofficially, it
aimed to set a new standard of national aggrandizement after the
French Exposition Universelle of 1890, which had established the
Eiffel Tower as a Parisian icon.

The Chicago fair made the Great Exhibition of 1851 look like a
village fete. Frederick Law Olmsted, the designer of Central Park,
and Daniel Burnham, Chicago's city architect, had turned a wedge of
boggy parkland into a Beaux Arts vision. More than two hundred
exhibition halls, all painted white, were arranged around a central

basin and linked by waterways and lagoons on a scale so great that boats ferried visitors between the halls. For the first time, an exhibition had national pavilions, capsules of pride in products and culture, each commanded by a quasi-parliamentary "delegate." A gaggle of "auxiliary congresses" met on the fringes, like provincial assemblies. At dusk thousands of electric bulbs lit up the fairground. Visitors praised its electrified extravagances as a "vision of fairyland," a "sudden vision of heaven."

Chicago, devastated by fire in 1871, was rising again as an industrial behemoth. In October, "Chicago Day" set a new world record by attracting 716,881 visitors in a single day. The novelties included a "moving sidewalk" and a Mormon choir; Frederick Douglass's grandson, the violinist Joseph Douglass, and the Hungarian Jewish escape artist Harry Houdini; the first fully electrified kitchen, dishwasher included, and the public recitation of the Pledge of Allegiance. In the sky over the "White City," the first Ferris wheel revolved on its axis—a giant glowing, spinning wheel. The future, as Hegel had predicted, would have an American accent.

The most popular auxiliary congress opened in Columbus Hall on September 11, 1893. The World's Parliament of Religions was a watershed in the history of religion: the first meeting of representatives from all the "great Historic Religions of the world," as well as the Theosophists, whose faith was great, historic, and global in its own way. In seventeen days of lectures, speakers from across the world presented the tenets and history of their religion, and searched for common ground in the human family of belief.

There had never been such a meeting, so extensive a public display of religious amity. In the third century CE, only Buddhists had attended the Great Council of King Ashoka. In 325 CE, only Christians had attended the Council of Nicaea. In the sixteenth century, when the Mughal emperor Akbar decided to found his own religion, the Zoroastrians had offered only select translations from the *Zend Avesta*, and the Brahmins had refused to translate the Vedas at all; Akbar's Muslim ministers had been so suspicious that he had been obliged to interview some of his informants on his balcony at night, after his servants had hauled them up by a rope. The Parliament of Religions met in the spotlight of global attention and with the blessing of bishops and cardinals. In its design, its universality, and its hope that mutual tolerance would generate spiritual answers to social problems such as "Temperance, Labor, Education, Wealth, and Poverty," the parliament was the first global "interfaith" meeting. Unlike the Council of Nicaea, it was thoroughly harmonious.

Though common humanity leveled the field, Christianity had the home advantage. As the historian Walter R. Houghton noted, the power of the West made Christianity "more potent than at any preceding period." Only the power of the West, and the West's belief in the universality of its outlook, could have made the global parliament "a possibility and a fact." A Presbyterian, Dr. John Barrows, led the proceedings. Those on his fifteen-man committee were all Christian, apart from Rabbi Emil Hirsch of Chicago. Of the two hundred papers to be read, three-quarters were by Christians. Hindus, Jains, Muslims, Buddhists, and Jews were to speak early in each day's schedule, warming up for the main act, the "lowly Nazarene."

This, at least, was the divines' plan. But on the first two days, the parliament witnessed a revolt of public opinion. The mainly female audience was much more interested in the speakers from Eastern religions. When the Christians took the stage, they found themselves addressing a half-empty hall. This insurgency in the pews forced the committee to invert the schedule. For the rest of the session, the Christians spoke earlier in the day, and the non-Christians topped the bill. This ensured the Christian speakers a full house and the audience a daily dose of the exotic and charismatic.

On the afternoon of the fourth day, crowds of women besieged the hall and the organizers had to commandeer the adjoining room. The star of the East had arrived—not from Bethlehem but Calcutta: a Hindu monk named Swami Vivekananda.

"Sisters and brothers of America!"

• • •

A bullish, muscular man with a head heaped with black curls, Vivekananda was dark of skin and sensuous of eye. Onstage he wore red- or saffron-colored robes, a girdle of deep rose-red silk, and a white turban shot with golden thread. His English was eloquent and melodious. Harriet Monroe, the founder of *Poetry* magazine, thought the "handsome monk" in the orange robe had a voice as "rich as a bronze bell."

Vivekananda had not been invited to the Parliament of Religions. He had heard of it in India and invited himself. He had been in this strange western land since April 1893, on a solitary mission for the regeneration of India. It was not going well. Vivekananda wanted to recapture the warrior spirit of the ancients and to import technology, not missionaries, to India, but, he complained, his handlers treated him like a "circus turn." They billed him as the "Hindoo Rajah" and, though he had a perfectly fine brown suit, insisted that he wear his robes, as advertised.

The exposition's nobler precedents included the World's Peace Jubilee and International Music Festival, held in Boston in 1872. At the Boston festival, the first of many gatherings to link world peace and popular music, an African American choir, the Fisk Singers, shared a stage with European performers including Johann Strauss, the master of the Viennese waltz, and those notorious pacifists from London, the band of the Grenadier Guards. The exposition's less dignified precedents included the Congress of Nations (1874) and the Ethnological Congress (1884), global freak shows choreographed by P. T. Barnum. Vivekananda saw the Parliament of Religions as a kind of heathen circus: an exotic theatrical, like the exposition's Native American dances, its model village with a "Chinese joss house" decked with idols, and its Egyptian street, where the "coochee-coochee" gyrations of the belly dancer Little Egypt showed new uses for the human stomach.

Vivekananda despised Oriental clichés, but he exploited his name and costume to pursue his mission. Until 1893, he had been Narendranath Datta the *parivrajaka*, a wandering monk who usually wandered by train, frequently to arrive at a rich man's gate. One of these wealthy patrons, Ajit Singh, the maharajah of Ketri, had funded Datta's American tour. Singh paid for his silk robes and turban, gave him spending money, and upgraded him to a first-class cabin for the sea voyage to Vancouver via Yokohama. When Datta asked, Singh wired more money and sent a monthly stipend to Datta's mother too. The maharajah also showed Datta how to wrap his turban in the Rajastani style and, just before he left for the West, suggested a stage name: Vivekananda, "the bliss of discerning wisdom."

The swami knew how to work an audience. "All religions are true," he said at the parliament. "We accept all religions to be true." All souls were equal: men and women were brothers and sisters. Yet if all religions shared in a universal spirituality, his had the largest share. Hinduism was the mother of the family of religions—and that made the Aryan wisdom of the Hindu the foundation of the modern truth of science.

"From the high spiritual flights of Vedantic philosophy of which the latest discoveries of science seem like echoes, from the agnosticism of the Buddhist and the atheism of the Jains to the low ideas of idolatry and the multifarious mythologies, each and all have a place in the Hindu's religion."

After the lecture, Dr. Barrows took Vivekananda to the restaurant in the Art Institute.

"What shall I get you to eat?" Barrows asked.

"Give me beef!"

Vivekananda was an ideological carnivore. The ancient Brahmins had eaten beef and they had been warriors, not clerks and coolies. Since then, he complained, religion had "got into the kitchen." The Hindu nationalists in the Cow Protection Society claimed that political freedom would come from dietary restraint, but vegetarianism made men weak and womanly, and Hindus the servants of British beefeaters. To build their political muscle, Hindus needed to revitalize the fiber of their minds by Western ideas and the Western diet.

Vivekananda prescribed the "three B's": "beef, biceps and the Bhagavad Gita."

To his audience, Vivekananda's costume radiated a "more-than-
Oriental splendour," like the hat of the otherwise naked Parsi in
Kipling's *Just So Stories*. The press dubbed him the "Napoléon" of the
parliament after Vivekananda claimed that he was from the Kshatriya, the warrior element in the four *varnas*, the Hindu social orders.
In truth, he was from the Kayastha, a mixed caste of scribes, their
blood mingling Brahminic and Kshatriya lineages with the servile
taint of the Shudras, the lowest *varna*. He said little about his early
life, and his Western admirers did not ask. Nor, as they ingested his
faith, did he tell them that he had ingested theirs.

Asked about his spiritual training, Vivekananda described how,
aged eighteen, he had found his guru in the late Ramakrishna, a
deeply eccentric holy man from Calcutta.

But Vivekananda was also a discreet socialist. He saw the physical
and spiritual exercises of yoga as tools for a revolution in consciousness. Explaining his revolution to Americans, he quoted Ramakrishna's doctrines of *bhakti*, universal compassion. Explaining it to
Hindus, Vivekananda quoted the less compassionate doctrines of
Marx and Engels. The regeneration of Vedic and Aryan religion
would lead to the "withering away of the state." The "ideal man" of
the past was the Brahmin, who "killed all selfishness and who lives
and works to acquire and propagate wisdom and the power of love."
This was also the "ideal of the Hindu race" in the future. The "scientific" purification of a "degenerate" Hindu culture, and the beefy diets
of the ancient Brahmins and modern Britons, would converge in spiritual perfection. An entire nation would achieve the Brahmin ideal of
"spiritual culture and renunciation." Every man and woman would
be "spiritual and moral and good." They would have no caste division,
no need for police or soldiers. "Why should anyone govern them at
all? Why should they live under a government?"

Vivekananda discerned the ratio of bliss to wisdom. Hindus needed science, to overthrow an empire. Americans hungered for spiritual consolation, to make modern freedom tolerable. They were as credulous as children. "I want to give them dry, hard reason, softened in the sweetest syrup of love and made spicy with intense work, and cooked in the kitchen of Yoga, so that even a baby can easily digest it."

Vivekananda's father was a skeptic, a lawyer in the high court in Calcutta, and his mother was traditionally devout. While Gandhi had floundered amid the British curriculum, Vivekananda had excelled. He was a scholar and a sportsman, he knew the Hindu scriptures, and he played Indian music too. After his schooling at Calcutta's prestigious Presidency College, he had read for a B.A. at the Scottish Church College. He had studied Sanskrit and Bengali as well as European philosophy. He was so taken with Herbert Spencer's blending of evolution and utilitarianism that he corresponded with Spencer and translated his "Education" into Bengali.

The intellectual omnivore struggled to digest his reading. Ancestral piety did not agree with imported rationality. A crisis of belief led Vivekananda to join the Hindu reformers of the Brahmo Samaj, which Keshab Chandra Sen was leading toward a fusion of Christianity and Hinduism. Next, Vivekananda's search led him into the streets, like Diogenes with his lamp, asking passersby if they had seen God. Then it led him to Debendranath Tagore, the leader of the Arya Samaj. Asked the same question, Tagore did not reply directly but told Vivekananda he had a yogi's eyes and that he should practice meditation. Finally, it led to Ramakrishna.

Vivekananda had first heard of Ramakrishna in a class at the Scottish Church College. The boys were studying "The Wanderer," the first book of Wordsworth's autobiography, *The Excursion.* The class tried to imagine the English poet walking the hills of the Lake District, where, haunted by the memory of his beloved, he falls into a "momentary trance." What, a boy asked, was a trance?

A trance, explained William Hastie, principal of the college, was a psychological state. It was usually a flight of imagination but, in rare and elevated minds, it could reveal the inner and total nature of reality. Hindus called this insight *samadhi*, the dissolution of individual consciousness into the physical world. This, the highest of meditative states, needed not just intense concentration but also purity of mind—and that, Hastie reminded his youths, was very rare. "I have seen only one person who has experienced that blessed state of mind," he reflected, "and he is Ramakrishna Paramahamsa of Dakshineswar. You can understand it if you go there and see for yourself."

In November 1881, Vivekananda met Ramakrishna at the house of Surendranath Mitra, a wealthy admirer. Ramakrishna spoke to the guests and, after hearing Vivekananda sing, invited the youth to visit him. A few weeks later, Vivekananda and a friend went to the temple at Dakshineswar.

Thin and wizened, the fifty-five-year-old Ramakrishna lived in a small hut as a priest and worshipper of Kali. He spoke in village dialect like a peasant, not a city dweller or a scholar, and seemed almost childishly simple, talking in parables and paradoxes. Prone to daily episodes of *samadhi*, he would suddenly break out in song and dance, tearing off his clothes, his face in a rictus of ecstasy. In his twenties, Ramakrishna had seen a vision of Kali, not in her usual aspect as a terrifying killer, but as the "universal mother." Materiality had dissolved around him, and the universe had revealed itself as waves of energy: "And what I saw was an infinite shoreless sea of light; a sea that was consciousness. However far and in whatever direction I looked, I saw shining waves, one after another, coming towards me."

Ramakrishna started to worship Rama in the form of Hanuman the monkey god. This made sense to him because, he said, he could feel a tail extending from the base of his spine. His family decided that he was losing his mind, so they arranged a marriage. As his wife was five years old, Ramakrishna had plenty of time to get closer to the universal mother. He studied tantra and yoga with a middle-aged female teacher, Bhairavi Brahmani. She taught him the worship of Shakti, the feminine power of the cosmos, and how yoga, chanting, and meditation could raise the dormant energy of *kundalini* from the base of his spine to his brain, a serpentine ascent that triggered the bliss of *samadhi*. Ramakrishna disliked the *vamachara*, or "left hand," aspects of his tantra training. The attainment of liberation through transgression, notably forbidden foods, alcohol, and ritualized sex, seemed like "entering a house through the back door." He preferred the gentler paths of *bhakti*, the populist faith of affection and compassion that had arisen in Bengal in the same years that "soulful" Protestants had developed Europe's ideals of personal spirituality.

Ramakrishna never consummated his marriage. "I am very much afraid of women," he said. "When I look at one, I feel as if a tigress were coming to devour me. Besides, I find that their bodies, their limbs, and even their pores are very large. This makes me look upon them as she-monsters." When he looked at a woman, he saw "entrails, blood, filth, worms, phlegm." It took great effort to look past her corporeal monstrosity and see the "Blissful mother" within. Even then, Ramakrishna used "woman and gold" as shorthand for worldly error and corruption. A *sannyasin* must shun women, and worship the cosmic feminine not as a lover but as her handmaid. When Ramakrishna's wife eventually joined him, he joined her, dressing and living as a woman for several days at a time. Subsequent experiments in truth included periods living as a Muslim and a Christian. In these cases, Ramakrishna lived as a man and experienced a visionary merging of his body with those of Muhammad and Jesus.

Ramakrishna's adepts did more than sit at his feet. In his education of his boys, his right foot played a role similar to that of the wizened brown hand in Blavatsky's transcriptions. He would invite a boy to a private meeting in his bedroom, go into a trance, and then place his right foot in the boy's lap. The boys reported that he kept it there until they experienced an onrush of divine joy. Questioned on his methods of enlightenment, Ramakrishna pleaded diminished responsibility by heightened consciousness. He had been in *samadhi*. How could the "supreme swan" know what his foot had done?

At their first meeting, Ramakrishna told Vivekananda that he had seen God. On their second, he used his nimble footwork. Vivekananda panicked and resisted, believing himself to be hypnotized by a madman. Yet though his sudden weakness disgusted him, he was intrigued. When he returned, Ramakrishna led him into a garden and touched him again. This time Vivekananda did not resist.

In Nietzsche's psychology of religion, Ramakrishna was a "decadent" out of Dostoevsky, a case of "sublimity, sickness and childishness." The Hindu reformers in Calcutta, alienated from their roots by Western education and city life, cherished Ramakrishna as their holy fool. Even as they rationalized the idols, sex, and mysticism out of Hindu tradition, they idealized him as an incontinent truth-teller. For Keshab Chandra Sen and Debendranath Tagore, the folk wisdom of *bhakti* consoled a divided heart and promised to unite a nation. And so Vivekananda persisted in his studies with Ramakrishna.

Ramakrishna adored Vivekananda's masculine vigor and his heroic stamina in meditation. He sought out Vivekananda at Brahmo Samaj meetings or at home and would go into a trance when Vivekananda sang. He encouraged Vivekananda to argue and cross-examine him, to pit intellectual brawn against pliant *bhakti*. "Try to see the truth from all angles," he suggested.

In 1884, Vivekananda's father died and his family went bankrupt. Vivekananda moved to Dakshineswar and became Ramakrishna's pupil. They were inseparable for the next two years. After Ramakrishna's death in 1886, Vivekananda and a small group of disciples set up a *math*, or monastery, in a ruined house at Baranagar, near Calcutta. They begged for food, got up at three in the morning to pray, and studied Christian texts and European philosophy as well as Hindu scriptures. In early 1887, Vivekananda took his monk's vow. For five years he traveled around northern India. He carried only a water pot, a staff, and two books: the Bhagavad Gita and a Catholic devotional, Thomas à Kempis's *Imitation of Christ.*

The historical significance of a holy man, Nietzsche had written, lies not in what he is but in what he *"signifies* in the eyes of those who are not holy."

Vivekananda was a modern hybrid, a blend of Hinduism and Herbert Spencer, of Ramakrishna's revivalism and the Brahmo Samaj's Christian idealism. His spiritual quest reflected the disruptions of the modern West, but his audience saw him as an image of the ancient East. He profited from this perception by playing to the gallery. So did two Buddhists who found spiritual celebrity in Chicago, Angarika Dharmapala and D. T. Suzuki.

Daisetzu Teitaro Suzuki came to Chicago as the interpreter for Soyen Shaku, a Zen monk from Japan. Together, they were to introduce Zen to America. Shaku and Suzuki spoke of ancient Zen but, like most Japanese, they were fluent in the imported vocabulary of race and nation. In 1853, U.S. commodore Matthew Perry's "black ships" had forced the Tokugawa shogunate to open Japan to foreign trade. A closed, feudal society buckled, and the shogunate's reforms could not prevent a revolt by an alliance of rebellious regional prefects and the young emperor Meiji. In 1868, the shogunate collapsed and the victors declared the restoration of Japan's ancient empire. They set up the emperor as an object of national worship, purged Shinto, Japan's indigenous religion, of foreign Buddhist impurities, and began a program of rapid modernization along Western lines. They called their coup the Meiji *Ishin,* a "restoration" or "renovation," but the new Japan was a centralized, industrialized military power, with much the same relation to its past as the new Germany bore to the Holy Roman Empire.

Born in 1870, Suzuki was a member of two groups humbled by the new regime: the samurai class, which had maintained the feudal system, and the Buddhist minority, most of them followers of the

"Pure Land" Mahayana school. At Tokyo's new university, Suzuki studied the Western curriculum with *keimo gakusha*, "scholars who illuminate the darkness." Just as Vivekananda's studies led to Ramakrishna, Suzuki's led him to Zen—or rather, to a hybrid form influenced by Western-style reform. At Tokyo University, two American Buddhists, Lafcadio Hearn and Ernest Fenollosa, explained the evolution of Buddhism through the ideas of Herbert Spencer. Young Japanese Buddhists were writing "Essentials of the Buddhist Sects" and editing "Buddhist bibles" for a *shin bukkyo*, a "New Buddhism," rational and unitarian like the Brahmo Samaj. The name echoed the Japanese terms for Catholicism and Protestantism, *kyo bukkyo* and *shin-kyo*, the "old doctrine" and "new doctrine."

For the Chicago Parliament of Religions, Suzuki translated Shaku's "Law of Cause and Effect, as Taught by Buddha," rendering traditional Buddhist terms into Theosophical English. Afterward, Shaku recommended Suzuki to Paul Carus, editor of the Open Court Press. Founded in 1887 to disseminate cheap editions of philosophical and religious classics, Open Court was owned by Edward Hegeler, a successful German immigrant. Hegeler poured his profits from mining and zinc processing into the search for a scientific religion, funding Open Court and *The Monist*, a journal of "philosophical enquiry." Carus, a scholar of religion and fellow German emigrant, was married to Hegeler's daughter Marie. The Hegeler-Carus family lived in LaSalle, Illinois—"Zinc City"—in one of the Midwest's finest buildings, a Second Empire mansion designed by William Boyington, the architect of the Chicago Water Tower and the Illinois State Capitol. In Open Court's offices on the second story, Suzuki helped Carus translate the *Tao Te-Ching* from Chinese into English. In 1895, he translated Carus's *Gospel of Buddha* from English into Japanese; in its preface, Soyen Shaku describes Buddhism as superior to all Western faiths. Carus published two primers for Western Buddhists, Suzuki's *Outlines of Mahayana Buddhism* and Shaku's *Zen for Americans*.

In 1905, Shaku would teach America's first Zen classes in a house near San Francisco. His *Zen for Americans* would become the primer of Western Zen and Suzuki, the author of over a hundred books, Zen's foremost Western interpreter, if not its monopolist. Yet he was not a monk. He was an academic philosopher, a reader of Emerson and William James. He became a frequent visiting professor at American universities and a recurrent presence at interfaith conferences, assisting Western theologians and psychologists in the search for the grail of faith's common "essence." If he spoke intimately to the dilemmas of Romantic nihilism, it was because he knew them so well. In the 1910s, he joined a group of scholars at Kyoto University whose work aimed to integrate German Romantic philosophy and Meiji nationalism. Soon afterward, Suzuki became a Theosophist and married an American member of the Society, Beatrice Erskine Lane. It would be all too easy for Carl Jung, an admirer of Carus, to anoint Suzuki as the authentic voice of Zen.

While Suzuki steered Zen westward toward philosophy and Theosophy, Angarika Dharmapala extracted himself and Theravada Buddhism from the stifling intimacy of their alien embrace.

Dharmapala was a slim, gentle Sinhalese, born in 1864. Instead of the monk's yellow robe and shaven head, he wore the white robe of a layman, and combed and coiffed his hair like a Westerner. His real name was Don David Hewavitharana. His father, Don Carolis, was one of Ceylon's richest merchants and one of Asia's largest furniture producers. Don Carolis sent his sons to Ceylon's best British schools but was also a lay leader in Olcott's Buddhist revival. He was vice president of Olcott's Buddhist Protection Committee; the president was Don Carolis's father-in-law.

At eight, Don David took a vow of celibacy. At sixteen, he was active in the movement. Like Gandhi, he discovered his ancestral faith through English translations and Theosophical interpretations. Olcott employed him as a translator, and Blavatsky groomed Don David for leadership, telling him to learn Pali and to align the Theravada revival with universal humanity. Don David changed his name to

Angarika Dharmapala: an *angarika* was a "homeless" man, a renouncer, and *dharmapala* meant "guardian of the dharma."

In a modern innovation, Dharmapala extended his vows to cover the eight precepts but, though honoring them every day like a monk, he remained a layperson. His reinterpretation of the *angarika* drew on the Theosophical interpretation of *brahmacharya*: the ascetic's control of the body, especially its sexual needs, created a store of energy to be directed into society—in modern, political form. As Vivekananda was doing, and as Gandhi was later to do, Dharmapala was creating a political persona that carried the authority of religion: a layman who lived like a monk, a monk who worked like a politician, a politician who cultivated the charisma of a prophet.

The further Dharmapala, Vivekananda, and Gandhi developed this persona, the less they liked its Western, imported elements, and the more they presented themselves in purely Eastern and indigenous terms. Aptly, Dharmapala's crisis of faith was Theosophical. In 1885, Edwin Arnold, the author of *The Light of Asia*, had visited the temple at Bodh Gaya in northeastern India, where the Buddha first attained enlightenment. To Arnold's dismay, the Buddhist shrine built by the Emperor Ashoka was now a Hindu temple. The statue of Buddha had become a Hindu icon, a priest of Shiva presided, and Buddhists were not allowed to worship. Prompted by his friend Weligama Sumangala, the high priest of Ceylon, Arnold had called for the British to restore the site to Buddhist control.

In 1891, Dharmapala followed Arnold's footsteps to Bodh Gaya and was similarly appalled. Sacred statues were buried in piles of garbage, and the head priest was using pillars from Ashoka's temple to prop up his kitchen ceiling. Back at Ceylon, Dharmapala founded the Maha Bodhi Society for the revival of Buddhism in India, and the recovery of Bodh Gaya in particular. Dharmapala dreamed of recreating Bodh Gaya as a global center of pilgrimage, a new heart for Buddhism in the subcontinent. He sued its Hindu proprietors for control of the temple, arguing that Bodh Gaya was the Buddhist's Zion or Mecca. Already a vicious critic of the Christian missionaries at

Ceylon, he now attacked Hinduism as obscurantist and bullying, and Islam, too, for causing the decay of Buddhism in India.

Nor did Dharmapala's revaluation spare the Theosophical Society. He and Colonel Olcott now held antagonistic visions of the future of Buddhism. Olcott, who listed Emperor Ashoka as one of his earlier incarnations, wanted to incorporate Ceylon into the Buddhist wing of Theosophy's universalist empire. Dharmapala began to see Olcott as a spiritual imperialist, in league with the British. In late 1892, Olcott and Dharmapala toured India to raise funds for the Maha Bodhi Society. In Calcutta, Hindu Theosophists accused Olcott of secretly turning Theosophy toward Buddhism. When Olcott placated them, Ceylonese Buddhists accused him of turning Theosophy toward Hinduism. Annie Besant's arrival in India in October 1893 only worsened Olcott's position. Blavatsky had been a Buddhist and a universalist, and Olcott remained a woolly "eclectic," but Besant insisted that she and Theosophy were essentially Hindu. The Theosophical consensus was fragmenting into nationalism and sectarian conflict, the Blavatskyite empire fissuring into small kingdoms. Its constituents, fulfilling Blavatsky's orders if not her ambitions, were taking charge of their spiritual futures.

Dharmapala mentioned none of this in Chicago. Instead he emphasized his Theosophical training: the Ceylonese were the original Aryans; Theravada Buddhism was the world's original faith, and also ideal for the rational, scientific future. Offstage, Dharmapala and his three companions circulated thousands of Maha Bodhi pamphlets. He befriended Paul Carus, who invited him to return to America; later, Carus would chair America's first Maha Bodhi chapter.

Dharmapala also befriended Vivekananda. In India, Dharmapala and Vivekananda had been rivals. In Chicago, they discovered how much they shared. Initially, Vivekananda had planned to present himself as a Theosophist. Before leaving Calcutta, he had asked Olcott for his blessing. But Olcott, worried by the chauvinism of the Hindu Theosophists, had refused to give Vivekananda letters of introduction. Retaliating, Vivekananda attacked Olcott as an imperialist. India had no need to import religion from the West—and no need for the "dead ghosts of Russians and Americans" either.

The Parliament of Religions was an imperial market of the spirit, revealing the tensions of a globalized age. Its traveling salesmen pitched their product like diplomats, using what D. T. Suzuki called *upaya,* "expedient means." Ramakrishna had licensed Vivekananda to preach, and Vivekananda created an international network in Ramakrishna's name. Its missionaries preached a dogma in his name, but in photographs Ramakrishna's expression is one of ecstatic confusion. His method was to baffle by free association and then enlighten by sudden *samadhi.* His disciples turned his ramblings into a written philosophy that was compatible with the Western education he had lacked, and directed this interpretation toward a global audience.

In Vivekananda's gospel, Ramakrishna preached love: emotion over intellect, *bhakti* over theology, universal harmony over sectarian dissent. In ritual, Ramakrishna taught yoga as the route to *samadhi,* and the control of *kundalini* as the key to personal enlightenment. And when Ramakrishna expressed a preference in philosophy, he endorsed the Advaita school, which had first been codified around 800 CE by Adi Shankara of Kerala. Ramakrishna did not believe in the duality of matter and spirit, but in their singularity. Spirit and matter might be perceived as discrete, but they were identical aspects of a single substance, the matter of the universe.

In Western terms this made Ramakrishna a Monist: spirit was everywhere present in matter. This encouraged Westerners to align Ramakrishna with Heraclitus and other pre-Socratics; with the mystical strains in Judaism, Christianity, and Islam; with the most adventurous efforts of Renaissance Neoplatonism; with the panentheism of Spinoza and the transcendental realism of Kant. Ramakrishna, it seemed, had been an Indian Emerson: a messiah for the age of Blavatsky, a philosopher born for the pages of Paul Carus's *Monist.*

It was, Carus said, a "New Religious Era." East and West, past and present, matter and spirit were collapsing into the new singularity of science and the soul.

In June 1894, Vivekananda went to Green Acre, a hotel in Eliot, Maine, sixty miles north of Boston. The hotel's owner, Sarah Farmer, had heard him speak in Chicago and invited him to join her Green Acre Conference, an annual eight-week festival intended to "quicken and energize the spiritual, mental and moral natures." An eighty-five-foot flagpole, repurposed from a ship's mast, rose over the resort. A thirty-six-foot white banner floated from it, carrying the universal message of all religions in green letters: PEACE. The banner may have been the first "peace flag."

The guests stayed in the hotel or camped for free in the field next door. The lectures, held in a large tent on the hotel grounds, were also free, as were the many smaller classes. There were talks on Christian Science, Spiritualism, and Theosophy; Farmer's friend and fellow organizer Sara Bull had a strong Theosophical pedigree, for she had been converted by Blavatsky's disgraced aide Mohini Chatterjee. In the tent, Vivekananda gave America's first lectures on yoga. In the trees, he taught America's first yoga classes. The locals complained about single women going "a-niggering in the pines."

"Emerson and Bronson Alcott and all of the old Concord set would have enjoyed sitting out under the stars at Greenacre," a reporter reflected in *The Portsmouth Daily Chronicle*. If they had, they would have sat among friends. Sarah Farmer's parents were Transcendentalist reformers; it was their poet friend John Greenleaf Whittier who had suggested the name Green Acre. Sara Bull was related to Longfellow by marriage, and she had known Emerson. The old Concord set would have recognized Vivekananda's language too. He translated *Brahman*, absolute reality, as "God," and quoted Adi Shankara on Advaita monism. Still, though the guru catered to the needs of his freethinking pupils, he was puzzled by their camping etiquette: "Women sometimes are not embarrassed to expose their bodies above the waist, but they say that to go barefoot is as bad as being naked."

In December 1894, Bull organized a second series of talks near her house on Brattle Street, Cambridge. Vivekananda gave two of the seven lectures to audiences whose members included William James; Charles Lanham, the chair of Harvard's department of Indo-Aryan languages; and Ernest Fenollosa, who had lately returned from Tokyo. During the "Cambridge Conferences," Vivekananda stayed at Bull's house, where the Sanskrit phrase "Truth is One; the wise call it variously" was inscribed over the fireplace in the music room. In six private lessons, he taught Raja yoga to Bull, Farmer, and their friends.

After washing themselves thoroughly, the women were shown how to sit in *asana*, with their spines erect and their heads and hips aligned. On Vivekananda's instruction, they told themselves that every part of their bodies was perfect, the sex organs included. From toes to head, the body was a divine "instrument," a "vessel" that could sail to "the shores of eternal truth." After breathing deeply through the nostrils, they meditated for ten to fifteen minutes on the "being who created the universe."

In further sessions, Vivekananda taught breath control and meditation techniques, and told the women about the ascent of *kundalini* toward *samadhi*. The "nerve center" at the base of the spine was the "seat of the generative substance of the sexual energy." The class imagined a triangle containing a tiny coiled serpent. This was Ramakrishna's path of enlightenment by *bhakti*, a rapid and effective method.

Sara Bull was a widow; her husband, forty years her senior, had died in 1880. Sarah Farmer never married; nor had another of Vivekananda's first pupils, the singer Emma Thursby. They were educated women, and their independence of mind and professional ambition had reduced their chance of marriage. They knew Emerson's philosophy of cosmic compensation. Vivekananda revealed the path to the monist revelation within: an overpowering subjectivity, simultaneously liberating the spirit and body.

"The sleeping serpent is called Kundalini," Bull noted, "and to raise the Kundalini is the whole object of Raja-Yoga."

*Vivekananda's yoga was a motley blend. He mixed the dualist meta-*physics of the *Yoga Sutras* with the monism of Advaita. His description of the "subtle body" came from Hatha yoga, not Raja yoga. His instructions for meditation mixed Ramakrishna's folk wisdom with the self-helping platitudes of Theosophy, New Thought, and Christian Science. "This whole universe is my body," he taught, "all health, all happiness, is mine, because all is in the universe. Say, 'I am the universe.'"

The spiritual appetites of the West were whetted. A new generation was hungry for an Indian Emerson. The religious revolutionaries of both the West and the East needed a philosophy capable of reconciling the intolerable paradoxes and confusions of modern life.

The new mental universe that Farmer and her friends discovered was populated not just by yogis and holy men but also by physicists and developers of technology. In the last years of the nineteenth century, a series of scientific discoveries revealed a new physics, and a new perception of the world inside matter that accorded with the Monist spirituality. In 1887, Heinrich Hertz proved James Clerk Maxwell's inference that electromagnetic waves could travel over distance. Hertz built machines to transmit and receive these invisible "wireless" waves; their rate of frequency was named for him. The next step was commercial wireless communication. Its pioneers included Nikola Tesla, who encountered Hertz's work at the Paris Exposition of 1889; and Jagadish Chandra Bose, a Cambridge graduate whose research at Presidency College, Calcutta, was partly funded by Sara Bull. Bose was the first to detect radio waves by a semiconductor junction, and the first to demonstrate the military uses of *adrisya alok*, "invisible light." In December 1895, as Vivekananda lectured at the second series of Cambridge Conferences, at Calcutta's town hall Bose used millimeter-length waves to detonate gunpowder from a distance.

In 1896, Wilhelm Röntgen developed X-ray photography and

Antoine Becquerel discovered radioactivity. In 1897, Sir Joseph Thomson identified the electron. In 1898, Tesla launched a radio-controlled boat and the Italian entrepreneur Guglielmo Marconi opened the first radio factory. In the same year, Marconi achieved the first ship-to-shore communication, and a promotional coup; when Edward, the portly Prince of Wales, hurt his knee, a Marconi wireless was placed on the royal ship so that he could follow yacht races. In 1899, Marconi's signals crossed first the English Channel and then the Atlantic Ocean.

For decades, science had eroded the established Western concepts of space and time. The new physics weakened Euclid's geometry and Newton's physics, just as the new cities altered the experience of social life. The sacred space of the church became the concert hall, and then the sports stadium. The sacred time of the sabbath turned into the weekend, and the daily newspaper replaced the morning prayer. Technology had changed the relationship between social space and social time.

Monism contradicted none of the new physics; if anything, the new physics reinforced Monism. Had not Blavatsky predicted the rending of the Veil of Nature between 1888 and 1897, and the dealing of a "death blow" to "materialistic science"? Had not Nietzsche predicted the collapse of the Idealist division between matter and spirit? Monism seemed the only philosophical doctrine capable of containing the yogi and the physicist. In an age of religious doubt, Monism saved the soul: spirit existed within matter, as the essence of the atom. In an age of culture wars, Monism brokered peace: the race scientist and the priest both saw a spiritual essence at the heart of human biology. In an age of political passions, Monism consoled and inspired: amid radical subjectivity and secret doctrines, Monism united all in a single objective truth. It carried a revelation of shared identity, as clear as a radio signal: "I am the universe."

*"The sickness goes deep." Professor Binswanger had found no im-*provement in the patient's condition, and in the spring of 1892, he

had returned Nietzsche to the bosom of his family. The great circle was closing.

The recurring motif of religion, Sir James Frazier observed, was the related cults of the great mother and the sacrificed son. This, the riddle of the Sphinx, now revealed itself to Nietzsche. Oedipus, blind and crippled, was borne back by the eternal recurrence, back to his mother's house. By 1893 Nietzsche was paralyzed on his right side and bedbound. His sister, Elisabeth, returned from Paraguay to care for him. Nueva Germania had failed and Bernhard Förster, addled by debt, malaria, drink, and opiates, had shot himself in a hotel room. Elisabeth had previously dismissed her brother's work as "frightful . . . the self-admiration of egoism," and called him the victim of his own "furious egotism which tears apart everything in its path." Now, she appointed herself manager of his estate.

In the morning, Nietzsche's mother and sister, two bacchantes in widow's weeds, washed and dressed him, then hauled him into his wheelchair. If he was quiet, they propped him up on a sofa for visitors or, if the sun was out, on a bench on the porch, with a blanket on his legs. His theologian friend Franz Overbeck found him speechless, "half-crouching, like a mortally wounded animal" on one of the days of "total prostration" that alternated with days of "dreadful excitability, which rose to a pitch of roaring and shouting." When John Mackay, a Scottish American anarchist and Uranian propagandist, asked about his inspirations, Nietzsche could only mumble incoherently and shake his head.

The man who believes he has killed his sensuality, Nietzsche had written, is "deceiving himself: it lives on in an uncanny vampire form and torments him in repulsive disguises." Elisabeth created a false icon while Nietzsche was still alive. Planning his immortality, she engaged another young admirer, Rudolf Steiner, to catalog Nietzsche's library. "It was a wonderful task," Steiner recalled, to read Nietzsche's "passionate, critical" annotations and the mass of marginal comments that showed "the seeds of his ideas sprouting." In January 1896, Elisabeth rewarded Steiner by admitting him to Nietzsche's presence. "Have just seen Nietzsche," Steiner wrote in his diary. "He lay on the sofa, like a thinker who is tired and continues to think through a problem, long wrestled with, lying down. His appearance is that of a healthy person. No paleness. No white hair. The powerful moustache as in the Zarathustra picture. O, this powerful forehead, simultaneously betraying thinker and artist. Radiating the peace of the sage. One has the impression of a powerful world of thought lying hibernating behind this forehead."

Nietzsche had feared the consequences when he raised an ax against the ideals of his age. All great insights had a split head, and their knower perceived the world through a Janus face, a double mask of stone. Were his treacherous perceptions a blessing or a curse? He had discovered the Monist life of instinct. Man interpreted the world according to his needs and drives. Each drive was a "lust for domination," and each tried to impose its "perspective" on its body or its society. If no single point of observation was more valid than another, then the conflict of perspectives could not generate independent facts or objective truths—only "interpretations" and subjective inferences. The ideal of individual conscience was one of those subjective inferences too. The thinking, reasoning individual was a hypothesis disproved, the dream of conscience a fiction.

"Inasmuch as the word 'knowledge' has any meaning at all, the world is knowable," he had written in 1887, "but it is variously *interpretable*; it has no meaning behind it, but countless meanings."

Nietzsche had called this "Perspectivism." In the same year, Paul Cézanne had arranged a bowl or two of fruit and one or two vases on a flat table in Aix-en-Provence and painted what he saw. Sometimes the table seemed to tip toward Cézanne, with one of its edges weirdly curved. Sometimes a bowl lifted up, making the cherries and peaches strangely round and flat. Sometimes the neck of a vase expanded, and an ellipse turned into a thick circle, as though he was looking at it from above.

Cézanne's experiments followed earlier hints from the Impressionists, who, equipped with mass-produced tubes of portable, stable oil paint, had been able to leave their studios. Unmoored in a field, or rocking on a houseboat like Daubigny, the painter moved in an unsteady, subjective relation to canvas and subject. The still life is a study of nature, but Cézanne's view of nature was no longer still. Objects were no longer held in place by a single and fixed perspective, the mathematical principle that, laid out by Leon Battista Alberti in the fifteenth century, had defined four centuries of Western art and architecture. Instead, plural perspectives create distortions in a moving field of vision. Straight lines develop curves, planes begin to buckle and bulge, and light polarizes into sudden contrasts: Perspectivism in art. In the early 1900s, the continued effort to see "from all sides" would produce Cubism, a further dissolution of fixed perspective.

The perception "I am the universe" leads from the individual to the universal, from Perspectivism to Monism. The inference that follows—"The universe is me"—returns from Monism to Perspectivism, from the universal to the individual. Modern spirituality is Monist in framework, but it is Perspectivist in the details. And the details, as the Bauhaus architect Mies van der Rohe was to say, were where God could be found.

As the Perspectivist-Monist condition was a modern one, it was strongest at the nodes of technical civilization. In 1895, two significant symptoms appeared in Paris, the City of Light and the capital of nineteenth-century culture. One was technical and commercial: an ingenious application of light waves. The other was nationalist and political: a vision of an ancient people resurrected in modern form. Both were harbingers of the new century.

In February 1895, Auguste and Louis Lumière, two brothers from Lyon whose name happened to be "light," patented their Cinématographe, a device for recording, developing, and projecting moving images. The Lumière brothers were not the first in the field; rather, their machine collated earlier developments and directed them toward commercial ends. For nearly thirty years, photographers had been capturing individual images, often with multiple cameras and lenses, and replaying them in sequence to create the impression of movement. In the 1870s, Eadweard Muybridge had used chronophotography to show that a horse leaves the ground when it gallops, and Albert Londe had sequenced the fleeting facial expressions of neurotics for Jean-Martin Charcot. In the 1880s, as projectors improved and lens speeds accelerated, the sequences became smoother. In 1891, the Edison company's Kinetoscope ran a perforated reel of images at high speed over a light source; above it, the viewer put an eye to a "peephole." But the Lumière Cinématographe was a shared experience and an entertainment.

On December 28, 1895, the brothers held the first public screening for ticketholders in the Indian Salon of the Grand Café in central Paris. Their customers saw ten short films, each around forty seconds in length. The first showed workers leaving the Lumière factory in Lyon. The second was a slapstick: a boy steps on a garden hose and lifts his foot when the gardener looks into the hose. The rest were documentaries: fishing, feeding a baby, swimming, a Lyon street scene. In 1896, the brothers showed their films in Bombay, London, and New York. After that, though, they abandoned cinema; the future, they said, belonged to color photography. By then, their competitors had caught up and were giving the public what it really wanted. In April 1896, the Edison Company's Vitascope displayed the first screen kiss: the actors John C. Rice and May Irwin reenacting the onstage kiss with which they ended the hit musical comedy *The Widow Jones*. This was Edison's bestselling reel of 1896. In the same year, the French photographer Eugène Pirou filmed the striptease artist Louise Willy and an unknown male actor in one of the first pornographic films, *Le coucher de la mariée*, or "Bedtime for the bride."

The camera's single eye set a new standard of reality and a new standard of unreality. Just when linear perspective succumbed to the distortions and disturbances of fine art and physics, cinema reasserted it as mass entertainment. For nearly two hundred years, Westerners had accused Easterners of passivity, and invariably blamed religion and climate. In the cinema, Westerners had created a new church of passivity, a technological dreamworld like Plato's cave. The winking light from the projector linked the erotic impulse to the machine pulse and cast prepared images onto a blank screen. In time, cinema would be turned to the service of art, and art to the service of politics. The cinema was to become a great illuminator, a democratizer of other people's experience. It was also to become a great distractor, and a great inciter. Technological enchantment had, as Olcott said of Blavatsky, a hypnotic glamour.

"Again I considered the phenomenon of the crowd," wrote Theodor Herzl, the Paris correspondent of the Vienna *Neue Freie Presse*, after attending an early cinema screening. "There they sat for hours, tightly packed, motionless, in bodily torture—and for what? For an imponderable . . . For sounds, tones, and pictures!"

Born in 1860, Herzl was the stocky, dark-eyed, square-bearded son of German-speaking Jews who had migrated from Budapest to Vienna. His body carried two marks of male passage. On his eighth day, the infant Herzl received a metaphysical reminder of his hereditary difference as a Jew. The mark of circumcision bound him to a people, and to a history as profound in religious significance as it was extensive in persecution. More visibly, just after Herzl's twenty-first birthday, a small saber nick on his cheek marked his acculturation as a Germanic gentleman. A student of law at Vienna University, he joined a *Burschenschaft*, a dueling society of patriotic students. His choice of fraternity name was "Tancred," after the hero of Disraeli's novel. An evening with the *Burschenschaft* was a Wagnerian affair. It began in chivalry and song but ended in German nationalism and antisemitic grievance, with an occasional coda of a *Liebestod* of street violence against Jews. Herzl did not attend the revels regularly. When Wagner died in February 1883, the thousands of German students at Vienna gathered in mourning. The tributes and drink flowed, and the evening ended as an antisemitic rally. When Herzl wrote to a newspaper in complaint, his fraternity expelled him.

In the next decade, Herzl married a Jewish woman. He fathered three children, failed as a novelist, and struggled as a playwright, but prospered as a journalist. All the time, the "Jewish Question" gnawed at him. The contradiction between his ideals of masculinity, Jewish and Germanic, made him profoundly unhappy. He was a *Grenzjude*, an assimilated "border Jew," homeless within and without. He was a modern Austrian, an artist in the German language, but he lived "constantly" in fear of a medieval assault. He was elegant and educated, but his "Jewish nose and beard" licensed street urchins to shout, *"Saujud!"*—"Jew pig!"—at his carriage, and drunks to mock him with the rioter's cry *"Hep! Hep!"*; allegedly an acronym for the Crusaders' war cry, *Hierosolymna est perdita*: "Jerusalem is lost." It felt ignoble to cringe inwardly, perpetually fearing the blow. It seemed no less ignoble to surrender by rejecting his father's faith and surname. He was caught in what he called a "New Ghetto," estranged from Jews and Christians alike. Jerusalem was lost, but the New Jerusalem of liberal Europe treated him as an interloper in its gates.

Herzl was glad to escape Vienna for Paris, the capital of European universalism and the Rights of Man. The French seemed more civilized and tolerant: "Here I pass through the crowd unrecognized." The Jewish flâneur hoped he had outrun his dilemma, but in reality he was strolling toward it. In Vienna, Herzl had been a feuilletonist and a "chatterer," an anecdotal artist of modern life, diversifying lightly on the distractions of literature and culture. In Paris, his reportage for the *Neue Freie Presse* included politics. France, too, had its antisemitic parties and newspapers, its demagogues and mobs. Just as in Vienna, a citadel of liberal civilization was besieged from within. Mass democracy gave voice to irrational, violent urges; the liberal system would elevate tyrants to power. "I saw how the world is governed. I stared, too, at the phenomenon of the crowd."

In this capacity, Herzl witnessed the first act of the drama that would soon symbolize the crisis of Europe. Just before Christmas 1894, a closed court-martial convicted Alfred Dreyfus, a Jewish officer in the French artillery, of passing secrets to the Germans. His sentence was life imprisonment on Devil's Island in French Guiana. On January 5, 1895, Dreyfus was paraded before the cadets of the École Militaire and formally degraded. Dreyfus's officer's braid, buttons, and insignia were torn off, and his sword broken.

"I swear I am innocent!" he protested. "Long live France! Long live the Army!"

"*À mort les Juifs!*" the mob screamed from behind the railings. "Death to the Jews!"

Herzl had attended the court's early, public sessions, and he witnessed Dreyfus's degradation. The vast majority of observers believed that Dreyfus was guilty: two years would pass before proof of Dreyfus's innocence would come to light, and an incident of espionage metastasize into *l'Affaire*, an ideological civil war over the future of French politics. Already Herzl doubted Dreyfus's guilt. He understood the psychology of assimilation. A Jewish officer, he felt, would want to compensate for a millennium of "civic dishonor" by proving his "almost pathological desire for honor."

In late May 1895, Herzl witnessed French parliamentarians debating proposals to prevent Jews from immigrating into France. At the end of the month, the Christian Socialists swept the Viennese elections, making the antisemite Karl Lueger the city's next mayor. The eruption of Jew-hatred in Paris and Vienna forced Herzl to confront what he already knew. Perhaps, too, the desiccation of his marriage and artistic ambitions left him with nowhere to hide. Either way, by June 1895, Herzl felt certain that he could read the future. The "Great Revolution" of enlightenment and universalism was over. "Things cannot improve but must get worse—until the massacres. Governments can no longer prevent it, even if they wanted to. Also, there is socialism lurking behind."

On June 4, 1895, Herzl attended Wagner's *Tannhäuser*. Herzl sensed himself the target of racial nationalism, the monism of the body politic. The revelation panicked him: "So wildly the streams of thought raced through my soul." The words poured out so quickly and strangely that he feared he was going mad. He felt his personality dissolving into the wide river of world history. He felt sure that his "spiritual legacy" would make him one of the great benefactors of mankind. "Or is this belief the onset of megalomania?"

The Jews needed to answer the "Jewish Question" before their enemies did. The answer was a revolutionary leap forward into the past: the recovery of the lost Jerusalem, the return to Zion.

"My conception of God," Herzl reflected, "is, to be sure, Spinozistic" and approaches the natural philosophy of the monists." God, Herzl thought, was a "beautiful, beloved old word." It allowed the "childlike or constricted mind" to conceive the otherwise inconceivable. This Gladstone bag of the spirit was wanted on voyage. The votaries of Yahweh would carry their historical God out of Europe as once they had carried the Ark of the Covenant. In Zion, they would become a caste of "high priests" and don "impressive robes." The wonder-working Hasidic rabbi of Sadgora would be installed as a kind of provincial bishop. Herzl did not say if the robes would be traditional, as described in the Talmud, or modern. As a child, he had dreamed of emulating de Lesseps's Suez Canal. Perhaps the hierophants of Judea would resemble the priests in *Aïda*.

"We recognize ourselves as a nation through our religion." Zion would retain Judaism as Wagner retained the trappings of Christianity. The old faith dressed the stage as a mythical proscenium, framing the political artwork of the future. As it would be for historical time, so it must be for historical space. The Promised Land was hot, small, and too close to Europe. It was also subject to the whim of the Turkish sultan and, by all reports, desolate and infested with bandits. But Palestine possessed the magic of history. In exile, the Jews had been sustained by faith in the glories of their past. As *Tannhäuser* showed, only a "mighty legend" could rouse a people to believe in its future.

"Do not think this is a fantasy. I am no architect of castles in the air. I build a real house, with materials you can see, touch, examine. Here are the blue-prints." There would be a bank funded by the Rothschilds and other plutocrats, and a national fund for land purchases. The constitution would resemble the merchant oligarchy of Venice, modernized by way of English liberalism; the first Jewish doge would be a Rothschild. The state would thwart radical agitation by the Prussian method, the partnership of private capital and "state socialism." There would be universal welfare and a corps of "spinsters" trained as governesses, with ranks and pensions like all civil servants. There would be a seven-hour workday and a small professional army, enlisting no more than a tenth of the male population. Hungarian Jews would be the "hussars of Judea," a cavalry with magnificent yellow-and-white uniforms. Dueling with sabers would be encouraged. To train the youth of Judea to answer the call to "freedom and manliness," the schools would teach English sports and "the Maccabean tradition."

If the Jewish state was to convince the Jewish masses to forsake the fleshpots of modern Egypt, it would have to create "the desirable illusion of the old environment." Herzl was not thinking of the synagogue of his childhood or the shtetl of the Russian Pale. He wanted opera houses and "genuine Vienna cafés." Hebrew was ossified in the prayer book. "Who among us knows enough Hebrew to ask for a train ticket?" Yiddish was a vulgarity, to be cast off with the deformations of exile. German was the future language of the Jews. But the Mediterranean zephyrs of French civilization would soften its harsh moods. Zion would be like Trieste for the new Jews, an Austro-Hungarian outpost in the south.

"German theater, international theater, opera, musical comedy, circus, café-concert, Café Champs-Elysées."

Jerusalem had a Jewish majority by the 1850s. The revivalist mysticism of the Hasidic movement and improved transportation networks in eastern Europe had caused the Jewish population to overflow the

Jewish quarter of the Old City and the sixteenth-century fortifica-
tions of Suleiman the Magnificent. Emancipated Western Jews led by
Britain's Moses Montefiore began to construct Jewish neighborhoods
outside the city walls. If these demographic and spatial changes reflected tremors in the Jewish perception of time and space, they did
not yet amount to an organized political program. Jewish Jerusalem,
religious or artisanal, was sustained by charity from the Diaspora.
Montefiore's neighborhood of Yemin Moshe, with its windmill set in
a model Ottoman village, was a personal project. Zionism would be a
greater breach, redrawing boundaries not just between nations but
also between Jews.

The program for Jewish revival in the form of modern statehood
began a few months before Herzl's birth. In 1862, the German socialist Moses Hess wrote *Rome and Jerusalem*, the first formal proposal
for turning millennial prayers into a political program. In the 1840s,
Hess had associated with Marx and Engels; he may have supplied
Marx with the slogan "Religion is the opiate of the people." By the
early 1860s, Hess had realized that Jews were not welcome in the universal family of European socialism. His answer was to transfer the
revolution to ancestral soil and "redeem" the Land of Israel as a socialist republic.

In 1882, Yehudah Leib Pinsker, a doctor appalled by the pogroms
in his native Odessa, reached similar conclusions. In *Auto-Emancipation*,
Pinsker explained the Jewish predicament in almost Nietzschean
psychological terms. The Jews had lost their ancient state but they
survived spiritually as a ghost among the nations. Their uncanny survival, and the absence of the nationhood that this had caused, created
"an indelible stigma, repellent to non-Jews and painful to the Jews
themselves." The "fear of ghosts" was universal and, Pinsker allowed,
it even had a "certain justification in the psychic life of humanity."
Among Christians, the Jewish ghost raised fear, prejudice, and
persecution.

Pinsker refused to use the language of his persecutors. He called antisemitism by its real name: "Judeophobia" was a "hereditary form of demonopathy," expressed as a pathological fear of Jews. The antisemite imagined himself to be menaced by a monolithic "Semitism," and saw individual Jews as the material forms of his "Platonic hatred." Judeophobia was a psychic aberration, and perhaps incurable: after two thousand years, the universal impulse to torment the scapegoat was firmly attached to the Jews. Even if they abandoned their distinctiveness, they would remain a chosen people—the "people chosen for universal hatred."

The only answer to the metaphysics of Judeophobia was "autoemancipation," the revival of Jewish national consciousness. Pinsker became the leader of an Odessa socialist group named Chovevei Tzion, the "Lovers of Zion." In July 1882, ten of its members and a group from Bilu, another Jewish socialist movement, founded an agricultural colony on land bought from an Arab village near Jaffa. They named it Rishon le-Tzion, "First in Zion." This new phase of Jewish history, Bilu announced, would create new foundations for the "neglected Jewish economic reality," according to science and "the latest word of European culture." Several more colonies were planted on the coastal plain over the next decade, most of them wineries or artisanal villages. The pioneers brought socialist ideals but they had little farming experience and no running water. They lived in tents, then shacks. Malaria was endemic and suicide frequent. The weather was brutal and the Arabs were suspicious. The new lovers of Zion soon found themselves in the same position as older lovers of Zion. Chovevei Tzion survived on the patronage of Edmond de Rothschild.

Herzl did not invent Zionism, but Zionism reinvented Herzl. He took the term "Zionism" from *Self-Emancipation*, a pamphlet of 1890 by an Austrian Jewish student named Nathan Birnbaum. Herzl had not read Hess or Pinsker; when he did read *Rome and Jerusalem*, he called Hess the most important Jewish thinker since Spinoza. Nor had Herzl read George Eliot's novel on Jewish identity, *Daniel Deronda*

(1876). Herzl had, however, read Disraeli's meditation on racial chivalry and national redemption, *Tancred*. The Jews needed a champion: a Hebrew knight, a Tancred or a Tannhäuser, a Quixote willing to charge the windmills of race and nation. Herzl elected himself as a messiah.

If Zionism reinvented Herzl, Nietzsche supplied the template. Herzl was distant enough from his roots to find them exotic: he was more of a Gandhi than a Vivekananda or a Dharmapala. The god of Herzl's Zionism was not the God of Moses, but the god of Zarathustra, the inner god of history and biology, the humiliated, burdened camel who dares to become a lion in the desert. Like Nietzsche, Herzl was a defector from Wagner's Germania. In flight and confrontation, he bore the antipodal imprint of its spiritual politics. Zionism was the first Nietzschean political movement and the first national movement of the New Age.

Nietzsche's ideas had been in the air at Vienna University, especially among Jewish students. Herzl, a wide reader in philosophy, had been close to the Pernerstorfer circle, a group of Jewish intellectuals known as "Nietzsche's Society in Vienna." Its members included the socialist leader Victor Adler, the feuilletonist Arthur Schnitzler, and Josef Paneth, a medical student and friend of Sigmund Freud's. Paneth was an early admirer of Nietzsche, and in January 1884 he had come across his idol in Nice. Paneth was on holiday, and Nietzsche was writing the third part of *Zarathustra*. When Nietzsche learned that Paneth was Jewish, he praised the nascent movement for the "regeneration" of the Jews in their ancient land. Nietzsche was "quite disappointed," Paneth recalled, "that I did not wish to hear anything about the restoration."

In 1891, Herzl asked in print when Nietzsche's "new European man" would appear. In 1895, he identified him as a "new Jew," the Hebrew Superman. Nietzsche called antisemitism a neurosis. Herzl was the doctor who would cure it. He saw the sickness and its crisis in Nietzschean terms. Adversity was part of his biological destiny, history a duel of races: "We must have been a highly gifted people to have endured twenty centuries of slaughter and remain undestroyed."

"*Wollen macht frei,*" said Herzl the Jewish Zarathustra: will, or desire, liberates. Zionism was to be a faith for life after God, a transvaluing dream lived in defiance of the world. Herzl did not describe Zionism in the archaic language of Moses, the prophets, or the Talmudic sages. He used the fresh language of Nietzsche: the spiritual daring, the dynamic psychology, the imagery of physics and perspectivism: "Great things need no firm foundation. An apple must be placed on the table to keep it from falling. The earth hovers in the air. Thus I can perhaps secure and found the Jewish state without any firm anchorage. The secret lies in movement. Hence I believe that somewhere a guidable aircraft will be discovered. Gravity overcome through movement."

Zionism was the Perspectivism of the Jews. Beginning an ostensibly rational political program where Nietzsche's delusions had stopped, Herzl, the Hebrew Caesar, wrote letters to Bismarck and the pope. He imagined himself convening the Rothschild clan in conclave. When he began to write them a letter petitioning for their patronage and money, his flood of inspiration turned into a book. In February 1896, *Der Judenstaat, The Jewish State*, was published in Vienna.

"*As there was no hocus-pocus from the beginning, the Vedanta is draw*ing the highest classes of American society," Swami Vivekananda reported from New York that month.

The night before, Sarah Bernhardt, the toast of the age, had spotted him in the audience at *Iziel*, a "sort of Frenchified life of Buddha," and invited him to dinner. Bernhardt, a French Jew, played Iziel, a courtesan who sits in the Buddha's lap and tries to seduce him as he preaches the "vanity of the world." The Buddha in *Iziel* persists in *brahmacharya*, holy celibacy, and carries on preaching. Vivekananda found his own vow somewhat burdensome. He had "fallen" before, as a wandering monk in India, and it was rumored that he had tumbled into the long grass at Green Acre too. He enjoyed American life: its beef and ice cream, its candid, clever women. Perhaps too much: he worried that he was getting fat.

At dinner, he diverted his attention away from the "divine Sarah" and toward Nikola Tesla. The inventor of the AC motor and a pioneer of wireless communication, Tesla was working on a global wireless system, despite the recent immolation of his laboratory in an electrical fire. He wanted to create a global network of information exchange, with the earth as a giant conductor. When Vivekananda related the Vedantic concepts of *prana* and *akasha* to the physicist's "force" and "matter," and *Brahman* to the immanent "energy" of the universe, Tesla lit up like one of his light bulbs. This, he said, was the only kind of spirituality that "modern science can contain." He invited Vivekananda to visit him in the remains of his laboratory.

"In that case, the Vedantic cosmology will be placed on the surest of foundations," Vivekananda predicted. "I can clearly see their perfect union with modern science, and the elucidation of the one will be followed by the other." The union would not be a marriage of equal partners. Tesla hoped to incorporate spiritual yearnings into science. Vivekananda wanted to incorporate science into religion, and Western technology into Hindu nationalism: "If India is to rise again, it will be only through 'religion,' and not through any other idea, though there will be room for many other things as well, like politics, economics, and so forth, but all within this framework of religion."

In January 1897, Vivekananda left for India. After stopping in London and Colombo, he landed at Madras to a hero's welcome. News of his Western success had preceded him. He progressed to Calcutta in triumph and rejoined his monks. In May, he used the money he had collected in his Western travels to found the Ramakrishna Mission. His first work at the mission was to codify its monastic rules. His second was to launch a famine relief program, the beginnings of spreading the social gospel among the Hindu masses.

Absence had not made his heart fonder of the ordinary Hindu male. He criticized Hindus in the same language as the early Zionists criticized their fellow Jews. The Hindu masses were prisoners of ritual and superstition. If someone tried to improve or lead them, they thwarted him with "the malicious nature befitting a slave." They were passive and docile: "The whole nation has become effeminate—a race of women!" They needed a dose of Western manliness, the rational cure of technology, political organization, and a work ethic. "What we want is muscles of iron and nerves of steel. We have wept long enough. No more weeping, but stand on your feet and be men. It is a man-making religion that we want. It is man-making all-around education that we want."

This, though, was all Hindus needed from the West. Vivekananda's travels confirmed his faith that the Vedanta was the original and supreme spirituality, and that Hindus were its bearers. The West was "gross, material, selfish, and sensual." The East was spiritual. This was the commodity that the West wanted most of all, and it could become India's greatest export. "Spirituality must conquer the West," he announced when he landed in Colombo. "This is the great ideal before us, and everyone must be ready for it—the conquest of the world by India . . . Up, India, conquer the world with our spirituality."

Elisabeth Nietzsche moved her brother to Weimar. She wanted him to die in Goethe's city. His deathbed and his archive would be conveniently close to the Goethe-Schiller archive, so tourists could bless all their houses in a single excursion.

"Above all," Nietzsche had asked in his last lucid hours in Turin, "do not mistake me for someone else." He may have recognized that this was Elisabeth's intention. She dressed him in loose white robes. She grew his mustache to an absurd length. She was embalming him alive, preparing his myth. Soon Nietzsche, like a half-flayed martyr, could only receive the torments but not speak of them.

He had become the chief mourner at his own funeral. The world of thought was beyond his control, and others were already reaping the growths he had sown. In 1894, Lou Andreas-Salomé wrote a candid biography of her erstwhile friend. Elisabeth Förster-Nietzsche swiftly countered with the idyllic and hygienic *Young Nietzsche*, the first volume of a two-part hagiography. In November 1896, Richard Strauss's tone poem *Also Sprach Zarathustra* premiered in Frankfurt. In 1900, a complete German edition began to appear, heavily edited by Elisabeth. Nietzsche now attracted the kind of educated rabble that the young art historian Aby Warburg called "the *Ubermensch* on his Easter holiday, with *Zarathustra* in the pocket of his tweed cape, seeking fresh courage from its mad cascadings for his struggle for life, even against political authority."

Elisabeth's edition suppressed Nietzsche's homoeroticism, his eventual renunciation of German nationalism, and his rejection of Wagner as neurotic and decadent. The philosophical anti-Judaic material was turned to the politically antisemitic ends that Nietzsche had come to despise. Still bemused by the details of her brother's philosophy, Elisabeth engaged Rudolf Steiner as her teacher. He found her unteachable and they gave up. She had, though, understood enough for her needs. In 1887, the *Antisemitische Correspondenz* had attacked Nietzsche as "eccentric," "pathological," and "psychiatric." Now, the racial demagogues and vulgar Darwinians embraced him as she embraced them. Traduced and transvalued, Nietzsche once again became a perfect Wagnerite.

As did Wagner, albeit with less damage to the record. In 1882, Ludwig Schemann, one of Wagner's pan-Germanist acolytes, had met Arthur de Gobineau at Wagner's house. Schemann heard his master's voice in his head: Wagner would want him to help the ailing, aging Gobineau. Schemann set to translating Gobineau into German, publicized him as the founding theorist of degeneration and, less accurately, characterized him as a Wagnerian visionary of racial regeneration. In 1894, while Andreas-Salomé and Elisabeth Nietzsche competed over Nietzsche's biography, Schemann launched the Gobineau Society.

Closely identified with Wagner's philosophical followers and Cosima Wagner's circle of racist sycophants, the society disseminated an antisemitic version of Gobineau's mildly philosemitic theories, and collected his manuscripts and his correspondence with other racial philosophers, Renan among them. Henry Hotze, who thirty years earlier had carried Gobineau into the Anglophone world, was one of the Gobineau Society's founding members. Zarathustra had been dragged down from his mountain and into the marketplace of resentment.

The First Zionist Congress met on August 29, 1897. Herzl had planned to hold the conference in Munich, but the leaders of the local Jewish community had disapproved, so he moved the parliament of the Jews to a hotel on Nietzsche's old ground, Basel. Nearly two hundred delegates from fifteen countries gathered in the hotel's ballroom. It was the largest gathering of Jewish leaders since the Romans dissolved the Sanhedrin.

A six-pointed Shield of David was above the door. A long banner hung on each side of the entrance, white with blue stripes at the edges, like a *tallit*, the prayer shawl. Many of the delegates thought the banner resurrected the flag of the ancient Jews, but no one knew if the ancient Maccabeans had used a flag; the banner was the work of Herzl's friend David Wolffsohn. And if the variety of factions would have been familiar to the ancient Judeans, their ideological differences were entirely modern: Orthodox Jews, Jewish atheists, Jewish capitalists, Jewish anarchists, Jewish aristocrats, Jewish proletarians.

The Anglo-Jewish writer Israel Zangwill, author of *Children of the Ghetto* and *The Melting Pot*, thought Herzl the king of the Jews: "a majestic Oriental figure," square-bearded and "serene" like an Assyrian king. Amid passionate declarations and rhetoric, Herzl spoke softly, defining the ancient dream in the language of a moderate, practical lawyer. Yet beneath this "statesmanlike prose" and placid exterior, Zangwill detected the quintessence of wild modernity: "the romance of the poet, the purposeful vagueness of the modern evolutionist, the fantasy of the Hungarian, the dramatic self-consciousness of the literary artists, the heart of the Jew."

"At Basel," Herzl declared, "I founded the Jewish state." The Basel platform defined the goals of Zionism as both cultural and political. The political object was to be achieved diplomatically and institutionally, not by piecemeal charity or farming collectives. The newly founded Zionist Organization was to lobby the Great Powers for a "publicly recognized, legally secured homeland in Palestine." Meanwhile, it would prepare for the arrival of the Jewish masses by creating a constitution, a bank, and a national fund for land purchases. The cultural object was to convince the Jewish masses to take part in the inner revolution of "strengthening the Jewish national sentiment and national consciousness."

Zionism, Herzl said, was not a party, but a national renaissance: "the Jewish people on the move" through history. Eight in every ten Jews lived in the Russian Empire. After the pogroms of the early 1880s, hundreds of thousands were already on the move. But almost all of them were heading west to Vienna, Berlin, Paris, London, and New York. By 1897, only twenty-five thousand had gone to Palestine. Still, Herzl felt sure that he had read the future correctly. The fact of the Basel conference and the founding of the Zionist Organization proved that the Jews were returning to the "stream of history." At Basel, he prophesied that the Jewish state would arise in 1947.

On August 15, 1947, the British left their Indian empire, and Pakistan and India became independent states. On November 29, the League of Nations voted to partition the British-controlled Palestine Mandate into two states, Jewish and Arab.

The public careers of Herzl and Vivekananda lasted little more than a decade. But in that time each performed a massive and crucial labor for his people. Both understood that transvaluing ancient religious communities into modern political nations was as much a spiritual revolt as a practical and political process. They looked back across centuries of degeneration and decay to a golden age of Vedic or

Maccabean glory. They looked forward to a future where scientific methods and central authority would rebuild the masculine virtues of an emasculated people. They saw their peoples imprisoned by historical time and imagined them freed in political space. They were Perspectivist politicians, auto-emancipators of the spirit in a Monist universe.

EPILOGUE: 1898

The Psychopathology of Everyday Life

> When the New Age is at leisure to pronounce, all will be
> set right. —*William Blake*, Milton: A Poem *(1804)*

In the first-floor consulting room at 19 Berggasse, the patient re-
clines on a rug-draped couch as if in a rowboat. Above her head is a
framed print, *The Rock-Cut Temple at Abu Simbel*, and a reproduction
of Ingres's *Oedipus and Sphinx*. There are prints from Renaissance
Florence, and copies of vases and statuary from Greece and Rome.
The doctor is a collector. When he takes his annual walking holiday
in the Alpine foothills, he brings his favorite items with him, as well
as his wife and children. When he sits at his writing desk, he cordially
salutes the statues lining its periphery: Thoth the Egyptian baboon
god of the moon, Athena the goddess of war and wisdom, Imhotep
the architect and healer. Behind them is a Chinese table screen, an aid
to scholarly contemplation.

Eventually, the doctor will possess more than two thousand items,
many of them ancient and expensive. All will be displayed in his professional rooms, none in the family quarters. He will create a living
museum of gods and images, stimuli to legends and stories. In front
of his recumbent patients he will place a cabinet containing six different statues of Eros. The cabinet's mirrored back will show them the

god of love from all angles; possibly, it also allows the doctor to observe his patients without them noticing.

The doctor sits behind the patient's head, saying little, out of sight but inside the mind. The patient's eyes and thoughts wander among the idols and ruins of the ancient Mediterranean. If she flinches from the life erotic and turns her head away from the wall, she will find herself facing the scientific facts that underlie the inner drama of dreams and evasions, the proofs that the doctor already knows her innermost secrets. Her eyes will meet an engraving that shows the office of Dr. Charcot and then, through doors left open during consultations, the doctor's study, thick with books and statues. Her field of vision will terminate in a wall of antiquities on the theme of death, its centerpiece a large Egyptian funerary boat.

Sigmund Freud developed psychoanalysis to be a science of the mind. The sickness that the talking cure was meant to heal was individual and social. The crisis of the inner life was the crisis of Western society, and Freud's reduction of intolerable distress to "ordinary unhappiness" a primer for containing the passions of politics within a liberal, rational civilization. Instead, the twentieth century became a century of irrationalism and murder: nationalism and socialism, New Age democracy and popular Theosophy, the slaughter in the trenches and the genocide of the Jews. When the prophetic visions of eccentrics became part of everyone's political language, the radical individualism of spirituality produced a radical conformity in politics. The Religious Revolution became what Freud called a "psychopathology of everyday life."

Karl Marx's socialism was fashionably reworked by Friedrich Engels into "scientific socialism," then reworked again by Lenin and Mao. Mass-produced, socialism spread across the globe, mutating to adapt to local conditions. In Germany, class war mutated into race war and national socialism. In Russia and China, socialism supplied a new imperial doctrine. In India and Europe, it supplied an anti-imperial doctrine. The greater the application of socialist theory, the worse the human, ethical, and environmental cost. Yet socialism retains its appeal: it speaks of justice and economy, but it appeals to the religious impulse and the power of resentment. Socialism's only challenger as the most successful of all post-Christian ideologies is antisemitism.

Henry David Thoreau's nonviolent retreat from society returned to the streets in the mass protests led by Gandhi in India and Martin Luther King, Jr., in the United States. Thoreau's *Walden* is on American high school reading lists. Walden Pond is a pilgrimage site, with a replica of his hut in the car park. **Walt Whitman** suffered a stroke in 1873 and retired to his brother's house in Camden, New Jersey. He was still revising *Leaves of Grass* when he died, a white-bearded sage, in 1892. His poetic style and radical stance made him the direct ancestor of the Beat writers, notably Allen Ginsberg. Today, Whitman is an icon of gay liberation and the quintessential American poet.

Transcendentalist thought became the religion of upwardly mobile white Americans in the Sixties, and it remains so today. Meanwhile, the standing of its greatest mind slowly declines. Once the central intellect of his age, and the American peer of Thomas Carlyle, **Ralph Waldo Emerson** is now more likely to be seen as a precursor of more radical spirits: Whitman, Thoreau, and, in recent years, Nietzsche. Emerson's house in Concord is a museum, but his writings are slipping off the American curriculum.

John Ruskin died in January 1900 as a global eminence. His rage against the machine deeply influenced the radical politics of Tolstoy and Gandhi. His aesthetic theories influenced Marcel Proust and William Morris and inspired the Arts and Crafts movement. His Pre-Raphaelites, part of the first modern art movement, continue to fascinate the public, though not the critics, through exhibitions and films. Yet Ruskin's reputation declined sharply in the decades after his death. The modernist revolt in art rejected his tastes in design and morality. His humane and artisanal socialism was crushed by the socialism of the state and heavy industry. The aspect of his biography that most interests the twenty-first century is his sexual psychology: his cruelty to Effie Gray; his obsession with Rose de la Touche, the juvenile daughter of two of his friends; and his nervous collapse in late life. Still, visitors to Venice take Ruskin as their guide, and artists are trained at the Ruskin School of Drawing at Oxford University. The Guild of Saint George survives too, though today its activities tend to concentrate on environmentalism and the Ruskin Museum at Sheffield.

Charles Baudelaire, the inventor of *modernité*, died in 1867, aged forty-six. Penniless and debilitated by drink, laudanum, and syphilis, he spent his last years living with his mother and then, after a stroke in 1864, in nursing homes. The posthumous publication of his verse and criticism gratified his mother and received an acclaim that has never abated. His literary children include Verlaine, Rimbaud, and Mallarmé; his admirers, T. S. Eliot, Edmund Wilson, Marcel Proust, and Walter Benjamin.

Charles Darwin, who had been accused of confusing evolution with English liberalism, became so synonymous with rationalism that, today, American liberals ward off religion and right-wingers by sporting one-word bumper stickers bearing his name. His defender **Thomas Henry Huxley** died in 1895. The first "agnostic," Huxley is remembered as "Darwin's bulldog" and as the uncle of Aldous Huxley, whose essays retain the imprint of his Victorian uncle's humane and scientific rationalism, even after their author's midlife turn to mysticism and psychedelic drugs.

Arthur, Comte de Gobineau, died in 1882. After the founding of the Gobineau Society, his racial theories were popularized by Richard Wagner's Scottish son-in-law, Houston Stewart Chamberlain. In 1899, the Munich publisher Hugo Bruckmann, who would later publish *Mein Kampf*, published Chamberlain's racist history of the modern age, *The Foundations of the Nineteenth Century* (1899). During World War I, Chamberlain renounced his British citizenship and propagandized for Germany. Afterward, he blamed Germany's defeat on the Jews and became the first public figure to acclaim Adolf Hitler as "Germany's savior."

Chamberlain, who died in 1927, is almost forgotten today, and so is Gobineau. But **Richard Wagner** remains the object of the cult that he and Cosima worked so hard to create. Wagner is the most consequential composer in the history of music: his racial revolt into nationalism and socialism was fulfilled in the national socialism of Adolf Hitler. By the mid-1920s, Wagner's heirs, Chamberlain among them, had turned Bayreuth into a shrine of the racial aesthetic and the Nazi leadership's favorite holiday destination. After the interval of World War II, the Wagner Festival was revived in 1951 under the leadership of Wagner's grandsons Wieland Wagner, who had worked at the Bayreuth satellite of the Flossenbürg concentration camp, and Wolfgang Wagner, who, according to his son, continued to admire Hitler.

Colonel Henry Olcott led the Theosophical Society until his death in 1907. The "Protestant Buddhism" that he founded in Ceylon became integral to the Sri Lankan independence movement. In 1915, when Buddhists rioted in Colombo against Muslims, the British authorities reacted by imprisoning hundreds of Buddhists, including Olcott's ally **Angarika Dharmapala**. Four years later, Dharmapala was one of the founders of the Ceylon National Congress, which was modeled on the Indian National Congress. He became increasingly nationalistic, as well as hostile to Muslims and critical of Christianity. He died in 1933, fifteen years before Ceylon achieved independence. In 1972, Ceylon became the Republic of Sri Lanka. Streets in Colombo are named after both Olcott and Dharmapala.

Annie Besant succeeded Olcott as leader of the Theosophical Society and ruled it until her death in Adyar in 1933. The Theosophical Society is still there. Descendants of the eighty-five American lodges that split off from the Adyar mother ship in 1895 also still exist. So does the Theosophical Society in America, which was formed by the five lodges that stayed loyal to the faith. Recent lecturers at its headquarters at Wheaton, Illinois, have included the Dalai Lama, Ram Dass, and Rupert Sheldrake.

In 1908, Besant's aide Charles Leadbeater met a thirteen-year-old boy on the beach in Adyar. His name was Krishnamurti; he was the son of an Indian clerk who worked for the society. Leadbeater and

Besant groomed Krishnamurti as the Maitreya, the Theosophical messiah. They separated him from his family, dressed him in Western clothes, spoon-fed him Dostoevsky and Nietzsche, and made him do vigorous English sports. In 1911, Besant launched Krishnamurti in London with his first lecture to the Order of the Star in the East.

In the years before and after World War I, Krishnamurti carried the Theosophical gospel, and the burden of Besant's and Leadbeater's expectations, around the world, closely chaperoned by the leaders of the Theosophical Society. In 1922, Krishnamurti, now twenty-seven years old and living in the Theosophical community in Ojai, California, suffered a two-month-long collapse, possibly psychological, possibly epileptic, whose symptoms included disassociation, the perception of bright colors, a sense of "otherness," and visions of an infinite and benign cosmos. The "process," as Krishnamurti called it, would return periodically throughout his life. When he recovered, he began to drift away from Besant, despite her plans to announce his messiahship in 1925, the fiftieth anniversary of the society's founding. In 1929, Krishnamurti dissolved the Order of the Star in the East, but he continued to live and lecture in Ojai.

Krishnamurti became close friends with another émigré seeker, Aldous Huxley, who had moved to California in 1938. His lectures, disseminated by tape recordings, an innovation that Blavatsky and the Coulombs would have known how to use, made Krishnamurti a significant influence on the growth of neo-Vedanta in the West, and a central figure in its expansion in the Sixties. Krishnamurti may not have been the Theosophical messiah, but he did represent the fulfillment of Blavatsky's dream, a spiritual revolutionary who answered the existential crisis of the West with the wisdom of the East. The sources of that wisdom presumably included his exploitation as a child by the Theosophists. "There is no teacher, no pupil; for there is no leader, no guru; there is no Master, no Saviour," he told an audience in 1966. "You yourself are the teacher and the pupil; you are the Master; you are the guru; you are the leader; you are everything."

The Sixties resurrected **Helena Blavatsky**. Credited or not, she

was the founder of the cod-religious medley that the Sixties' generation acclaimed as New Age thought. She was also the forerunner of
the thousands of young Westerners who went east to India in search
of meaning. The Western appetite for drugs and occultism was now so
great that **Éliphas Lévi**'s books were republished for the first time in
fifty years. Lévi might have felt cheated all over again when he noticed
the *correspondance* between his *Satanisme* and the decade that saw the
birth of heavy metal and the popularization of his version of the tarot.
The internet, another medium for unifying the peoples of the world in
dematerialized mystification, secures Blavatsky's posterity in a new
century.

Friedrich Nietzsche also enjoyed a posthumous surge in popularity in the Sixties. But this was one among the many, apparently unending, surges in Nietzsche's significance. No modern philosopher
has had greater influence on the arts, from Richard Strauss to Kelly
Clarkson, the chorus of whose 2011 hit reprised the one Nietzsche
line that everyone knows: "What doesn't kill me makes me stronger."
No modern philosopher, not even Bertrand Russell or Ayn Rand, has
had such a profound influence on the world beyond the ivory tower as
Nietzsche. The speed with which he was recognized as the supreme
analyst of the spiritual crisis of his time is remarkable. By the time of
his death in August 1900, he was well known outside the German-
speaking world, and mostly admired by anarchists, aesthetes, and the
occasional academic. Yet during World War I, Nietzsche was so much
part of Germany's patriotic consensus that one hundred thousand
copies of *Zarathustra* were distributed to German soldiers in the
trenches. Naturally, the edition was designed to survive in the field,
and possessed the Nietzschean virtue of hardness.

"I should think there is no instance since history began of a country being so demoralized by a single writer," Thomas Hardy wrote in
1914. The war, one London bookseller noticed from his sales ledger
that year, looked like a "Euro-Nietzschean War." It was, in that Nietzsche's growing international audience saw the conflict in his terms:
Herbert Read, the future Surrealist, found himself discussing Nietzsche

with a German prisoner minutes after nearly killing him in trench fighting. Nietzsche had anatomized the decadence of mass society and prescribed salutary violence as the cure. Artists had responded first to this strong imagery, but politicians and propagandists made more creative use of it. Nietzsche, as he had foreseen, was drawn into the vortex of other people's rituals of violence. "All power structures of the old society will have been exploded—all of them are based on lies," he had written in *Ecce Homo*. "There will be wars the like of which have never been seen on earth. It is only beginning with me that the earth knows metapolitics."

This was not the only Nietzsche prophecy that was fulfilled in the early decades of the twentieth century. The selective editing of his writings by his sister, Elisabeth, and his long immersion in racial theories endeared Nietzsche to a German veteran of the trenches. Adolf Hitler, the great popularizer of the swastika that Madame Blavatsky had placed on the Theosophists' icon and Nietzsche's editors had placed on the spines of the first complete edition of his works in German, had absorbed the New Age's spiritual politics in his youth. He was prone to quote Nietzsche as well as Schopenhauer all through his life. Elisabeth Nietzsche even made a gift to Hitler of the Holy Grail of the German racial spirit, her brother's walking stick.

It would be unfair to say that Nazi Germany was an accurate reflection of Nietzsche's philosophy. But it would be false to say that central elements of Nietzsche's thought were incompatible with the ethos and actions of Nazi Germany. His state-sanctioned popularity is proof enough. Nietzsche's thought emerged from the same nineteenth-century stew of race politics and Romantic spirituality as Wagner's operas, Nietzsche himself, and the would-be intellectuals of German fascism. Nietzsche had called for a new and pitiless morality of hardness for his "blond beasts," the "lords of the earth" (a phrase that appeared in *Mein Kampf*). He had identified the Jews as the source of the "slave morality" that restrained the Germans from attaining their fullest historical development and that had to be violently overthrown.

"You say that it is the good cause that hallows even war?" Zarathustra had said. "I say unto you: it is the good war that hallows any cause."

As Nietzsche's Socrates contained multitudes, so there are many Nietzsches. There is the Nietzsche of Sigmund Freud, the modern Socrates who, in his determination to build a rational and liberal science of the mind, downplayed the influence of Nietzsche as the modern Alcibiades. There is the Nietzsche of Carl Jung, who admitted the influence and became a racial mystic, soaked in Blavatskyite fantasies about the Aryan Jesus. There is the American Nietzsche of H. L. Mencken, whose *Philosophy of Nietzsche* (1907) introduced Nietzsche as sharing Mencken's dislike of Jews and democracy. There is the American Nietzsche of Walter Kaufmann, the Jewish fugitive from Nazism whose translations of the 1950s defined the Nietzsche of the Sixties, a Dionysiac rebel against spiritual and sexual conformity. There is the Nietzsche of the Classicists, who eventually accepted his theories about the Dionysian origins of the theater, and there is now also the Nietzsche of the online alt-right. If the West is not finished with Nietzsche, it is because the nihilism that he called "western Buddhism" and the response that he called "metapolitics" are not finished with us.

Swami Vivekananda's Ramakrishna Mission grew into a global network of monasteries. These became conduits for the westward flow of "neo-Vedanta," the revivalist Hinduism that Ramakrishna had inspired in his disciples. The mission raised Ramakrishna into a figure of international importance, but Vivekananda would not live to see his dream fulfilled. Diabetic and exhausted by his travels, he died of an aneurysm in 1902.

Theodor Herzl, similarly debilitated by his work, died in 1906. As he had predicted at Basel, the revived Jewish state was born in 1947, when the United Nations voted to divide the British-controlled Palestine Mandate into Jewish and Arab states; the old-new State of Israel survived Arab attempts to destroy it after its independence on May 14, 1948. By then, the Germans and their collaborators had murdered six million of Herzl's people, including his youngest daughter, Trude, who died at the Theresienstadt concentration camp in 1943 and whose body was incinerated.

It was, however, suicide, not murder, that ended Herzl's family line. Trude's siblings were already dead. Her older sister Pauline had died from a heroin overdose in 1930, and her brother Hans had committed suicide on the day of her funeral. Stephan Neumann, Herzl's lone grandson, was the only one of his heirs to become an active Zionist. After Anglicizing his name to Stephen Norman and serving as a British artillery officer, he despaired at the refusal of Britain's Labour government to allow Holocaust survivors into Palestine and committed suicide in Washington, D.C., in 1946. Theodor Herzl's remains, along with those of Pauline and Hans Herzl and Stephan Neumann, were disinterred and reburied in Israel's national cemetery on Mount Herzl in Jerusalem.

In 1915, **Mohandas Gandhi** returned to India preceded by his South African reputation as an anti-imperial strategist and a polemicist of Hindu liberation in *Hind Swaraj* (1909). In 1920, having exchanged his lawyer's suit for the legendary *dhoti*, Gandhi became the leader of the Indian National Congress. Thoreau's strategy of nonviolence, milled through the Hindu ideal of *satyagraha*, "soul force," mobilized unarmed, ordinary Hindus against an empire. The newsreel made Gandhi a global celebrity and he remains one still, though he is now more likely to be invoked alongside Thoreau on the bumper stickers of Americans than on the hustings by Indian politicians. Gandhi is a secular saint in the West, so his standing is immune to the facts of his kind words for Hitler; his attempt to sabotage the British-led armies that saved India from being turned into a Japanese slave plantation; the intriguing and undermining of initiatives by both allies and enemies that contributed to the catastrophic violence of Partition; and even his habit of sleeping naked with his young great-nieces, in order, he claimed, to test his celibate resolve.

India, the world's largest democracy, became an independent nation for the first time in its history in June 1947. Just over six months later, in January 1948, Gandhi was shot to death. His assassin, Nathu-ram Godse, was a member of the Hindu Mahasabha, a Hindu nation-alist group with roots in the Arya Samaj of Dayananda Saraswati. Godse was also an erstwhile member of another Hindu nationalist group, the Rashtriya Swayamsevak Sangh (RSS), or National Volun-teer Association, a group strongly influenced by the thought of Swami Vivekananda. The RSS's current members include India's prime min-ister, Narendra Modi.

Today, one in three Americans believes in reincarnation. Nearly one in eight practices yoga. Nearly one in five describes themselves as "spiritual but not religious." The Religious Revolution is not over.

NOTES

Prologue

3 *"We, the witnesses"*: Kern Holoman, *Berlioz*, 335.

4 *"From Boulogne"*: Emerson, May 6, 1848: *Journals*, VII, 450.

8 *"All religious movements in history"*: Emerson, *Early Lectures*, I, 181.

10 *"once omnipotent"*: Emerson, *Journals*, XV, 228.

11 *"The powers that make a capitalist"*: Emerson, *Journals*, XI, 9.

11 *"Rouse up"*: W. Blake, preface to *Milton: A Poem* (1804).

11 *"Torchlight processions"*: Emerson, *Journals*, X, 329.

12 *"For the matter of socialism"*: Emerson, *Journals*, X, 310.

1. The New Prometheus

15 *"If there is any period"*: Emerson, "The American Scholar" (1837), *Collected Works*, I, 67.

16 *"Until now"*: Marx and Engels, preface to "The German Ideology" (1844), *Writings of the Young Karl Marx*, Easton (ed.), 404.

16–17 *"But what is most interesting"* . . . *"We are a link in the chain"*: Disraeli, *Tancred*, I, 225–26.

20 *"Think over the confession"*: Engels to Marx, cit. Mehring, *Karl Marx*, 147.

20 *"God has set me"*: Noyes to a follower, cit. Blake and Wells (eds.), *Oneida Community Collection*, 3.

20 *"the work of Antichrist"*: Noyes, *Way of Holiness*, 10.

20 *"redeem man"*: Noyes, *Way of Holiness*, ii.

21 *"true holiness"* . . . *"creed and constitution"*: Noyes, *Bible Communism*, 6.

21 *"seven holy days"*: Noyes, *Way of Holiness*, 177.

21 *"mutual criticism"* . . . *"complex marriage"*: Noyes, *Bible Communism*, 6.

22 *"First we abolish sin"*: Noyes, *Way of Holiness*, 177.

22 *"Between this present time"*: Noyes to a follower, cit. Blake and Wells (eds.), *Oneida Community Collection*, 3.

22–23 *"subjection of Nature's forces"* . . . *"bourgeois prejudices"*: Marx and Engels, "Communist Manifesto," *Marx and Engels: The Political Writings,* 66.

23 *"swindlers, confidence tricksters"*: Marx and Engels, "The Eighteenth Brumaire of Louis Napoleon" (1852), *Marx and Engels: The Political Writings,* 531.

25 *"All that is solid"*: Marx and Engels, "Communist Manifesto," *Marx and Engels: The Political Writings,* I, 64.

25 *"the vices"* . . . *"Faith is dead"*: Mazzini to Pius IX, M. Fuller [Ossoli], *At Home and Abroad,* 285–87.

26 *"My most secret thought is that"*: Metternich, *Nachgelassene papiere,* ed. R. Metternich-Winneburg (Berlin, 1880–84), III, 348; cit. Löwith and Wolin, *Heidegger and European Nihilism,* 184.

26 *loud knockings*: The account of the Hydesville events is from the "Certificate of Mrs. Margaret Fox, Wife of John D. Fox," April 11, 1848, repr. Underhill, *The Missing Link in Modern Spiritualism,* 4–10.

26–28 *"Mr. Splitfoot"* . . . *"Dear friends"*: Underhill, *Missing Link in Modern Spiritualism,* 48–49.

29 *"Resolved. That woman"*: Seneca Falls Convention, Seneca Falls, New York, July 19–20, 1848, Cady Stanton et al. (eds.), *History of Woman Suffrage,* I, 67.

29 *"busy time"*: Mott to Stanton, cit. L. Mott, *Selected Letters of Lucretia Coffin Mott,* 163.

29 *"greatest rebellion"*: Cady Stanton et al. (eds.), *Woman Suffrage,* I, 68.

29 *"Oh my daughter"*: Cady Stanton, *Eighty Years,* 20.

29 *"gloomy superstitions"* . . . *"The old bondage"*: Cady Stanton, *Eighty Years,* 44–45.

30 *"After battling"*: Stanton and Stanton Blatch (eds.), *Cady Stanton,* I, 79.

30 *"magnetic circle"*: Stanton and Stanton Blatch (eds.), *Cady Stanton,* I, 141.

30 *"wife, mother"* . . . *"odious"*: Cady Stanton, *Eighty Years,* 147–48, 145–46, 50.

31 *"masculine productions"* . . . *"helpless and hopeless"*: Cady Stanton et al. (eds.), *Woman Suffrage,* I, 67–68.

31 *"Oh Lizzie"*: Lutz, *Created Equal,* 46.

31 *"the sacred right"*: Stanton and Stanton Blatch (eds.), *Cady Stanton,* I, 146.

31–32 *"republican principles"* . . . *"great precept of nature"*: Cady Stanton, *Eighty Years,* 59.

32 *"new inspiration"* . . . *"the injustice"*: Cady Stanton, *Eighty Years,* 149.

32 *"to be smart"* . . . *"Female Reformers"*: Cady Stanton et al. (eds.), *Woman Suffrage,* I, 74.

32 *"spirited and spicey"* . . . *"able"*: *Seneca County Courier,* July 21, 1848, cit. Griffith, *In Her Own Right,* 58.

33 *"encompassed and overcanopied"* . . . *"barnyard Conflagrations"*: Carlyle, "Characteristics," *Collected Works of Carlyle,* IV, 23, 30.

34 *"Babylonish confusion"*: Carlyle, "Characteristics," *Collected Works,* IV, 120.

34 *"an iron, ignoble"* . . . *"The Divinity"*: Carlyle, "Characteristics," *Collected Works*, IV, 23, 22.

34 *"realize a Worship"* . . . *"abysses of mystery"*: Carlyle, "Characteristics," *Collected Works*, IV, 24, 30.

34 *"Nay"* . . . *"in the higher"*: Carlyle, "Characteristics," *Collected Works*, IV, 31.

34–35 *"cry of their soul's agony"* . . . *"Godlike in human"*: Carlyle, "Characteristics," *Collected Works*, IV, 24, 32.

37 *"Thus is Art"*: Emerson, "Nature," *Nature: Addresses, and Lectures*, ed. Cabot, 29.

37 *"Standing on the bare ground"*: Emerson, "Nature," 15.

37 *"Calvinism rushes to be Unitarianism"*: Emerson, "Character," *Lectures and Biographical Sketches*, ed. Cabot, 116.

38 *"I shall speak"* . . . *"we are unable"*: F. von Schelling [?], "The First Systematic Program of German Idealism" (1797), cit. Calasso, *Literature and the Gods*, 57–60.

40 *"The main fruit"*: Marx and Engels, *Neue Rheinische Zeitung*, December 24, 1848; *Marx/Engels Collected Works*, VI, 138.

2. The Stones of Venice

41 *The gondola*: The gondola ride is described in Ruskin, *Stones of Venice*, I, 47ff.

42 *"delicacy"* . . . *"partly feminine"*: Ruskin's friend F. J. Furnivall, cit. Batchelor, *John Ruskin*, 74.

43 *"golden clasp"* . . . *"world-wide pulsation"*: Ruskin, *Stones of Venice*, I, 49.

43 *"with the quietness"*: Ruskin to his father, Bradley (ed.), *Letters from Venice*, 37.

43 *"pestilence"* . . . *"At first I thought"*: Ruskin, *Stones of Venice*, I, 30, 31.

44 *"The foundations of society"*: Ruskin, *Stones of Venice*, II, 163.

44 *"The last few eventful years"*: Ruskin, *Stones of Venice*, III, 4.

45 *"Laissez-faire the only . . ."*: Emerson, *Journals*, XI, 45.

46 *"It is not, truly speaking"* . . . *"You must either"*: Ruskin, *Stones of Venice*, II, 165, 162, 161.

46 *"at every grasp"*: Emerson, "Thoreau" (1862), *Lectures and Biographical Sketches*, ed. Cabot, 431.

47 *"Would it not"*: Thoreau, "Paradise (to Be) Regained," *A Yankee in Canada*, 184.

47 *"second breakfast"*: Emerson, "Seventh of March Speech," *Later Lectures*, ed. Cabot, I, 334.

47 *"compact system"*: Hegel, *Philosophy of History*, 142.

47 *"We will not be imposed upon"*: Thoreau, "Paradise (to Be) Regained," 198.

47 *"eye right inward"*: Thoreau, *Walden*, 343.

47 *"little world"*: Thoreau, *Walden*, 142.

48 *"Time is but the stream"* . . . *"God Himself culminates"*: Thoreau, *Walden*, 82, 81.

Notes

48 *"The yogi absorbed in contemplation"*: Thoreau to Harrison Blake, *Familiar Letters*, ed. Sanborn, 175.

48–49 *"There was nothing for me"* . . . *"It is of no use"*: Emerson to Samuel Grey Ward, *Letters from Emerson to a Friend*, ed. Norton, 27.

49–50 *"declarations of Birma"* . . . *"Is it not likely"*: Voltaire, *Philosophical Dictionary* (1764), 286, 278; cit. Gunn, *First Globalization*, 165.

50 *"relatively insignificant"* . . . *"local varieties"*: App, *Birth of Orientalism*, xiii–xiv.

51 hot afternoons: Kopf, *British Orientalism and the Bengal Renaissance*, 29.

51 *"volume of sound"*: Thoreau, May 31, 1841, *Journal of Thoreau*, ed. Torrey and Allen, 261.

52 *"Im Orient müssen wir das höchste Romantische suchen"*: Schwab, *Oriental Renaissance*, 13.

52 *"expert in home-cosmography"*: Thoreau, *Walden*, 259.

52 *"a loftier course"*: Thoreau, *Journal of Thoreau*, II, 4.

52 *"confidently in the direction"* . . . *"new, universal"*: Thoreau, *Walden*, 261.

53 *"If we could draw"* . . . *"sagacity and science"*: Wood to Dalhousie, 1859, cit. Headrick, *Tentacles of Progress*, 60, 64.

53 *"How much more admirable"*: Thoreau, *Walden*, 49.

54 *"On approaching Calcutta"*: Stocqueler, *Handbook of British India*, 179.

54 specter of a second Lancashire: Tripathi, *Trade and Finance in the Bengal Presidency*, 228.

54 *"waves of people"*: T. H. Huxley to H. A. Huxley, Desmond, *Huxley*, 151.

55 *"Truly it was astonishing"*: Victoria to Leopold, *Letters of Queen Victoria*, II, 317–18.

55 *"revolutionary crisis"*: Comte, *System of Positive Polity*, IV, 346.

55 *"The Principle, Love"*: Comte, *System of Positive Polity*, I, 58.

55–56 *"Your success as a philosopher"* . . . *"the European race"*: Booth, *Saint-Simon and Saint-Simonism*, 5, 37.

56 *"How can a man"* . . . *"social institutions"*: Hubbard, *Saint-Simon*, 95, 102.

56 *"Nature uniformly does one thing"*: Emerson, *Journals*, XI, 8.

57 *"vast intellectual operation"*: Comte, *The Positive Philosophy*, I, 15–16.

57 *"general elements"* . . . *"altruism"*: Comte, *System of Positive Polity*, I, 65–66.

57 *"universal Humanity"*: Comte, *System of Positive Polity*, IV, 346.

57–58 *"science of production"* . . . *"Great Being"*: Comte, *System of Positive Polity*, I, 64–65.

58 *"natural intermediaries"* . . . *"subjective nature"*: Comte, *System of Positive Polity*, I, 58, 56.

58 Jesuits: Chadwick, *Secularization of the European Mind*, 238.

58 *"With this exhibition"*: Marx and Engels, *Neue Rheinische Zeitung* (March–April 1850); *Marx and Engels: The Political Writings*, 289.

59 *"For the first time"*: Ruskin, "The Opening of the Crystal Palace Considered in Some of Its Relations to the Prospects of Art" (1854), *Works*, XII, 417–18.

59 *"concentrated power"*: Marx, "Revolutions of 1848," *Marx and Engels: The Political Writings*, 289.

59 *"beneath the wheels of the Juggernaut"*: Marx, *Capital*, I, 661.

60 *"sixpenny dollops of pork pie"*: Letter to the *Morning Chronicle*, cit. Gibbs-Smith, *The Great Exhibition of 1851*, 21.

60 *"false consciousness"*: Engels to Franz Mehring, T. Eagleton, *Ideology: An Introduction*, 89.

60 *"quite bewildered"* . . . *"iron death mask"*: Marx to Engels, *Collected Works*, XXVII, 384.

60–61 *"industrial and scientific"* . . . *"In our days"*: Marx, *The People's Paper*, April 19, 1856, cit. Wheen, *Karl Marx*, 201.

61 *"absolute protection"* . . . *"exasperate the persons"*: J. Lowis, "Note upon Mr. Commissioner Mills's Letter, 15th May, 1845," *Papers Relating to Juggernauth* (London: J. H. Cox, 1848), 19.

62–63 *"Reason is confounded"* . . . *"superior either in talents"* . . . *"most delicate matter"*: Macaulay, "Government of India" (1833), *Speeches of Lord Macaulay*, 138, 136, 161.

64 *"The day is not far"*: Marx, "The Future Results of British Rule in India," *New-York Tribune*, August 8, 1853; *Marx and Engels: The Political Writings*, 321.

64 *"fourth-class"*: Hunter, *Marquess of Dalhousie*, 191.

65 *"social change"*: Headrick, *Tentacles of Progress*, 63.

65 *"What is really desired"* . . . *"the humble"*: Ruskin, *Unto This Last* (1860), *Works*, XVII, 90.

3. The French Revelation

67 *"pendulum clock"*: T. Gauthier, "Le Club des Hachichins," *Revue des Deux Mondes*, 16, no. 3 (January–February 1846), 522.

68 *long, narrow*: de Beauvoir, *Les mystères de l'Île Saint-Louis*, I, 10; R. Calasso, *La Folie Baudelaire*, 32.

69 *"machine à penser"*: Hayter, *Opium and the Romantic Imagination*, 155.

69 *"Nature is a temple"*: "La nature est un temple où de vivants piliers / Laissent parfois sortir de confuses paroles; / L'homme y passé à travers des forêts de symbols / Qui l'observent avec des regards familiers" (Baudelaire, "Correspondances," *Les fleurs du mal*).

70 *"explosion"*: Constant, *La Bible de la liberté*, 30.

70 *"vapors and shadows"* . . . *"From now on"*: Constant, *Mère de Dieu*, 169–71.

70 *"dead faith"* . . . *"Nature, no longer"*: Constant, *Mère de Dieu*, 293.

71 *"Nothing in Nature"*: "Rien n'est muet dans la nature / Pour qui sait en suivre les lois: / Les astres ont une écriture, les fleurs des champs ont une voix": M. A. Constant ["de Baucour"], "Correspondances," *Les trois harmonies, chansons, et poesies*, 300.

71 *"began in absurdity"* . . . *"absolute truths"*: Lévi, *Histoire de la magie*, trans. Waite, 327, 32.

72 *"sign of the microcosm"*: Lévi to Spedalieri, after May 1869: Lévi–Spedalieri Letters (Verginelli-Rota Collection), Accademia dei Lincei, Rome, VII/ LXIII, f.60.

72 *"supernatural"* . . . *"physical laws"*: Lévi, *Dogme et rituel de la haute magie*, trans. Waite, 192, 331.

73–74 *"excitement"* . . . *"magnetic breath"*: Lévi, *Histoire de la magie*, trans. Waite, 39.

74 *"adapt or direct"* . . . *"the face"*: Lévi, *Dogme et rituel de la haute magie*, trans. Waite, 7.

74 *"Scientifically provable"*: Lévi, *Histoire de la magie*, trans. Waite, 36.

74 *Cornelius Agrippa's*: Katz, *Occult Tradition*, 14.

74 *"man of science"*: Lévi, "Appendix" (September 1, 1859), *Histoire de la magie*, trans. Waite, 376.

74 *"everywhere in conspiracy"*: Emerson, *Collected Works*, II, 29.

77 *"I have been magnetised"*: Sprague, Diary, April 30, 1850, "Selections from Sprague's Diary and Journal," ed. Twynham, 131–40.

77 *"hope and all"*: Sprague, Diary, May 21, 1850, 141.

77 *"Spirit Agency"* . . . *"chains of disease"*: Sprague, Diary, February 9, 1853, 147.

77 *"Summer-Land"*: Sprague, Diary, November 17, 1855, 148.

77 *"Spirit Guides"*: Sprague, Diary, February 9, 1853, 147–48.

77–78 *"ruined church"* . . . *"shrine of thought"*: Sprague, "The Ruined Church," *The Poet and Other Poems*, 214.

78 *"literary celebrities"* . . . *"Our senses"*: Underhill, *Missing Link*, 137.

78 *"The piano was sweetly played"*: Braude, *Radical Spirits*, 17.

78 *"Why is it not"*: Sprague, Diary, May 12, 1849, 140.

79 *"patient, rigid"*: Davenport, *The Death-Blow to Spiritualism*, 154.

79 *"sublime"* . . . *"the filthiest selfishness"*: Emerson, *Journals*, XI, 284.

79–80 *"abused Red Man"* . . . *"enemies of Republican Liberty"*: Brigham, *Twelve Messages from the Spirit of John Quincy Adams*, 83, 89, 318–19.

80 *"Spiritualism will work miracles"*: Braude, *Radical Spirits*, 17.

80 *"large-hearted women"* . . . *"whole conception"*: Holmes, "The Professor at the Breakfast Table," *Atlantic Monthly*, III (January 1856), 90.

80 *"If the spirits"*: Braude, *Radical Spirits*, 96.

81 *"persons in whom"*: Braude, *Radical Spirits*, 23.

82 *"There are two"*: Lévi to Spedalieri, after August 21, 1871: Lévi–Spedalieri Letters, IX/LXXXVII, f.73.

82 *"law of equilibrium"* . . . *"mysteries of sexual love"*: Lévi, *Histoire de la magie*, trans. Waite, 45.

82 *"grey on grey"*: Marx and Engels, *The Class Struggles in France*, 110–11.

83 *"distinction of contraries"* . . . *"a soft voice"*: Lévi, *Histoire de la magie*, trans. Waite, 46.

83 *"indifferent"*: Lévi, *Dogme et rituel de la haute magie*, trans. Waite, 71.

83 *"falsehood in action"*: Lévi, *Histoire de la magie*, trans. Waite, 46.

83 *"way of feeling"*: Blanning, *The Romantic Revolution*, 6.

84 *"phenomenal"*: Kant, *Critique of Pure Reason* (1792), A359.

84 *"beauty & power"* . . . *"claims to his rights"*: Emerson, *Journals*, I, 138.

84 *"caves of ice"*: Coleridge, "Kubla Khan" (1797).

85 *"exceptional wills"*: Lévi, *Histoire de la magie*, trans. Waite, 292.

85 *"the Absolute"* . . . *"revolving in the circle"*: Lévi, *Dogme et rituel de la haute magie*, trans. Waite, 13.

85 *"Mary, the Divine Mother"* . . . *"all traditions"*: Lévi, *History of Magic*, trans. Waite, 38–39, 41.

86 *"At this point"*: Lévi, *Dogme et rituel de la haute magie*, trans. Waite, 13.

86 *"Spiritual New-birth"*: Carlyle, *Sartor Resartus* (1833–34; 1836), *Collected Works*, I, 242.

86 *"gold, secret instructions"* . . . *"phantoms of nightmare"*: Lévi, *Dogme et rituel de la haute magie*, trans. Waite, 73–74.

87 *"How many ova"* . . . *"I caught him"*: Thoreau, *Journal*, ed. Torrey and Allen, I, 275.

87 *"One may discover"*: Thoreau, *Journal*, ed. Torrey and Allen, I, 88.

88 *"I have, as it were"* . . . *"material was pure"*: Thoreau, *Walden*, 109–10.

88 *"great-grandmother"* . . . *"I lay down"*: Thoreau, *Walden*, 230.

88 *"religion of Hindostan"*: Marx, "The British Rule in India," June 10, 1853; *New-York Tribune*, June 25, 1853; *Marx/Engels Collected Works*, XII, 125.

88 *"I want the flower"*: Thoreau, *Walden*, 59.

89 *"purer stratum"*: Thoreau, *Journal*, ed. Torrey and Allen, II, 4.

89 *"meanly, like ants"*: Thoreau, *Walden*, 64.

89 *"different drummer"* . . . *"the divine life"*: Thoreau, *Walden*, 80–81.

89–90 *"truly spiritual"* . . . *"old and terrible"*: Baudelaire, "La Chambre Double," *Petits poèmes en prose* (1869), trans. Scarfe, *Baudelaire: The Poems in Prose*, 37.

90 *"Go, wake up"*: Lévi, *Dogme et rituel de la haute magie*, trans. Waite, 74–75.

4. The Descent of Man

92 *"heart-sickening atrocities"*: Desmond and Moore, *Darwin's Sacred Cause*, 1.

92 *"If only the Geologists"*: Ruskin to Dr. Henry Acland, Ruskin, *Works*, XXXVI, 114–15.

93 *"I find the noddle"*: Darwin, *Correspondence of Charles Darwin*, ed. Burkhardt and Smith, II, 85.

93 *"Wherefore my bowels"*: Isaiah 16:11.

94 *"The varieties of man"*: Darwin, *Journal* (1839), 520; Lander, *Lincoln and Darwin*, 33.

94 *"most interesting"* . . . *"own dear Nigger"*: Desmond and Moore, *Darwin's Sacred Cause*, 135, 137.

97 *Louis XV*: de Gercy, *Une vie de femme liée aux événements de l'époque*, I, 181.

97 *His aunt died young*: L. Schemann, "Drei biographischen Skizzen von Gobineau," *Quellen und Untersuchungen zum Leben Gobineaus*, I, 175.

97 *"passionate character"*: Gercy, *Une vie de femme*, II ,2.

97 *"All his aspirations"*: Buenzod, *Formation de la pensée de Gobineau*, 58; Bookhut, "Arthur de Gobineau and His Philosophical History," 41.

99 *"democratic inanities"*: Bookhut, "Arthur de Gobineau," 106; A. B. Duff, "Un fragment inédit des *Souvenirs* de Diane de Guldencrone," *Études Gobiniennes*, 1 (1966), 72.

102 *"the most beautiful"*: J. F. Blumenbach, *De generis humani varietate nativa*, trans. Benshye, 269.

103 *"distinguished naturalist"*: Nott, "Sketch of the Epidemic of Yellow Fever of 1847 in Mobile," *Charleston Medical Journal and Review*, 3 (1848), 1–21, and "Yellow Fever Contrasted with Bilious Fever," *New Orleans Medical and Surgical Journal*, 4 (1848), 563–601; E. Chernin, "Josiah Clark Nott, Insects, and Yellow Fever," 790–802, 793.

104 *"substantially in that same"*: Nott and Gliddon, *Types of Mankind*, II, 189.

105 *"I have a friend"*: Nott to Gobineau, March 7, 1855, Schemann, *Gobineau's Rassenwerk*, 192.

105 *"fanaticism of two-thirds"*: Hotze to Gobineau, July 11, 1856, Schemann, *Gobineau's Rassenwerk*, 199–200.

105 *"moral and intellectual"* . . . *"scientific fact"*: Gobineau, *Essai sur l'inégalité des races humaines*, trans. Hotze, 27, 16.

105 *"No change"*: *Mobile Register*, December 19, 1855.

106 *"Calvinistic dogma"* . . . *"authority of the Bible"*: Hotze to Gobineau, July 11, 1856, Schemann, *Gobineau's Rassenwerk*, 197, 205.

106 *"intermixture"* . . . *"ethnic disorder"*: Gobineau, *Essai sur la inégalité des races humaines*, II, 536; trans. E. Beasley, *The Victorian Reinvention of Race*, 51.

106 *"poor wretches"*: Darwin, *What Mr. Darwin Saw in His Voyage Round the World*, 99–100; Lander, *Lincoln and Darwin*, 33–34.

107 *"grand style"*: Emerson, *Journals and Miscellaneous Notebooks*, IX, 124.

107–108 *"Our planet"* . . . *"insignificance"*: Emerson, *An Address Delivered in the Court-House*, 31–32.

108 *"superior individual"* . . . *"all the ancestors"*: Emerson, 1851, *Journals*, XI, 377.

108 *"mummified"*: Eden, *The Search for Nitre*, 95.

108 *"Below some small"*: Darwin, *The Voyage of the* Beagle, 19.

109 *"for a long term"*: Secretary of State William L. Marcy, August 1854, cit. Pineo, *Ecuador and the United States*, 39.

109 *"melting & intermixture"* . . . *"Irish, Germans"*: Emerson, *Journals*, IX, 299.

109 *"Too much guano"*: Emerson, 1851, *Journals*, XI, 376.

110 "Fate. The classes": Marx, "Forced Emigration," *New-York Tribune*, March 22, 1853; Emerson, *Journals*, XIII, 127; see L. S. Feuer, "Emerson's Reference to Karl Marx," *New England Quarterly*, 33, no. 3 (September 1960), 378–79.

110 *"Out of its own entrails"*: Marx, "On the Jewish Question" ("Zur Judenfrage," 1843), Raines (ed.), *Marx on Religion*, 45–69, 65, 67.

110 *"The next world war"* . . . *"complete extirpation"*: Engels, "The Magyar Struggle," *Neue Rheinische Zeitung*, 1849; Marx and Engels, *Marx/Engels Collected Works*, VIII, 230, 234.

111 *"social emancipation"*: Marx, "On the Jewish Question," Raines (ed.), *Marx on Religion*, 69.

111 *"free, strong"*: Gobineau, *Essai sur l'inégalité des races*, trans. Collins, 59.

111 *"Whoever saw"*: Nott, *The Physical History of the Jewish Race*, 11.

111 *"a most ancient"* . . . *"ancient Semitism"*: O'Donoghue (trans.) and Nash (ed.), *Gobineau and Orientalism*, 5, 6, 7, 128.

112 *"revelation is unsuspended"*: Report of Ibn Alusi, Mufti of Baghdad, Abd al-Husayn Ayati Tafti Avarih, *Al-Kawatib al-Durriya fi Ma'athir al-Bahariya*, 2 vols. (Cairo, 1923–24), I, 64; trans. Amanat, *Resurrection and Renewal*, 310.

112 *"comfortable blanket"* . . . *"hybrid ideas"*: O'Donoghue (trans.) and Nash (ed.), *Gobineau and Orientalism*, 7.

113 *"incomprehensibly vast"* . . . *"vain endeavour"*: Darwin, *On the Origin of Species*, I, 34, 56.

114 *"I do not discuss"*: Burkhardt et al. (eds.), *Correspondence of Darwin*, VII, 270.

114 *"I have been"*: Burkhardt et al. (eds.), *Correspondence of Darwin*, VII, 247.

115 *"Much light will be thrown"*: Darwin, *On the Origin of Species*, I, 304.

115 *"prophetic germ"*: Irvine, *Apes, Angels, and Victorians*, 107.

116 *"I am sorry"*: F. Darwin (ed.), *Life and Letters of Darwin*, II, 56.

116 *"descent with modification"*: Darwin, *On the Origin of Species*, I, 126.

116 *"contented face"*: Stauffer (ed.), *Charles Darwin's Natural Selection*, 175.

117 *"execrated as an atheist"*: F. Darwin (ed.), *Life and Letters of Darwin*, II, 25.

117 *"fiery Boils"*: Burkhardt et al. (eds.), *Correspondence of Darwin*, VII, 362.

5. The New Chronology

119 *"man-Bloomer"*: Loving, *Walt Whitman*, 224.

120 *"naively"*: Krieg, *A Whitman Chronology*, 34.

120 *"I too, following many"*: Whitman, "Starting from Paumanok," *Leaves of Grass* (6th ed., 1881), 7.

120 *"most extraordinary"*: Emerson, introductory letter to Whitman, *Leaves of Grass* (1856 ed.), n.p.

120 *"more truth"* . . . *"strange"*: Thoreau, *Correspondence of Thoreau*, ed. Hudspeth, I, 445.

120 *"If you would obtain"*: Thoreau, *Journals*, IV, 9.

121 *"It is as if the beasts"*: Thoreau, *Correspondence of Thoreau*, ed. Hudspeth, I, 445.

121 *"cold compliments"*: Loving, *Whitman: The Song of Himself*, 168.

121 *"great American poem"*: Emerson, "The Poet" (1842), *Collected Works of Emerson*, ed. Ferguson, 22.

121 *"I was simmering"*: Loving, *Whitman: The Song of Himself*, 168.

121 *"eats dirt and excrement"*: Whitman, "The Eighteenth Presidency!" (unpublished), cit. Reynolds, *Walt Whitman's America*, 140.

122 *"Sex"* . . . *"contains all"*: Whitman, "A Woman Waits for Me" (1856), *Leaves of Grass* (6th ed.), 88.

122 *"voices of sexes"* . . . *"I resist anything"*: Whitman, "Song of Myself" (1855), *Leaves of Grass* (6th ed.), 29, 24.

123 *"antiseptic of the soul"*: Whitman, preface to *Leaves of Grass* (1855 ed.), v.

123 *"spirituality the translatress"*: Whitman, "Starting from Paumanok," *Leaves of Grass* (6th ed.), 21.

123 *"beginning of a great"*: Emerson, introductory letter to Whitman, *Leaves of Grass* (1856 ed.), n.p.

124 *"Democracy's lands"* . . . *"See, ploughmen"*: Whitman, "Starting from Paumanok," *Leaves of Grass* (6th ed.), 26, 18.

124 *"great power"*: Emerson, introductory letter to Whitman, *Leaves of Grass* (1856 ed.), n.p.

124 *"Who, for instance"*: Huxley, "The Darwin Hypothesis," *The Times*, December 26, 1859; Huxley, *Darwiniana*, 1–21, 17, 18.

125 *"indifference"* . . . *"I am sharpening"*: L. Huxley (ed.), *Life and Letters of Thomas Henry Huxley*, I, 183, 189.

125 *"The individuals of a species"*: Huxley, "Darwin Hypothesis," *Darwiniana*, 18.

126–127 *"the supreme question"* . . . *"transmuted ape"*: Owen, *Edinburgh Review*, CXI (1860), 487–532, 495–97.

127 *"I, at least"*: "Senex" [FitzRoy], *The Times*, December 1, 1859; Mellersh, *FitzRoy of the Beagle*, 271–72.

127 *"our duty towards God"*: Holyoake, *Sixty Years of an Agitator's Life*, I, 142.

128 *"What a book it is!"*: Martineau to Holyoake, [December] 1859, BL Add. Mss. 42, 726, f.26.

129 *"ABC of the great"*: Huxley, "Preface" (1893), *Darwiniana*, vii.

129 *"Well, Sam Oxon got up"*: Hooker to Darwin, L. Huxley (ed.), *Life and Letters of Sir Joseph Dalton Hooker*, I, 526.

129 *"I would sooner claim kindred"*: Alfred Newton to Edward Newton, Wollaston, *Life of Alfred Newton*, 119.

129 *"Darwinism"*: Huxley, "The Origin of Species," *Darwiniana*, 22–79, 78.

130 *"masterly"*: Baden Powell, "On the Study of the Evidences of Christianity," Parker (ed.), *Essays and Reviews*, 94–144, 139.

130–131 *"It seemed to me"* . . . *"theistical or other doctrine"*: Holyoake, *Limits of Atheism*, II, 292–93.

131 *"this age"*: Holyoake in *The Reasoner*, December 3, 1851; Holyoake, *The Origin and Nature of Secularism*, 51.

131 *"Clearly science"*: Holyoake, *Limits of Atheism*, II, 291–92.

133 *"There will soon be no more"*: Whitman, preface to *Leaves of Grass* (1855 ed.), xi.

133 *"year of the struggle"* ... *"masculine voice"*: Whitman, "Eighteen Sixty-One," *Leaves of Grass* (6th ed.), 221.

133 *"My heart goes"*: Desmond and Moore, *Darwin's Sacred Cause*, 334.

134 *"I have managed to skim"*: F. L. Darwin (ed.), *More Letters of Darwin*, I, 203.

134 *"baptize"* ... *"Natural selection"*: Desmond and Moore, *Darwin's Sacred Cause*, 324, 326.

135 *"Nevertheless, the doctrine"*: Darwin, *Natural Selection*, II, 175–76.

135 *"Yesterday, I was influenced"*: Thoreau, January 21, 1853, *Journal*, IV, 472.

136 *"He never married"* ... *"contempt"*: Emerson, "Thoreau," *Lectures and Biographical Sketches*, ed. Cabot, 424.

136 *"mild, humane"*: "The Natural History of Man," *The Index*, July 23, 1863.

137 *"Mr. de Gobineau"*: [Anon.], "The Distinctions of Race," *The Index*, October 23, 1862.

137 *"The Cannon will not suffer"*: Emerson, *Journals*, XV, 55.

137 *"a chronic puzzle"*: Emerson, *Journals*, XV, 267.

137 *"the gallows"*: Emerson, *Journals*, XIV, 333.

138 *"The world is ever equal"* ... *"searches character"*: Emerson, *Journals*, XV, 450, 148.

138 *"hurried and slipshod"*: Emerson, "Fortune of the Republic," *Later Lectures*, ed. Bosco and Meyerson, II, 334.

138 *"wholesome disinfectants"*: Emerson, *Journals*, XV, 266.

138 *"Sometimes,"* ... *"gunpowder smells good"*: Allen, *Waldo Emerson*, 608.

138 *"It is a potent"*: Emerson, "Fortune of the Republic," *Later Lectures*, ed. Bosco and Meyerson, II, 334.

139 *"cannot be burned"*: Emerson, *Journals*, XV, 286.

139 *"completeness of system"* ... *"What is life"*: Emerson, "Natural History of the Intellect," *Lectures and Biographical Sketches*, ed. Cabot, 12, 10.

139 *"analogy of spatial distance"*: Emerson, *Journals*, XV, 423.

140 *"I believe"* ... *"in the existence"*: Emerson, "Natural History of the Intellect," *Lectures and Biographical Sketches*, ed. Cabot, 5.

142 *"the terrible reality"*: *New York Times*, October 20, 1862.

142 *"Were you ever Daguerrotyped"*: Emerson, *Journals*, VIII, 100.

142 *"rushing stream"*: Emerson, "The Method of Nature" (1841), *Nature, Addresses and Lectures*, ed. Cabot, 190.

142 *"a fit"*: Emerson, *Journals*, VIII, 100.

142 *"This Image is altogether"*: Carlyle to Emerson, *Correspondence of Carlyle and Emerson*, II, 109–10.

142 *"It is hard to extract"*: Traubel, *With Walt Whitman in Camden*, I, 108.

143 *"set up my hope"*: Traubel, *With Walt Whitman in Camden*, I, 405.

143 *"noble, sturdy"*: Traubel, *With Walt Whitman in Camden*, I, 183.

143 *"long rows"* ... *"dying kiss"*: Whitman, "The Wound Dresser" (1865), *Leaves of Grass* (1881 ed.), 242.

143 *"The days in the hospitals"*: Traubel, *With Walt Whitman in Camden*, VI, 194.

143 *"reflected in Nature"*: Whitman, "Children of Adam," *Leaves of Grass* (6th ed.), 79.

143 *"I will lift"*: Whitman, "Starting from Paumanok," *Leaves of Grass* (6th ed.), 18.

144 *"struggle for the life"*: Lincoln, "Address to the 148th Ohio Regiment," *Collected Works of Abraham Lincoln*, VII, 529.

144 *"damned war business"*: Traubel, *With Walt Whitman in Camden*, III, 293.

144 *"burning flame"*: Whitman, "The Wound Dresser," *Leaves of Grass* (6th ed.), 287.

144 *"entire is saturated"*: Whitman, *Memoranda During the War*, 57.

144 *"divine impressions"*: Mallarmé, letter to Cazalis, 886; De Man, "Poetic Nothingness: On a Hermetic Sonnet by Mallarmé," *Critical Writings*, 18–29, 24.

145 *"Meanings, proofs"*: Whitman, "A Woman Waits for Me," *Leaves of Grass* (6th ed.), 88.

145 *"It was a religion"*: Traubel, *With Walt Whitman in Camden*, III, 581.

145–146 *"involved, baffling"* . . . *"altogether to our own"*: "Death of Abraham Lincoln," Whitman, *Specimen Days*, 311–15.

6. The Origin of the World

149 *"different kind"*: Wagner to Eliza Wille, Barth, Mack, and Voss (eds.), *Wagner: A Documentary Study*, 204.

149 *"glinting, overbrimming stream"*: Wagner, "The Music of the Future" ["Zukunftsmusik"] , *Richard Wagner's Prose Works*, III, 339–40.

149 *"the curse that annihilates"*: Wagner to Theodor Apel, Watson, *Wagner: A Biography*, 64.

150 *"darkling things"* . . . *"radically transformed"*: Wagner to Uhlig, Wagner, *Letters of Richard Wagner*, ed. and trans. Burk, 618.

150 *"infinite diversity"*: Wagner, "The Music of the Future," *Richard Wagner's Prose Works*, III, 339.

151 *"the man we wait"*: Wagner to Roeckel, cit. Rolland, "Wagner: A Note on *Siegfried* and *Tristran*," *Musicians of Today*, 74.

151 *"I know now"*: Wagner to Uhlig, cit. Rose, *Wagner: Race and Revolution*, 90.

151 *"I have no money"*: Wagner to Liszt, *Selected Letters of Wagner*, ed. Spencer and Millington, 171.

152 *"synagogue-song"* . . . *"floating in the air"* . . . *"Judaism is"*: Wagner, "Judaism in Music" ["Das Judenthum in der Musik"], *Richard Wagner's Prose Works*, III, 91, 81, 100.

152 *"wandering chord"*: Schoenberg, *Harmonienlehre* (Leipzig: Verlaseigentum, 1911), 284.

154 *"To-day we need"*: Wagner, "Opera and Drama" ["Oper und Drama"], *Richard Wagner's Prose Works*, III, 191.

155 *"recognition that the only God"*: Wagner, "Jesus of Nazareth" (unpub., 1843); Rose, *Wagner*, 55.

155 *"true spirit and kernel"*: Schopenhauer, *The World as Will and Representation*, III, 226.

155 *"sneaking, dirty race"*: Schopenhauer, "On Religion," *Parerga and Paralipomena*, II, 357.

156 *"atheistic Buddhism"*: Schopenhauer, *The World as Will and Representation*, II, 444.

156 *"Christ's teaching"*: Schopenhauer, *Parerga and Paralipomena*, II, 357.

156 *"Every moving thing"*: Genesis 9:3.

157 *"the flesh with the life"*: Numbers 18:29.

157 *"eternal essence"* . . . *"barbarism of the West"*: Schopenhauer, *On the Basis of Morality*, 218.

157 *"Out of all"*: Numbers 18:29.

157 *"bad blood"* . . . *"I cannot abide"*: Marx and Engels, *Marx/Engels Collected Works*, XXXXII, 231.

158 *"perfidious Christian illness"*: Marx to Engels, cit. Raines (ed.), *Marx on Religion*, 238.

158 *"With this delay"* . . . *"My illness"*: Engels to Marx and Marx to Engels, cit. Manuel, *A Requiem for Karl Marx*, 84, 86.

158 *"a metaphysical image"*: Steger, *The Quest for Evolutionary Socialism*, 126.

159 *"If progress is the aim"*: Herzen, *From the Other Shore*, 37.

159 *"Man in his arrogance"*: Darwin, cit. Thomas, *Scientific Socialism: From Engels to Althusser*, 58.

159 *"horrify the world"* . . . *"How I should be abused"*: Darwin to Kingsley and Lyell, cit. Desmond and Moore, *Darwin's Sacred Cause*, 318–19.

159 *"Creator"*: Darwin, *Origin of Species*, II, 306.

159 *"moral and intellectual supremacy"*: Lyell, *The Geological Evidences of the Antiquity of Man*, 474, xii.

159–160 *"homogenous"* . . . *"Power"*: Wallace, *Alfred Russel Wallace: An Anthology*, 22, 26.

160 *"essential part"*: Fichman, *An Elusive Victorian: The Evolution of Alfred Russel Wallace*, 175.

160 *"It is remarkable"*: Marx to Engels, *Marx/Engels Collected Works*, XXX, 249.

161 *"The great questions"*: Bismarck, cit. Steinberg, *Bismarck: A Life*, 465.

162 *"Our success sure"*: Emerson, *Journals*, XV, 65.

162 *"a word the meaning of which"*: Tolstoy, "Second Epilogue," *War and Peace*, III, 499.

162 *"fist that"* . . . *"Asceticism"*: Emerson, *Journals*, XV, 63–64, 469.

162 *"Hebrew superstition"*: Wagner to Roeckel, cit. Rose, *Race and Revolution*, 97.

162 *"I must have"*: Wagner to Eliza Wille, cit. Watson, *Richard Wagner*, 131.

163 *"most joyous musical"*: Baudelaire, cit. Large et al. (eds.), *Wagnerism in European Culture and Politics*, 144.

164 *"My trust in our strength"*: Ludwig II to Wagner, Strobel (ed.), *König Ludwig II und Richard Wagner*, I, 44; cit. Salmi, *Imagined Germany: Richard Wagner's National Utopia*, 100.

165 *"grand performance"*: Wagner to von Bülow, *Selected Letters of Wagner*, ed. Spencer and Millington, 609.

165 *"Let us present"*: Ludwig II to Wagner, Strobel (ed.), *König Ludwig II und Richard Wagner*, IV, 24, cit. Salmi, *Imagined Germany*, 100.

166 Schutzgeiste Deutschlands: Strobel (ed.), *König Ludwig II und Richard Wagner*, IV, 150.

166 *"Honour your German masters"*: Wagner, *Die Meistersinger*, cit. Salmi, *Imagined Germany*, 49.

166 *"I do so hate controversy"*: Darwin to Wallace, F. Darwin (ed.), *Life and Letters of Charles Darwin*, II, 326.

166–167 *"Among savages"* . . . *"pick of the women"*: Darwin to Wallace, F. Darwin (ed.), *Life and Letters of Charles Darwin*, II, 272–73.

167 *"noble families"* . . . *"like rabbits"*: Darwin, *The Descent of Man and Selection in Relation to Sex*, I, 164, 167; citing Galton, *Hereditary Genius*, 132–40.

167 *"pulling off the coloured"*: Spencer, *Social Statics*, 379.

167 *"sounder and stronger"*: Greg, "On the Failure of 'Natural Selection' in the Case of Man," *Fraser's Magazine*, 78 (1868), 359; cit. McDonagh, *Idiocy: A Cultural History*, 267.

167 *"We are living"*: Galton, "Hereditary Talent and Character," *Macmillan's Magazine*, 12 (1865), 326, 319.

168 *"law of the Prophet"*: *L'Artiste*, cit. Shaw, *Ottoman Painting*, 47.

168 *"sisters"*: Whitman, "The Sleepers," *Leaves of Grass* (6th ed.), 325.

168 *"Moslem who paid"*: Du Camp, *Les convulsions de Paris* (1878–81), cit. A. Jones, "Meaning, Identity, Embodiment: The Uses of Merleau-Ponty's Phenomenology in Art History," *Art and Thought*, ed. Arnold and Iversen, 71–90, 72.

169 *"represent things"*: Baudelaire, "The Life and Work of Eugène Delacroix," *Baudelaire: Selected Writings on Art and Artists*, trans. Charvet, 358–89, 367.

169 *"the spirit has an existence"*: Ravaisson-Mollien, *La philosophie en France au XIXème siècle*, 258.

169 *"In the beauty of poems"*: Whitman, preface to *Leaves of Grass* (1855 ed.), vii.

170 *"Joyous we too"* . . . *"The earth to be spann'd"*: Whitman, "Passage to India" (1868), *Leaves of Grass* (6th ed., 1881 ed.), 321, 319, 316.

170 *"freetrade"* . . . *"nothing too close"*: Whitman, preface to *Leaves of Grass* (1855 ed.), v.

170–171 *"The key to an understanding"* . . . *"something in our soul"*: Carus, *Psyche*, trans. Welch, 1, 23.

171 *"sum of the activities"*: Hartmann, *Philosophy of the Unconscious*, II, 279.

172 *"The whole theory"*: Whitman, preface to *Leaves of Grass* (1855 ed.), v.

172 *"This preservation"*: Darwin, *On the Origin of Species*, 5th ed. (London: John Murray, 1869), 92.

172 *"helpless"*: Darwin, *The Descent of Man*, I, 162.

172 *"extinction of less-improved forms"*: Darwin, *On the Origin of Species*, I, 162.

173 *"an ascending organic scale"* . . . *"utter idiot"*: Darwin, *The Descent of Man*, I, 101, 102.

174 *"natural objects and agencies"* . . . *"a dog looks"*: Darwin, *The Descent of Man*, I, 62, 65, 64, 66.

174 *"The master"*: Whitman, preface to *Leaves of Grass* (1855 ed.), viii.

174–175 *"God-implanted conscience"* . . . *"The question is"*: Darwin, *The Descent of Man*, II, 114, 302–3.

176 *"the great stream"*: Zincke, "Last Winter in the United States"; Darwin, *The Descent of Man*, I, 179.

177 *"misfortune for science"*: Darwin to J. V. Carus, *Correspondence of Charles Darwin*, ed. Burkhardt and Smith, XVIII, 231.

178 *"dense crowd"*: Dicey, *The Egypt of the Future*, 10.

178 *"accursed"*: Darwin to Hooker, F. Darwin (ed.), *Life and Letters of Charles Darwin*, I, 515.

178 *"Romanic and Teutonic"*: Carus to Darwin, *Correspondence of Charles Darwin*, ed. Burkhardt and Smith, XVIII, 258.

178 *"German revolution"*: Disraeli to the Commons, cit. Wawro, *The Franco-Prussian War*, 305.

178–179 *"Wonderful progress"* . . . *"My aim"*: Salmi, *Imagined Germany*, 149, 153.

179 *"festive wedding day"*: Billington, *Fire in the Minds of Men*, 348.

181 *"soon overwhelmed"*: Gibbon, *The Decline and Fall of the Roman Empire*, III, 460.

181 *"new barbarians"*: Gibbon to Lord Loughborough, *Letters of Gibbon*, ed. Norton, III, 321.

181 *"the Church of the Antichrist"* . . . *"revealed"*: Lévi to Spedalieri [1871], Lévi–Spedalieri Letters, Accademia dei Lincei, Rome, IX/LIII, ff.45–46.

181 *"Incidentally"* . . . *"the fact"*: C. Wagner, *Cosima Wagner's Diaries*, ed. Gregor-Dellin and Mack, I, 377.

7. Passage to India

186 *"limbs, heads and trunks"*: Blavatsky to Olcott, *Letters of H. P. Blavatsky*, 43.

187 *"astrological formulas"*: A. L. Rawson, "Mme. Blavatsky: A Theosophical Occult Apology," repr. *Theosophical History*, II/6 (1988), 209–20, 210–11.

188 *"a gentleman student"*: Blavatsky to Sinnett, *The Letters of H. P. Blavatsky to A. P. Sinnett*, 151.

188 *"closet"*: E. Cutting Coulomb, *Some Account of My Intercourse with Madame Blavatsky*, 3.

188 *"beggarly tramps"*: Blavatsky, cit. Sinnett, *Incidents in the Life of Madame Blavatsky*, 159.

188 *"disagreeable scenes"*: Blavatsky, cit. Cranston, *H.P.B.*, 117.

188 *"kind-hearted Hebrew"*: Olcott, *Old Diary Leaves*, I, 20.

189 *"Good gracious"* . . . *"Permettez-moi"*: Murphet, *Yankee Beacon of Buddhist Light: Life of Colonel H. S. Olcott*, 24.

189 *"the filling of their pockets"*: Olcott, cit. Goodwin, *The Theosophical Enlightenment*, 299.

190 *"spooks of other personalities"* . . . *"European gentleman"*: Olcott, *Old Diary Leaves*, I, 8–9.

190 *"solitary travels"*: Sinnett, *Incidents in the Life of Madame Blavatsky*, 134.

190 *"witnessing the mysteries"*: Olcott, *People from the Other World*, 293–94.

191 *"crazy delusion"* . . . *"partial mortification of the leg"*: Blavatsky, *Letters of Blavatsky*, ed. Algeo, I, 110, 58.

192 *"Whenever I was called"*: Blavatsky, *Letters of Blavatsky*, ed. Algeo, I, 10.

192 *"In the night"*: Blavatsky, *Letters of Blavatsky*, ed. Algeo, I, 192.

192–193 *"Sometimes, it seems"* . . . *"old Negro"*: Blavatsky, *Letters of Blavatsky*, ed. Algeo, I, 177, 354.

193 *"very strange"* . . . *"I never lose"*: Blavatsky, *Letters of Blavatsky*, ed. Algeo, I, 192.

193 *"wonderful psycho-physiological"*: Olcott, *Old Diary Leaves*, I, 18.

193–194 *"dregs"* . . . *"truly wonderful"*: Sinnett, *Incidents in the Life of Madame Blavatsky*, 177–79.

194 *"Everything is double"*: Blavatsky, *Isis Unveiled*, I, xxvi.

194 *"Her mediumship"*: Olcott, *People from the Other World*, 453.

195 *"God's Law"*: *New York Times*, July 17, 1874.

195 *"society for this kind"*: Olcott, cit. Cranston, *H.P.B.*, 143.

195 *"sharp-witted savant"*: Blavatsky, *From the Caves and Jungles of Hindostan*, 21.

196 *"a science and a thing"*: Olcott, *Old Diary Leaves*, I, 108.

196 *"learned occultists"*: Blavatsky, cit. Godwin, *The Theosophical Enlightenment*, 289.

196 *"secret Society"*: Blavatsky, *Collected Writings*, I, 124.

196–197 *"beatific vision"* . . . *"$four a bottle"*: Deveney, *Paschal Beverly Randolph*, 69, 217, 70.

197 *"It is a wonderful drug"*: Blavatsky to Albert Rawson, cit. Johnson, *In Search of the Masters*, 21.

197 *"mighty moment"* . . . *"Oriental Breast-Love"*: Deveney, *Paschal Beverly Randolph*, 218, 219.

197 *"somnambulist"*: Britten, "Occultism Defined," *Two Worlds*, November 18, 1887.

198 *"decidedly opposed"* . . . *"slim, brown"*: Gomes, *The Dawning of the Theosophical Society*, 89, 88, 114.

198 *"astral music and bells"*: William Judge, "Habitations of H.P.B., III," *The Path,* November 1893, 237–39.

199 *"secret Bohemians"* . . . *"Indian philosophers"*: Cranston, *H.P.B.,* 182–83.

199 *"the most attractive"*: Olcott, *Old Diary Leaves,* I, 417.

200 *"Pythagorean numbers"* . . . *"the very language"*: *Hartford Daily Times,* December 2, 1878, cit. Cranston, *H.P.B.,* 170.

200 *"neo-Platonists"*: Gomes, *The Dawning of the Theosophical Society,* 88.

200 *"the ancient Baloochistan city"*: Blavatsky, *Isis Unveiled,* II, 308.

201 *"my first Guru"*: Olcott, *Old Diary Leaves,* I, 19.

201 Dogme et rituel: Alden, "The Book Hunter," *The Idler Magazine,* ed. J. K. Jerome et al., VII: February–July 1895 (London: Chatto and Windus, 1895), 280.

202 *"philosophies and sciences of antiquity"* . . . *"identical with the Hindu"*: Blavatsky, *Isis Unveiled,* I, xi, xxvii.

202–203 *"branch nations"* . . . *"local allegory"*: Blavatsky, *Isis Unveiled,* II, 434–35.

203 *"far-away countries"*: Blavatsky, *The Caves and Jungles of Hindostan,* 21.

204 *"a pendulum"* . . . *"All dark"*: Olcott, *Old Diary Leaves,* I, 467, 480, 481.

204 *"Have you seen the lighthouse?"*: Blavatsky, *The Caves and Jungles of Hindostan,* 3–7.

205 *"the goddess Mamba"*: Olcott, *Old Diary Leaves,* II, 13–14.

8. The Revolt of Zarathustra

207 *"What a glorious time!"*: Nietzsche, cit. Kohler, *Zarathustra's Secret,* 168.

207 *"great health"*: Nietzsche, *Ecce Homo,* ed. Ridley and Norman, trans. Norman, *The Anti-Christ, Ecce Homo, Twilight of the Idols,* 2.

208 *"Never have I been"*: Nietzsche, cit. Kohler, *Zarathustra's Secret,* 176.

208 *"little pastor"*: E. Förster-Nietzsche, *Der werdende Nietzsche* (Munich: Musarion, 1924), 196.

209 *"degradation and pride"*: Byron, "Manfred," *The Works of Lord Byron* (London: John Murray, 1821), II, 19.

209 *"superman"*: Nietzsche, cit. Hollingdale, *Nietzsche: The Man and His Philosophy,* 23.

210 *"terrifyingly inarticulate"*: Nietzsche, cit. Kohler, *Zarathustra's Secret,* 54.

210–211 *"vigorous, mysterious"* . . . *"Who knows"*: Nietzsche, cit. Kreel and Bates, *The Good European,* 40.

211 *"simply in itself"* . . . *"heavenly Aphrodite"*: Plato, *Symposium,* trans. Griffith, 19.

211–212 *"financial or political inducements"* . . . *"improve in wisdom"*: Plato, *Symposium,* trans. Griffith, 24.

212 *"reveals those"* . . . *"You can open them up"*: Plato, *Symposium,* trans. Griffith, 73–75.

Notes

212 *"lifeless mask"*: Ludwig von Scheffler, cit. Gilman (ed.), *Conversations with Nietzsche*, 74.

212 *"Nietzsche cannot even"*: Burckhardt, cit. Kohler, *Zarathustra's Secret*, 121.

213 *"noble simplicity"*: Winckelmann, *History of the Art of Antiquity*, trans. Mallgrave, 343, ix.

213–214 *"as they really are"* . . . *"He who works"*: Arnold, *Culture and Anarchy*, 145, 143, 271, 47.

214 *"all manifestations of the terrible"*: Nietzsche, notes for *The Birth of Tragedy*, cit. Kohler, *Zarathustra's Secret*, 74.

216 *"How could I think"*: Nietzsche, *The Gay Science*, trans. Kaufmann, 248.

216 *"new human flora and fauna"* . . . *"infinite white mane"*: Nietzsche, *The Gay Science*, trans. Kaufmann, 303, 248.

216 *"new Greek academy"*: Nietzsche to Rohde, *Selected Letters of Nietzsche*, ed. Levy, 73.

216 *"dangerous, creeping"*: Nietzsche, *Ecce Homo*, ed. Ridley and Norman, trans. Norman, *The Anti-Christ, Ecce Homo, Twilight of the Idols*, 105.

216 *"make music and discuss philosophy"*: Wagner to Nietzsche, cit. Safranski, *Nietzsche: A Philosophical Biography*, 57.

217 *"oracles"* . . . *"everywhere corpses"*: Cosima Wagner, cit. Kohler, *Nietzsche and Wagner*, 56; and Nietzsche, "Socrates and Tragedy," *Nietzsche and Wagner*, 79.

218 *"spiritual"* . . . *"soulful explanation"*: Nietzsche, cit. Silk and Stern, *Nietzsche on Tragedy*, 57.

218 *"We were giving chloroform"*: Nietzsche, cit. Kohler, *Zarathustra's Secret*, 83.

219 *"gulf of oblivion"* . . . *"nausea of the absurd"*: Nietzsche, *The Birth of Tragedy*, trans. Kaufmann, 41.

219 *"longing for the nothing"* . . . *"mere masks"*: Nietzsche, *The Birth of Tragedy*, trans. Kaufmann, 79–80, 73.

219–220 *"spiritualized introspective"* . . . *"fraternal union"*: Nietzsche, *The Birth of Tragedy*, trans. Kaufmann, 82–83, 41–42, 33.

220–221 *"higher egoism"* . . . *"renovation and purification"*: Nietzsche, *The Birth of Tragedy*, trans. Kaufmann, 79, 63, 14.

221 *"A more beautiful"* . . . *"inspired waste"*: Wagner to Nietzsche, cit. Pletsch, *Young Nietzsche*, 140, 143.

221 *"I had discovered"*: Nietzsche, *Ecce Homo*, trans. Kaufmann, 272.

222 *"I have never in my life"*: Wagner to Nietzsche, cit. Safranski, *Nietzsche*, 248.

222 *"Israelite"*: Cosima Wagner, cit. Kohler, *Wagner: Last of the Titans*, 523.

223 *"As I follow"*: Wagner to Eiser, Gregor-Dellin, *Wagner: His Life, His Work, His Century*, 750.

223 *"spiteful tricks"* . . . *"wrote letters"*: Nietzsche to Gast, cit. Kohler, *Zarathustra's Secret*, 103.

224 *"house of the scholars"*: Nietzsche, *Thus Spoke Zarathustra*, trans. Kaufmann, 290.

224 *"a bitter undertaste"*: Flaubert to Louise Colet, Steegmuller, *Letters of Gustave Flaubert*, 181.

224 *"blessed isles"*: Nietzsche, *Thus Spoke Zarathustra*, trans. Kaufmann, 55.

224 *"foremost saint and martyr"*: Nietzsche, *Thus Spoke Zarathustra*, trans. Kaufmann, 70.

224–225 *"We have killed him"* . . . *"Whither are we moving?"*: Nietzsche, *The Gay Science*, trans. Kaufmann, 181.

225 *"great ladder"* . . . *"oddly painful"*: Nietzsche, *Beyond Good and Evil*, trans. Kaufmann, 67, 75.

225–226 *"precipitate"* . . . *"decisive value"*: Nietzsche, *Beyond Good and Evil*, trans. Kaufmann, 44.

226 *"O you dolts"* . . *"the stone, stupidity"*: Nietzsche, *Beyond Good and Evil*, trans. Kaufmann, 75.

226 *"religious instinct"* . . . *"growth in profundity"*: Nietzsche, *Beyond Good and Evil*, trans. Kaufmann, 66, 44.

226 *"If I do not discover"*: Nietzsche to Overbeck, cit. Kaufmann, *Nietzsche: Philosopher, Psychologist, Antichrist*, 59.

226 *"Verily like the sun"*: Nietzsche, *Thus Spake Zarathustra*, trans. Kaufmann, 124.

226 *"professor of the Joyous Science"*: Emerson, *Journals*, VIII, 8.

227 *"Ascending souls"*: Emerson, "Prospects" (1842), *Early Lectures*, ed. Whicher and Spiller, III, 368.

227 *"Life is a search"*: Emerson, "Power" (1860), *The Conduct of Life*, 53.

227 *"the moment of transition"*: "Self-Reliance" (1841), Emerson, *Collected Works*, ed. Ferguson et al., II, 240.

227 *"affirm liberty"*: Emerson, "Power," *The Conduct of Life*, 4

227–228 *"pagan"* . . . *"perfected his reconciliation"*: Pater, *The Renaissance*, 191.

228 *"the most advanced"*: Dawson, *Darwin, Literature, and Victorian Respectability*, 99.

228 *"To burn always"*: Pater, *The Renaissance*, 238, 236.

228 *"With knowledge"*: Nietzsche, *Thus Spake Zarathustra*, trans. Kaufmann, 77.

228 *"It is not enough"* . . . *"Brave is he"*: Nietzsche, *Thus Spake Zarathustra*, trans. Kaufmann, 288–89.

229 *"Zarathustra the dancer"*: Nietzsche, *Thus Spake Zarathustra*, trans. Kaufmann, 294.

9. The Eternal Return

231 "Sadhu! Sadhu!" . . . *"took pansil"*: Olcott, *Old Diary Leaves*, II, 196.

232 *"benighted Buddhist"*: Blavatsky to *The World*, January 23, 1877, *Collected Writings*, ed. de Zirkoff, I, 238.

233 *"the most perfect"*: Buchanan, "On the Religion and Literature of the Burmas," *Asiatic Researches*, 179–80, 258.

Notes

234 *"old religion"*: Olcott, *Old Diary Leaves*, II, 167–69.

235 *"condensed statement"* . . . *"The Past"*: Olcott, *Old Diary Leaves*, II, 371.

235–236 *"God-send"* . . . *"certain painful occurrences"*: Coulomb, *Some Account of My Intercourse with Madame Blavatsky*, 6, 9.

236–237 *"resuscitation of the pure"* . . . *"great shock"*: Olcott, *Old Diary Leaves*, I, 395, 397.

237 *"naked coolies"*: Blavatsky, *From the Caves and Jungles of Hindostan*, 32.

237–238 *"sweet, almost feminine"* . . . *"Luther of India"*: Blavatsky, cit. Johnson, *The Masters Revealed*, 108, 107.

238 *"Look at us"*: Olcott to Dayananda, cit. Johnson, *The Masters Revealed*, 110.

240 *"most influential"* . . . *charming hostess*: Olcott, *Old Diary Leaves*, II, 28, 115, 29.

241 *"prolonged and careful"* . . . *"reintegrated at its destination"*: Sinnett, *The Occult World*, 81, 86.

241 *"I have it"*: Olcott's account, mailed to Mavalankar, repr. *The Times of India*, cit. Vania, *Madame Blavatsky: Her Occult Phenomena and the Society for Psychical Research*, 65–66.

241–242 *"Timbuctoo"* . . . *"vacillating and whimsical"*: Olcott, *Old Diary Leaves*, II, 294.

242 *"with the Govt. seal"*: Blavatsky, cit. Prothero, *The White Buddhist*, 71.

242 *"primitive nature-worship"*: Olcott, "Preface to the Adyar Library Edition," *A Buddhist Catechism*, 6.

242 *"dense popular ignorance"* . . . *"antidote"*: Prothero, *The White Buddhist*, 99, 102.

243–244 *"1. Q. Of what religion"* . . . *"men of science"*: Olcott, *A Buddhist Catechism*, 11, 30–31, 33.

244 *"Let us pursue"*: Nietzsche, *The Will to Power*, trans. Hill and Scarpitti, 55.

245 *"huge, pyramidal"* . . . *"This is the most extreme"*: Nietzsche, *Ecce Homo*, ed. Ridley and Norman, trans. Norman, *The Anti-Christ, Ecce Homo, Twilight of the Idols*, 123.

245 *"evolutionary course"*: Nietzsche, *On the Genealogy of Morals*, trans. Kaufmann, 160.

245 *"the ape, together"*: Nietzsche, *Daybreak*, trans. Hollingdale, 32.

246 *"It is a European"*: Nietzsche, *The Will to Power*, trans. Hill and Scarpitti, 57.

246 *"passive nihilism"*: Nietzsche, *The Will to Power*, trans. Hill and Scarpitti, 38.

246 *"half-Christian, half-German"* . . . *"super-Asiatic eye"*: Nietzsche, *Beyond Good and Evil*, trans. Kaufmann, 68.

246 *"6000 feet"*: Nietzsche, *Ecce Homo*, ed. Ridley and Norman, trans. Norman, *The Anti-Christ, Ecce Homo, Twilight of the Idols*, 123.

246 *"appeared to savour"*: Buck, *Simla Past and Present*, 120.

247 *"The inexorable shadow"*: Sinnett, *The Occult World*, 96–97; see Barker (ed.), *The Mahatma Letters*, 1–4.

247 *"mother source"* . . . *"popular religion"*: Blavatsky, *La revue spirité*, October 1878, *Collected Writings*, ed. Zirkoff, I, 402.

247–248 *"dozen Babu-Theosophists"* . . . *"I spent hours"*: Blavatsky to Prince Alexander Dondoukoff-Korsakoff, Cranston, *H.P.B.*, 230.

248 *"humbug"* . . . *"But we can't"*: Olcott, *Old Diary Leaves*, II, 374–75.

248–249 *"necessary experiments"* . . . *"vibratory thrills"*: Olcott, *Old Diary Leaves*, II, 406–7.

249–250 *"something superhuman"* . . . *"The most difficult lesson"*: Olcott, *Old Diary Leaves*, II, 374–77, 383.

250 *"What air!"*: Blavatsky, cit. Cranston, *H.P.B.*, 235.

250 *"Happy days"* . . . *"flounder about"*: Olcott, *Old Diary Leaves*, II, 393, 397.

251 *"I could be the Buddha"*: Nietzsche, 1883, cit. Panaïoti, *Nietzsche and Buddhist Philosophy*, 2.

252 *"This last bite"*: Nietzsche to Overbeck, cit. Kaufmann, *Nietzsche: Philosopher, Psychologist, Antichrist*, 59.

252 *"Could you create a god?"*: Nietzsche, *Thus Spoke Zarathustra*, trans. Kaufmann, 43.

252 *"ready and ripe"* . . . *"clouds pregnant"*: Nietzsche, *Thus Spoke Zarathustra*, trans. Kaufmann, 214–15.

253 *"I draw circles"*: Nietzsche, *Thus Spoke Zarathustra*, trans. Kaufmann, 209.

253 *"Is it not better"*: Nietzsche, *Thus Spoke Zarathustra*, trans. Kaufmann, 54.

253 *"a bow lusting for its arrow"*: Nietzsche, *Thus Spoke Zarathustra*, trans. Kaufmann, 214–15.

253 *"I have discovered the Greeks"*: Nietzsche, unpublished note, cit. Bishop, *Nietzsche and Antiquity: His Reaction and Response to the Classical Tradition*, 455 (n.28).

254 *"Just as Darwin"*: Engels, *Der Sozialdemokrat*, March 22, 1883, cit. Thomas, *Scientific Socialism*, 188.

254–255 *"gospel of contemporary socialism"* . . . *"Science is the liberator"*: Marx and Engels, *Marx/Engels Collected Works*, XXIV, 69–70.

255 *"Sexual unions"* . . . *"diet, intemperance"*: Olcott, *Old Diary Leaves*, III, 70.

255 *"mesmerized water"* . . . *"aura meter"*: Olcott, *Old Diary Leaves*, II, 407–8.

255–256 *"rail, steamboat"* . . . *"hysteric"*: Olcott, *Old Diary Leaves*, II, 440, 418, 404.

256 *"heavy black snake"* . . . *"victorious one"*: Nietzsche, *Thus Spoke Zarathustra*, trans. Kaufmann, 20, 69–70.

256 *"Once you said"*: Nietzsche, *Thus Spoke Zarathustra*, trans. Kaufmann, 109.

256 *"polluted stream"*: Nietzsche, *Thus Spoke Zarathustra*, trans. Kaufmann, 13.

257 *"This figure of eighteen months"*: Nietzsche, *Ecce Homo*, ed. Ridley and Norman, trans. Norman, *The Anti-Christ, Ecce Homo, Twilight of the Idols*, 124.

257 *"One has to impress them"*: Blavatsky, cit. Cranston, *H.P.B.*, 254–55.

10. The Will to Power

261 *"entered India and toyed"*: Afghani, "The Materialists in India" (1884), trans. Keddie, *An Islamic Response to Imperialism*, 175.

261–262 *"the strength of ten"* . . . *"idols, cows"*: "Commentary on the Commentator" (1882), trans. Keddie, *An Islamic Response to Imperialism,* 129, 101–3, 129, 127–28.

263 *"Aryan spirit"* . . . *"superficial layer"*: Renan, cit. Keddie, *Afghani: A Political Biography,* 197.

263 *"Islam and Science"*: Renan, *L'Islamisme et la science,* 2.

264 *"intellectual nullity"* . . . *"certain regret"*: Renan, *L'Islamisme et la science,* 16, 14, 7, 19–20.

264 *"species of Protestantism"* . . . *"hatred of science"*: Renan, *L'Islamisme et la science,* 14, 12, 19–20.

264 *"free thought"* . . . *"heaviest chain"*: Renan, *L'Islamisme et la science,* 17–19.

264–265 *"In truth"* . . . *"more advanced civilization"*: Afghani, "Answer to Renan," trans. Keddie, *An Islamic Response to Imperialism,* 183, 187, 182.

265 *"What is heavy?"*: Nietzsche, *Thus Spoke Zarathustra,* trans. Kaufmann, 214.

266 *"mechanistic and the Platonic"*: Nietzsche, *The Will to Power,* trans. Hill and Scarpitti, 591.

266 *"plant called Man"*: Nietzsche, *Beyond Good and Evil,* trans. Kaufmann, 54.

266 *"Countless dark bodies"* . . . *"inversion of values"*: Nietzsche, *Beyond Good and Evil,* trans. Kaufmann, 108, 60.

267 *"general uglification"* . . . *"heritage of multiple origins"*: Nietzsche, *Beyond Good and Evil,* trans. Kaufmann, 301.

267 *"ludicrous species"* . . . *"obnoxious and ridiculous"*: Nietzsche, *Beyond Good and Evil,* trans. Kaufmann, 352, 340, 358.

267 *"dwarfing of man"* . . . *"sand and slime"*: Nietzsche, *The Gay Science,* trans. Kaufmann, 255, 228.

267 *"the body and physiology"*: Nietzsche, *The Will to Power,* trans. Hill and Scarpitti, 304.

268 *"physiology, medicine"*: Nietzsche, *Ecce Homo,* ed. Ridley and Norman, trans. Norman, *The Anti-Christ, Ecce Homo, Twilight of the Idols,* 118.

268 *"hard particles"* . . . *"Materialism is the root"*: Afghani, "The Truth About the Materialists" (1881), trans. Keddie, *An Islamic Response to Imperialism,* 132–33, 141, 53.

269 *"Thou shalt not propagate"*: Nietzsche, *Thus Spoke Zarathustra,* trans. Kaufmann, 216.

269 *"Intellect alone"*: Nietzsche, *The Will to Power,* trans. Hill and Scarpitti, 540.

270 *"I am a pure-blooded"*: Nietzsche, *Ecce Homo,* ed. Ridley and Norman, trans. Norman, *The Anti-Christ, Ecce Homo, Twilight of the Idols,* 77.

270 *"strongest, toughest"* . . . *"mastery over Europe"*: Nietzsche, *Beyond Good and Evil,* trans. Kaufmann, 378.

271 *"You taught me language"*: Shakespeare, *The Tempest,* I.ii, 362–63.

272 *"Something extraordinarily nasty and evil"*: Nietzsche, *The Gay Science,* trans. Kaufmann, 172.

Notes

272 *"The problem of the value"*: Nietzsche, *Beyond Good and Evil*, trans. Kaufmann, 9.

274 *"I know my fate"*: Nietzsche, *On the Genealogy of Morals*, trans. Kaufmann, 326.

274 *"make no end of coin"*: Conrad, *Heart of Darkness*, 12.

274 *"much spite"*: Nietzsche to Overbeck, cit. W. Santianello, "A Post-Holocaust Examination of Nietzsche and the Jews: Vis-à-Vis Christendom and Nazism," ed. J. Golomb, *Nietzsche and Jewish Culture*, 21–54, 51.

275 *"antipode"*: Nietzsche, *Beyond Good and Evil*, trans. Kaufmann, 253.

275 *"the last Christian died"*: Nietzsche, cit. Santianello, "A Post-Holocaust Examination of Nietzsche and the Jews," ed. Golomb, *Nietzsche and Jewish Culture*, 51.

275 *"I want to live for a while"*: Nietzsche to Köselitz, cit. Emden, *Friedrich Nietzsche and the Politics of History*, 176.

275 *"In these days"*: Froude, *Oceana, or, England and Her Colonies* (London: Longmans, Green, 1886), 389.

276 *"Verily, Allah"*: Koran, 13:11; Afghani, "The Truth About the Neicheri Sect," trans. Keddie, *An Islamic Response to Imperalism*, 173.

276 *"He excelled"*: M. R. Rida, *Tarikh al-ustadh al-imam ash-sheikh Muhammad Abduh*, I (Cairo, 1931), 43; trans. Kedourie, *Afghani and Abdu*, 15.

277 *"sect of* neichiris *"* . . . *"pure ears of children"*: Afghani, "The Truth About the Neichiri Sect," trans. Keddie, *An Islamic Response to Imperalism*, 160, 150, 160–61.

277 *"seduce the sons"* . . . *"bringing in a girl"*: Afghani, "The Materialists in India" (1884), trans. Keddie, *Islamic Response*, 177–78, 148–49, 159.

277 *"England believes"*: Afghani, cit. Rochefort, *Les aventures de ma vie*, IV, 345.

278 *"vile animal qualities"*: Afghani, *Misr*, II, no. 45 (April 25, 1879), trans. Keddie, *Afghani: A Political Biography*, 107.

278 *"body and soul"*: Kathi [Dreesen] to Afghani, July 22, 1885, I. Afshar and A. Mahdavi (eds.), *Documents inédits concernant Sayyid Jamal-al-Din Afghani* (Tehran, 1963), 66–67; trans. Keddie, *Afghani: A Political Biography*, 269.

278 *"Owing to his preoccupation"*: Rida, *Tarikh*, I, 72.

278 *"cut the organ"*: Muhammad al-Makhzumi, *Khatirat Jamal al-Din al-Afghani* (Beirut, 1931), 43; trans. Kedourie, *Afghani and Abdu*, 8–9.

278 *"ecstatic"* . . . *"morbid nutrition"*: Nietzsche, *The Will to Power*, trans. Hill and Scarpitti, 52.

278 *"Wherever on earth"*: Nietzsche, *Beyond Good and Evil*, trans. Kaufmann, 61.

279 *"It was because one was wrong"*: Nietzsche, *On the Genealogy of Morals*, trans. Kaufmann, 173.

279 *"the cream of the nobility"*: Olcott, *Old Diary Leaves*, III, 79.

281 *"humanitarian"* . . . *"how much slaves"*: Blunt, *Gordon at Khartoum*, 208–9.

281 *"abnormal"* . . . *"pleuritic cold"*: Olcott, *Old Diary Leaves*, II, 159, 161.

282 *"Are the much despised"* . . . *"one of the first-rate"*: James to Davison and to
Alice Gibbens James, cit. Blum, *Ghost Hunters*, 82, 79.

282 *"Truly a brilliant company"*: Olcott, *Old Diary Leaves*, III, 95.

283 *"spirit of justice"*: Schultz, *Henry Sidgwick: Eye of the Universe*, 19.

284 *"mad turmoil"*: Blavatsky, cit. Cranston, *H.P.B.*, 261.

284 *"crowded to overflowing"* . . . *"She is extremely unattractive"*: Sidgwick's diary,
cit. Sidgwick and Sidgwick, *Henry Sidgwick*, 385.

285 *"the flimsiest of screens"* . . . *"No account"*: James, *The Varieties of Religious
Experience*, 307–8.

285 *"wonderful stream"*: Richardson, *William James*, 234.

286 *"I have urged you forward"*: Whitman, "As I Lay with My Head in Your Lap,
Camerado," *Leaves of Grass* (6th ed.), 190; cit. Schultz, *Henry Sidgwick: Eye
of the Universe*, 20.

286–287 *"You have harboured"* . . . *"You see, the back"*: Hodgson, "Report of the
Committee," 280, 224.

287 *"Sorry you go"*: Blavatsky to the Coulombs, cit. Cranston, *H.P.B.*, 268.

287 *"fabrication"*: Blavatsky, *The Times*, October 9, 1885.

288 *"I am returning"* . . . *"Success complete"*: Blavatsky, cit. Cranston, *H.P.B.*,
278–79.

288 *"huge fraudulent"* . . . *"carefully filled"*: Hodgson, "Report of the Committee,"
208, 252–53.

289 *"reintegrated"*: *Bombay Gazette*, October 13, 1880; letter to *Times of India*,
October 16, 1880; Coulomb, *Some Account*, 23–25; Hodgson, "Report of the
Committee," 267.

289 *"Indian head"*: Hodgson, "Report of the Committee," 209–10.

289 *"For our own part"*: Hodgson, "Report of the Committee," 206.

290 *"vapour"* . . . *"wilful deception"*: Hodgson, Report of the Committee," 252–
53, 210, 239.

290 *"Wonderful woman!"* . . . *"quite unfit"*: Olcott, *Old Diary Leaves*, II, 206–7.

291–292 *"She is indeed"* . . . *"foment as widely"*: Hodgson, "Report of the Committee," 313–14.

292 *"a European form of Buddhism"*: Nietzsche, *The Will to Power*, trans. Hill
and Scarpitti, 57.

292 *"Petersburg metapolitics"*: Nietzsche, *On the Genealogy of Morals*, trans.
Kaufmann, 157.

293 *"the most marvellous liar"*: Hume, cit. Cain, *The Cornchest for Scotland*, 39.

294 *"And do you know"*: Nietzsche, *The Will to Power*, trans. Hill and Scarpitti,
595–96.

295 *"intelligible world"*: Nietzsche, *Human, All Too Human*, trans. Hollingdale,
33.

295 *"Do you want a name"*: Nietzsche, *The Will to Power*, trans. Hill and Scarpitti, 595–96.

11. Culture and Anarchy

299–300 *"disasters of lustful love"* . . . *"long and healthy"*: Gandhi, *An Autobiography, or My Experiments with Truth,* 67–68, 90, 93.

300 *"Behold the mighty Englishman"*: Gandhi, *An Autobiography,* 78.

301 *"meat-feasts"* . . . *"pearl-drops of love"*: Gandhi, *An Autobiography,* 81, 83, 88.

301–302 *"playing the English"* . . . *"God had come"*: Gandhi, *An Autobiography,* 119, 118.

302 *"a very fine specimen"*: Guha, *Gandhi Before India,* 49.

302 *"instinctive repulsion"*: K. Joynes Salt to Carpenter, cit. G. Hendrick, *Henry Salt,* 148.

303 *"return to Nature"*: Carpenter, *Civilisation,* 38.

303 *"only man"*: Winsten, *Salt and His Circle,* 65.

303–304 *"vivisection"* . . . *"We may become"*: Shaw, cit. Dervin, *Shaw,* 107–8.

305 *"trembling, panting"*: Miller, *The Destruction of Gotham,* 7, 213.

305 *"This is the era"*: Carpenter, *Civilisation,* 33.

306 *"counter culture"*: Roszak, *The Making of a Counter Culture.*

308 *"sun-baths"*: Carpenter, *Adam's Peak to Elephanta,* ix.

309 *"This is the way back"*: Carpenter, *Civilisation,* 35.

309 *"The new aristocracy"*: Nietzsche, *The Will to Power,* trans. Hill and Scarpitti, 544.

309 *"one day, at some future time"*: Nietzsche, *Ecce Homo,* ed. Ridley and Norman, trans. Norman, *The Anti-Christ, Ecce Homo, Twilight of the Idols,* 120.

309 *"redeemer"* . . . *"He has to be the bad"*: Nietzsche, "The Case of Wagner," *Basic Writings,* trans. Kaufmann, 641, 612.

309 *"spiritualization"*: Nietzsche, *On the Genealogy of Morals,* trans. Kaufmann, 66, 100.

309 *"perfection in being"* . . . *"levelling"*: Nietzsche, *The Will to Power,* trans. Hill and Scarpitti, 66, 42, 17.

310 *"long legs"*: Nietzsche, "The Case of Wagner," *Basic Writings,* trans. Kaufmann, 636.

310 *"ruling race"* . . . *"philosophical authorities"*: Nietzsche, *The Will to Power,* trans. Hill and Scarpitti, 545–48.

310 *"ill-constituted, sickly"* . . . *"maggot-man"*: Nietzsche, *On the Genealogy of Morals,* trans. Kaufmann, 480, 478–79.

310 *"Who can say"*: Nietzsche, *On the Genealogy of Morals,* trans. Kaufmann, 467.

310 *"machinists"* . . . *"plebiscite against good taste"*: Nietzsche, "The Case of Wagner," *Basic Writings,* trans. Kaufmann, 635, 637, 623.

310 *"And when you look"*: Nietzsche, *Beyond Good and Evil,* trans. Kaufmann, 279.

311 *"Dionysus versus the Crucified"* . . . *"assassinate two thousand years"*: Nietzsche,

Ecce Homo, ed. Ridley and Norman, trans. Norman, *The Anti-Christ, Ecce Homo, Twilight of the Idols*, 110.

311 *"In a significant sense"* . . . *"My entire used-to-be"*: Nietzsche to von Gersdorff, cit. Kreel and Bates, *The Good European*, 144.

311 *"accidental contact"*: Nietzsche to Gast, cit. Grillaert, *What the God-Seekers Found in Nietzsche*, 38.

311 *"Two thousand years"*: Nietzsche, *The Anti-Christ*, ed. Ridley and Norman, trans. Norman, *The Anti-Christ, Ecce Homo, Twilight of the Idols*, 16.

311 *"Through Wagner"* . . . *"One has almost completed"*: Nietzsche, "The Case of Wagner," *Basic Writings*, trans. Kaufmann, 612.

312 *"I took the same"* . . . *"projected into the infinite"*: Nietzsche, *Ecce Homo*, ed. Ridley and Norman, trans. Norman, *The Anti-Christ, Ecce Homo, Twlight of the Idols*, 138.

312 *"monotono-theism"*: Nietzsche, cit. Azzam, *Nietzsche Versus Paul*, 29.

312 *"split the history"*: Nietzsche, cit. Young, *Friedrich Nietzsche: A Philosophical Biography*, 541.

312 *"Good; even very good"*: Nietzsche, Fragment, "Final Consideration": *Basic Writings*, trans. Kaufmann, 800.

313 *"You are sanctified"*: Nietzsche, *The Anti-Christ*, ed. Ridley and Norman, trans. Norman, *The Anti-Christ, Ecce Homo, Twlight of the Idols*, 11.

313 *"lie"* . . . *"ideal"*: "The Case of Wagner," *Basic Writings*, trans. Kaufmann, 613.

313 *"a serpent"* . . . *"every evil"*: Nietzsche, *The Anti-Christ*, ed. Ridley and Norman, trans. Norman, *The Anti-Christ, Ecce Homo, Twlight of the Idols*, 47.

313 *"holy parasite"* . . . *"corrupt"*: Nietzsche, *The Anti-Christ*, ed. Ridley and Norman, trans. Norman, *The Anti-Christ, Ecce Homo, Twilight of the Idols*, 26.

313 *"Islam at least assumes"*: Nietzsche, *The Anti-Christ*, ed. Ridley and Norman, trans. Norman, *The Anti-Christ, Ecce Homo, Twilight of the Idols*, 63.

313 *"idiot"* . . . *"It is a pity"*: Nietzsche, *The Anti-Christ*, ed. Ridley and Norman, trans. Norman, *The Anti-Christ, Ecce Homo, Twilight of the Idols*, 27–28.

313 *"Either you* are *a Chandala"*: Nietzsche, *The Anti-Christ*, ed. Ridley and Norman, trans. Norman, *The Anti-Christ, Ecce Homo, Twilight of the Idols*, 64.

314 *"scabies of the heart"*: Nietzsche, *The Gay Science*, trans. Kaufmann, 339.

314 *"I never speak to masses"*: Nietzsche, *Ecce Homo*, trans. Kaufmann, 326.

314 *"For when truth enters"*: Nietzsche, *Ecce Homo*, trans. Kaufmann, 327.

315 *"Nothing like this"*: Nietzsche, *Ecce Homo*, trans. Kaufmann, 284.

315–316 *"story of the twentieth century"* . . . *"death and burial"*: Donnelly, *Caesar's Column*, 37–38, 329.

316 *"resistance to natural instincts"*: Nietzsche, *The Anti-Christ*, ed. Ridley and Norman, trans. Norman, *The Anti-Christ, Ecce Homo, Twilight of the Idols*, 122.

316 *"This book is about me"*: Nietzsche to Deussen, cit. C. Crawford, "Nietzsche's

Psychology and Rhetoric of World Redemption: Dionysus Versus the Crucified," Golomb, Santaniello, and Lehrer (eds.), *Nietzsche and Depth Psychology*, 271–94, 287.

317 *"Alas . . . no more!"*: Nietzsche to Strindberg, Levy (ed.), *Selected Letters of Friedrich Nietzsche*, 311.

317–318 *"bands of unselfish" . . . "dazzled, blinded"*: Cranston, *H.P.B.*, 363.

319 *"atomic matter"*: Blavatsky, *The Secret Doctrine*, I, 620, 638.

319 *"disabused me"*: Gandhi, *An Autobiography*, 148.

320 *"Hinduism at its best"*: Gandhi, cit. Fischer, *The Life of Mahatma Gandhi*, 559.

320 *"crowded round" . . . "physical instrument"*: Ross, cit. Cranston, *H.P.B.*, 410.

320 *"H.P.B. stands"*: Indian Mirror, cit. Cranston, *H.P.B.*, 81.

321 *"reopen the long sealed treasures" . . . "A broader humanity"*: New-York Tribune, cit. Cranston, *H.P.B.*, 195.

321 *"race of inquirers" . . . "very heart of Europe"*: Stead, *Review of Reviews: An International Magazine*, III (January–July 1891), 613–14.

322 *"Reincarnation may or may not"*: Stead, "Borderlander: Olcott's Madame Blavatsky," *Borderland: A Quarterly Review*, I, no. 6 (October 1894); Olcott, *Old Diary Leaves*, IV, 250–51.

322–323 *"identical" . . . "We seem to move"*: Frazer, *The Golden Bough*, 49, 55–56.

325 *"squeamishness and suspiciousness"*: Gandhi, *An Autobiography*, 181.

326 *"snobbishness" . . . "coolie barrister"*: Gandhi, *An Autobiography*, 200, 203.

326 *"Is this Christian-like?"*: Gandhi, *Satyagraha in South Africa*, 77.

327 *"Hottentot servant" . . . "If you want"*: Gandhi, *An Autobiography*, 212–16.

328 *"The Asiatic"*: Natal Mercury, cit. Gandhi, *Satyagraha in South Africa*, 151.

328 *"God-forsaken continent"*: Gandhi, cit. Jordens, *Gandhi's Religion*, 43.

12. The Perspectivists

330–331 *"delegate" . . . "Temperance, Labor"*: Syman, *The Subtle Body*, 41, 304 (n.18), 42.

331 *"lowly Nazarene"*: Houghton (ed.), *The Parliament of Religions and Religious Congresses at the World's Columbian Exposition*, I, 13.

331–332 *"Sisters and brothers" . . . "rich as a bronze bell"*: Jackson, *Vedanta for the West*, 26.

332 *"circus turn"*: Romain, *Prophets of the New India*, v.

332 *"Chinese joss house"*: Syman, *The Subtle Body*, 43.

333 *"From the high spiritual"*: Vivekananda, Parliament address, *Complete Works of Vivekananda*, I, v.

333 *"What shall I get"*: The Outlook, July 17, 1897; Doniger, *The Hindus: An Alternative History*, 639.

333 *"got into the kitchen"*: Vivekananda, *Complete Works of Vivekananda*, III, 703.

334 *"beef, biceps"*: Vivekananda, cit. Sharma, *A Restatement of Religion*, xii.

334 *"withering away of the state"* . . . *"Why should anyone"*: Renade (ed.), *Vivekananda's Rousing Call to Hindu Nation*, 62.

335 *"I want to give them"*: Vivekananda to Sturdy, *Complete Works of Vivekananda*, V, 150.

336 *"I have seen only one"*: Anon., *The Life of Swami Vivekananda*, I, 24.

336 *"And what I saw"*: Isherwood, *Ramakrishna and His Disciples*, 65.

337 *"entering a house"* . . . *"entrails, blood"*: Sharma, *A Restatement of Religion*, 28, 32.

338 *"Try to see the truth"*: Banhatti, *Life and Philosophy of Swami Vivekananda*, 276.

339 *"signifies in the eyes"*: Nietzsche, *On the Genealogy of Morals*, trans. Kaufmann, 173.

344 *"dead ghosts of Russians"*: Vivekananda, *The Hindu*, February 8–11, 1897; Vivekananda, *Complete Works*, IV, 318.

345 *"quicken and energize"* . . . *"Emerson and Bronson Alcott"*: *Portsmouth Daily Chronicle*, cit. Syman, *The Subtle Body*, 49–51.

345 *"Women sometimes"*: Vivekananda, *Complete Works*, VII, 469.

346 *"Cambridge Conferences"*: Bull lived at 168 Brattle Street.

346–347 *"instrument"* . . . *"This whole universe"*: Syman, *The Subtle Body*, 58.

348 *"The sickness goes deep"*: Nietzsche, "The Case of Wagner," *Basic Writings*, trans. Kaufmann, 642.

349 *"frightful"* . . . *"furious egotism"*: Elisabeth Förster-Nietzsche, cit. D. Hayden, "Nietzsche's Secrets," eds. Golomb et al., *Nietzsche and Depth Psychology*, 295–316, 299.

349 *"half-crouching, like a mortally wounded"*: Overbeck to Rohde, cit. Hollingdale, *Nietzsche*, 247.

349 *"deceiving himself"*: Nietzsche, *Human, All Too Human*, trans. Hollingdale, 331.

349 *"It was a wonderful"*: Steiner, diary, cit. Hoffman, *Zur Geschichte des Nietzsche Archivs*, 183–85.

350 *"Inasmuch as the word"*: Nietzsche, *Writings from the Late Notebooks*, ed. Bittner, 139.

353 *"Again I considered"*: Herzl, *Diaries of Herzl*, ed. Lowenthal, 33.

354 *"Jewish nose"* . . . *"Hep! Hep!"*: Herzl, *Diaries of Herzl*, ed. Lowenthal, 6, 10.

354 *"Here I pass"* . . . *"I saw how the world"*: Herzl, *Diaries of Herzl*, ed. Lowenthal, 5.

355 *"I swear I am innocent"*: Read, *The Dreyfus Affair*, 113.

355 *"civic dishonor"*: Herzl to Pannizardi, cit. Schorske, *Fin-de-Siècle Vienna*, 162.

355–356 *"Things cannot improve"* . . . *"Or is this belief"*: Herzl, *Diaries of Herzl*, ed. Lowenthal, 35, 48.

356 *"My conception of God"*: Herzl, *Diaries of Herzl*, ed. Lowenthal, 62.

357 *"high priests"* . . . *"hussars of Judea"*: Herzl, *Diaries of Herzl*, ed. Lowenthal, 41, 43.

357 *"freedom and manliness"* . . . *"the Maccabean tradition"*: Herzl, *Diaries of Herzl*, ed. Lowenthal, 39, 37.

357 *"the desirable illusion"* . . . *"German theater"*: Herzl, *Diaries of Herzl*, ed. Lowenthal, 41, 37.

358–359 *"fear of ghosts"* . . . *"auto-emancipation"*: Pinsker, *Auto-Emancipation*, trans. Blondheim, 2–4.

359 *"neglected Jewish economic reality"*: Reinharz and Shavit, *Glorious, Accursed Europe*, 38.

360 *"regeneration"* . . . *"that I did not wish"*: Nietzsche-Förster, *Das Leben Friedrich Nietzsche*, II, 474–75; R. F. Krummel, "Joseph Paneth über seine Begegnung mit Nietzsche in der Zarathustra-Zeit," *Nietzsche-Studien*, 17 (1988), 478–95; W. J. McGrath, "Mahler and the Vienna Nietzsche Society," in *Nietzsche and Jewish Culture*, ed. Golomb, 218–32, 219.

360 *"new European man"*: Herzl, "Frankreich im Jahre 1891," *Neue Freie Presse*, cit. Golomb, *Nietzsche and Zion*, 25.

361 *"We must have been"*: Herzl, *Diaries of Herzl*, ed. Lowenthal, 9.

361 *"Great things need"*: Herzl, cit. Schorske, *Fin-de-Siècle Vienna*, 164.

361–362 *"As there was no"* . . . *"In that case"*: Vivekananda to Sturdy, *Letters of Vivekananda*, 181.

362 *"If India is to rise again"*: Mohapatra, *Political Philosophy of Swami Vivekananda*, 7.

363 *"the malicious nature"* . . . *"The whole nation"*: Vivekananda, cit. Jones, *Socio-Religious Reform Movements in British India*, 44.

363 *"What we want is muscles"*: Vivekananda, cit. Chaube, *Recent Philosophies of Education in India*, 54.

363 *"gross, material"*: Vivekananda, cit. Jones, *Socio-Religious Reform Movements in British India*, 44.

363 *"Above all"*: Nietzsche, *Beyond Good and Evil*, trans. Kaufmann, 155.

364 *"the Ubermensch on his Easter holiday"*: Warburg to André Jolles, cit. Roeck, *Florence 1900*, 223.

364 *"eccentric"*: Santianello, "A Post-Holocaust Re-Examination of Nietzsche and the Jews," Golomb, *Nietzsche and Jewish Culture*, 50.

365–366 *"a majestic Oriental"* . . . *"the romance"*: Herzl, *Diaries of Herzl*, ed. Lowenthal, 215–16.

366 *"At Basel"*: Herzl, cit. Schorske, *Fin-de-Siècle Vienna*, 164.

Epilogue

374 *"There is no teacher"*: Krishnamurti, "2nd Public Talk," Ojai, November 5, 1966, http://jiddu-krishnamurti.net/en/1966/1966-11-05-jiddu-krishnamurti-3nd-public-talk.

375 *"I should think"*: Hardy, *Daily Mail*, September 27, 1914, cit. Bridgwater, *Nietzsche in Anglosaxony*, 144.

375 *"Euro-Nietzschean War"*: James Joll, "The English, Friedrich Nietzsche and the First World War," in Geiss and Wendt (eds.), *Deutschland in der Weltpolitik des 19 und 20 Jahrhunderts*, 305.

376 *"All power structures"*: Nietzsche, *Ecce Homo*, trans. Kaufmann; *On the Genealogy of Morals and Ecce Homo*, 327.

377 *"You say that it is"*: Nietzsche, *Thus Spoke Zarathustra*, trans. Kaufmann, 13.

BIBLIOGRAPHY

Allen, G. W., *Waldo Emerson: A Biography* (New York: Viking, 1981)

Amanat, A., *Resurrection and Renewal: The Making of the Babi Movement in Iran, 1844–1850* (Ithaca, NY: Cornell University Press, 1989)

Anonymous, *The Life of Swami Vivekananda, by His Eastern and Western Disciples*, 3 vols. (Mayavati: Prabuddha Bharata Office, 1914)

App, U., *The Birth of Orientalism* (Philadelphia: University of Pennsylvania Press, 2011)

Arnold, D., and M. Iversen, *Art and Thought* (Oxford: Blackwell, 2003)

Arnold, M., *Culture and Anarchy: An Essay in Political and Social Criticism* (1867; London: Smith, Elder, 1869)

Azzam, A., *Nietzsche Versus Paul* (New York: Columbia University Press, 2015)

Banhatti, G. S., *Life and Philosophy of Swami Vivekananda* (New Delhi: Atlantic, 1989)

Barker, A. T. (ed.), *The Mahatma Letters to A. P. Sinnett from the Mahatmas M. and K.H.*, 2nd ed. (Pasadena, CA: Theosophical University Press, 1926)

Barth, H., D. Mack, and E. Voss (eds.), *Wagner: A Documentary Study* (Oxford: Oxford University Press, 1975)

Batchelor, J., *John Ruskin: A Life* (New York: Carroll and Graf, 2000)

Baudelaire, C., *Les fleurs du mal* (Paris: Poulet-Malassie et de Broise, 1857)

———, *Petits poèmes en prose* (1869), trans. F. Scarfe, *Baudelaire: The Poems in Prose* (Manchester: Carcanet, 1989)

———, *Selected Writings on Art and Artists*, trans. P. E. Charvet (Cambridge: Cambridge University Press, 1972)

Beasley, E., *The Victorian Reinvention of Race: New Racisms and the Problem of Grouping in the Human Sciences* (New York: Taylor and Francis, 2010)

Beauvoir, R. de, *Les mystères de l'Île Saint-Louis: Chroniques de l'hôtel Pimodan*, 2 vols. (Paris, Bourdillat, 1859)

Billington, J. H., *Fire in the Minds of Men: Origins of the Revolutionary Faith* (New York: Basic Books, 1980)

Bishop, P. (ed.), *Nietzsche and Antiquity: His Reaction and Response to the Classical Tradition* (Rochester, NY: Camden House, 2004)

Blake, N. M., and L. G. Wells (eds.), *The Oneida Community Collection in the Syracuse University Library* (Syracuse, NY: Syracuse University Library, 1961)

Blanning, T., *The Romantic Revolution* (London: Weidenfeld and Nicolson, 2010)

Blavatsky, H. P., *Collected Writings of H. P. Blavatsky*, 14 vols., ed. B. de Zirkoff (Wheaton, IL: Theosophical, 1966–85)

————, *From the Caves and Jungles of Hindostan* (London: Theosophical, 1892)

————, *Isis Unveiled: A Master-Key to the Mysteries of Ancient and Modern Science and Theology*, 2 vols. (1877; Point Loma, CA: Theosophical, 1910)

————, *Letters of H. P. Blavatsky: Volume 1, 1861–1879*, ed. J. Algeo (Wheaton, IL: Quest, 2003)

————, *The Letters of H. P. Blavatsky to A. P. Sinnett and Other Miscellaneous Letters*, ed. A. T. Barker (London: T. Fisher Unwin, 1925)

————, *The Secret Doctrine: The Synthesis of Science, Religion, and Philosophy*, 3 vols. (London: Theosophical, 1888)

Blum, D., *Ghost Hunters: William James and the Search for Scientific Proof of Life After Death* (New York: Penguin, 2006)

Blumenbach, J. F., *De generis humani varietate nativa* (1775), trans. T. Benshye, *On the Natural Varieties of Mankind* (1865; New York: Bergman, 1969)

Blunt, W. S., *Gordon at Khartoum: Being a Personal Narrative of Events in Continuation of "A Secret History"* (London: Stephen Swift, 1911)

Bookhut, F. R., "Arthur de Gobineau and His Philosophical History" (PhD diss., New York University, 1973)

Booth, A. J., *Saint-Simon and Saint-Simonism: A Chapter in the History of Socialism in France* (London, 1871)

Bradley, J. L. (ed.), *Ruskin's Letters from Venice, 1851–1852* (Yale, 1955)

Braude, A., *Radical Spirits: Spiritualism and Women's Rights in Nineteenth-Century America* (Bloomington: Indiana University Press, 2001)

Bridgwater, P., *Nietzsche in Anglosaxony: A Study of Nietzsche's Impact on English and American Literature* (Leicester: Leicester University Press, 1972)

Brigham, J., *Twelve Messages from the Spirit of John Quincy Adams, Through Joseph Stiles, Medium, to Josiah Brigham* (Boston: Bela Marsh, 1859)

Buchanan, F., "On the Religion and Literature of the Burmas," *Asiatic Researches, or Transactions of the Society Instituted in Bengal*, vol. 2 (Calcutta: Cantopher, 1790), 163–368.

Buck, E., *Simla Past and Present* (Calcutta: Thacker, Spink, 1904)

Buenzod, J., *La formation de la pensée de Gobineau et l'Essai sur l'inegalité des races* (Paris: Nizet, 1967)

Byron, [Lord] G. G., *The Works of Lord Byron*, 17 vols. (London: John Murray, 1821–25)

Bibliography

Cady Stanton, E., *Eighty Years and More (1815–1897): Reminiscences* (New York: European, 1898)

Cady Stanton, E., S. B. Anthony, and M. J. Gage (eds.), *History of Woman Suffrage*, 3 vols. (Rochester, NY: Susan B. Anthony, 1889)

Cain, A. M., *The Cornchest for Scotland: Scots in India* (Edinburgh: National Library of Scotland, 1986)

Calasso, R., *La Folie Baudelaire*, trans. A. McEwen (New York: Farrar, Straus and Giroux, 2012)

———, *Literature and the Gods*, trans. T. Parks (New York: Knopf, 2001)

Carlyle, T., *Collected Works of Thomas Carlyle*, 16 vols. (London: Chapman and Hall, 1864)

Carlyle, T., and R. W. Emerson, *The Correspondence of Thomas Carlyle and Ralph Waldo Emerson, 1834–1872*, 2 vols. (London: Chatto and Windus, 1883)

Carpenter, E., *Adam's Peak to Elephanta* (1890; 2nd ed., New York: Dutton, 1904)

———, *Civilisation: Its Cause and Cure* (London: George Allen and Unwin, 1889)

Carus, C., *Psyche: On the Developmental History of the Soul: Part 1*, trans. R. Welch (1846; Dallas: Spring, 1989)

Chadwick, O., *The Secularization of the European Mind in the Nineteenth Century* (Cambridge: Cambridge University Press, 1975)

Chaube, S. P., *Recent Philosophies of Education in India* (New Delhi: Concept, 2005)

Chernin, E., "Josiah Clark Nott, Insects, and Yellow Fever," *Bulletin of the New York Academy of Medicine*, 59, no. 9 (November 1983)

Comte, A., *The Positive Philosophy*, 2 vols., trans. H. Martineau (London: Chapman and Hall, 1853)

———, *System of Positive Polity; or, Treatise on Sociology, Instituting the Religion of Humanity*, 4 vols. (London: Longmans, Green, 1877)

Conrad, J., *Heart of Darkness* (1899; London: Everyman, 1992)

Constant, M. A., *La Bible de la liberté* (Paris: Gosselin, 1841)

———, *La mère de Dieu: Épopée religieuse et humanitaire* (Paris: Gosselin, 1844)

———, *Les trois harmonies, chansons, et poesies* (Paris: Fellens et Dufour, 1845)

[Cooper, L. M., et al.], *H.P.B.: In Memory of H. P. Blavatsky, by Some of Her Pupils* (London, Madras, New York: Theosophical Society, 1891)

Coulomb, E. Cutting [Madame Coulomb], *Some Account of My Intercourse with Madame Blavatsky from 1872 to 1884; with a Number of Additional Letters and a Full Explanation of the Most Marvellous Theosophical Phenomena* (London: Stock, 1884)

Cranston, S. *H.P.B: The Extraordinary Life and Influence of Helena Blavatsky, Founder of the Modern Theosophical Movement* (New York: Putnam's, 1993)

Darwin, C., *Correspondence of Charles Darwin*, ed. F. Burkhardt, S. Smith, J. A. Secord, et al., 21 vols. (Cambridge: Cambridge University Press, 1985–2014)

———, *The Descent of Man and Selection in Relation to Sex*, 2 vols. (New York: Appleton, 1871)

———, ed., *The Life and Letters of Charles Darwin, Including an Autobiographical Chapter*, 2 vols. (New York: Appleton, 1887)

———, ed., *More Letters of Charles Darwin: A Record of His Work in a Series of Hitherto Unpublished Letters*, 2 vols. (London: John Murray, 1903)

———, *Natural Selection: Being the Second Part of His Big Species Book, Written from 1856 to 1858*, ed. R. C. Stauffer (Cambridge: Cambridge University Press, 1975)

———, *Origin of Species by Means of Natural Selection; or, The Preservation of Favored Races in the Struggle for Life*, 2 vols. (1859; New York: Appleton, 1896)

———, *The Voyage of the* Beagle (New York: Collier and Son, 1909)

———, *What Mr. Darwin Saw in His Voyage Round the World in the Ship* Beagle (New York: Weathervane, 1879)

Davenport, R. B., *The Death-Blow to Spiritualism: Being the True Story of the Fox Sisters* (New York: G. W. Dillingham, 1898)

Dawson, G., *Darwin, Literature, and Victorian Respectability* (Cambridge: Cambridge University Press, 2007)

Dervin, D., *Shaw: A Psychological Study* (Lewisburg, PA: Bucknell University Press, 1975)

Desmond, A. J., *Huxley: The Devil's Disciple* (London: Michael Joseph, 2009)

Desmond, A. J., and J. Moore, *Darwin's Sacred Cause: How a Hatred of Slavery Shaped Darwin's Views on Human Evolution* (Boston: Houghton Mifflin Harcourt, 2009)

Deveney, J. P., *Paschal Beverly Randolph: A Nineteenth-Century Black American Spiritualist, Rosicrucian, and Sex Magician* (Albany: State University of New York Press, 1997)

Dicey, E., *The Egypt of the Future* (London: Heinemann, 1907)

Disraeli, B., *Tancred; or, The New Crusade*, 3 vols. (London: Henry Colburn, 1847)

Doniger, W., *The Hindus: An Alternative History* (Oxford: Oxford University Press, 2009)

Donnelly, *Caesar's Column: A Story of the Twentieth Century* (New York: Shulte, 1889)

Eagleton, T., *Ideology: An Introduction* (London: Routledge, 1994)

Eden, T. E., *The Search for Nitre and the True Nature of Guano, Being an Account of a Voyage to the South-West Coast of Africa* (London: Groombridge, 1846)

Emden, C., *Friedrich Nietzsche and the Politics of History* (Cambridge: Cambridge University Press, 2008)

Emerson, R. W., *An Address Delivered in the Court-House in Concord 1st August, 1844 on the Anniversary of the Negroes in the West Indies* (Boston: Munroe, 1844)

————, *Collected Works of Ralph Waldo Emerson*, 13 vols., ed. R. A. Bosco, P. Burkholder, J. Carr Ferguson, A. R. Ferguson et al. (Cambridge, MA: Belknap Press of Harvard University Press, 1971–2013)

————, *The Conduct of Life* (Boston: Houghton Mifflin, 1860)

————, *Early Lectures of R. W. Emerson*, 3 vols., ed. S. E. Whicher and R. E. Spiller (Cambridge, MA: Belknap Press of Harvard University Press, 1966)

————, *The Journals and Miscellaneous Notebooks of Ralph Waldo Emerson*, 16 vols., ed. A. Ferguson, W. Gilman, G. P. Clark, and M. R. Davis (Cambridge, MA: Belknap Press of Harvard University Press, 1960–82)

————, *Later Lectures of Ralph Waldo Emerson, 1843–1871*, 2 vols., ed. R. A. Bosco and J. Meyerson (Athens: University of Georgia Press, 2001)

————, *Lectures and Biographical Sketches by R. W. Emerson*, ed. J. E. Cabot (Boston: Houghton Mifflin, 1870)

————, *Letters from R. W. Emerson to a Friend, 1838–1853*, ed. C. E. Norton (Boston: Houghton Mifflin, 1899)

————, *Natural History of Intellect and Other Papers* (Cambridge, MA: Riverside, 1893)

————, *Nature: Addresses, and Lectures*, ed. J. E. Cabot (Cambridge, MA: Riverside, 1883)

Fichman, M., *An Elusive Victorian: The Evolution of Alfred Russel Wallace* (Chicago: University of Chicago Press, 2004)

Fischer, L., *The Life of Mahatma Gandhi* (New York: Harper, 1950)

Flaubert, G., *Letters of Gustave Flaubert: 1830–1857*, trans. F. Steegmuller (Cambridge, MA: Belknap Press of Harvard University Press, 1980)

Förster-Nietzsche, E., *Das Leben Friedrich Nietzsche*, 2 vols. (Leipzig: Naumann, 1904)

————, *Der werdende Nietzsche* (Munich: Musarion, 1924)

Frazer, J., *The Golden Bough: A Study in Magic and Religion* (1922; New York: Doubleday, 1961)

Fuller [Ossoli], M., *At Home and Abroad; or, Things and Thoughts in America and Europe*, ed. A. Buckminster Fuller (1856; Boston: Roberts Bros., 1895)

Galton, F., *Hereditary Genius: An Inquiry into Its Laws and Consequences* (London: Macmillan, 1869)

Gandhi, M. K., *An Autobiography, or My Experiments with Truth: A Critical Edition*, ed. T. Suhrud (New Haven, CT: Yale University Press, 2018)

————, *Satyagraha in South Africa* (Ahmedabad: Navajivan, 1928)

Geiss, I., and B. J. Wendt (eds.), *Deutschland in der Weltpolitik des 19 und 20 Jahrhunderts* (Dusseldorf: Bertelsmann, 1973)

Gercy, Mme. [Marie] de, *Une vie de femme liée aux événements de l'époque*, 2 vols. (Paris: Corbet, 1853)

Gibbon, E., *The Decline and Fall of the Roman Empire*, 6 vols. (London: Everyman, 1993)

————, *Letters of Gibbon*, ed. J. E. Norton, 3 vols. (London: Cassell, 1956)

Gibbs-Smith, C. H., *The Great Exhibition of 1851* (London: HMSO, 1981)

Gilman, S. L. (ed.), *Conversations with Nietzsche: A Life in the Words of His Contemporaries*, trans. D. J. Parent (Oxford: Oxford University Press, 1987)

Gobineau, A. de, *Essai sur l'inégalité des races humaines*, 5 vols. (Paris: Firmin-Didot, 1853–55), ed. and trans. H. Hotz [Hotze], *The Moral and Intellectual Diversity of the Races* (Philadelphia: Lippincott, 1856), and A. Collins (Los Angeles: Noontide Press, 1966)

Golomb, J. (ed.), *Nietzsche and Jewish Culture* (Routledge: London, 1997)

———, *Nietzsche and Zion* (Ithaca, NY: Cornell University Press, 2004)

Golomb, J., W. Santaniello, and R. Lehrer (eds.), *Nietzsche and Depth Psychology* (Albany: State University of New York Press, 1999)

Gomes, M., *The Dawning of the Theosophical Society* (Wheaton, IL: Theosophical, 1987)

Goodwin, J., *The Theosophical Enlightenment* (Albany: State University of New York Press, 1994)

Gregor-Dellin, M., *Wagner: His Life, His Work, His Century* (London: Collins, 1983)

Griffith, E., *In Her Own Right: The Life of Elizabeth Cady Stanton* (New York: Oxford University Press, 1984)

Grillaert, N., *What the God-Seekers Found in Nietzsche: The Reception of Nietzsche's* Übermensch *by the Philosophers of the Russian Religious Renaissance* (Amsterdam: Rodolphi, 2008)

Guha, R., *Gandhi Before India* (New York: Random House, 2014)

Gunn, G. C., *First Globalization: The Eurasian Exchange, 1500 to 1800* (Lanham, MD: Rowman and Littlefield, 2003)

Halsted, J. B. (ed.), *Romanticism: Selected Documents* (London: Palgrave Macmillan, 1969)

Hartmann, K.R.E. von, *Philosophy of the Unconscious*, 2nd ed., 3 vols., trans. W. C. Coupland (London: Kegan Paul, Trench, Trübner, 1893)

Hayter, A., *Opium and the Romantic Imagination* (London: Faber and Faber, 1968)

Headrick, D. R. *Tentacles of Progress: Technology Transfer in the Age of Imperialism* (New York: Oxford University Press, 1988)

Hegel, G. W., *Philosophy of History*, trans. J. Sibree (New York: American Home Library, 1902)

Hendrick, G., *Henry Salt: Humanitarian Reformer and Man of Letters* (Urbana: University of Illinois Press, 1978)

Herzen, A., *From the Other Shore: An Open Letter to Jules Michelet*, trans. R. Wollheim (Westport, CT: Hyperion, 1981)

Herzl, T., *The Diaries of Theodor Herzl*, ed. and trans. M. Lowenthal (New York: Dial, 1956)

Himmelfarb, G. (ed.), *The Spirit of the Age: Victorian Essays* (New Haven, CT: Yale University Press, 1962)

Hodgson, R., "Report of the Committee Appointed to Investigate Phenomena Connected with the Theosophical Society" [*"The Hodgson Report"*], *Proceedings of the Society for Psychical Research*, 3, pts. viii and ix (London: Trübner, 1885)

Hoffman, D. M., *Zur Geschichte des Nietzsche Archivs* (Berlin: De Gruyter, 1991)

Hollingdale, J., *Nietzsche: The Man and His Philosophy*, rev. ed. (Cambridge: Cambridge University Press, 1965)

Holyoake, G., *The Limits of Atheism; or, Why Should Skeptics Be Outlaws?*, 2 vols. (London: Brook, 1874)

———, *The Origin and Nature of Secularism; Showing That Where Freethought Commonly Ends Secularism Begins* (London: Watts, 1896)

———, *Sixty Years of an Agitator's Life*, 3rd ed., 2 vols. (London: Unwin, 1893)

Houghton, W. R. (ed.), *The Parliament of Religions and Religious Congresses at the World's Columbian Exposition*, 2 vols. (New York: Neely, 1894)

Hubbard, M. G., *Saint-Simon, sa vie et ses travaux* (Paris: Guillaumin, 1857)

Huxley, L. (ed.), *Life and Letters of Sir Joseph Dalton Hooker*, 2 vols. (Cambridge: Cambridge University Press, 1918)

———, ed., *Life and Letters of Thomas Henry Huxley*, 2 vols. (London: Macmillan, 1903)

Huxley, T. H., *Darwiniana: Essays* (New York: Appleton, 1896)

Hunter, W. W., *The Marquess of Dalhousie* (Oxford: Clarendon, 1890)

Irvine, W., *Apes, Angels, and Victorians* (London: Weidenfeld, 1955)

Isherwood, C., *Ramakrishna and His Disciples* (London: Methuen, 1965)

Jackson, C. T., *Vedanta for the West: The Ramakrishna Movement in the United States* (Bloomington: Indiana University Press, 1994)

James, W., *The Varieties of Religious Experience* (1902; New York: Modern Library, 1936)

Johnson, K. Paul, *In Search of the Masters: Behind the Occult Myth* (self-published, 1990)

Jones, K. W. *Socio-Religious Reform Movements in British India* (Cambridge: Cambridge University Press, 1999)

Jordens, J., *Gandhi's Religion: A Homespun Shawl* (London: Macmillan, 1998)

Katz, D. S., *The Occult Tradition: From the Renaissance to the Present Day* (London: Jonathan Cape, 2006)

Kaufmann, W., *Nietzsche: Philosopher, Psychologist, Antichrist* (Princeton, NJ: Princeton University Press, 1950)

Keddie, N. R., *Afghani: A Political Biography* (Berkeley: University of California Press, 1972)

———, *An Islamic Response to Imperialism: Political and Religious Writings of Sayyid Jamal ad-Din "al-Afghani"* (Berkeley: University of California Press, 1970)

Kedourie, E., *Afghani and Abdu: An Essay on Religious Unbelief and Political Activism in Modern Islam* (1966; London: Frank Cass, 1997)

Kern Holoman, D., *Berlioz* (Harvard University Press, 1989)

Kohler, J., *Nietzsche and Wagner: A Lesson in Subjugation*, trans. R. Taylor (New Haven, CT: Yale University Pres, 1998)

———, *Wagner: Last of the Titans*, trans. S. Spencer (New Haven, CT: Yale University Press, 2004)

———, *Zarathustra's Secret: The Interior Life of Friedrich Nietzsche*, trans. R. Taylor (New Haven, CT: Yale University Press, 1989)

Kopf, D., *British Orientalism and the Bengal Renaissance: The Dynamics of Indian Modernization* (Oakland: University of California Press, 1969)

Kreel, D. F., and D. L. Bates, *The Good European: Nietzsche's Work Sites in Word and Image* (Chicago: University of Chicago Press, 1997)

Krieg, J. P., *A Whitman Chronology* (Iowa City: University of Iowa Press, 1998)

Lander, J., *Lincoln and Darwin: Shared Visions of Race, Science, and Religion* (Carbondale: Southern Illinois University Press, 2010)

Large, D. C., W. Weber, and A. Dzamba Sesse (eds.), *Wagnerism in European Culture and Politics* (Ithaca, NY: Cornell University Press, 1984)

Lévi, E. *Dogme et rituel de la haute magie* (Paris: G. Ballière, 1856), 2 vols., trans. A. E. Waite, *Transcendental Magic* (London: Rider, 1923)

———, *Histoire de la magie* (Paris: G. Baillière, 1860), trans. A. E. Waite, *History of Magic* (London: Rider, 1913)

Lincoln, A., *Collected Works of Abraham Lincoln*, 9 vols., ed. R. P. Basler (New Brunswick, NJ: Rutgers University Press, 1953)

Loving, J., *Walt Whitman: The Song of Himself* (Berkeley: University of California Press, 1999)

Löwith, K., and R. Wolin, *Heidegger and European Nihilism* (New York: Columbia University Press, 1995)

Lutz, A., *Created Equal: A Biography of Elizabeth Cady Stanton* (New York: Octagon, 1974)

Lyell, C., *The Geological Evidences of the Antiquity of Man: With Remarks on the Theories of the Origin of Species by Variation* (London: John Murray, 1863)

Macaulay, T. B., *Speeches of Lord Macaulay: Corrected by Himself* (London: Longman, Green, Longman, and Roberts, 1860)

Manuel, F. E., *A Requiem for Karl Marx* (Cambridge, MA: Harvard University Press, 1995)

Marx, K., *Capital: A Critical Analysis of Capitalist Production*, 2 vols., trans. S. Moore and E. Aveling, ed. F. Engels (1867; London: Swan Sonnenschein, Lowrey, 1887)

———, *Marx on Religion*, ed. J. C. Raines (Philadelphia: Temple University Press, 2002)

———, *Writings of the Young Karl Marx*, ed. L. D. Easton (New York: Doubleday, 1967)

Marx, K., and F. Engels, *The Class Struggles in France* (1850; London: Martin Lawrence, 1964)

————, *Marx/Engels Collected Works*, 50 vols., various eds. (London: Lawrence and Wishart, 1975–2004)

————, *Marx and Engels: The Political Writings*, 3 vols. (London: Verso, 2019)

McDonagh, P., *Idiocy: A Cultural History* (Liverpool: Liverpool University Press, 2008)

Mehring, F., *Karl Marx: The Story of His Life* (1936; London: Routledge, 2003)

Mellersh, H.E.L., *FitzRoy of the* Beagle (London: Rupert Hart Davis, 1968)

Miller, J., *The Destruction of Gotham* (New York: Funk and Wagnalls, 1886)

Mohapatra, K., *Political Philosophy of Swami Vivekananda* (New Delhi: Northern Book Centre, 1996)

Mott, L., *Selected Letters of Lucretia Coffin Mott*, ed. B. Wilson Palmer (Champaign: University of Illinois Press, 2002)

Murphet, H., *Yankee Beacon of Buddhist Light: Life of Colonel H. S. Olcott* (Wheaton, IL: Quest, 1988)

Nietzsche, F., *The Anti-Christ, Ecce Homo, Twilight of the Idols*, ed. A. Ridley and J. Norman (Cambridge: Cambridge University Press, 2005)

————, *The Basic Writings of Nietzsche*, trans. and ed. W. Kaufmann (New York: Random House, 2000)

————, *Beyond Good and Evil: Prelude to a Philosophy of the Future*, trans. W. Kaufmann (New York: Vintage, 1966)

————, *The Birth of Tragedy from the Spirit of Music* (1872), trans. W. Kaufmann (New York: Vintage, 1968)

————, *Daybreak: Thoughts on the Prejudices of Morality*, trans. R. J. Hollingdale (Cambridge: Cambridge University Press, 1997)

————, *The Gay Science: With a Prelude in Rhymes and an Appendix of Songs* (1882), trans. W. Kaufmann (New York: Vintage, 1974)

————, *Human, All Too Human: A Book for Free Spirits* (1878), trans. R. J. Hollingdale (Cambridge: Cambridge University Press, 1986)

————, *On the Genealogy of Morals* (1887), trans. W. Kaufmann and R. J. Hollingdale, *On the Genealogy of Morals and Ecce Homo* (New York: Vintage, 1967)

————, *Sämtliche Briefe: Kritische Studieausgabe*, 8 vols., ed. G. Colli and M. Montinari (Munich: Deutscher Taschenbuch Verlag, 1986)

————, *Sämtliche Werke, Kritische Studieausgabe*, 15 vols., ed. G. Colli and M. Montinari (Munich: Deutscher Taschenbuch Verlag, 1980)

————, *Selected Letters of Friedrich Nietzsche*, ed. O. Levy, trans. A. M. Ludovici (Garden City, NY: Doubleday, Page, 1921)

————, *Thus Spoke Zarathustra: A Book for All and None* (1883–85), trans. and ed. W. Kaufmann (New York: Modern Library, 1968)

————, *The Will to Power: Selections from the Notebooks of the 1880s*, ed. R. K. Hill and M. A. Scarpitti (London: Penguin, 2017)

————, *Writings from the Late Notebooks*, ed. R. Bittner (Cambridge: Cambridge University Press, 2003)

Nott, J. C., *The Physical History of the Jewish Race* (Charleston, SC: Walker and James, 1850)

Nott, J. C., and G. R. Gliddon, *Types of Mankind: or, Ethnological Researches Based upon the Ancient Monuments, Paintings, Sculptures, and Crania of Races*, 2 vols. (Philadelphia: Lippincott, 1855)

Noyes, H., *Bible Communism: A Compilation from the Annual Reports and Other Publications of the Oneida Association and Its Branches* (1848; Brooklyn, NY: 1853)

————, *The Way of Holiness: A Series of Papers Formerly Published in "The Perfectionist," at New Haven* (Putney, VT: Noyes, 1838)

O'Donoghue, D. (trans.), and G. Nash (ed.), *Comte de Gobineau and Orientalism: Selected Eastern Writings* (New York: Routledge, 2009)

Olcott, H. S., *A Buddhist Catechism According to the Sinhalese Canon* (Madras: Scottish Press, 1887)

————, *Old Diary Leaves: The True History of the Theosophical Society*, 6 vols. (New York: Putnam's, 1895)

————, *People from the Other World* (Hartford, CT: American, 1875)

Panaoïti, A., *Nietzsche and Buddhist Philosophy* (Cambridge: Cambridge University Press, 2013)

Parker, J. W. (ed.), *Essays and Reviews* (London: Parker, 1860)

Pater, W., *The Renaissance: Studies in Art and Poetry* (1873; London: Macmillan, 1910)

Pineo, R. F., *Ecuador and the United States: Useful Strangers* (Athens: University of Georgia Press, 2007)

Pinsker, Y. L., *Auto-Emancipation: An Appeal to His People by a Russian Jew* (1882), trans. D. S. Blondheim (New York: Maccabean, 1906)

Plato, *Symposium and Phaedrus*, trans. T. Griffith (1986; London: Everyman, 2000)

Pletsch, C., *Young Nietzsche: Becoming a Genius* (New York: Free Press, 1991)

Prothero, S., *The White Buddhist: The Asian Odyssey of Henry Steel Olcott* (Bloomington: Indiana University Press, 1996)

Ravaisson-Mollien, F., *La philosophie en France au XIXème siècle* (Paris: Imprimerie Impériale, 1868)

Read, P. P., *The Dreyfus Affair: The Story of the Most Infamous Miscarriage of Justice in French History* (London: Bloomsbury, 2012)

Reinharz Y., and Y. Shavit, *Glorious, Accursed Europe: An Essay on Jewish Ambivalence*, trans. M. Engel (Waltham, MA: Brandeis University Press, 2010)

Renade, M.S.E. (ed.), *Vivekananda's Rousing Call to Hindu Nation* (Chennai: Vivekananda Kendra Prakashan Trust, 1963)

Renan, E., *L'Islamisme et la science: Conférence faite à la Sorbonne le 29 Mars 1883* (Paris: Calmann Lévy, 1883)

Reynolds, D. S., *Walt Whitman's America: A Cultural Biography* (New York: Vintage, 1995)

Richardson, R. D., *William James: In the Maelstrom of American Modernism* (Boston: Houghton Mifflin Harcourt, 2006)

Rochefort, H., *Les aventures de ma vie*, 4 vols. (Paris: Dupont, 1894)

Roeck, B., *Florence 1900: The Quest for Arcadia*, trans. S. Spencer (New Haven, CT: Yale University Press, 2009)

Rolland, R., *Musicians of Today*, trans. M. Blaiklock (New York: Henry Holt, 1914)

Romain, R., *Prophets of the New India*, trans. E. F. Malcolm-Smith (London: Cassell, 1930)

Rose, P. L., *Wagner: Race and Revolution* (New Haven, CT: Yale University Press, 1992)

Roszak, T., *The Making of a Counter Culture: Reflection on the Technocratic Society and Its Youthful Opposition* (Berkeley: University of California Press, 1969)

Ruskin, J., *The Stones of Venice*, 3 vols. (1851–53; New York: Wiley and Sons, 1880)

———, *The Works of John Ruskin*, 39 vols., ed. E. T. Cook and A. Wedderburn (London: George Allen, 1904)

Safranski, R., *Nietzsche: A Philosophical Biography*, trans. S. Frisch (New York: W. W. Norton, 2002)

Salmi, H., *Imagined Germany: Richard Wagner's National Utopia* (Oxford: Oxford University Press, 1999)

Schemann, L., "Drei biographischen Skizzen von Gobineau," *Quellen und Untersuchungen zum Leben Gobineaus*, 2 vols (Strassburg: Trübner, 1914)

———, *Gobineau's Rassenwerk* (Stuttgart: Frommans, 1910)

Schopenhauer, A., *On the Basis of Morality*, trans. A. B. Bull (London: Swan Sonnenschein, 1903)

———, *Parerga and Paralipomena: Short Philosophical Essays*, 2 vols., trans. E.F.J. Payne (Oxford: Clarendon, 2001)

———, *The World as Will and Representation*, 3 vols., trans. R. B. Haldane and J. Kemp (London: Kegan Paul, Trench, Trübner, 1906)

Schorske, C. E., *Fin-de-Siècle Vienna: Politics and Culture* (New York: Vintage, 1981)

Schultz, B., *Henry Sidgwick: Eye of the Universe, an Intellectual Biography* (Cambridge: Cambridge University Press, 2004)

Schwab, R., *Oriental Renaissance: Europe's Rediscovery of India and the East* (New York: Columbia University Press, 1984)

Sharma, J., *A Restatement of Religion: Swami Vivekananda and the Making of Hindu Nationalism* (New Haven, CT: Yale University Press, 2013)

Shaw, W.M.K., *Ottoman Painting: Reflections of Western Art from the Ottoman Empire to the Turkish Republic* (London: I. B. Tauris, 2011)

Shively, C., *Calamus Lovers: Walt Whitman's Working-Class Camerados* (San Francisco: Gay Sunshine, 1987)

Sidgwick, A. S., and E. M. Sidgwick, *Henry Sidgwick: A Memoir* (London: Macmillan, 1906)

Silk, M. S., and J. P. Stern, *Nietzsche on Tragedy* (Cambridge: Cambridge University Press, 1981)

Sinnett, A. P., *Incidents in the Life of Madame Blavatsky Compiled from Information Supplied by Her Relatives and Friends* (London: George Redway, 1886)

———, *The Occult World* (Boston: Houghton Mifflin, 1885)

Spencer, H., *Social Statics* (London: Chapman, 1851)

Sprague, A., *The Poet and Other Poems* (Boston: White, 1864)

———, "Selections from Achsa W. Sprague's Diary and Journal," ed. L. Twynham, *Proceedings of the Vermont Historical Society*, IX, no. 3 (September 1941)

Stanton, T., and H. Stanton Blatch (eds.), *Elizabeth Cady Stanton, As Revealed in Her Letters, Diary and Reminiscences*, 2 vols. (New York: Harper, 1922)

Steger, M. B., *The Quest for Evolutionary Socialism: Eduard Bernstein and Social Democracy* (Cambridge: Cambridge University Press, 1997)

Steinberg, J., *Bismarck: A Life* (Oxford: Oxford University Press, 2011)

Stocqueler, J. H., *The Handbook of British India: A Guide to the Stranger, the Traveller, the Resident* (1844; London: W. H. Allen, 1854)

Strobel, O. (ed.), *König Ludwig II und Richard Wagner: Briefwechsel*, 5 vols. (Karlsruhe: Braun, 1936–39)

Syman, S., *The Subtle Body: The Story of Yoga in America* (New York: Farrar, Straus and Giroux, 2010)

Thomas, P., *Scientific Socialism: From Engels to Althusser* (New York: Routledge, 2008)

Thoreau, H. D., *The Correspondence of Henry David Thoreau*, 3 vols., ed. R. N. Hudspeth (Princeton, NJ: Princeton University Press, 2013)

———, *Familiar Letters*, ed. F. B. Sanborn (Boston: Houghton Mifflin, 1906)

———, *The Journal of Henry D. Thoreau*, 2 vols., ed. B. Torrey and F. H. Allen (Boston: Houghton Mifflin, 1906)

———, *Walden; or, Life in the Woods* (1854; Boston: James R. Osgood, 1878)

———, *A Yankee in Canada, with Anti-slavery and Reform Papers* (Boston: James R. Osgood, 1878)

Tolstoy, L., *War and Peace*, trans. L. and A. Maude, 3 vols (London: Everyman, 1992)

Traubel, H. L., *With Walt Whitman in Camden*, 3 vols. (Boston: Small, Maynard: 1906–14); subsequent vols. various eds. (Carbondale: Southern Illinois University Press, 1982–92)

Tripathi, A., *Trade and Finance in the Bengal Presidency, 1793–1833* (Oxford: Oxford University Press, 1979)

Underhill, A. L., *The Missing Link in Modern Spiritualism* (New York: Knox, 1885)

Vania, K. F., *Madame Blavatsky: Her Occult Phenomena and the Society for Psychical Research* (Bombay: Sat, 1951)

Bibliography

Victoria, *Letters of Queen Victoria: A Selection from Her Majesty's Correspondence Between the Years 1837 and 1861*, 3 vols., ed. A. C Benson and Viscount Esher (London: John Murray, 1908)

Vivekananda, *The Complete Works of the Swami Vivekananda*, 9 vols. (Mayavati: Prabuddha Bharata Office, 1915)

———, *Letters of Swami Vivekananda* (Calcutta: Modern Art, 1940)

Voltaire, *An Essay on Universal History, and the Manners and Spirit of Nations*, 2nd ed., 4 vols., trans. T. Nugent (London: J. Nourse, 1774)

Wagner, C., *Cosima Wagner's Diaries*, 2 vols., ed. M. Gregor-Dellin and D. Mack, trans. G. Skelton (New York: Harcourt Brace Jovanovich, 1978–80)

Wagner, R., *Letters of Richard Wagner: The Burrell Collection*, ed. and trans. J. N. Burk (London: Macmillan, 1950)

———, *Richard Wagner's Prose Works*, 8 vols. (London: Kegan, Paul, Trench, Trübner, 1892, etc.)

———, *Selected Letters of Richard Wagner*, ed. S. Spencer, and B. Millington (London: Dent, 1987)

Wallace, A. R., *Alfred Russel Wallace: An Anthology of His Shorter Writings* (Oxford: Oxford University Press, 1991)

Watson, D., *Wagner: A Biography* (New York: Scribner, 1981)

Wawro, G., *The Franco-Prussian War: The German Conquest of France in 1870–1871* (Cambridge: Cambridge University Press, 2003)

Wheen, F., *Karl Marx: A Life* (New York: W. W. Norton, 2000)

Whitman, W., *Leaves of Grass*, 6th ed. (Boston: James Osgood, 1881)

———, *Memoranda During the War* (Camden, NJ: author's publication, 1875–76)

———, *Specimen Days and Collect, November Boughs and Good Bye My Fancy* (Philadelphia: Rees Welsh, 1882)

Winckelmann, J. J., *History of the Art of Antiquity*, trans. H. F. Mallgrave (1755; Los Angeles: Getty Research Institute, 2006)

Winsten, S., *Salt and His Circle* (London: Hutchinson, 1951)

Wollaston, A.F.R., *Life of Alfred Newton, Late Professor of Comparative Anatomy, Cambridge University, 1866–1907* (New York: Dutton, 1921)

Young, J., *Friedrich Nietzsche: A Philosophical Biography* (Cambridge: Cambridge University Press, 2010)

ACKNOWLEDGMENTS

My thanks to George Lucas at InkWell Management in New York, Lizzy Kremer at David Higham Associates in London, and Eric Chinski at Farrar, Straus and Giroux.

Alex Self, Michael Abrams, and Natasha Green McDonagh helped with research, as did the staffs of the Accademia dei Lincei (Rome), the Bodleian Library (Oxford), the British Library (London), and the Widener Library at Harvard University (Cambridge, Massachusetts). Rony Alfandary, Billy Apt, Kapil Komireddi, Francesca Lidia Viano, and Sophus Reinert read my drafts.

Thank you, Fay, Alma, and Edie, and above all, Maja. This book is dedicated to you with love and gratitude.

INDEX

Gersdorff, Karl, 275
Geyer, Gottfried Benjamin, 153
Geyer, Ludwig, 153
Ghanim, Khalil, 263
Gibbon, Edward, 44, 181
Ginsberg, Allen, 371
Gladstone, William, 212–13
Gliddon, George Robins, 104
globalization, 59, 169, 176
gnosis, 74
Gobineau, Arthur de, 96–103,
    105–106, 111, 112, 116, 137, 202,
    228, 263, 372–73; Schemann and,
    364–65
Gobineau Society, 364–65, 372
God, 36, 37, 73, 113, 181; Darwin's
    views on, 159, 173–75; existence
    of, 76, 127–28, 131, 132;
    Holyoake's view of, 130–31;
    Nietzsche on death of, 6, 224,
    226, 231, 245, 312; Noah and,
    156–57
Godse, Nathuram, 379
Goethe, Johann Wolfgang von, 34,
    84, 153, 363
Gogol, Nikolai, 193, 194
Golden Bough, The (Frazer), 322
Gordon, Charles, 260, 281, 283,
    288, 293
Gordon, William and Alice, 240
Gospel of Buddha, The (Carus), 340
Gospels, 49, 156, 204, 232, 293, 313
Gosse, Edmund, 281
Götterdämmerung (Wagner), 151,
    163
Götzendämmerung (Nietzsche),
    310–13
Gray, Asa, 115, 134
Gray, Elisha, 194
Greater Britain (Dilke), 175
Great Exhibition and Crystal
    Palace, 54–55, 58–61, 113, 187,
    291, 329

Great Expectations (Dickens), 72
Greece, ancient, 50, 51, 100,
    145–46, 155, 208, 211–14,
    218–21, 253, 261, 264, 266; art
    of, 103, 104, 149, 213, 227–28
Greeley, Horace, 32, 47, 78
Greeley, Molly, 78
Green Acre Conference, 345, 362
Greg, W. R., 167
Grenadier Guards, 332
Grimm, Jacob, 101, 151
Grimm, Wilhelm, 101
Griswold, Rufus, 143
guano, 108–10
Guild of Saint George, 66
Guizot, François, 261
Gunananda, Migettuwatte, 234–35,
    242
Gurney, Edmund, 282, 284

Haeckel, Ernst, 269
Hamlet (Shakespeare), 221
Hardy, Thomas, 375
Hare, Robert, 81
Harpers Ferry raid, 115
Hart, Ernest, 281
Hartmann, Eduard von, 170, 171,
    176, 226
Hartmann, Franz, 286, 287
Harvard Divinity School, 11
hashish, 68–69, 90, 196–97
Hastie, William, 335–36
Hastings, Warren, 51, 62
Hawkins, Benjamin Waterhouse,
    113
Hearn, Lafcadio, 340
Hebraists versus Hellenizers,
    213–14
Hegel, Georg Friedrich, 12, 35–38,
    47, 83, 107, 110, 124, 161, 162,
    171, 227, 330
Hegeler, Edward, 340
Heine, Heinrich, 150, 154, 155